LOUISE BOURGEOIS

The Secret of the Cells

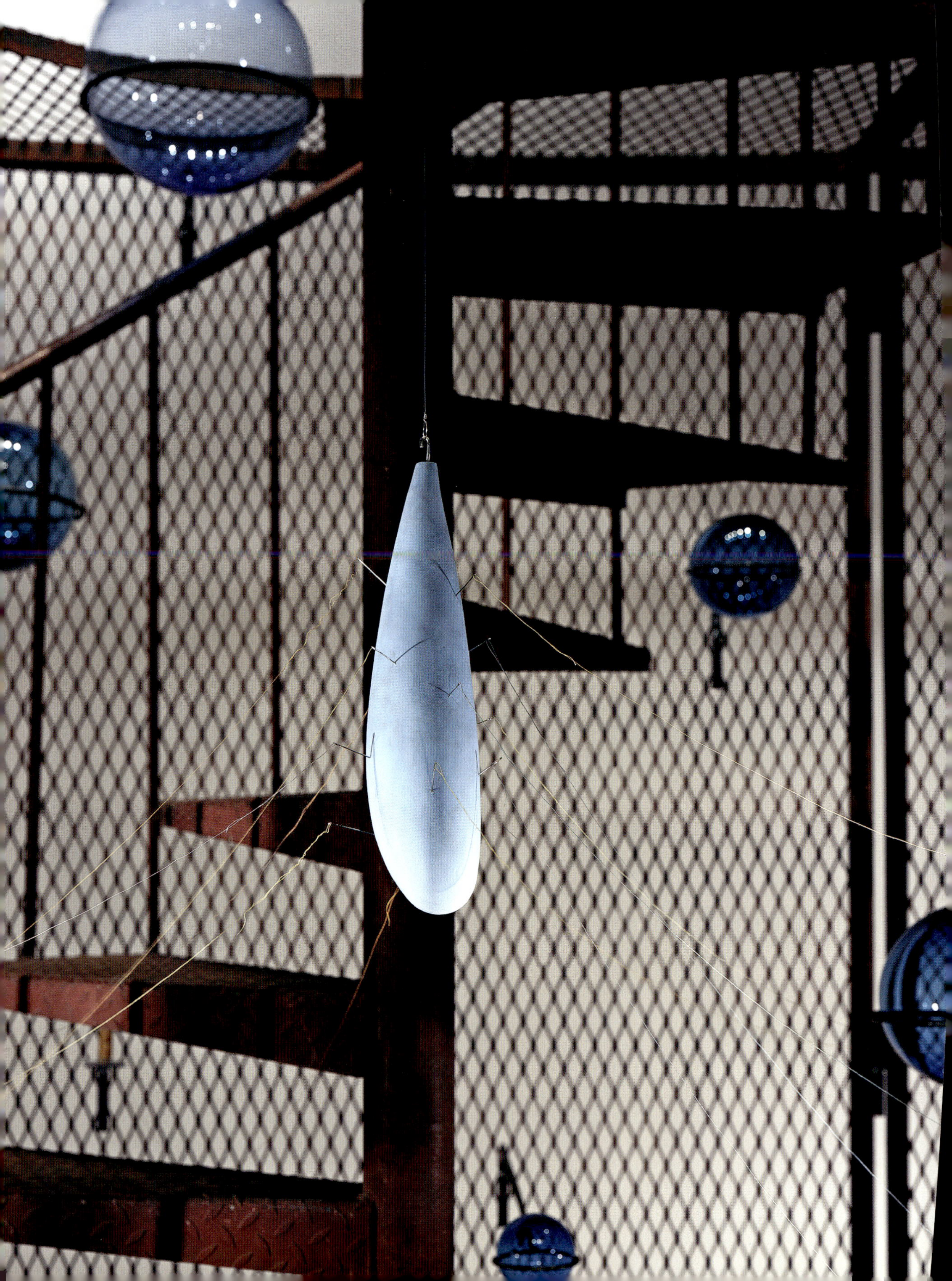

LOUISE BOURGEOIS

The Secret of the Cells

Rainer Crone
Petrus Graf Schaesberg

REVISED AND EXPANDED EDITION

PRESTEL
MUNICH · LONDON · NEW YORK

CONTENTS

PREFACE TO THE REVISED EDITION

Remembering Louise Bourgeois, there is every reason to marvel not only at the quality and longevity of her life, but also of her artistic production, a record rarely equaled. But it is another matter to consider the aesthetic implications of this longevity—especially since it is impossible that the artist would have excluded from her work a consciousness of her life's impending end.

We know that Bourgeois's work in general was acutely self-conscious and autobiographical. She made no secret of this fact, reaffirming it numerous times in public statements. And despite a critical mythology that attributes to artists of her generation the aim of making works that are entirely self-referential, she did so knowing full well that this autobiographical element in her work presupposes an external referent. To be sure, her specific formal means of invoking an external referent employed an element of symbolism. But it was symbolism that used the implicit character of the reference object to generate a tension between the conventional assumptions associated with it and the new ones she attributed to it.

The spiders for which she remains most famous become a diagram of her method. Needless to say, the spider is a universal image of repugnance and fear: "Along came a spider, who sat down beside her, and frightened Miss Muffet away," as the nursery rhyme has it. Spiders, bones, severed body parts, bodies tortuously twisted—in all these, Bourgeois's method is to take such elements with fearful associations and transmute them into something more truthful by virtue of a dispassionate, even scientific examination of their functional aspects. The spider weaves and protects by devouring less loathsome but genuinely harmful insects. Her spider thereby becomes *Maman* with all the warm associations of maternity that any child could desire. But this sense is even more powerful precisely because of the tension it generates with the conventional fearful associations of the image.

The term *Cells* evokes various linguistic associations, three of which are treated in depth in the work that follows:

1. A fundamental unit of life and its origin (as with the enclosure of a membrane, this meaning evokes the fact of being enclosed within a body).
2. Imprisonment (enclosure by definition, but with the negative association of punishment, and also numerous metaphorical associations).
3. Contemplation (self-imposed enclosure, but with the positive connotation of spiritual liberation, which juxtaposes a conceptual tension with the physical confinement contemplation requires). Recall that Bourgeois was a professed atheist who described herself as having "a religious temperament."

The first represents the past, the beginning of her life, including her childhood traumas, and the well of images from which she drew throughout her artistic life. Second is the self-conscious reflection on this experience, the realization that her being is contained by this past experience that threatens to become a prison. The third is the transcendence of this experience through the contemplation inherent in the aesthetic act. Made at the end of her life, the *Cells* stand in dialectical relation to her life's beginning and middle, the dialectic of the immediacy of artistic expression, self-conscious reflection on this immediate experience, and, finally, its transcendence.

Artists invented the installation partially in order to overcome an intrinsic limitation of sculpture, its tendency to resist an artist's effort to control the spectator's point of view with regard to the artistic object. But it is precisely because of their materiality that sculptures, and many installations, are the media most suitable for certain themes of transcendence because their very mass and physicality are in conceptual opposition with all that is weightless and metaphysical.

This is certainly an underlying assumption of Brancusi, and it cannot be mere accident that certain *Cells* of the last years of Bourgeois's life, illustrated in this revised edition, allude to the most explicitly metaphysical of Brancusi's works, his great outdoor sculpture installation at Tîrgu Jiu. In 1938, when Brancusi already was past sixty, he made this monumental series in order to commemorate fighters from this village who had died in World War I. This allusion to Tîrgu Jiu in the *Cells* is most apparent in Bourgeois's *Twelve Oval Mirrors*, among other things an ironic and affectionate answer to Brancusi's *Table of Silence* from Tîrgu Jiu, and her *Cell* entitled *The Last Climb*, an allusion to the *Endless Column* at Tîrgu Jiu and the culmination of an aspiration to metaphysical transcendence that remains the ensemble's central theme.

With these and other new Cells of this final period, the artist used her undiminished imagination to have the theme of transcendence bring her life's work to its culmination by means of an elegant allusion to her own physical end. She must have known that this was certainly not the end for Louise Bourgeois.

* * *

It is an honor for me personally to be able to see these last nine *Cells* of the final decade of Louise Bourgeois's life, works that surely she would not have been able to give to the world but for the infinite loyalty and assistance of Jerry Gorovoy. But this honor mingles not only with the passing of a great artist who has stridden into history, but with a most poignant loss, of young Petrus Graf Schaesberg, my collaborator on the first edition, whose fond memory I wish to invoke here.

Rainer Crone

PUBLISHER'S NOTE

This revised edition adds illustrations of the ten *Cells* completed by Louise Bourgeois after publication of the first edition of *Louise Bourgeois: The Secret of the Cells*. They span a decade, from the 1998 *Cell (Twelve Oval Mirrors)* until *Cell (The Last Climb)* (2008), made just two years prior to the artist's death in 2010. In the back matter of this edition, the Index of the Cells has been brought up to date, as have the exhibition list, bibliography, and lists of videos and films.

1 Jorge Luis Borges, *History of Eternity*, 1935

ACKNOWLEDGMENTS

For sundry assistance and helpful advice in our undertaking we are deeply indebted to the artist herself, who generously allowed us to delve into her past and present. In addition, we owe our gratitude to her friend and assistant of long standing, Jerry Gorovoy, who responded to all our needs and queries with down-to-earth practicality; in view of the large number of requests, this would not have been possible without the help of Wendy Williams. Nor should we forget the exciting ideas that we exchanged with Louise Bourgeois' son, Jean-Louis.

Special thanks are due to Michael Maegraith, without whose support this book would never have gone forward. Our thanks, too, to John Cheim, and to Peter Blum for the critical encouragement which spurred us to write an important book on such a singular artist. Many friends and colleagues should certainly be mentioned here, but we would like especially to name the following, who contributed in very different ways to the successful completion of this book: Marie-Laure Bernadac, Robert Miller, Suzanne Pagé, Karsten Greve, Yoko Toda, Christopher Wynne, Irma Tanno-Stecher, Hans-Rudolf and Gianpiera Bühlmann, and, not least, Jürgen Tesch, whose ideas and initiative inspired the compilation of the book.

This book demonstrates how fruitful, creative and sensible it can be — not only in view of the large number of unemployed people with creative potential for students to collaborate with their teacher who, thanks to his established success, has no need to amass further honors for his curriculum vitae. The younger author effectively obtains a great deal of practical knowledge which is unobtainable through theoretical study, and which would otherwise have to be gained independently — often through bitter experience — after the completion of his studies. The generation difference can in itself be an advantage as regards both concept and execution, in that the authors are able to link historical perceptions with contemporary aesthetic positions. Such collaboration between anything up to six authors has, for decades, been common in the scientific field, and the humanities — encumbered, as usual, by tradition — have a great deal of catching up to do in this respect. The success of our teamwork is again evident in the co-operation of Matthias Kunz, with whom the book was originally conceived and who has helped us to render Louise Bourgeois' fascinating and exemplary life in a form that makes for compelling reading.

Rainer Crone
Petrus Graf Schaesberg

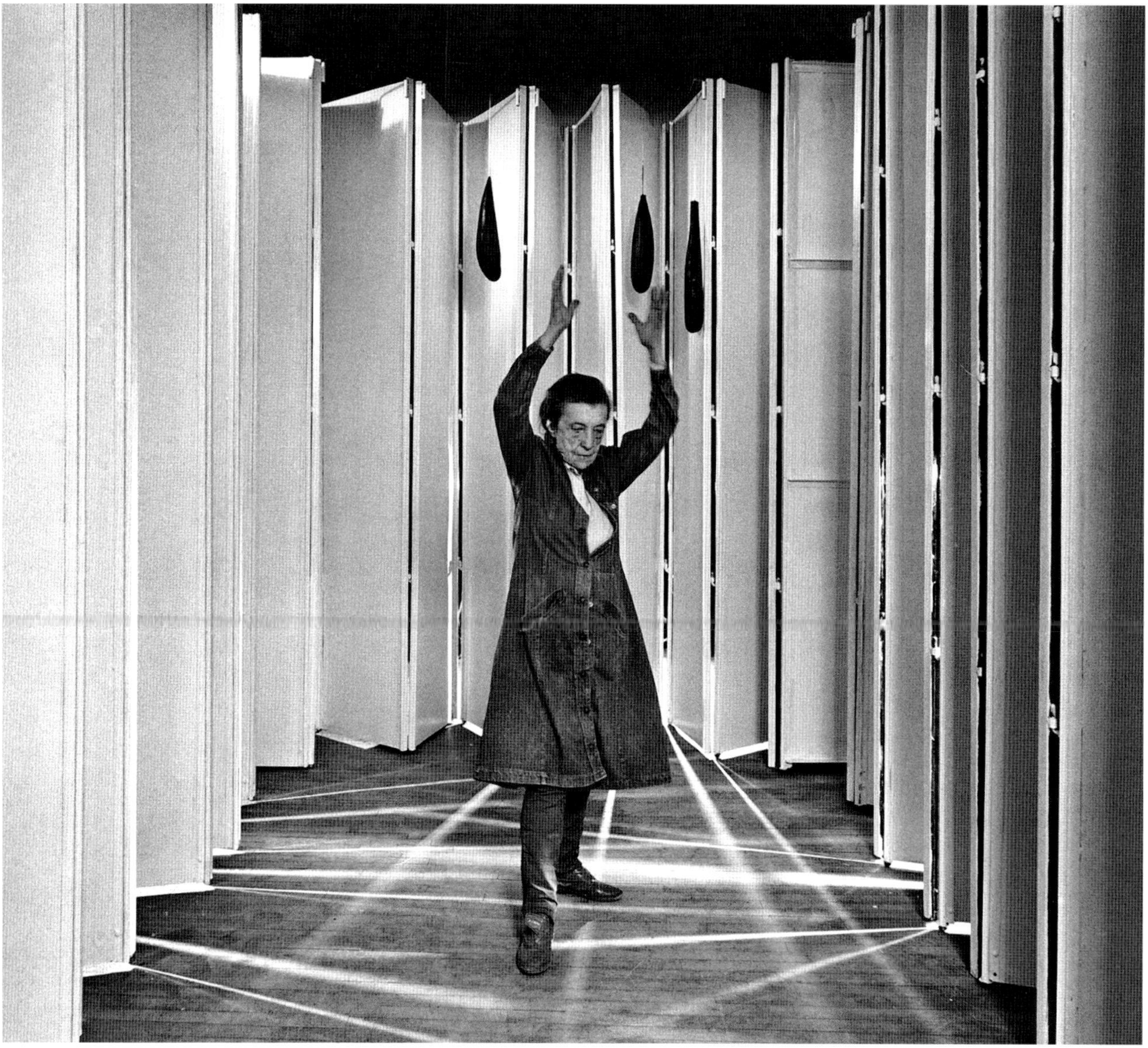

1 Louise Bourgeois in *Articulated Lair*, 1986

I. CONCEALED ZONES OF INTROSPECTION: *ARTICULATED LAIR* (1986)

A work of art does not need an explanation. The work has to speak for itself. The work may be subject to many interpretations, but only one was in the mind of the artist. Some artists say to make the work readable for the public is the artist's responsibility, but I don't agree with that. The only responsibility is to be absolutely truthful to the self.
My work disturbs people and nobody wants to be disturbed. They are not fully aware of the effect my work has on them, but they know it is disturbing.[1]

Louise Bourgeois, 1979

A dynamic figure in a denim dress flings her arms up into the air (Ill. 1). Does this gesture signify horror, annoyance, or even despair? Her face shows neither anger, fear, nor shock. Her serene features convey rather a sense of meditative concentration, unfaltering determination and immense emotional resources. Her undirected gaze is unseeing, for she is looking into an interior world. She surrenders to her own imagination, as though listening to an echo that reflects a wealth of memories abundant in experiences and allows her visions to generate new images in her mind's eye. Far from reacting impulsively to some external event, she seems to be creating a moment of undisturbed introspection, where she can sound into the depths of her own being. Her long jacket flows around her knees, while her feet, like those of a dancer, are planted gracefully yet firmly on the ground.

A photograph has frozen time into a single moment, capturing spontaneous movement, immortalizing it — a living monument, a statue of Louise Bourgeois at over seventy. We see her represented like a visitor in one of her own walk-in spatial sculptures, defining the location as here and now. Her eloquent gesture lends a particular expression to her intentions, which makes us want to learn more about them. This photo does not strike us as a document of some proud, self-satisfied sculptor posing in front of the work she has created. Instead it has the air of a theatrical performance by the artist, complementing the meaning of this installation already implicit in the title of the work.

She is surrounded by the rhythmically arranged folding walls of one of her major installations *Articulated Lair* of 1986, the first one of twenty-nine *Cells*. Gleaming shafts of light create a sectioning patchwork of corresponding planes on the floor. Sometimes they fan out and sometimes they combine to form broad corridors of light. Like the metal wall panels, hinged at three levels in such a way that the strange, outside world may be glimpsed through the slits between them, so, too, the light streaming in underlines the shady, protective twilight character of this space. It can be extended or decreased as desired with the help of the folding screen, since the metal wall panels are mounted on small casters. Through two small doors cut into the adjustable walls visitors enter and leave. Inside the space there is only one tiny, low, perforated stool with light shining on it from above. The shape of the circling, rounded enclosure, in which the doors are positioned in such a way that anyone entering the installation cannot immediately see the exit route (Ills 3, 6), contrasts starkly with the sharp-edged angles of the hinged walls. Encircling, enveloping sides heighten the protective character of the space, promising refuge, peace, and security to the intruder. Having been kept at bay outside by uniform black, once inside, the visitor feels sheltered by shades of white and the irregular light blue and black of the wall panels.

Hanging from black steel bands attached to the walls are groups of black rubber objects in various shapes and sizes. Their matt sheen, smooth surfaces and globular forms bring to mind thoughts of cudgels and clubs (Ills 3, 4). The black color and the soft, warm materiality of these objects precludes allusions to organic forms. No sooner does the viewer think he can identify a ham, sexual parts, limbs, sausages, or even bladders, stomachs, and intestines, than these quickly retreat back into the free, associative realms of independent abstraction as objects created by human hand. Their meaning and purpose are the subject of searching inquiry by a restless, volatile, free-floating imagination seeking

2 *Articulated Lair*, 1986

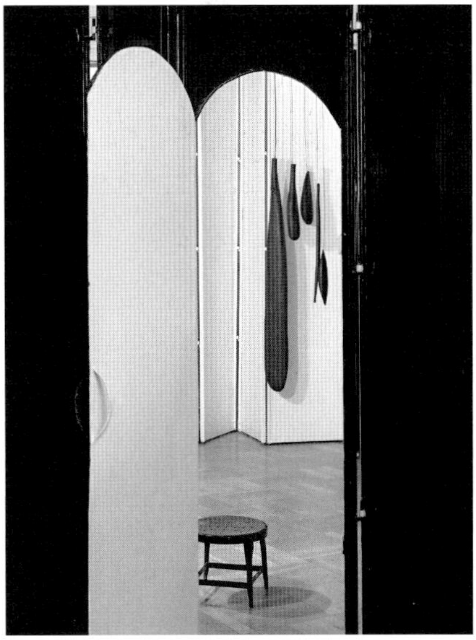

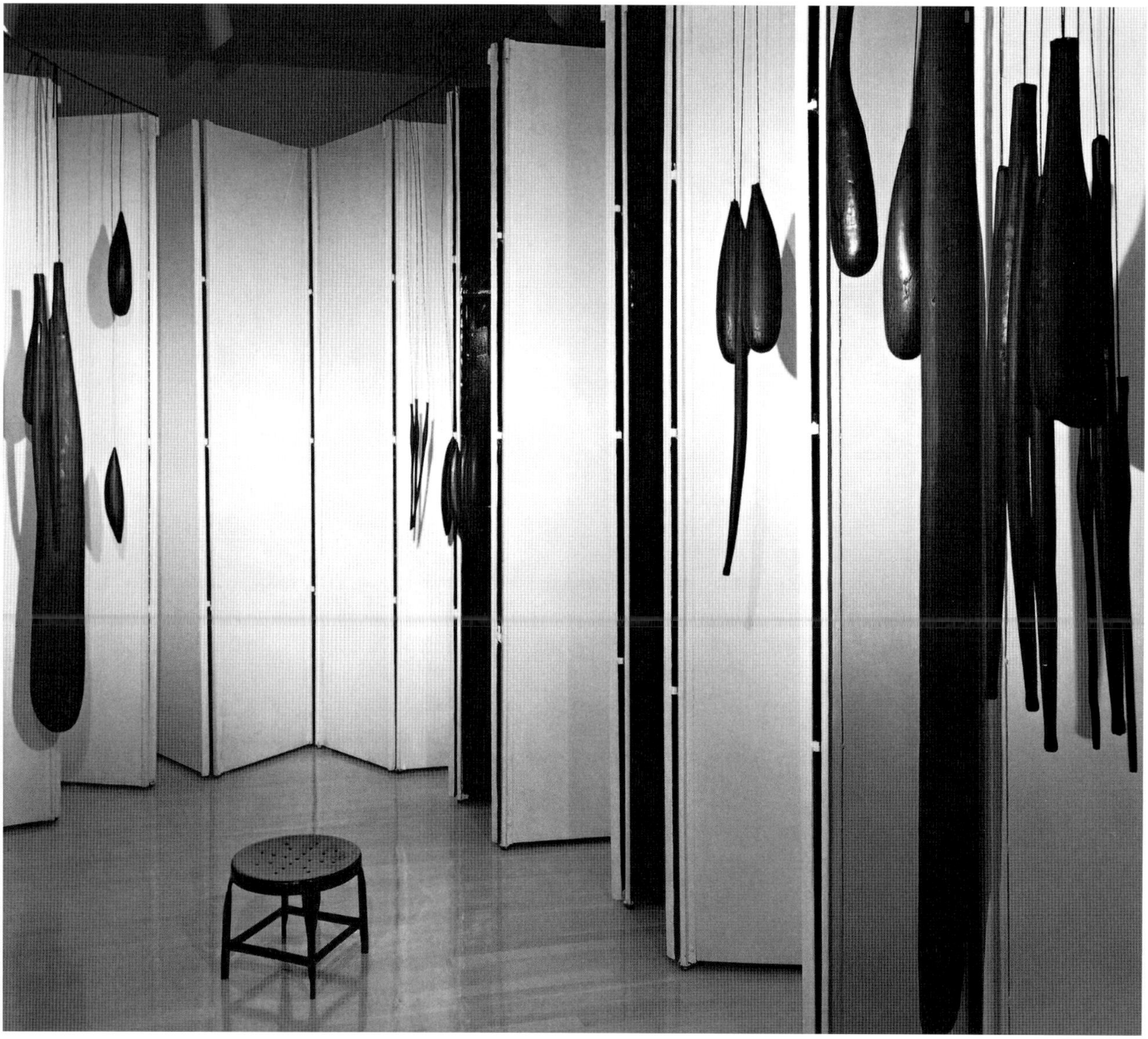

3 *Articulated Lair*, 1986
painted steel and rubber, height 132 in.

to interpret, to understand, and to fit what it sees into circumstantial reality as we know it. Louise Bourgeois calls these structures 'lairs' — in the sense of a den or a nest — intimate hiding places, concealed zones of introspection, where a creature might raise its brood or a person might live in safety.

In a discussion about the point of the installation, Louise Bourgeois described it as "a place to go, a place you need to go, a transitory protection." She continued:

> "The latest is called *Articulated Lair* because it has no fixed form; it is completely flexible, with forty-seven uprights, each of which has three hinges. If the circle were not completed, the parts would all fall down, like dominoes. And you can add or subtract.
> – And the two doors?
> LB: One is an entrance, and the other is an exit in order to escape if cornered.
> – For *you* to escape.
> LB: Right. For people without strategy. All they can muster is a lair.
> – Is escape a strategy?
> LB: It is a strategy all right, but a miserable one. It doesn't deserve the *title* of strategy, that's for sure. For me, strategy is always a move, not towards the self but towards someone else.
> – So you sit on your stool in the middle of your articulated lair.
> LB: And I enjoy it. It is a beautiful place.
> – And it's your nest, like an animal's.
> LB: Right. If this one is destroyed, I can make another.
> – So it's about lying low.
> LB: And watching. You watch to see whoever is coming and you have an attack of anxiety whenever a person is coming. But you recover and escape. It is a very considered way of living.
> – 'Articulated' means the lair is made in sections.
> LB: You can add or subtract. That's what 'articulated' means. So articulation is the symbol of a relationship that can change and improve."[2]

In *Articulated Lair* (Ills 1–4, 6) Louise Bourgeois has created a larger-than-life installation that transcends normal human dimensions: one does not merely observe it nor does one walk around it viewing it from all sides. The visitor does not admire it simply for its haptic structures, its refined materiality, its objective figuration, or its abstract formulation. Instead upon entering the installation, he squeezes ashamedly, almost surreptitiously, through a low door and succumbs to the architecture of the piece which is so ambiguously beguiling yet confusing. On closer examination, the apparent stasis of the rigid uprights turns out to be quite dynamic and flexible due to the casters and hinges that allow them to be extended or telescoped. The apparent impenetrability of this closed space reveals openings, gaps, and slits on all sides. The hermetic closure of its functional architectonics is broken open and called into question by the organic and vital structure of the spatial organism, variable in its elements and enriched by physical objects grouped together as living entities: warm, shifting, replete bodies whose presence fills the cold and stiff emptiness of the room. The naming of these corporeal objects and the title of the installation coincide: *Articulated Lair* — a jointed, eloquent, animalistic hiding-place that becomes an extended figure of meaning, a metaphor for domestic and human matters. Diametric opposites color the impression that this installation leaves with the viewer. Intimate, safe isolation is threatened by disturbing, inexplicable objects of rubber. Protective walls turn out to be a danger, for we could be trapped there at any moment. From having a sense of freedom and calm, the visitor suddenly realizes that this shelter could equally well become a prison.

Finally, it should be mentioned, the open ceiling and the lighting remind the visitor that this artificially installed room is itself only a part of a larger exhibition space: the piece has been constructed

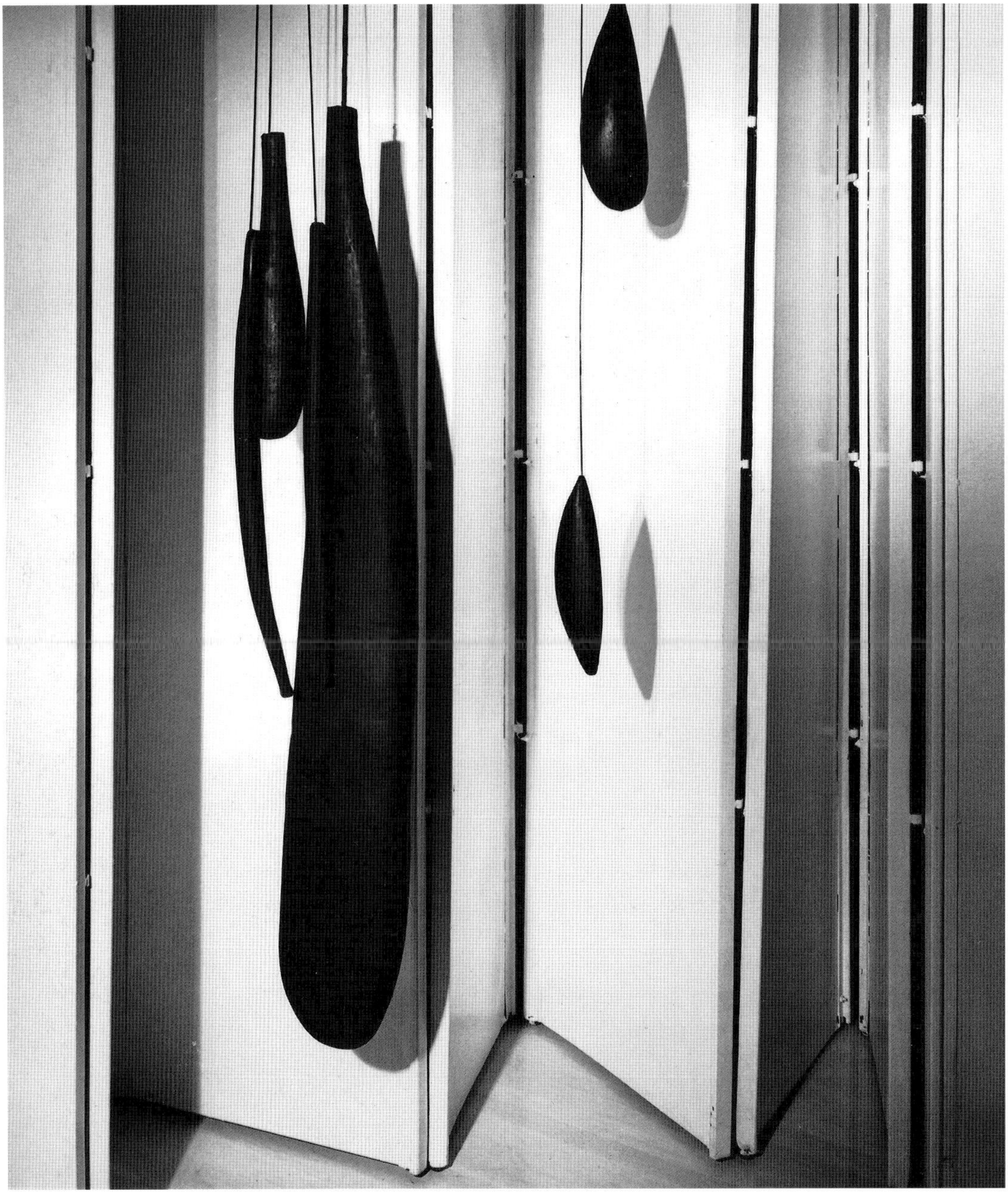

4 *Articulated Lair*, 1986

intentionally and for a specific purpose. Confronted with a work as impressive in its uniqueness as this is, the closer we try to come to it the more we are struck by its direct, simple visualization of fundamental, human life-experiences. And even though it seems to defy comprehension and to take on a puzzling, abstract dimension, we begin to appreciate its form, its color and material qualities, and its enigmatic allusions.

This perplexing withdrawal into the realms of abstraction should not however, obscure the fact that the viewer is faced here with a work that was created in the mid-1980s by a truly remarkable artist who was born in Paris in 1911; and that by the time she conceived *Articulated Lair*, she had been working in the tradition of Western, or rather West European, art for over forty-five years. Even as the twenty-seven-year-old Louise in a typically graceful pose, radiant with happiness, cheerfully self-confident and with the hint of a cheeky, rascally grin, her hair neatly tied back, was photographed on a Manhattan street in 1939 a year after her marriage to the American art historian, Robert Goldwater, she was already embarking on a long and fruitful artistic career. In France she had left behind the comfortable home of her youth and her early experiences in the art schools and academies where she had bravely enrolled after abandoning a degree in mathematics and philosophy at the Sorbonne. When asked what she found when she first came to America, she replied: "What I found and still find is the fact that in America everything is possible. There is room for everyone. It is very difficult to make a name, but no-one will stop you if you go on trying."[3]

Through her extreme and excessively articulated work Louise Bourgeois has, uniquely, altered the definition and parameters of sculpture that had prevailed since the Renaissance, from Michelangelo, Bernini and Antonio Canova to Rodin and the masters of the early twentieth century — parameters which had confined it to the faithful portrayal of the human body, the image of man, the image of humanity *per se*. Even though her modestly restrained installation *Articulated Lair* — conforming to the law of reduction — may at first sight appear to be constrained and indirect in its formulation, it will become apparent here, by observing it closely and putting it in its historical context, that it is singularly explosive in its conceptual power.

For the first time in its history, Louise Bourgeois has succeeded in turning the concept of 'sculpture' inside out. In her hands sculpture shakes off the shackles which bind it to a particular tangible object, and the practice of sculpting representations of individual objects is rendered obsolete. The criteria of sculptural production and the designation of an object as a work of art are no longer determined by the haptic qualities of its surface, its aesthetic or solely conceptual character. Consequently these criteria stand in the stead of, and now operate on, a metaphorical level which, in all its complexity, in its multiplicity of meaning, becomes the focus of the artist's conscious striving. Louise Bourgeois has created sculptures equal to and surpassing those of her contemporaries and predecessors in

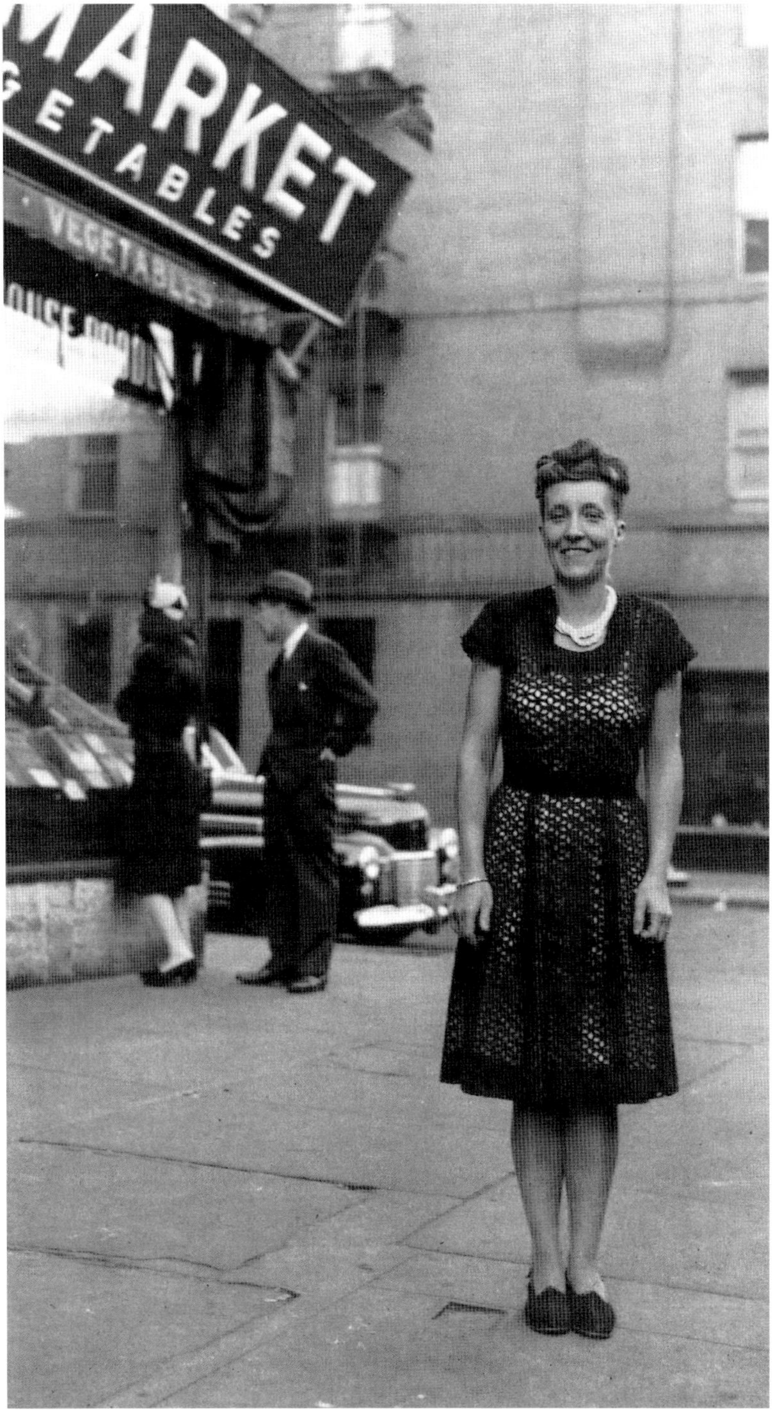

5 Louise Bourgeois, New York 1939

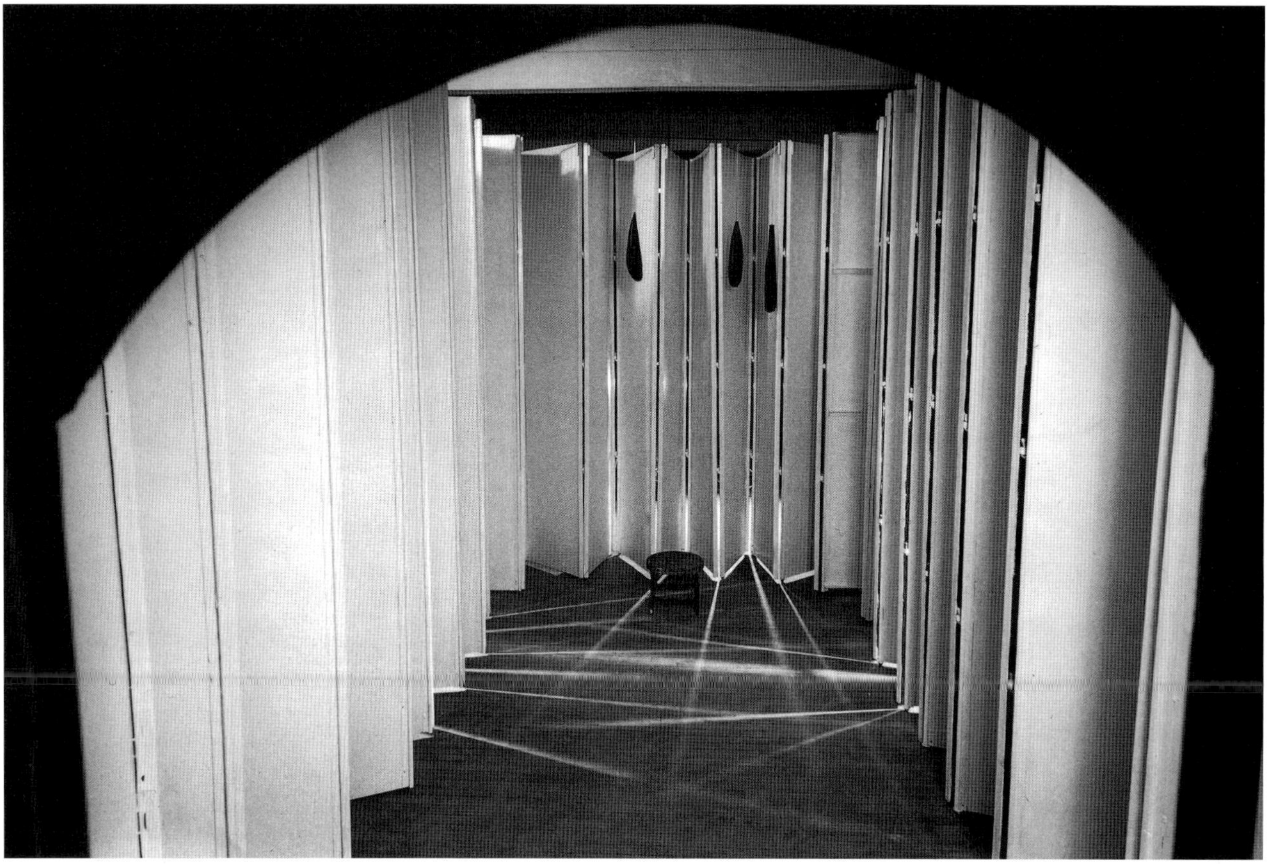

6 *Articulated Lair*, studio picture, 1986

twentieth-century sculpture — Constantin Brancusi, V.E. Tatlin, Alberto Giacometti, even Joseph Beuys and Bruce Nauman.

What artistic strength and energy lie behind this step that has been of such importance to Western art? Where has this woman come from with such an inexhaustible artistic will? What was the path that led her to this work?

II. THE LIFE OF AN ARTIST

Childhood, Youth, and her Years in New York: *The Destruction of the Father and Confrontation*

My childhood has never lost its magic, it has never lost its mystery, and it has never lost its drama. All my work in the past fifty years, all my subjects, have found their inspiration in my childhood.

Louise Bourgeois, 1997

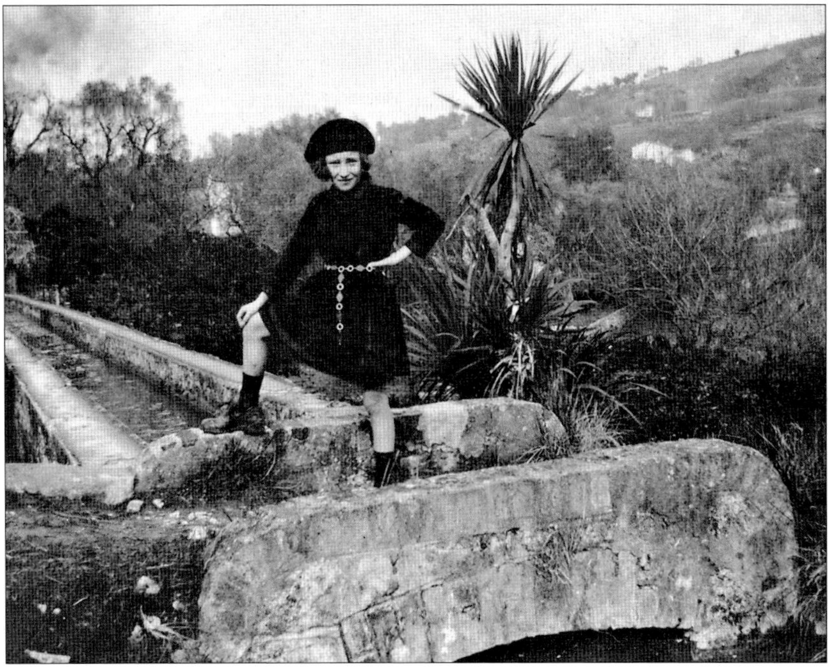

7 Louise in Le Cannet, 1922

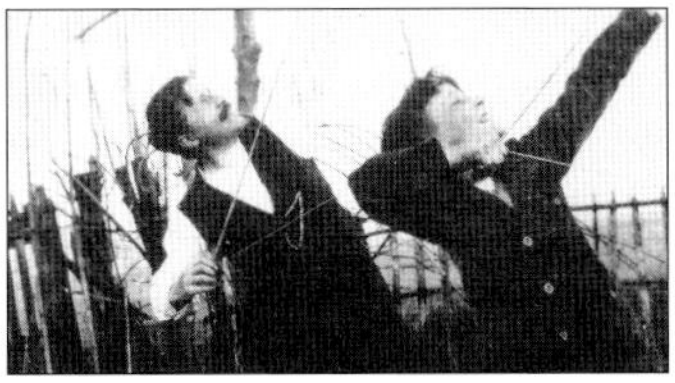

8 Pierre Bourgeois and his father practicing archery, c. 1923

"Straight to the stars!" The young Louise Bourgeois's joyful cry echoed through the garden as her brother set his sights on the stars. Father and son united in the noble sport, stood side by side, their bows taut. That was how she loved her father — youthful, high spirited, and full of vitality. At that moment all was still well with the world, and perhaps even the scepticism of a Zeno might have been dispelled by the young girl's infectious laughter. The heavenly bodies were not to lose their importance in the artist's life: "[...] And that explains my interest in the movement of the stars and the sun, which is absolutely basic for me. So that when I perceive where the sun is at a certain time of day, I relate to it as a *point fixe*. But this gets back to the panic. The panic means you have lost all frame of reference. And it is difficult to anticipate, so I find control by organizing my environment."[4]

smell that would come from the old tapestries as they were being dried. The colors from centuries gone by would take on new life and when the heavy tapestries had been wrung out and dried, they would await the skilled hands of the needlewomen like worn-out bodies after bathing, yearning for tenderness.

Her father had bought the house near the river in Choisy-le-Roi a year after Louise was born, by which time his tapestry and antiques business was firmly established. In the mornings, when daytime had not yet touched the dew-laden grass, the nearby river, still shrouded in mist, was propelling its green mass forwards. All around the sounds of the dawning day heralded its usual bustle in the steady crescendo of pots and pans in the kitchen and in the low babble of voices from behind the half-closed shutters. In this house overflowing with cooks, servants, restorers, washerwomen, brothers, and sisters — all combined with the background splashing of the waterfall — Louise would try to escape for a moment into her own morning, before her various tasks swept her up into the daily round.

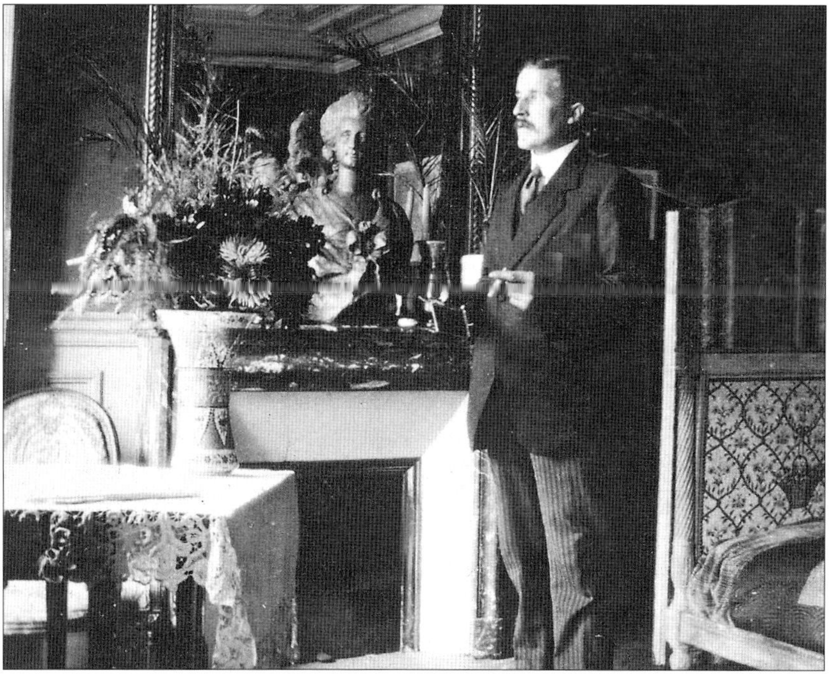

9 Louis Bourgeois, Louise's father, c. 1917

The sun broke through the heavy, milky clouds and lit up the facade of the grand house. The door to the garden was open as usual. The extensive roof terrace was empty and open to the fresh morning. Sometimes in her imagination Louise would summon up female figures there, with the pale, slightly pear-shaped faces of the women on the old tapestries in her father's business — their beautiful, sad eyes and their long, high-waisted, flowing gowns. She used to give them names and adorn them with brooches, earrings, and necklaces of gleaming precious stones. There was a river close by and she loved the

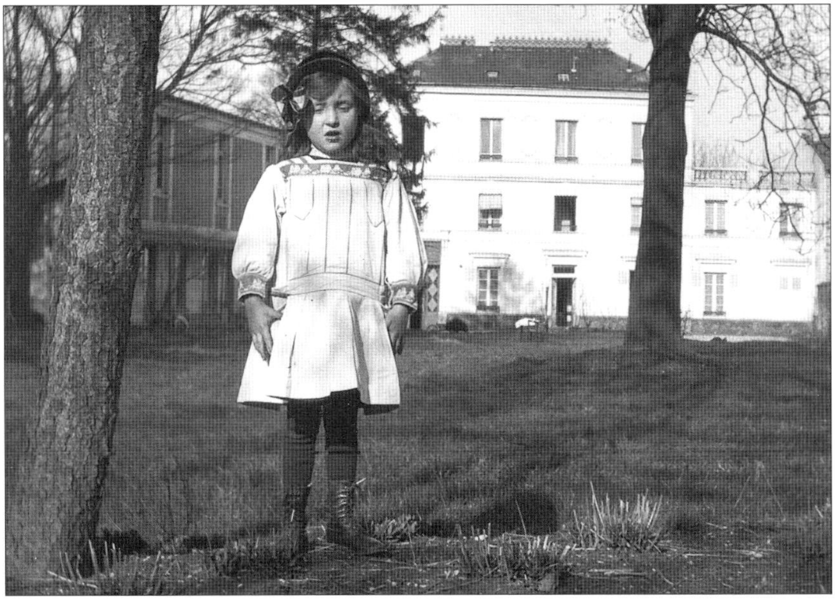

10 Louise in the garden of their house in Choisy-le-Roi, 1916

11 Louise in the garden of their house in Choisy-le-Roi, c. 1918

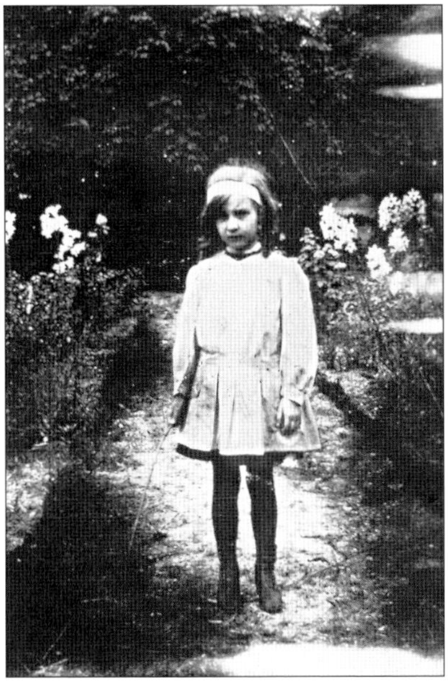

Louise Bourgeois was born on December 25, 1911 in Paris. The day before there had been a heavy fall of wet snow. The snow had frozen and crashed down in large, solid lumps from the roof of a nearby church. A servant, carrying the last supplies for the Christmas festivities, had trudged up to the delivery entrance of the grand apartment building on the left bank of the Seine in the center of Paris, and was now on the doorstep catching his breath and shaking the moisture out of his coat. The smell of Christmas cooking, the heavy aroma of fresh baking, and the sharp scent of citrus fruits pervaded the high rooms in the flat on the boulevard Saint Germain, mingling with the cold night air. Louis Bourgeois, entrepreneur and businessman, had been standing smoking at the window for a long time (Ill. 9). It took his eyes a while to accustom themselves to the light in the salon. He glanced several times at his wife, Josephine, and at the well-rounded shape of her stomach under the heavy folds of the dress he had given her when he knew she was expecting their second child. He could see from her face that she barely had the energy to follow the conversation that the doctor was conducting with their six-year-old daughter. Henriette, in the shadows of the candlelight, had virtually disappeared in amongst the upholstery cushions. Louis abruptly closed the windows, straightened his tie, and expressed his thanks rather pointedly to the doctor, who gave every appearance of intending to spend a good part of the Christmas period attending the birth of their child.

The story goes that the following day, Christmas Day 1911, when Louise's mother found she had a second daughter, she looked deep into her husband's eyes and quietly and calmly said: "She looks so very much like you, we must call her Louise" — thereby taking any sting from his potential disappointment at having fathered a second daughter. Later the artist commented on the situation: "If you bring a daughter into this world, you have to be forgiven, the way my mother was forgiven because I was the spitting image of my father. That was my first piece of luck. It may be why he treated me like the son he always wanted. I was gifted enough to satisfy my father. This was my second piece of luck."[5]

In 1916 the child with her father's name was four years old. Louise closed her eyes and tried to stand like a tree. The earth beneath her feet seemed to be growing into her through her tightly-laced boots, and the white dress with the flowered border around the neckline was turning into a leafy wood. She spread her hands a little, so that she could feel with her extended thumbs how the starched pleats of her dress were beginning to sway like branches in the wind. Her first memories were locking into position.

At the time, France was in a state of war. Josephine was hysterical when Louis went off to war and followed him from camp to camp with Louise. She had been relatively calm at the news that her husband had been wounded. After all, this was no more than she had been expecting daily since the moment when Louis had entered active service with his infantry unit. And somehow she was certain that now the worst had happened. The death of her brother-in-law — was that not enough? Desiré had died in the first days of the war, and at once everything that Louis had felt for his brother had become an act of remembrance. The deep affection that had bound the brothers together would never more be felt in the touch of a hand on a shoulder. And now Louis

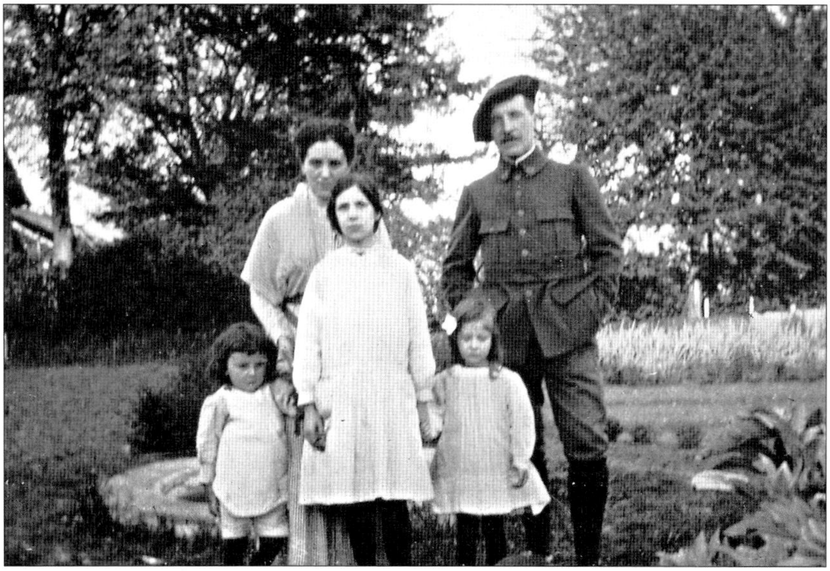

12 Louis Bourgeois in uniform with his wife and children (Pierre, Henriette, and Louise), Choisy-le-Roi, c. 1915

also had been drawn into that place where death took the center of the stage and every day, over and over, demanded payment for his role.

In 1915 Louis Bourgeois was taken to a military hospital in Chartres. The building was surrounded by a high wall, and just before Louise and her mother turned into the courtyard, the little girl saw the large red cross painted on a patch of pale brickwork. Holding her mother's hand, Louise had walked down the long room where nurses in white aprons hurried between the men lying in their wrought-iron beds. She ran the last few steps when she saw her father sitting contentedly on a chair by one of these beds. Louis was alive and, obviously feeling well, was perfectly happy to be photographed being attended to by a nurse.

Afterwards the four-year-old stood outside in the street again and took in the joy of seeing her father. That morning, still half asleep before their early departure, she had insisted on wearing her checked wool dress; had allowed her shoelaces to be tied tightly; and had looked in the mirror to see how the bow in her hair was sitting. Then she had graciously consented to being dressed in her knee-length velvet coat with the big golden buttons. The hat had caused heated discussion. Once they were settled on the long journey, it was only when she had tugged protractedly at its ribbon that the bow looked out under the rim; and she sank back against the leather seats to catch up on missed sleep. Now, standing in front of the hospital she was tired and happy, and the stone faces that she had seen on the cathedral walls as they drove by mingled with the looks of the many strange men who had watched from under their white sheets as her father took her in his arms.

13 Louis Bourgeois after being wounded in action, in hospital in Chartres, 1915

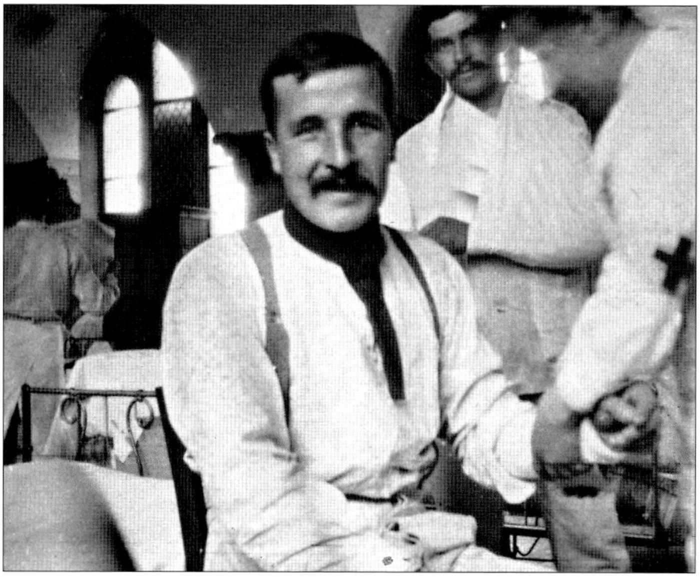

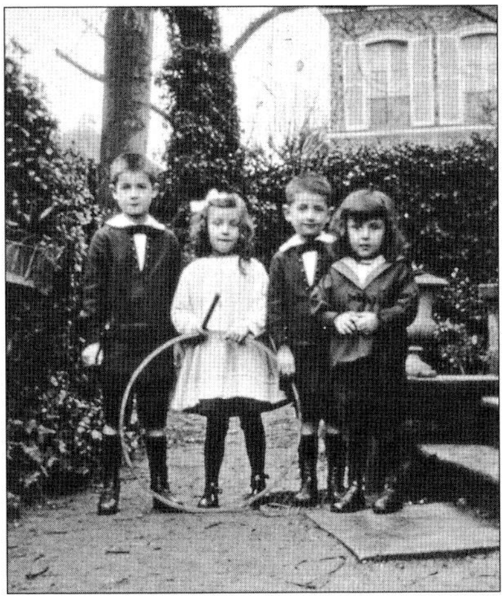

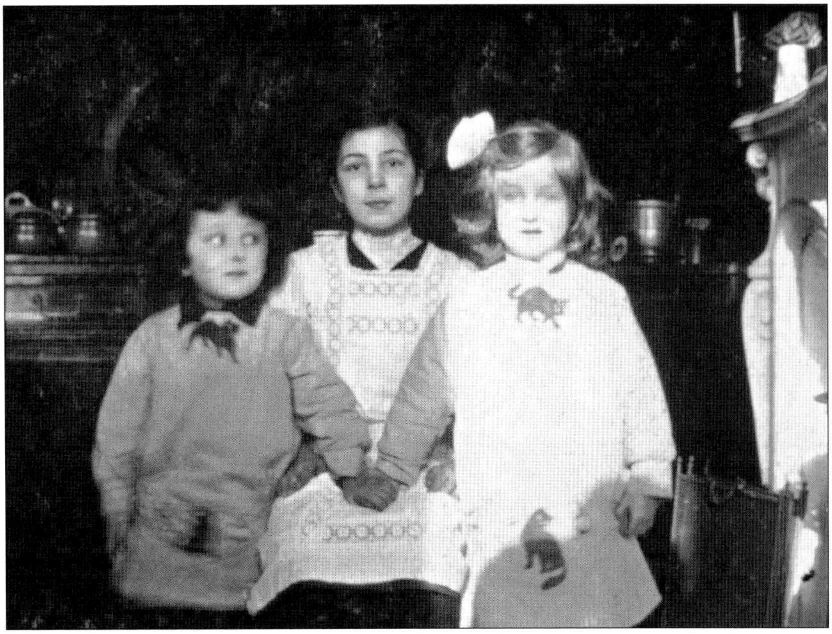

14 Louise and Pierre with their cousins, Jacques (left) and Maurice (second from right) in front of their grandparents' house, Clamart, c. 1917

15 The three siblings, Pierre, Henriette, and Louise, c. 1917

16 Louise in front of the hospital in Chartres when visiting her wounded father, 1915

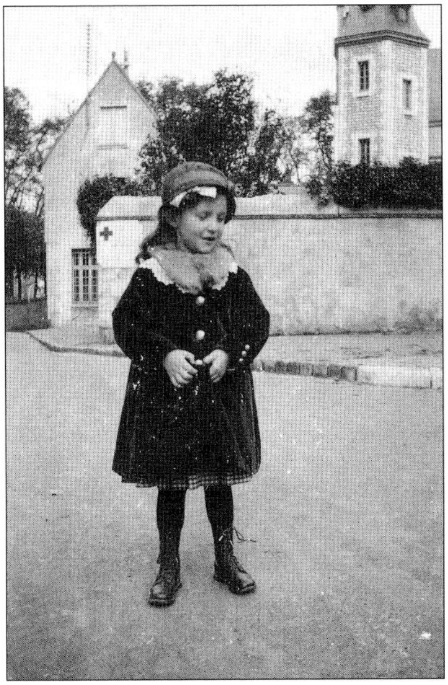

The First World War in fact increased the young Louise's immediate family. After her uncle's early death it was only natural that his two sons should come to live with her father's family. However, the inclusion of Jacques and Maurice (both older than Louise) in her family aroused in her a sense of now having to defend her territory (Ill. 14). And, according to the artist's own account in later years, the two boys were never really accepted. After all — as no one could deny — they were only cousins.

Her relationship with her younger brother, Pierre, was much more complex and affectionate (Ills 15, 21). When we listen to someone describing their past, a gentle laugh can sometimes conjure up a whole world. And it is not hard to imagine a torrent of childish yet cultured French clinging still in the thick wall-hangings. In 1917 we see the three siblings close together, the oldest sitting, the younger ones on either side, and, as before, we begin to read the photograph as the visual record of a memory. Just as in our own memories the truth of our lives always surfaces, so we take the various aspects of any image from someone else's past as a test of their account.

The metal fireguard in front of the fireplace is folded up. A cup of afternoon tea has been put down on the cast-iron stove in order not to miss the moment that would make a good photograph. Perhaps this was also a moment when the internal relationships within the family became visible. Pierre, startled by the click of the camera, has moved at just the precise moment that the shutter allowed the light into the black box. He wanted to see his sister Louise and could not quite keep his eyes still, as he had been told to do. The light of the afternoon sun streams into the room. Louise knows this full well and, in the shade of the window spars which casts a shadow across her eyes, looks calmly into the lens of the camera. She smiles quietly and remains still, knowing that the light is creating a special place for her and the blossom in her hair. The younger children's hands are safely clasped in the lap of their older sister, as Louise talks to her brother.

In 1919 the family moved to Antony on the Bièvre. The water of the River Bièvre had a sufficiently high natural tannic acid content to color the wool needed for repairing damaged areas in the tapestries. The river flowed through their garden, where, walking along the pebble paths winding around the groups of trees or isolated statues, they could easily find themselves face to face with a pig, or a flock of hens or a donkey.

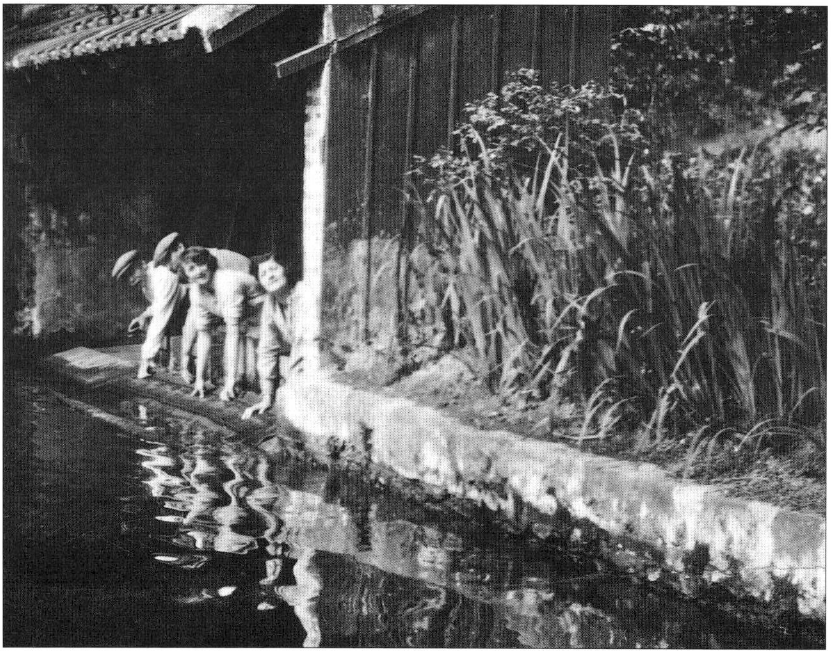

17 Weavers from the Bourgeois family business washing tapestries at the River Bièvre, c. 1920

Louise Bourgeois has described how this melee of creatures was part of a focused desire for harmony. Her father needed to convince himself after the war that the Germans and the French could indeed coexist. He wanted to show his children that mixtures are not impossible, and that even a dog and chickens, provided they were appropriately trained, could live together.[6]

On Sundays Louis and Louise took long walks from Antony to Clamart, where the young girl's grandparents used to live and now were buried. Father and daughter walked from one river valley to the next, from the Bièvre to the Seine. At some points they would stop to pay due respect to the sight of Paris in the changing daylight. Because of moments such as those, we can assume that Monsieur Bourgeois was relatively well in touch with the thoughts and dreams in his daughter's mind. Decades later Louise Bourgeois looked back to this time: "There is a very nice thing about my parents — that they were no social climbers, they were perfectly satisfied with their status. In these days it is very refreshing and there was no outlandish ambition in my family. There was no rat race, you see. They wanted to be independent. That was the password."[7]

At the end of the war in 1918, Spanish flu broke out in Europe and even more people perished. Louise's mother survived an attack but for years afterwards remained sickly and prone to emphysema. Now the family spent the winter months in the south, not least because of Josephine Bourgeois's delicate health (Ills 18, 19). For Louise, by now an adolescent, the twenties meant constantly widening horizons, partly as a result of the long journeys the family used to make to the Atlantic coast and to the mountains around Chamonix in summer, always returning to the Côte d'Azur in winter, first to Cimiez and later to Le Cannet (Ill. 23). The awakening and discovery of her own personality was bound up with a decade of extravagance, when a luxurious lifestyle was accompanied by the optimistic feeling of being part of an as yet unspoiled modern age.

In 1922 the swimming costume as a garment for female bathers was barely ten years old: we see father and daughter on a typical summer's day on the coast of Normandy, at the very spot where, two decades later, the soldiers from Louise's second home were to arrive to liberate Europe. As so often, the day had begun with a brilliant blue sky, so blue and glaring that Mme

18 Henriette, Louise's maternal grandmother, with Louise, Pierre, and Henriette on Mont Dore in the Auvergne, 1922

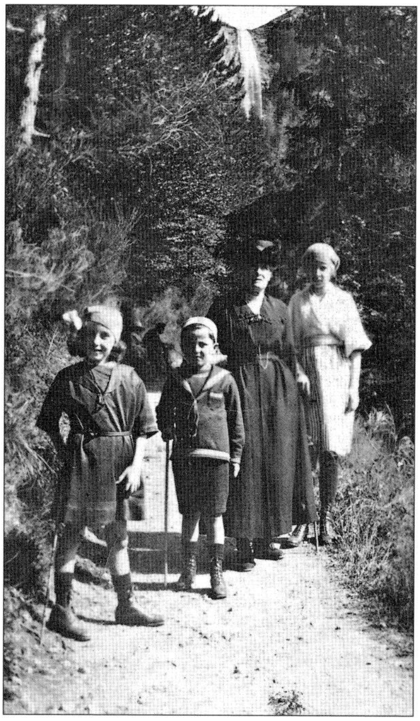

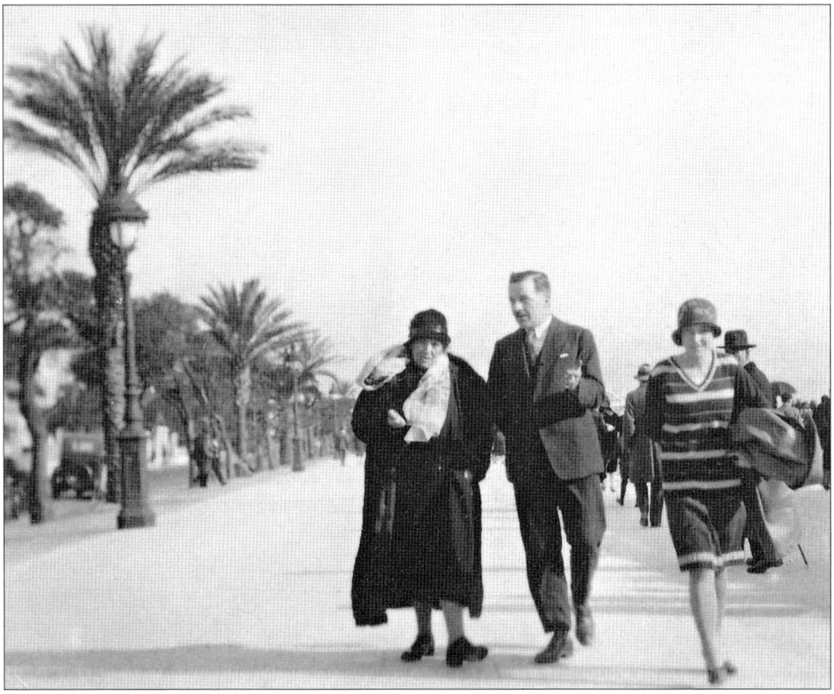

19 Louise, fashionably dressed in a Coco Chanel suit, with her parents, Nice, 1929

Bourgeois had had a searing headache since she woke up. They had gone to the beach early, had played in the water, and Louise had happily demonstrated her agility and physical coordination. No one had quite noticed the dark storm clouds gathering on the horizon. There was only a hectic scramble to leave when a powerful gust of wind blew over the deckchairs and sent the sunshades into the air like strange flying creatures. This was followed by a short lull, during which the distant roaring of the wind could be heard in concert with increasing crashing of the breakers: loud cries went up — *"Vite, vite, les parasols, les parasols"* — until the rain came pelting down. Louise and Louis had kept quite calm during the general uproar, watching the others' antics with amusement and exchanging glances, enjoying their own calm. With high-spirited abandon, Louise spun around with the white towel that she normally hid under in order to change into her tightly-fitting black bathing costume.

Sometimes Louise spent the summer in England. The intention was to improve her knowledge of English, which her father felt would be useful for business contacts. English was also the language of the young woman with whom Louise's father soon had a liaison. Sadie Gordon Richmond was engaged to give English lessons to the children and spent ten years with the Bourgeois family.

Louise was growing up now and it is difficult to resist a feeling of affection for her as she walks towards us on the promenade, ahead of her father and mother, or as she waves her changing towel, wearing a bathing costume of the sort that had revolutionized fashion and,

20 Louise with her father on the beach in Deauville (Normandy), 1922

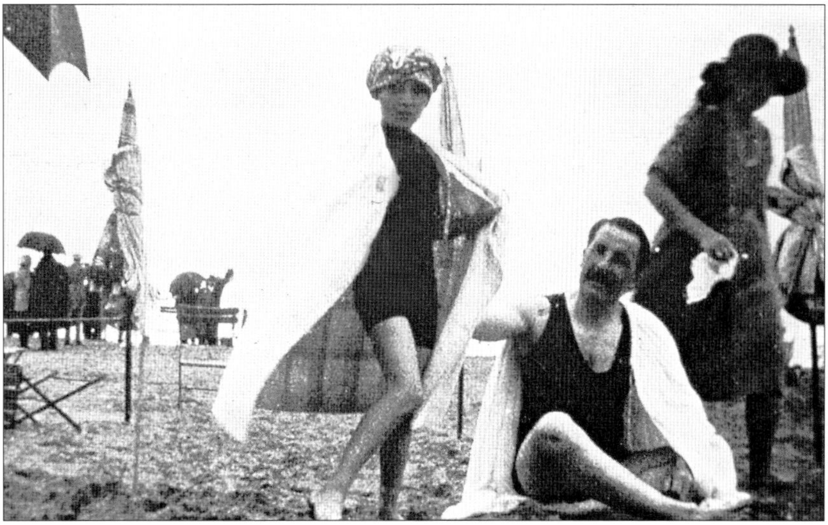

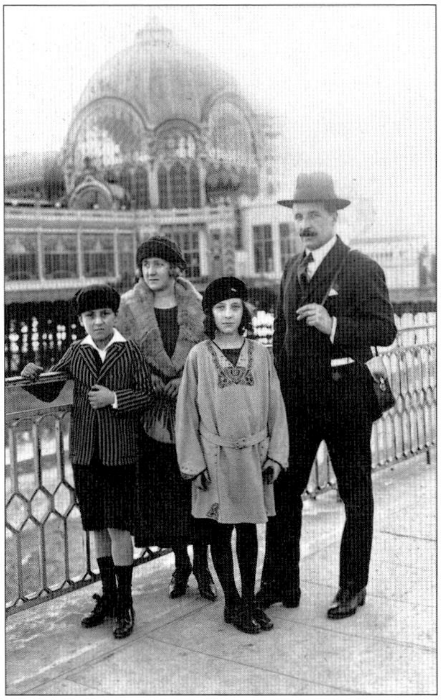

Left:
22 Pierre, Sadie, Louise, and her father on the Promenade des Anglais in Nice, c. 1923

with that, the image of women at the time. Her father must have delighted in matching her wit, taking a moment from his reading as he lay on the beach, and he glanced with pleasure at his daughter who cut such a pleasing figure in amongst the other water-sprites.

Some years before this, a young man named Marcel Proust had stood at the window of his hotel in Balbec and — vainly attempting to dry himself with a stiffly starched towel — had observed the mountains in the distance: "the snowy crests of its emerald waves, here and there polished and translucent."[8] Louise might perhaps also have been one of those who might have inspired the no-longer-young man to set out in search for a time that was now lost and which he described, page after page, conjuring up the atmosphere of those days: "In the midst of all these people, some of whom were pursuing a train of thought, but then betrayed its instability by a fitfulness of gesture, an aberrancy of gaze as inharmonious as the circumspect titubation of their neighbors, the girls whom I had noticed, with the control of gesture that comes from the perfect suppleness of one's own body and a sincere contempt for the rest of humanity, were advancing straight ahead, without hesitation or stiffness, performing exactly the movements that they wished to perform, each of their limbs completely independent of the others, the rest of the body preserving that immobility which is so noticeable in good waltzers."[9] Those long sentences: the desire to restrain the impatience of the new century, trying to force it to pay attention to a time that is now lost. "You cannot arrest the present", as Louise Bourgeois herself mused, "you just have to abandon every day to your past. And accept it. And if you can't accept it, then you have to do sculpture!"[10]

It was in Chamonix in 1929 (Ill. 24) that Louise first encountered mountains. Using long poles with iron tips which gripped the slippery, slightly thawing ice, they had set off up the glacier. The ground offered no secure foothold and Pierre flapped his left arm to keep his balance while Louise danced lightly from foot to foot to maintain hers. Despite the cold, the climb brought Louis out in a slight sweat. Only the mountain guide, true to his profession, was not to be thrown off balance.

The winter months in the south of France offered a rather more promising location: the rocky coastline, opening out into wide bays with views of the towns of the French Riviera, endless pine groves and the snow-covered peaks of the Alpes Maritimes. And all bathed in the light of the mild winter sun, suddenly turning the rocks glowing red and dipping the water in blue as though it were trying to invent a color that would dissolve sky and sea, casting an antique glow over the old fortress, and seemingly levitating the dour tower of the island monastery above the waters (Ill. 23). This was the light that had drawn Matisse south — in the afternoons one could wrap it around oneself like an Indian silk. Later it would settle over the whole landscape like a soft veil until the last lingering gleam of red slipped away over the horizon.

Since 1921 Louise had attended the Lycée Fénelon in Paris (Ill. 33), a school with a good reputation and a proud tradition. During the winter months she was enrolled at the Lycée Internationale in Cannes, just a few steps away from the long white beach that extended right around the bay. The girl with pigtails and bare knees sitting by her father on a wall was now a young lady, up-to-date with the latest fashions

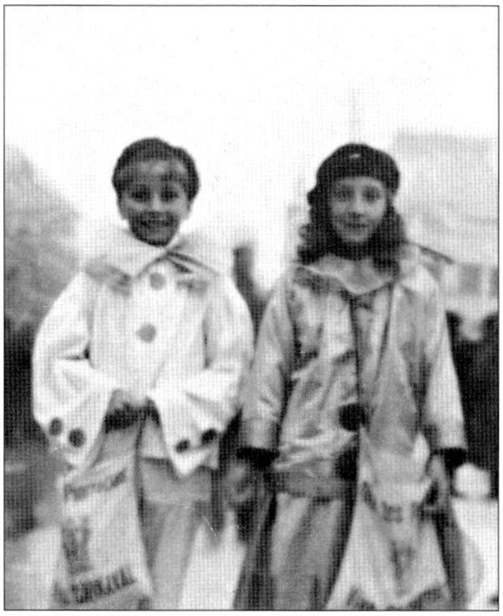

21 Louise and Pierre, dressed as Pierrot and Columbine, in Le Cannet, 1923

23 Louise with her parents in Le Cannet, 1922

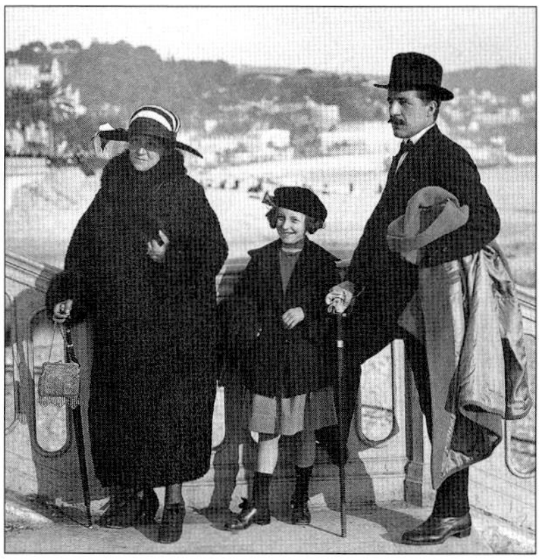

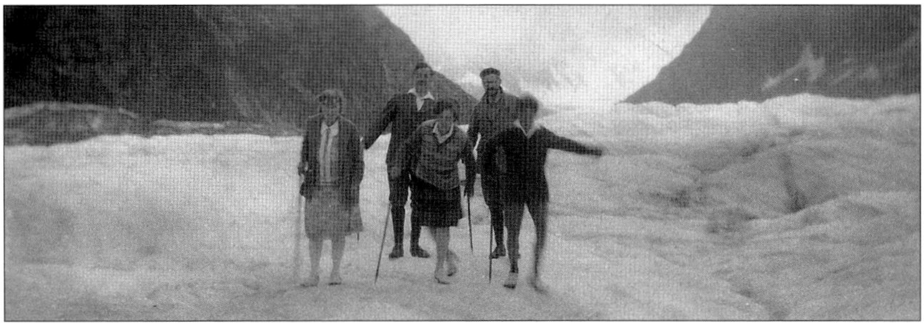

24 Sadie, Louis, Louise, M. Gonnet (a guide) and Pierre in Chamonix, 1929

and self-confident in her demeanor. In the mid-1920s we see her as a fourteen-year-old, already wearing a white, short-sleeved dress by Coco Chanel (Ill. 25), the designer who was to play such a major part in creating a new mood for the time. And Coco's competitor, the grand master of fashion, Paul Poiret, was also represented in the young Louise's wardrobe. Poiret is credited with having freed women from their corsets, straightening out the familiar S-curve of the previous era. By this time Coco Chanel was already deciding on new materials for women to wear. While Paul Poiret was contributing to the French war effort by rationalizing the production of military greatcoats so that sixty centimeters of material and four hours' labor were saved, Coco Chanel was employing over three hundred seamstresses. She introduced jersey — beige and machine-knitted — into the world of ladies' fashions. She dispensed with decoration for the clothes of the elegant élite and designated the line itself as the measure of style and affluence. With style replacing decorative accessories, and hitherto inferior materials receiving the blessing of top-class couturiers, a new image of womanhood was emerging, and fashion had successfully completed the leap into the new century. Coco wanted women to walk upright, wearing clothes that emphasized neither the waist nor the small of the back, and while Poiret was designing clothes that at last no longer pinched in the waist, Coco abandoned waists altogether. Hems crept upwards to allow the wearer to stride out freely. At the same time, however, these fashions were confusing, for they were unexpectedly free of allusion, and now a woman's wardrobe was no longer the subject of interested inquiry. From this point onwards there was a new set of rules.

And so we see Louise on the Promenade des Anglais in 1927, dressed in a style that was to change the world: a knee-length skirt with a long blouse hiding the waist and continuing the line of the skirt, a collar with a loose cravat and, drawn down over her short hair, the obligatory, bell-shaped hat with a narrow brim. Balancing a paper parasol on her shoulder, she stood in her high-heeled shoes in the midst of the passers-by under the palms in Nice (Ill. 28). Perhaps we might also have detected a touch of the designer perfume that neither revealed its contents nor alluded to the scent of some flower, but simply bore a number for a name. For Louise, the clothes she wore were a matter of conscious and individual choice — a Sonia Delaunay costume for the flight to London or for taking a walk with her father.

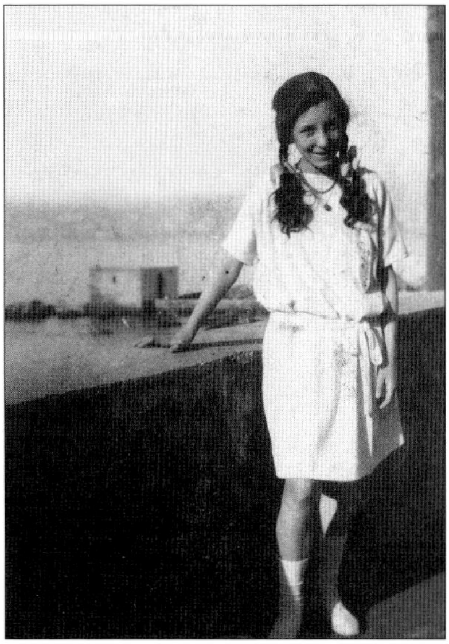

Right.
25 Louise, as a fourteen-year old, in a dress by Coco Chanel, 1925

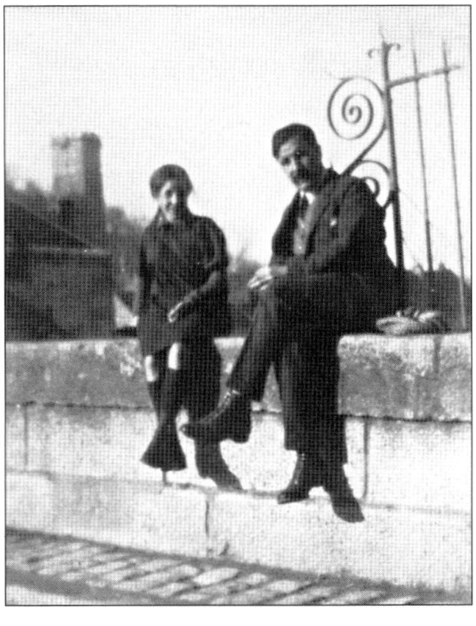

26 Louise with her father in Cannes, 1925

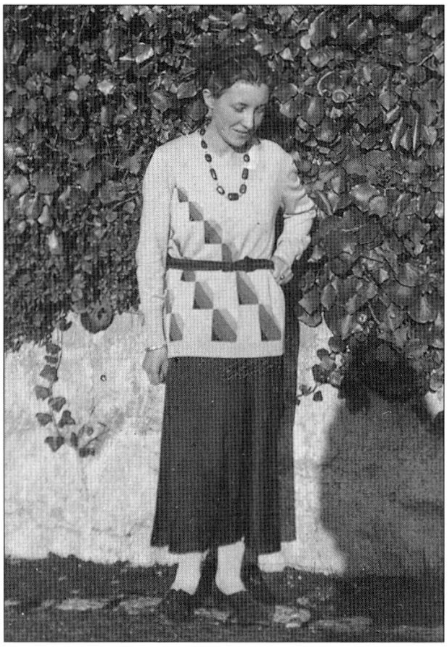

27 Louise in a suit by Sonia Delaunay, Nice, 1929

In 1929, when she had just turned eighteen, Louise got her driver's license (Ill. 30). After this she always drove the car, and her mother, who had previously had to rely on being driven by the governess, Sadie, now settled comfortably into the back seat of the large black car while Louise drove. We can only hope that Louise Bourgeois's own assessment of the differences between herself and her mother did not apply to her behavior on the roads: "My mother was a restorer, she repaired broken things. I don't do

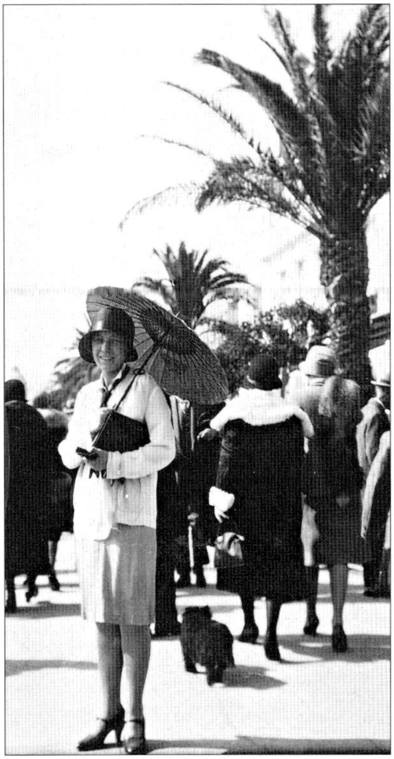

28 Louise on the Promenade des Anglais in Nice, 1927

that. I destroy things. I cannot go the straight line. I must destroy, rebuild, destroy again. My rhythm is not the same. My mother moved in a straight line: I go from one extreme to the other."[11] Louise now also took over responsibility for the care of her mother. Josephine Bourgeois needed regular care, and Louise set the cupping glasses.

Again and again we come across moments of peace in Louise's life: we find images that speak of recourse to an inner world — as, for example, if we were to stand on the steps of the Villa Pompeiana in Cimiez, not separated from the photographic subject by time and distance alone. Louise is leaning over the balustrade and her gaze travels freely from the steps out into nothingness, following the direction of a path without seeing it (Ill. 32). It is almost possible to

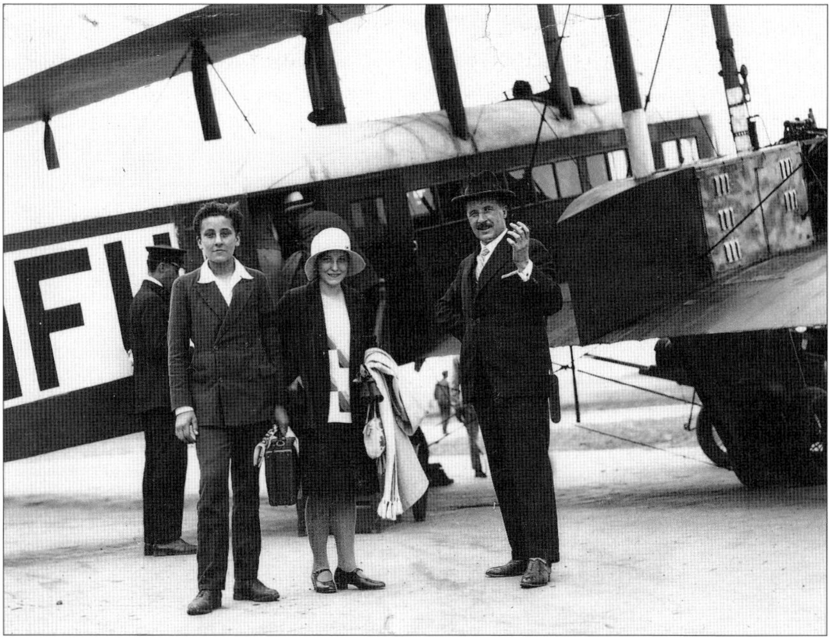

29 Pierre, Louise, and their father at Nice Airport before departing for London, 1929

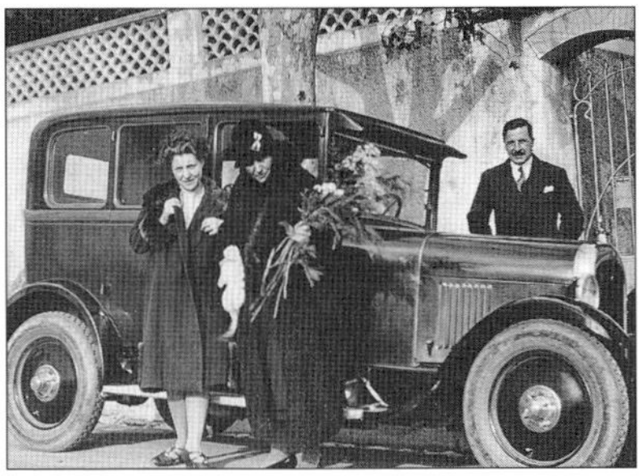

30 Louise with her parents and automobile in front of the Villa Pompeiana in Cimiez, Nice, 1928

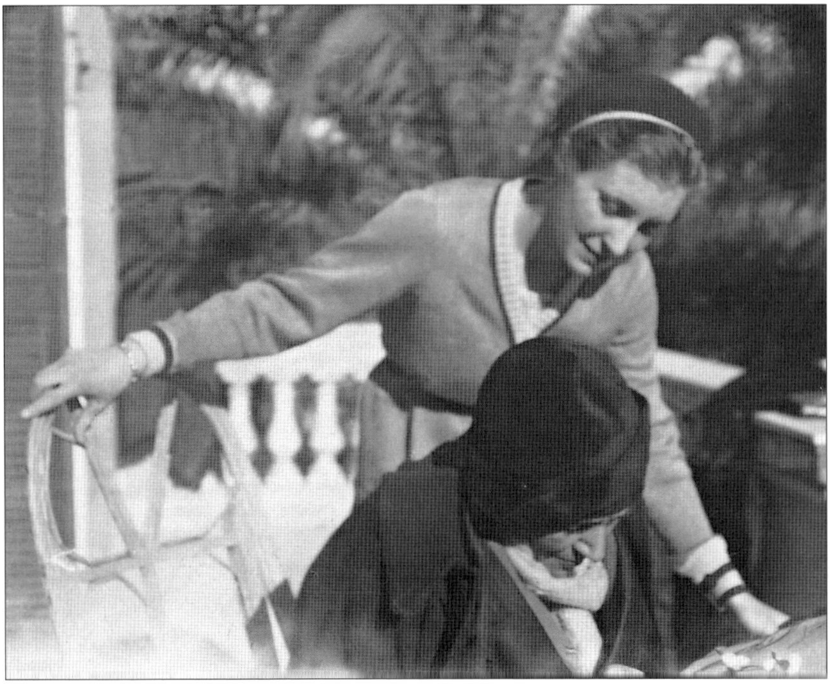

31 Louise with her mother in the garden of the Villa Pompeiana, 1932

32 Louise in the garden of the Villa Pompeiana, 1930

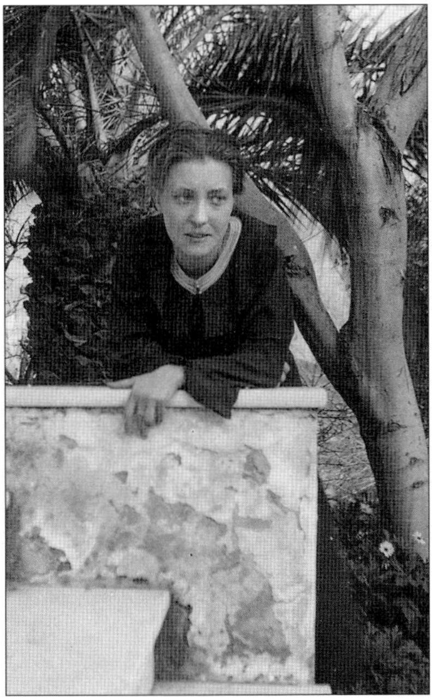

detect the slightly pungent scent of the eucalyptus trees and to hear the trilling of a single bird in the treetops.

As we linger for a moment in our narrative, is it altogether idle to speculate on the link between personal biography and an artist's later reputation? What role does individual character play, who determines the apportionment of creative potential which, as in the case we are considering here, is to produce works of epoch-making significance? We know that in 1925 Louise saw the *Exposition des Arts Décoratifs* and, in 1928, she met Pierre Bonnard in Le Cannet ...

However, Louise had first of all to finish high school, which she duly did in 1932. Her mother died that same year and Louise suffered deeply at her loss. She had, after all, made a pact with Fate to save her mother: "When I was afraid of my mother dying, a challenge I could not meet, the warding off of her death, not to let her disappear, I made a vow. I swore to myself if my mother survived that morning I would give up sex."[12] But in reality her reaction to her mother's death was even more desperate and she attempted to take her own life by jumping into the Bièvre. Her father had made light of her grief and when she really did jump he had to rescue her from the water. What should our response be to this decision to choose the only alternative to life? To give up life because it no longer seems bearable and one cannot imagine it continuing, is at least a decision — to choose the river. It should in no way be questioned, even if we know nothing of the condition of the Bièvre at the time, whether it was rushing and swirling, or even a realistic prospect for a suicide attempt. And these moments when desperation became a decision may well have played a part, years later, in the beginnings of Louise Bourgeois's endeavor to model a 'reality' that involved objects and spaces — '*Cells*' as she was to call them later — that provide a space where there may be a chance of bridging the gap between one's own existence and life itself.

What Louise Bourgeois had seen in 1925 at the age of thirteen at the *Exposition des Arts Décoratifs* had left its mark. "Those works were handcrafted and very beautifully made," she looked back with a degree of amusement. "Later I was taught by these artists. I have to say, I have a soft spot for all the people who taught me something. I liked all my teachers. The people I was revolting against were not my teachers."[13] As early as 1929, when she was still at school, Louise attended a drawing class at the Ecole Nationale d'Art Décoratif, even though she started to study mathematics and philosophy at the Sorbonne after her baccalaureate. Initially she took pleasure in the principles underlying mathematical constructions. However, as her studies brought her into contact with mathematical systems other than that of Euclid, she quickly became aware that any notion of mathematical certainty is wholly illusory. Nevertheless, her love of mathematical precision stayed with her and science remained for her the domain of one truth at least: "Science is truth. Art is pleasure, but, in the end, science has the last word. Life comes to an end and so do art and pleasure. Science is unerring, in the same way that we are born and that we die."[14] Meanwhile, from an early age, even as a child Louise had been taught by her parents to regard the ability to draw as something useful. "A lot of parents would make a career out of having children," as she later put it. "They lived through the child and destroyed him. It is better to have parents who use their children as unpaid labor."[15]

As a young girl, in 1921, Louise was one of the many draftsmen and women employed by her father, creating designs for missing sections in the tapestries. Often a leg or a horse's hoof had to be filled in, or sometimes it was a matter of creating innocuous flower patterns to conceal certain areas that were too much for the more puritan of the company's predominantly American clientele. Numerous cupids in compromising positions were snipped with a pair of sharp scissors and turned instead into the bearers of floral ornament. Louise was happy to find a degree of self-fulfillment in what she was doing: "*Cela a donné de la dignité à mon art. C'est tous ce que je demandais.*"[16] In the meantime the lines and shapes she drew in those days have come stunningly into their own in other media and, to this day, Louise Bourgeois's drawings collide with the web of our thinking and feeling until comprehension suddenly overtakes us with lightning speed on its long, spidery legs.

After Louise had finished school in 1932 she lived in Paris. A few weeks earlier she had still been shopping at the market in Nice. The weather had turned, and she felt that her pain at her mother's death must surely abate with time.

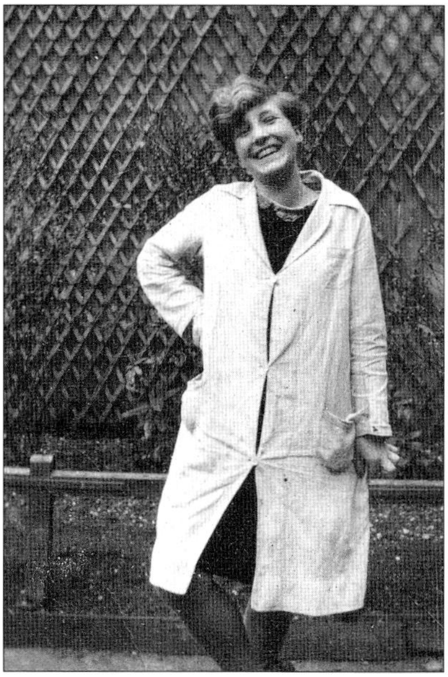

33 Louise Bourgeois as a student at the Lycée Fénelon in Paris, 1927

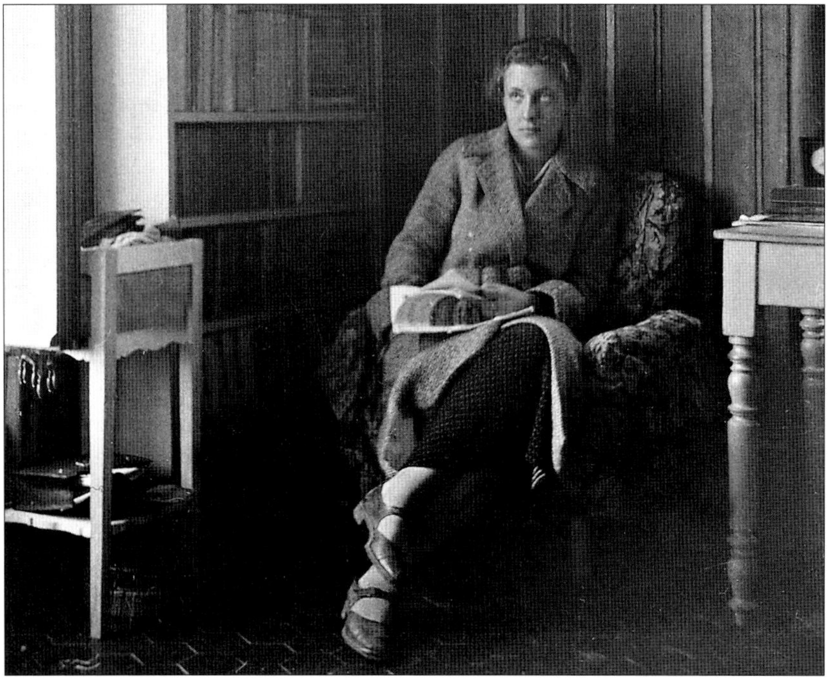

34 Louise preparing for the *Baccalauréat*, 1932

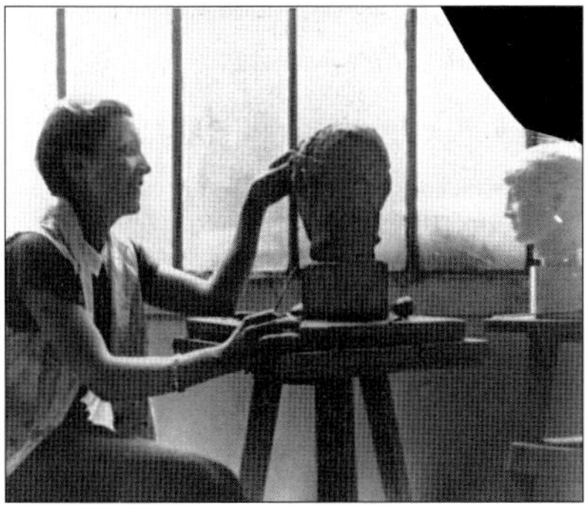

35 Louise photographed by Brassaï at the Académie de la Grande-Chaumière in Paris, 1937

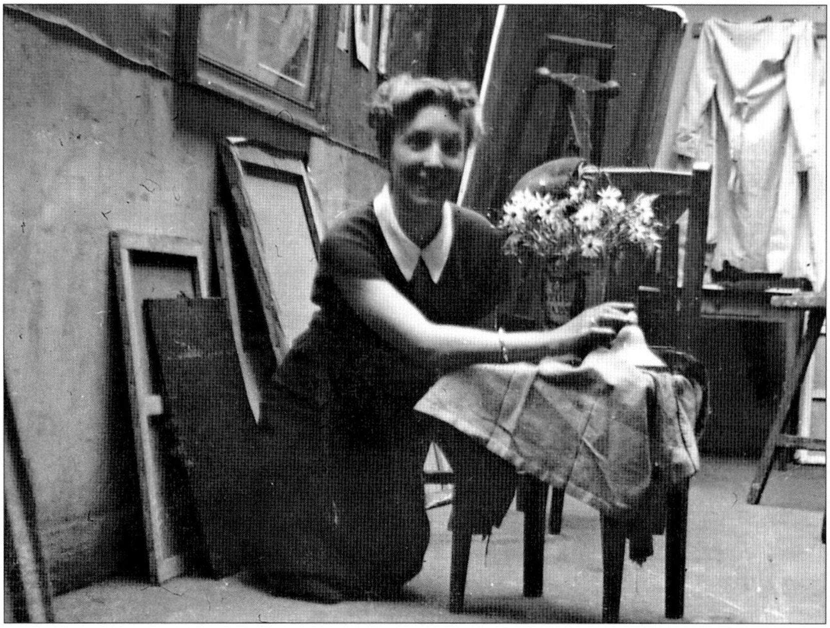

36 Louise at the Académie de la Grande-Chaumière, c. 1937

37 Louise in Nice, 1932

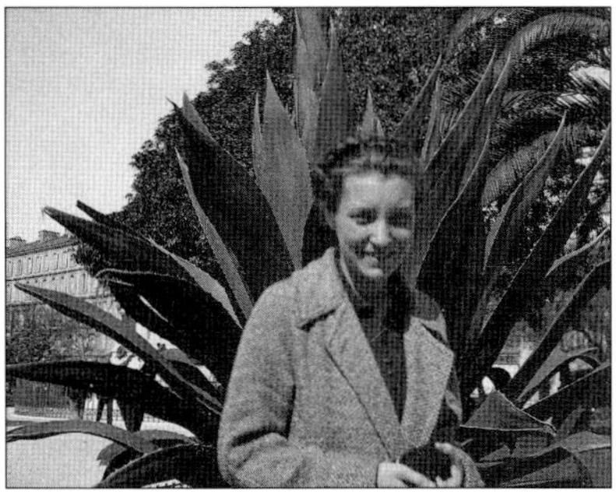

38 Louise in the marketplace in the old quarter of Nice, 1932

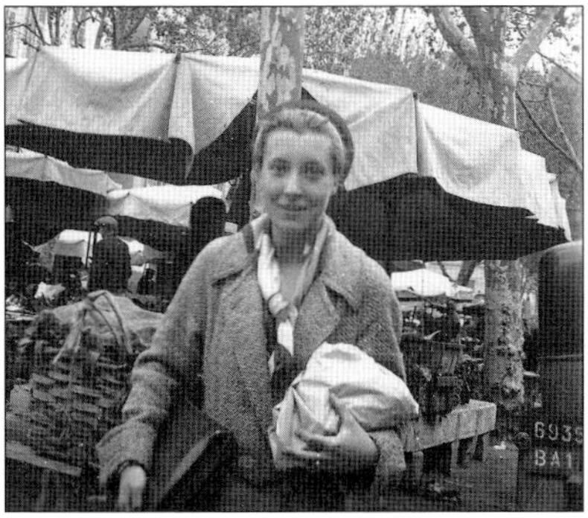

She was becoming increasingly subject to a specific form of disjointed memory that she felt the need to realize in visual terms. She sought out those who could teach her and ceased to take any notice of her father's antipathy towards people who called themselves artists.[17]

It was Fernand Léger who allowed her to attend his courses without having to pay fees, and who recognized her vocation as a sculptor in her response to an exercise he had set, which involved drawing wood-shavings floating in the air.

During this period, from 1933 onwards, Louise attended a variety of studios in Montparnasse and Montmartre (Ills 35, 36). "This brings back such a feeling of loneliness, it chokes me," she remembered later. "I went from studio to studio. [...] I wanted an art education, and I didn't want to go into the government schools; my way of doing it was to go from studio to studio. Let us say there were twelve — I went to every one of them, with an iron will that I was going to understand something I couldn't understand."[18] In the Atelier Wlerick at the Académie de la Grande-Chaumière she was entrusted with the task of choosing the models — without exception prostitutes with chalky white skin, violet lips, and orange-colored hair. They used to make jokes about the artist's innocence. Louise remembers their striking interest in cleanliness: "This is amazing, no? I learned more about life. I learned the most promiscuous people seem to have a fetish about cleanliness."[19]

She studied with Paul Colin, a relatively unknown artist, and went with his students to Moscow and Leningrad for a conference. In 1934 she went to Russia for the second time — eastwards through Germany, Denmark, Norway, and Sweden — to attend an International Festival of Theater in Moscow with Paul Colin and his more politically active students (Ill. 41). "I was attracted to Communism because it bothered my father," Louise comments with a wry smile. "I was brought up on teasing, and I returned the compliment whenever I could."[20] That year she attended the May Day celebrations in Red Square as a spectator but does not seem to have sacrificed anything of her own personal elegance for the sake of revolutionary ideals. The sight of her sitting on the railing on board the *Baltic Croisière* throws a revealing light on the way the *grande dame* of twentieth-century sculpture now describes that period, with her rough, girlish voice, lightly rouged lips, and the ghost of a French accent coloring her fluent American English: "I went

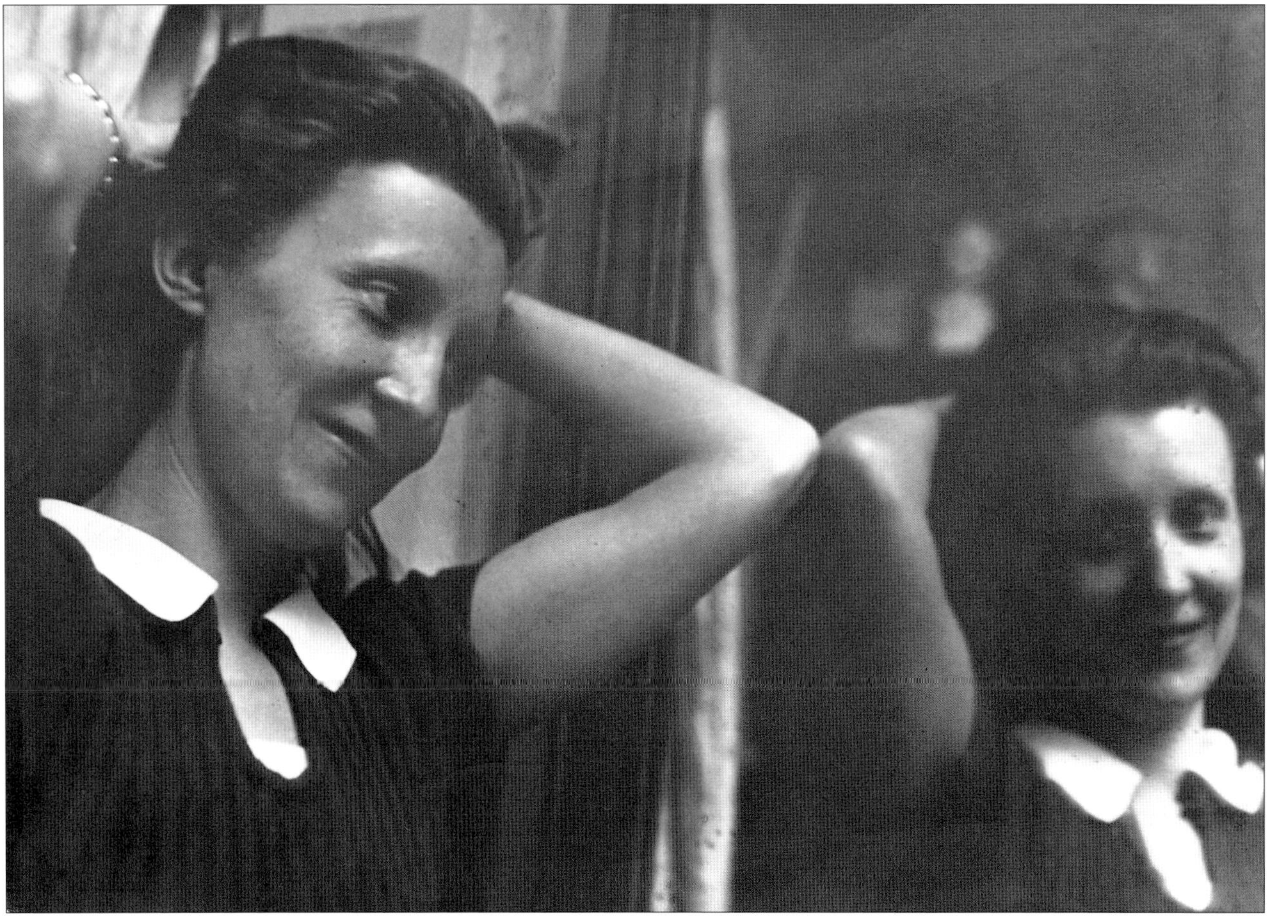

39 Louise posing for Brassaï, Paris 1937

40 Louise with Paul Colin's art students in Moscow, 1934

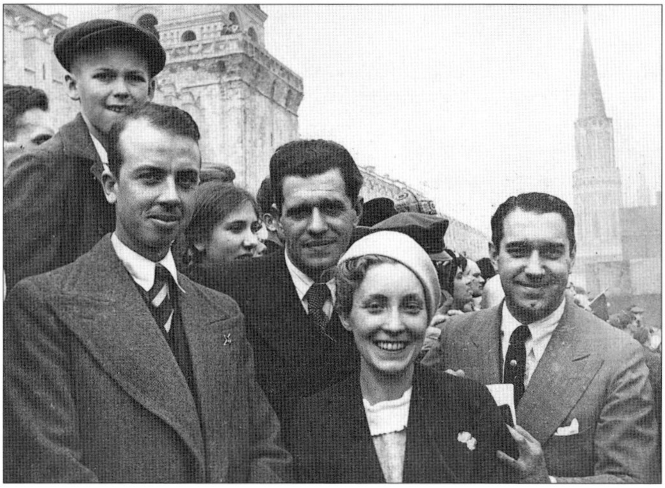

through a crisis of resented authority, the butt of which was Breton."[21] She had become acquainted with the Surrealists, but was too cool and too obviously intelligent for this to fan the flames of any warm sense of brotherhood.

In 1936 Louise moved to the rue de Seine, still in the St. Germain quarter, into a property that belonged to Isadora Duncan's brother, and where Breton had opened the Galerie Gradiva in the ground floor. As a consequence, she encountered the Surrealists almost daily near her flat after lunch.

At that time Louise started working in the Louvre. As she remembers, it was a good job and not without an element of prestige: "I got a job as a guide at the Louvre in Paris. Believe it or not I talked to Americans, and sometimes people from Australia. The Australians would say 'Gorgeous! Gorgeous!' I'd never heard that word before. Anyway, this was my job. I worked from nine to five. Now, the French are very strong on lunch. I was allowed to go to the basement and have lunch with the staff. [...] So I go downstairs and find a hell of people who had been wounded in the war. If you are in the war in France you are entitled to an official position. [...] And I walk in and look and a leg is cut off or an arm is gone and they are all in that basement eating their lunch."[22]

With these memories we will soon be leaving France and old Europe. Louise was now twenty-six years old and a woman with a strikingly radiant personality — not to mention her alarmingly wide-awake spirit and rapier-like wit. It was the photographer Brassaï who best understood how to capture these moments in his portraits: the glance of the woman in the mirror falls on us like a light summer shower (Ill. 39).

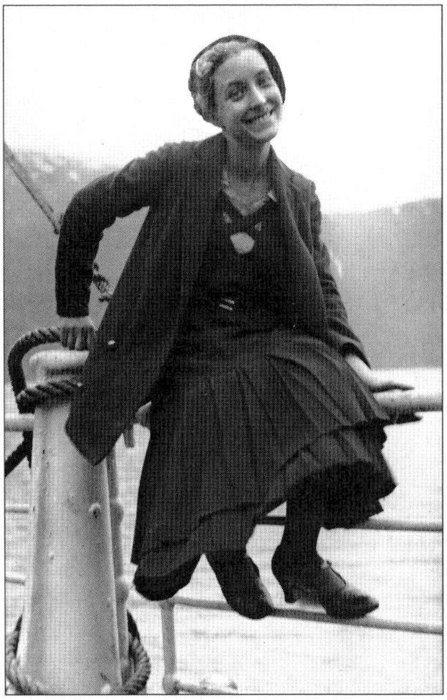

41 Louise on board the *Baltic Croisière*, 1932

Robert Goldwater was an American who looked rather like the young James Stewart but was a scholar or, to be more precise, an art historian. It is hardly surprising that he was the man to stand up to Father Bourgeois. One can well imagine the scene when Louis Bourgeois apparently finished one of his stories with an inviting laugh, only to be met by an impassive look from Robert Goldwater, accompanied by, "Is that supposed to be funny?" — which no doubt completely nonplussed the raconteur.[23] Perhaps it would be fair to call Robert Goldwater humorless, without necessarily viewing this as a negative character trait. At thiry-two years of age he was a serious student of the intellect, always sought evidence for any argument, and, as we can see, without being petty, had his writing desk completely under control. Small, dignified African figures stood next to each other and listened to

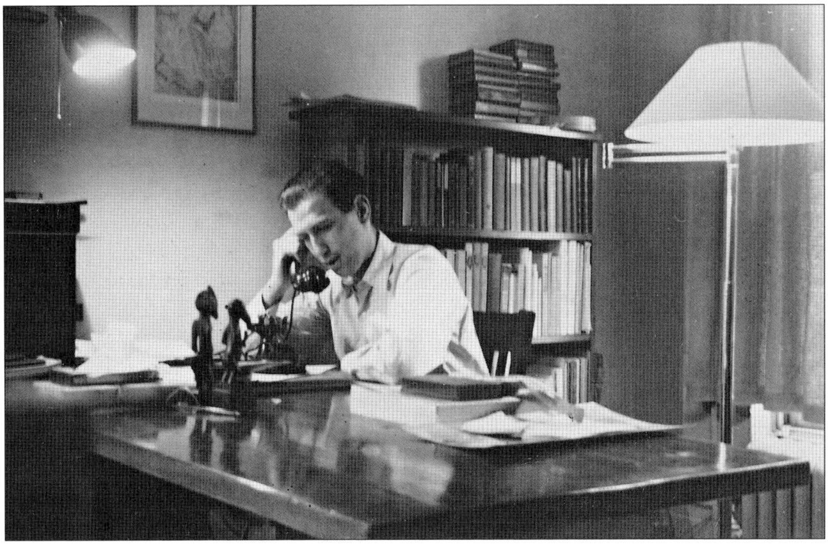

42 Robert Goldwater at his desk, New York, 1939

the conversation. "I married, first of all, an intellectual." Fifty years later Louise looked back on this time: "He was interested in nothing but ideas. That means he was interested in what is true and what is not true."[24] The apartment in Park Avenue that Robert and Louise had moved into, four blocks away from Grand Central Station, was not particularly quiet but Robert never actually raised his voice. Louise used to like watching him caught in the glow from two lamps as he sat at his writing desk by the window and telephoned — holding the black Bakelite receiver in his right hand and talking precisely into the mouthpiece — his upper body resting carefully on his lower left arm as he bent forwards slightly with his head bowed over the papers, not just hanging downwards, lanky yet disciplined. "Robert Goldwater was a completely rational person," Louise once characterized her husband, "he had the same qualities as my mother had. He did not betray me. He did not betray anyone. I never saw him angry in my life. Ever. And I never heard my mother raise her voice, ever. That is something."[25]

The couple had married in Paris in September 1938 and moved to New York one month later. Looking back, Louise becomes serious as she recalls: "He felt that he had found a diamond that he loved — rough, very rough — and I felt that he was really a catch. But we didn't understand each other, so that each of us remained forever, forever, mysterious to the other."[26] Louise left Europe, leaving behind her friends, her family, and the places she remembered. The passage to New York also gave her the opportunity to distance herself mentally from her past. Perhaps we can imagine coming across her in the evening before dinner, sitting on the ship's railing in a mood similar to that of a few years previously on the shores of the Mediterranean. At that time she had laid aside her notebook and the book she was reading and had rolled over on her side towards the land and away from the glittering surface of the evening sea. Suddenly everything had seemed too tame to her, too predictable and too restricted. The calm Mediterranean with scarcely perceptible high and low tides, the repeated journeys between Paris and the coast, the tedious studying for her baccalaureate. She dug her hands into the dense heap of seaweed she was lying on. The rays of the setting sun stole across her back. The feeling of warmth took the edge off her restless thoughts.

Now, barely six years later, her gaze was resting on the reflections of that same sun but on a very different ocean. She imagined drawing maps, three-dimensional maps like those she had seen in the Académie Militaire in Paris where each wave was illustrated showing its individual height, breadth, depth, and surface structure — a map which would constantly have to alter its appearance and yet, by definition, convey a sense of underlying continuity.

That same year, 1938, she made one trip back to France and adopted a child, a boy called Michel, who then returned with her to the New

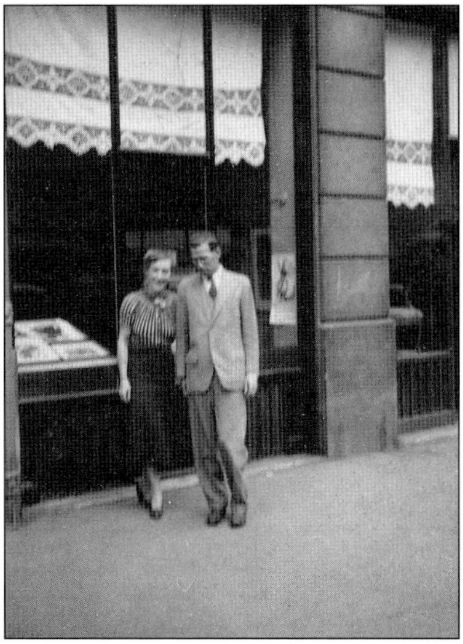

43 Louise and Robert in front of her father's tapestry gallery in Paris, 1938

44 Louise on the shore of the Mediterranean, c. 1932

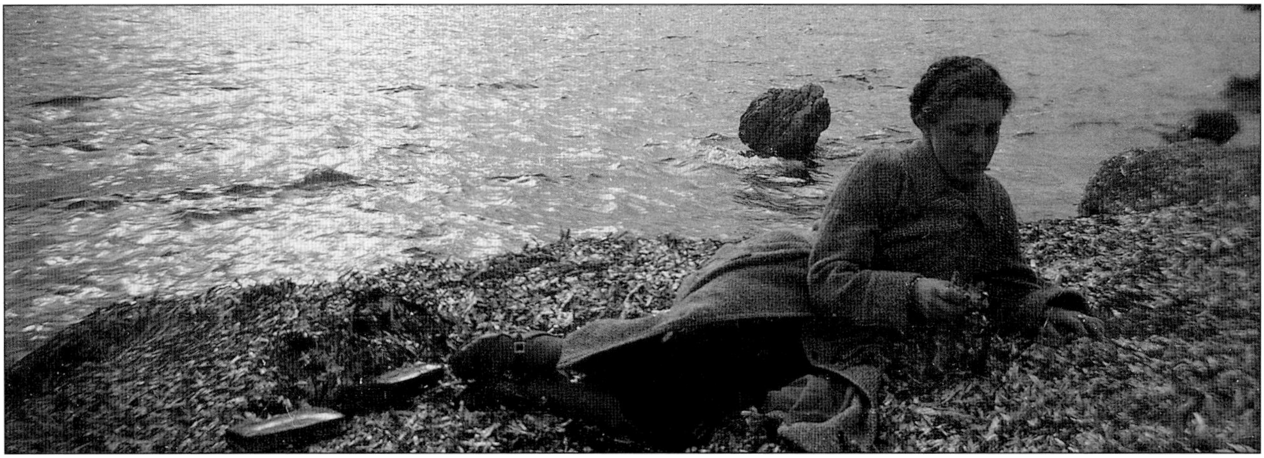

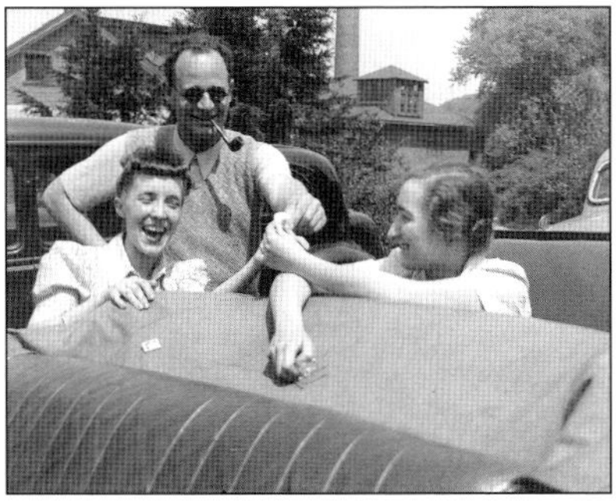

45 Louise with Andrew and Jane Ritchie in Huntington, Long Island, 1940

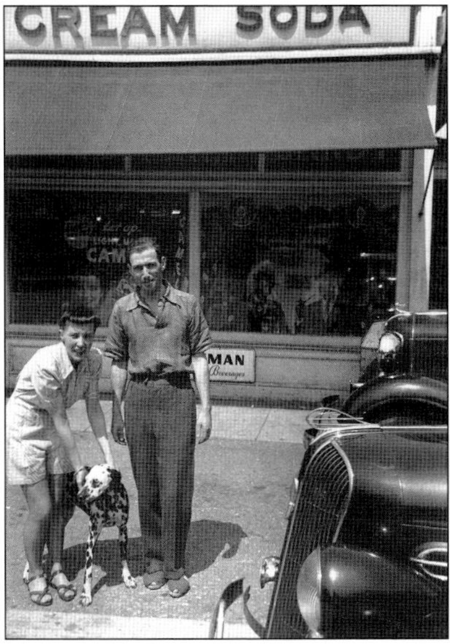

47 Louise and Robert in Huntington, Long Island, 1940

World. At the time the United States was in the slow process of freeing itself from the stranglehold of the Great Depression. So far, the preparations for war in Germany and Europe were no more than a matter of distant interest, and Louise was beginning to find her feet in her new cultural surroundings. After her initial arrival in New York in 1938 she had immediately enrolled in the Art Students League where she studied enthusiastically for two years with Vaclav Vytlacil, even if — as she remembers — she did not as a French national feel particularly welcome. During the daytime she used to spend a certain amount of time in the nearby Public Library "going back to the history of art. Our apartment was just two rooms, so small that I could not do anything there."[27] Later she claimed not to have had any real interest in art history: "My husband taught it, so I had my fill at home! I do believe in it as an activity, as a form of intellectual pursuit, but it did nothing for me — except that it kept me at a certain bracing level of intellectuality."[28]

Whereas today, South Beach, Miami — three hours away by plane — offers a welcome escape from the city, in the early 1940s New Yorkers had Long Island. In the summer of that year we see the couple in front of a shop in a street in Huntington, Long Island, where Robert Goldwater's parents owned a summer house. Concentrated heat rises in waves from the asphalt. People's eyes are half-closed against the glowing brightness of the day. Shiny Buicks and Packards reflect the midday sun. Coming into the picture from the right are the products of an economic world power. At this moment Robert and Louise present a not untypical image of a nation that has gradually overcome the shock of Black Friday — a nation that has perhaps become a little more cautious, yet which radiates optimism as it always did, and where the pursuit of happiness is even today still enshrined in the Constitution. Women pose with dazzling smiles to promote the joys of tobacco, men wear hats and smoke pipes. Louise is wearing long shorts and Robert is looking towards the sun with a relaxed air.

Their first son was born in 1940, the year of this photo, and a year later Jean-Louis was to be followed by his brother Alain. Three sons, four men in the house, mother, wife, and artist. On December 7, 1941 the Japanese attacked Pearl Harbor and the United States of America

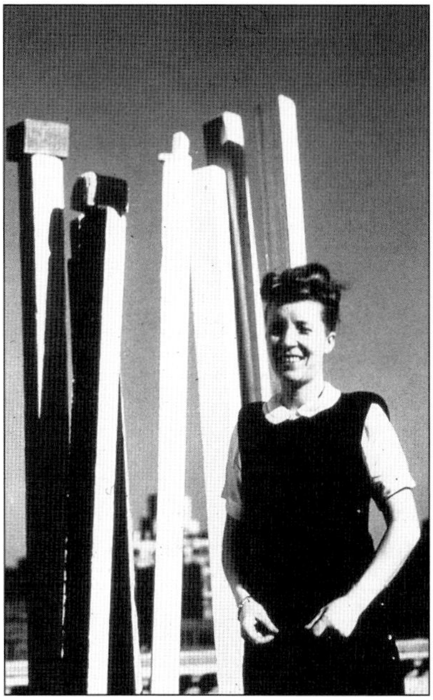

46 Louise with her sculpture *The Visitors Arrive at the Door* on the roof of Stuyvesant's Folly on 18th Street, New York, 1944

entered the Second World War. In 1941 the young family moved into an apartment block, Stuyvesant's Folly, on 18th Street. Towards the end of the war, on the roof of this apartment block, we are introduced for the first time to sculptures by Louise Bourgeois.

In 1943 Louise took part in the exhibition *The Arts in Therapy*, which was promoting artistic and craft activities as part of a rehabilitation program for the war wounded. Along with Alexander Calder and André Masson, she received an Honorary Award for her work. Louise was involved in a number of war-related projects of this kind. It is fascinating to contemplate the way that this young woman, in her early thirties, clearly fulfilled her various duties within the family and at the same time also managed to pursue her own individual path as an artist. It is, however, not just a matter of admiring some sublime, undaunted artistic vision that is able to hold its own through any difficulties. In Louise's case we see a young woman, a European, a Parisienne, who had left her home, her country,

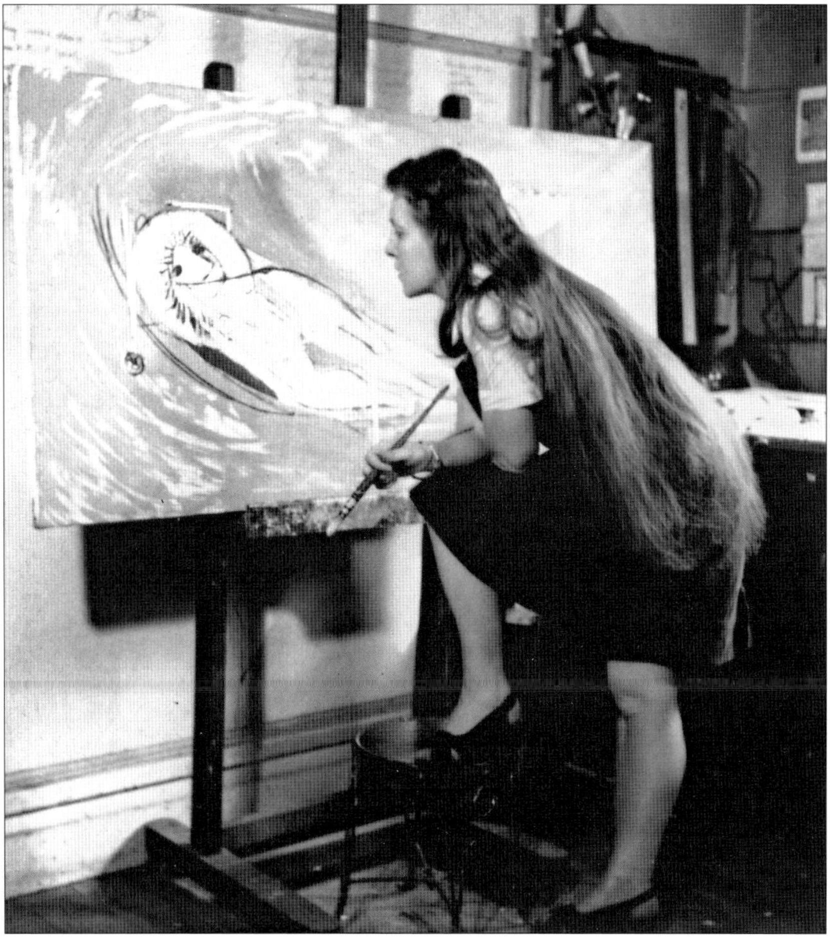

48 Louise in front of the easel in her studio on 18th Street, New York, c. 1946

her family and her friends, and set up home for her husband, an American academic, borne two children, and was bringing up three, engaging beyond the daily round in the politics of this time of war and at the same time continuing to follow her vocation as an artist.

In June 1945, at the age of thirty-three, Louise Bourgeois had her first solo exhibition, *Paintings by Louise Bourgeois,* in the Bertha Schaefer Gallery. "Even though I am French," she said, commenting on her work from the 1940s, "I cannot think of one of these pictures being painted in France. Everyone of these is American, from New York. I love this city, its clean cut look, its sky, its buildings, its scientific, cruel, romantic quality."[29] We see her standing at her easel, the artist in her studio. And her pose seems to reflect much of what she loves so much about this city: analytically sober in her observation, pragmatic execution, and stormy romanticism; a city that can change within the course of a single day from damp heat to ringing frost. Her long hair falls down her back, one knee is bent forwards and an elegantly shod foot rests on her painter's stool. She is holding her brush lightly between the fingers of her right hand. This situation, as it is captured in the photograph, corresponds exactly with her own self-image and has little in common with the heroically virile portraits of some of her painting contemporaries. She looks professional and completely capable of employing exactly as she wished any of the tools of her trade hanging next to the drawing board. Nor should we forget that at that time current modes of painting were determined by powerful male voices, with painters such as Jackson Pollock,

49 Louise in her studio, c. 1946

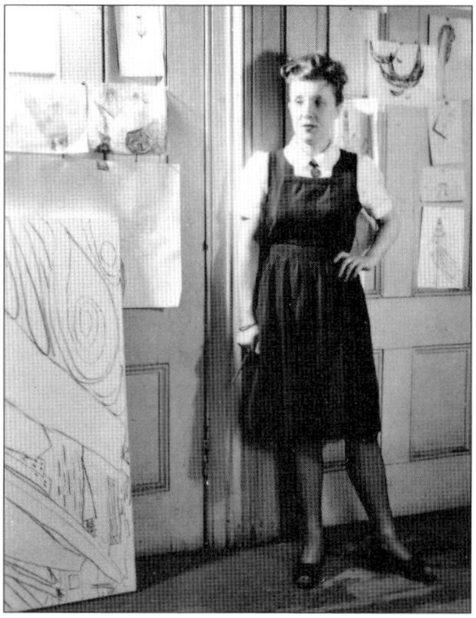

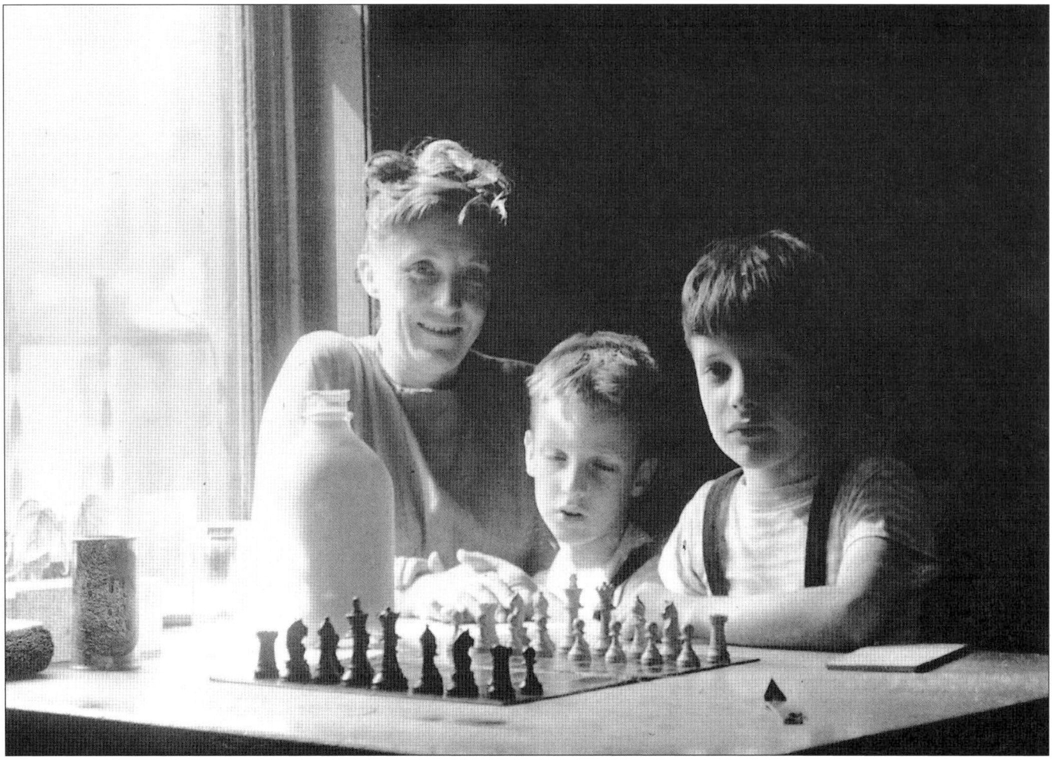

50 Louise with her sons Alain and Jean-Louis in New York, 1945

Clyfford Still, Robert Motherwell, Willem de Kooning, and Barnett Newman making their mark on canvas and poised to impress an American stamp on art history.

Other, older men, whom Louise did not greatly admire, had followed her to America: "Breton and Duchamp made me violent. They were too close to me and I objected [...] violently to their pontifications. Since I was a runaway, father figures on these shores rubbed me the wrong way."[30] In June of the same year, 1945, Louise took part in the exhibition, *The Woman*, in Peggy Guggenheim's gallery, Art of this Century; other participants included Leonora Carrington, Leonore Krasner, and Gypsy Rose Lee.

Louise's studio was open to the various members of her family. The light falling through the high city window shines brightly on a full bottle of milk standing next to a game of chess and smaller vessels on a table. The mother, her face largely in the shadows, is smiling. Even if there is a trace there of the tiredness that must have at times swamped her like a heavy downpour, her gaze is proudly and warmly alert. The light finds its way to the children's faces, bathing Alain in the contemplative beauty of a Botticelli figure, a childish beauty that allows the soul to shine through the relaxed features while his gently parted lips stop just short of words. Let us simply call it peace, the mood in this picture: the game has not yet begun, the first move has not yet been made. The mother's right hand rests in that of the older of the two boys. His glance from out of the dark shadows meets the camera with a serious air. Both children are holding their mother's hand, Alain's fingers are touching her wrist. If we wanted to find a place in this narrative for notions such as maternal happiness or family joy, then this would surely be it: "I only learned tenderness with the arrival of my children. Thus a new world was created."[31]

Meanwhile, in Europe, American soldiers were fighting side by side with the other Allies against the Germans. The second war in her lifetime, the second war in Europe; and before the atom bomb was dropped on Japan, Louise

Bourgeois organized an exhibition of documents relating to the French Resistance at the Norlyst Gallery in New York.

In this exhibition paintings, texts, poetry, and press articles combined to give a picture of French culture of the Resistance. Works by Picasso and Bonnard hung next to photographs of German tanks and soldiers and texts by Jean-Paul Sartre. Even if this campaign by Louise Bourgeois was instrumental in reminding the American public of the Resistance and of the occupation of France, it did not shed any light on how she herself stood in regard to the issue that was so important in the United States at the time, namely the question of left against right, of Communism against Capitalism. As a French Existentialist, Sartre, whose novel *La Nausée* was included in the exhibition, clearly counted as left-wing. Louis Aragon and Picasso were indeed Communists. But in this matter too, Louise kept her own counsel. In answer to a question about her attitude to politics, she once answered: "There is such a state where you are not for, you are not against, you are investigating. It is a much more intelligent attitude than to be committed to this and committed to that. You study, you consider, you have a scientific attitude, you do not have an emotional attitude."[32]

The war came to an end, and summer days in Connecticut in 1945 provided spiritual renewal. The country house in Easton was the center of endless activities for the three boys. Haystacks, trees that just asked to be climbed, the scent of fresh grass in the meadows, creamy milk for breakfast that they had seen flowing warm from the cow's full udder, made for halcyon days. The figures are gathered in front of the wooden facade of the house as though from a group by Piero della Francesca. The three children stand hand in hand in front of their mother, but Louise's features are warmed by a smile that is too immediate and lively ever to have been captured even by that master of Renaissance painting. By now Michel reaches her shoulder and Jean-Louis has the self-confident gaze of a young prince. The evening sun is setting rapidly and touches their heads with its last golden rays — an Indian summer. The younger boys' shorts are firmly attached to suspenders; only Michel has outgrown such childish dress. In the background, under a comet's tail of vine leaves, two men are deep in conversation. One is recognizable by his posture as Robert, a gently bowed head above relaxed shoulders, the weight on his right leg and the left leg bent — the other man is wearing a hat, elegant shoes, pale trousers, and a jacket that

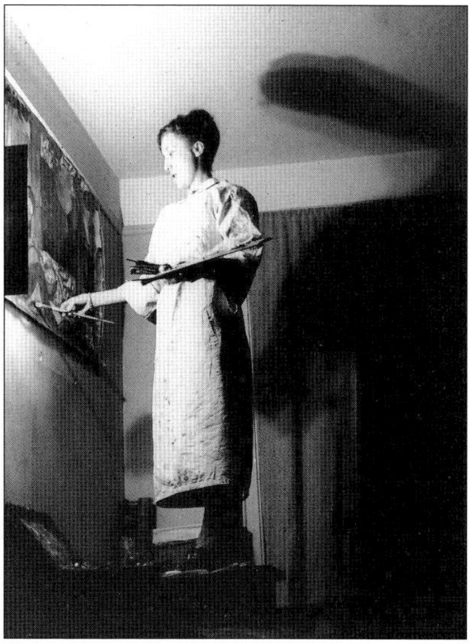

51 Louise in her studio, 1944

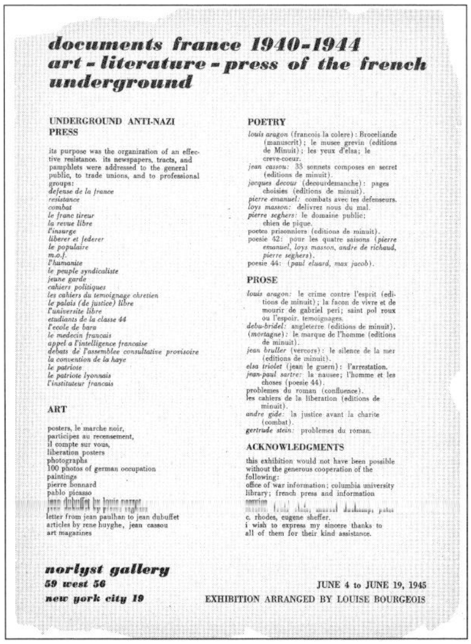

documents france 1940-1944
art - literature - press of the french underground

UNDERGROUND ANTI-NAZI PRESS

its purpose was the organization of an effective resistance. its newspapers, tracts, and pamphlets were addressed to the general public, to trade unions, and to professional groups:
defense de la france
resistance
combat
le franc tireur
la revue libre
l'insurge
liberer et federer
le populaire
m.o.f.
l'humanite
le peuple syndicaliste
jeune garde
cahiers politiques
les cahiers du temoignage chretien
le palais (de justice) libre
l'universite libre
etudiants de la classe 44
l'ecole de bara
le medecin francais
appel a l'intelligence francaise
debats de l'assemblee consultative provisoire
la convention de la haye
le patriote
le patriote lyonnais
l'instituteur francais

ART

posters, le marche noir,
participez au recensement,
il compte sur vous,
liberation posters
photographs
100 photos of german occupation
paintings
pierre bonnard
pablo picasso
jean dubuffet by louis parrot
[illegible]
letter from jean paulhan to jean dubuffet
articles by rene huyghe, jean cassou
art magazines

POETRY

louis aragon (francois la colere): Broceliande (manuscrit); le musee grevin (editions de Minuit); les yeux d'elsa; le creve-coeur.
jean cassou: 33 sonnets composes en secret (editions de minuit).
jacques decour (decourdemanche): pages choisies (editions de minuit).
pierre emanuel: combats avec tes defenseurs.
loys masson: delivrez nous du mal.
pierre seghers: le domaine public; chien de pique.
poetes prisonniers (editions de minuit).
poesie 42: pour les quatre saisons (*pierre emanuel, loys masson, andre de richaud, pierre seghers*).
poesie 44: (*paul eluard, max jacob*).

PROSE

louis aragon: le crime contre l'esprit (editions de minuit); la facon de vivre et de mourir de gabriel peri; saint pol roux ou l'espoir. temoignages.
debu-bridel: angleterre (editions de minuit).
(*mortagne*): le marque de l'homme (editions de minuit).
jean bruller (vercors): le silence de la mer (editions de minuit).
elsa triolet (jean le guern): l'arrestation.
jean-paul sartre: la nausee; l'homme et les choses (poesie 44).
problemes du roman (confluence).
les cahiers de la liberation (editions de minuit).
andre gide: la justice avant la charite (combat).
gertrude stein: problemes du roman.

ACKNOWLEDGMENTS

this exhibition would not have been possible without the generous cooperation of the following:
office of war information; columbia university library; french press and information service
[illegible]
c. rhodes, eugene sheffer.
i wish to express my sincere thanks to all of them for their kind assistance.

norlyst gallery
59 west 56
new york city 19

JUNE 4 to JUNE 19, 1945
EXHIBITION ARRANGED BY LOUISE BOURGEOIS

52 Invitation for the exhibition 'documents france 1940–1944 art – literature – press of the french underground', organized by Louise at the Norlyst Gallery, New York, in 1945

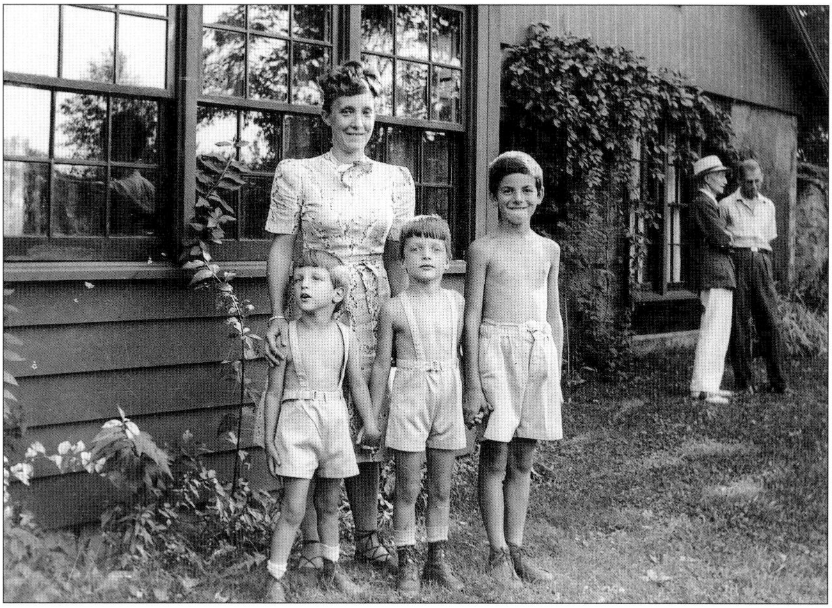

53 Louise with Alain, Jean-Louis and Michel in front of the house in Easton; in the background, Charles Prendergast and Robert Goldwater, 1945

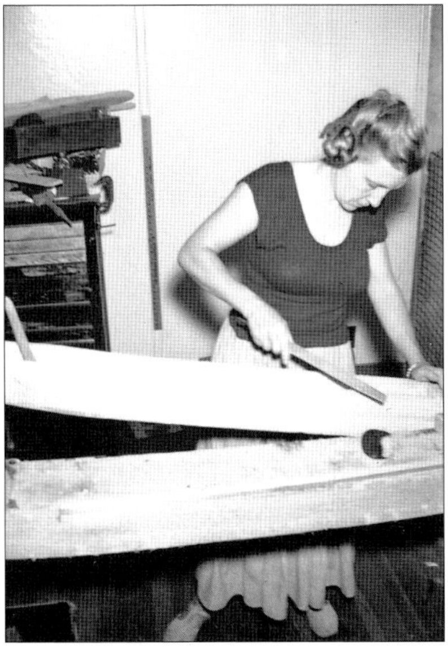

54 Louise working on a sculpture for her exhibition at the Peridot Gallery, 1949

55 Louise's personage sculptures in progress in Easton, Conn., c. 1947

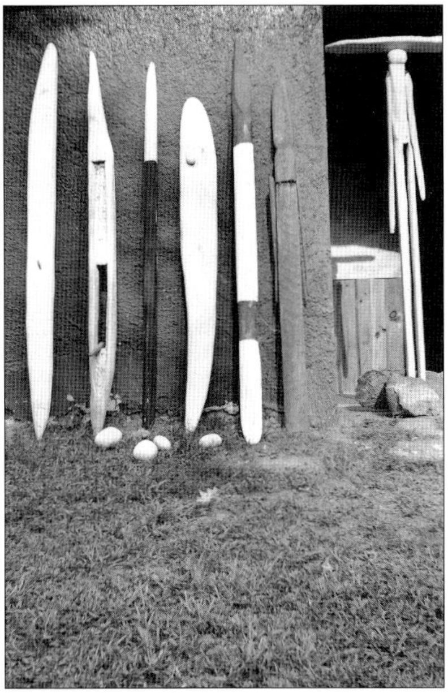

may be his concession to a stay in the country. Louise's husband is engrossed in conversation with Charles Prendergast, whose brother, Maurice, had exhibited work at the *Armory Show* in 1913 which had first introduced Modernism to the United States.

As far as we can ascertain, none of this deflected Louise from her chosen path (Ill. 51) — neither her duties as a wife and mother, nor her husband's professional life. It was not until 1956 that one of her sculptures in wood was illustrated in an article by her husband Robert on contemporary sculpture in New York. But all the time Louise had been working unremittingly. In 1947 she had her second solo exhibition, *Paintings*, in the Norlyst Gallery. Two years later, in October 1949, she showed her sculptures in public for the first time, having worked on them, simultaneously with her paintings, for a long time. This exhibition took place in the Peridot Gallery and was called *Louise Bourgeois, Recent Work 1947–1949: Seventeen Standing Figures in Wood.* Marcel Duchamp and Pierre Matisse visited the exhibition: "This is extraordinary!" was their verdict.[33] And yet it was to take more than three decades before the public realized what was emerging from this woman's hands. In this sense she shared the same fate as one of her contemporaries: her 'colleague' Barnett Newman was also largely denied the recognition in his own day that had been due to him at least since the 1940s. Born in 1906, five years before Louise Bourgeois, it was only in the 1950s that Newman had his first solo exhibition. This was in the Betty Parson Gallery in New York, which also had Louise Bourgeois on its books. Louise has her own explanation which makes it somehow plausible that recognition was denied her until she was well into old age, and why it should then have been all the greater: "It has to do with success. As the saying goes, nothing succeeds like success. Unless you break into what is called success, you simply don't exist. People are not going to hurt you, at least not deliberately; they are going to ignore you unless you have success. [...] I did not make my work for everybody, perhaps not for anybody. I made my art as a means of survival. It was a basic necessity for me. [...] I have ridden out my success because it was not really the purpose of my work to be successful. My work will outlive its success, be more enduring and stronger than success."[34]

Sales were intermittent but through the years Louise held on to her own achievements. In the 1960s she opened Erasmus Books and Prints, a shop on Madison Avenue, specializing in graphic works of the eighteenth to twentieth centuries.

In 1948 Louis Bourgeois visited his daughter and her family (Ill. 58). The man, who kept a small box on his desk, and put in it a pebble for every happy moment that proved that life was worth living, is sitting next to Louise at a table in a New York restaurant. The wine bottle has sunk right down into the cooler. Louise is drinking tea. Her father has crossed his legs with his customary nonchalance, holds a cigarette between his fingers, and pays court to his grown daughter (Ill. 56). Louise smiles. Three years later in 1951 Louis Bourgeois died. At his death, the box on his desk contained hundreds of stones.

That same year Louise had been granted American citizenship and with her sculpture, *Sleeping Figure*, had also been accepted by the Museum of Modern Art under the directorship of Alfred H. Barr, thereby becoming a figure of lasting public interest. From now on we have to divide our attention. Our focus on the past draws closer and the figures become more clearly defined. In May 1950 Louise supported the chorus of protest by a group of artists who were to become known as *The Irascible 18* and which included Willem de Kooning, Adolph Gottlieb, Ad Reinhardt, Jackson Pollock, Clyfford Still, Robert Motherwell, Barnett Newman, and Mark Rothko.[35] The group was united in protest at the conservative selection policies of the Metropolitan Museum with regard to the planned exhibition, *American Painting Today — 1950*. Its members — rather than emigrés from Paris — became Louise's friends: "I made friends with American artists who were my age and I showed with them at the Peridot Gallery from 1949 to 1953, at Norlyst and at Egan, which was one of the key galleries for the Abstract Expressionists. And Alfred Barr was a supporter from the beginning. He included me in an early panel discussion along with de Kooning and the rest [...]"[36]

Nevertheless, Louise and her works resisted categorization, thwarting any attempt to classify them as part of dominant art movements. At the last meeting of *Studio 35*, a three-day forum that attracted most of the Abstract Expressionists, Barnett Newman is seen sitting opposite to Louise Bourgeois. It is pleasing to imagine how their looks may have met across the table and the feelings that may have been reflected in those glances. Only Louise's pinned-up hair is visible, but what she is saying is clearly attracting attention. Whatever the case, she certainly refused to drink beer out of paper cups.

From 1951 onwards, Louise and her family regularly visited her old homeland in Europe. In 1951 they traveled to Holland and in 1953 they went to Italy for the first time. In 1952, Louise designed the sets for *The Bridegroom of the Moon*, a dance piece by Eric Hawkins, that was put on in the Hunter Playhouse in New York. The following year, 1953, she had her fifth solo exhibition (her third in the Peridot Gallery) in which she showed drawings and sculptures. After that, it was to be another eleven years before her next solo exhibition in any gallery. In 1954 she joined the American Abstract Artists group; in 1955 the Charles Egan Gallery put on a two-person exhibition with Franz Kline and Louise Bourgeois — a year previously the same gallery had shown Robert Rauschenberg's red paintings — and in 1956 the Whitney Museum purchased her sculpture *One and Others* (Ill. 102). Louise was known but she had not trumpeted her presence as loudly as some of her contemporaries. In 1947 her husband, Robert Goldwater, had been appointed editor of the *Magazine of Art*, the first journal that was to pay any attention to Abstract Expressionism. From 1960 onwards Louise regularly taught in numerous American institutions.

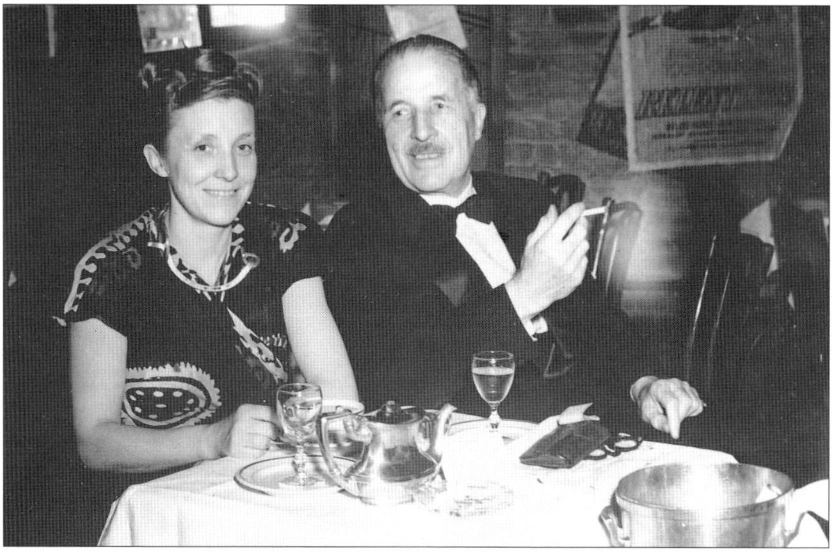

56 Louise with her father in the restaurant Leon & Eddie's in New York, 1948

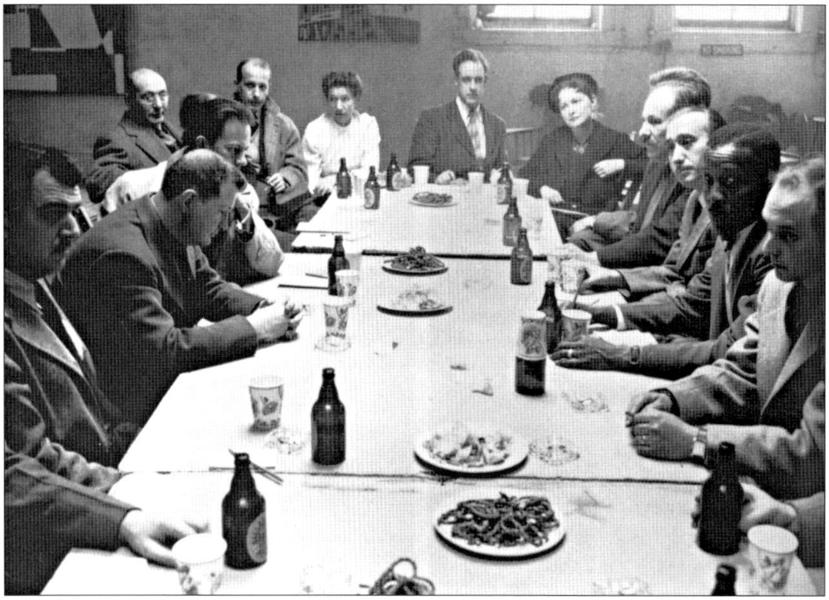

57 A meeting of artists in *Studio 35*, with Brooks, Reinhardt, Pousette-Dart, Bourgeois, Ferber, Tomlin, Biala, Goodnough, Sterne, Hare, Newman, Lipton, Lewis, and J. Ernst, New York, 1950

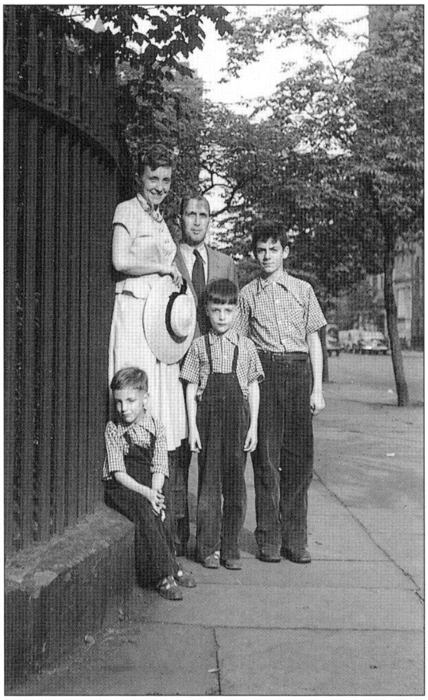

58 Louise with her husband and children, photographed by her father, New York, 1948

59 Louise in her studio, c. 1965, with works in plaster. *Clutching* (1962) is in the fireplace with *Amoeba* (1963–1965) in the background on the right.

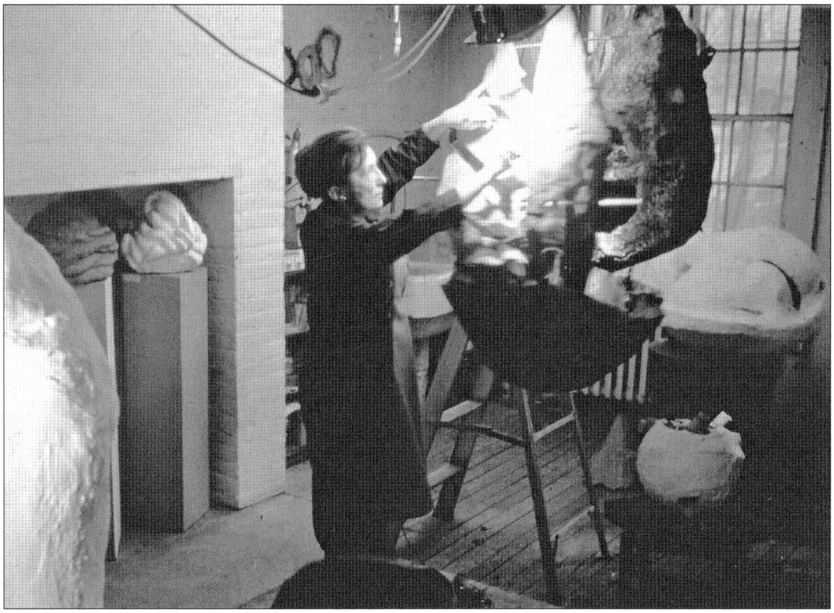

In January 1964 Louise Bourgeois showed plaster works in the Stable Gallery, which insiders considered the most important gallery for new talent; in the same year, 1964, Andy Warhol also exhibited there. The present curator of the Museum of Modern Art, Robert Storr, remembers the striking contrast between Louise Bourgeois's earlier work and the new work, as he saw it: "In place of wood she was using plaster, latex and various resins; instead of hard materials she had opted for soft ones; instead of cutting she was pouring and modeling."[37]

In 1959 in the French journal *Œil*, Michel Seuphor wrote about Louise Bourgeois's work under the headline 'Critic's Choice': "Contemporary sculpture seems to me more stimulating than contemporary painting [...] Louise Bourgeois in New York has been making 'totem figures' for some time now, succinct of form and yet with a remarkable aura. She calls them 'Astonished Forms' or 'Sleeping Figures.' [...] Her extraordinary work has clearly influenced a number of young American sculptors."[38]

This opinion, from a renowned French critic who had made his name with monographs on Piet Mondrian and the first generation of abstract artists, is particularly interesting when one takes into account the dominant features of sculpture in the United States in the 1960s: hard edges; smoothly polished surfaces; unyielding, industrially produced materials; serial structures with a brittle, intellectual kind of attraction. The viewer was being offered a new image of sculpture, with protagonists such as Donald Judd, Carl Andre, and Sol Lewitt, who required the viewer to meet and engage with their work on an intellectual level (see *Memling Dawn*, Ill. 94). At the same time, of course, Pop Art was also making acclaimed progress with fluidly soft, slack forms as exemplified in the sculptures of Claes Oldenburg.

But in the meantime a new generation of artisits was appearing: in 1966 Lucy Lippard organized an exhibition in the Fischbach Gallery called *Eccentric Abstraction*. In it she showed works by Louise Bourgeois, Bruce Nauman, Keith Sonnier, and Eva Hesse (to name but a few of the most significant participants). By now Louise Bourgeois was fifty-five and counted as a member of the older generation. Having produced work for a good twenty years now, she was clearly beginning to inspire and influence others. In 1967 she made a trip to Italy, to the marble quarries at Pietrasanta, where she worked many long hours lending form to a block of stone. Louise returned to Italy summer after summer, at least until 1972 (Ill. 99).

In April 1969 William Rubin, at the time Director of the Museum of Modern Art, devoted an article in the journal *Art International* to Louise Bourgeois: "There is a quality, integrity, and immediacy of feeling in Miss Bourgeois's work that we never feel in those occasional essays we see in painting where an attempt has been made to keep the language of organic forms alive. The implications of this seem to me to go beyond Miss Bourgeois's own work and to raise questions about the historicity of post-World War II sculpture, over and against painting."[39] (Ill. 60)

In January 1973 she showed her sculpture *Number seventy-two (The No March)* (Ill. 143) at the Whitney Biennale. In March 1973 Robert Goldwater died.

A year later, in 1974, Louise Bourgeois made *The Destruction of the Father*, a sculpture that creates its own space, a niche in our perception,

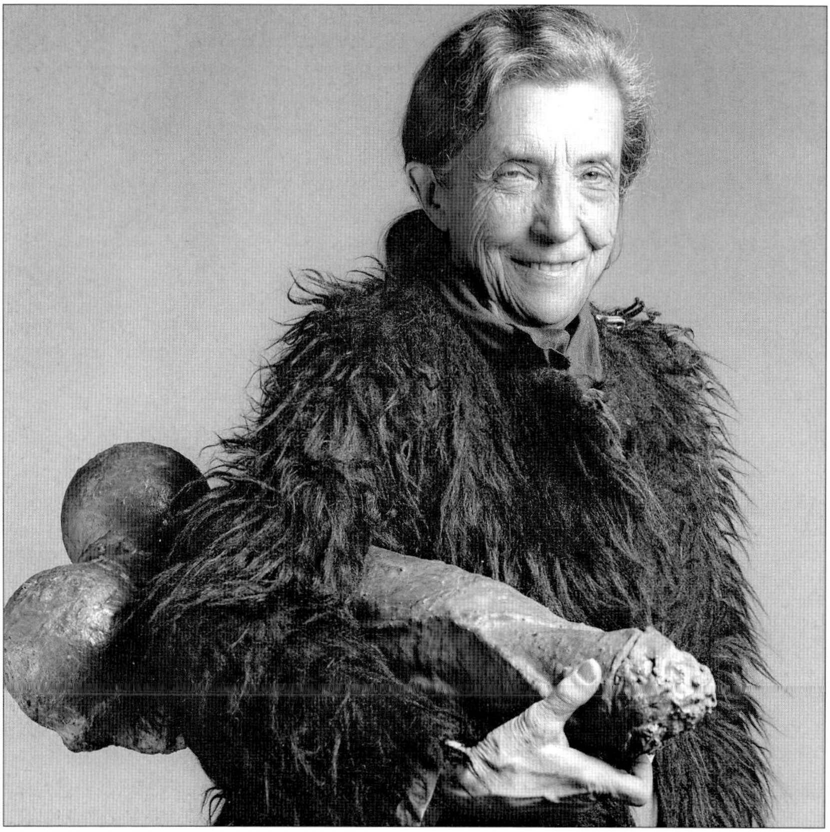

60 Portrait by Robert Mapplethorpe of Louise with *Fillette* (1968), 1982

61 Louise explaining her sculpture *Ventouse* to Arthur Miller during his visit to her studio in Brooklyn, 1991

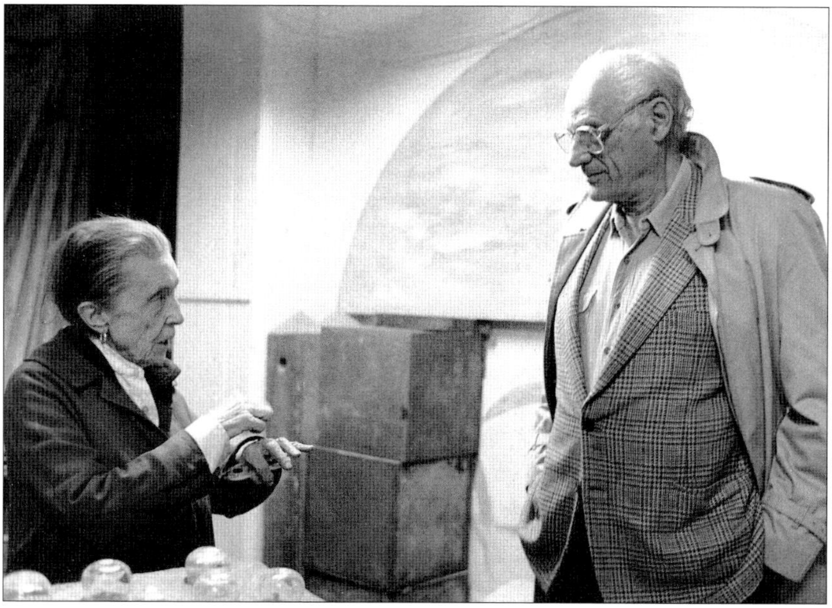

bathed in a reddish light. This sculpture does not so much occupy a particular volume by its presence as it opens up a new external space, a crevasse that absorbs our emotions (Ills 62, 63). Rotund forms hang like swords of Damocles from the ceiling, gathering like driving storm-clouds above a collection of club-like, egg-shaped forms that seem to be arranged on a table for some kind of meal. Latex domes crowd around the table, some stuffed full and bursting with life while others are limp and simply waiting. The space seems to have shrunk claustrophobically; tension demands to be released. The father dismembered, torn limb for limb, the death of the patriarch, caused by his offspring, the consumption of the progenitor — Louise has confirmed that this is about fear, the normal, perfectly ordinary, dull fear that she feels every day. How to escape this fear, to hide, to meet it, to drive it out, how to conquer the shame at having this fear, the fear of the fear? The Frenchman Marshall

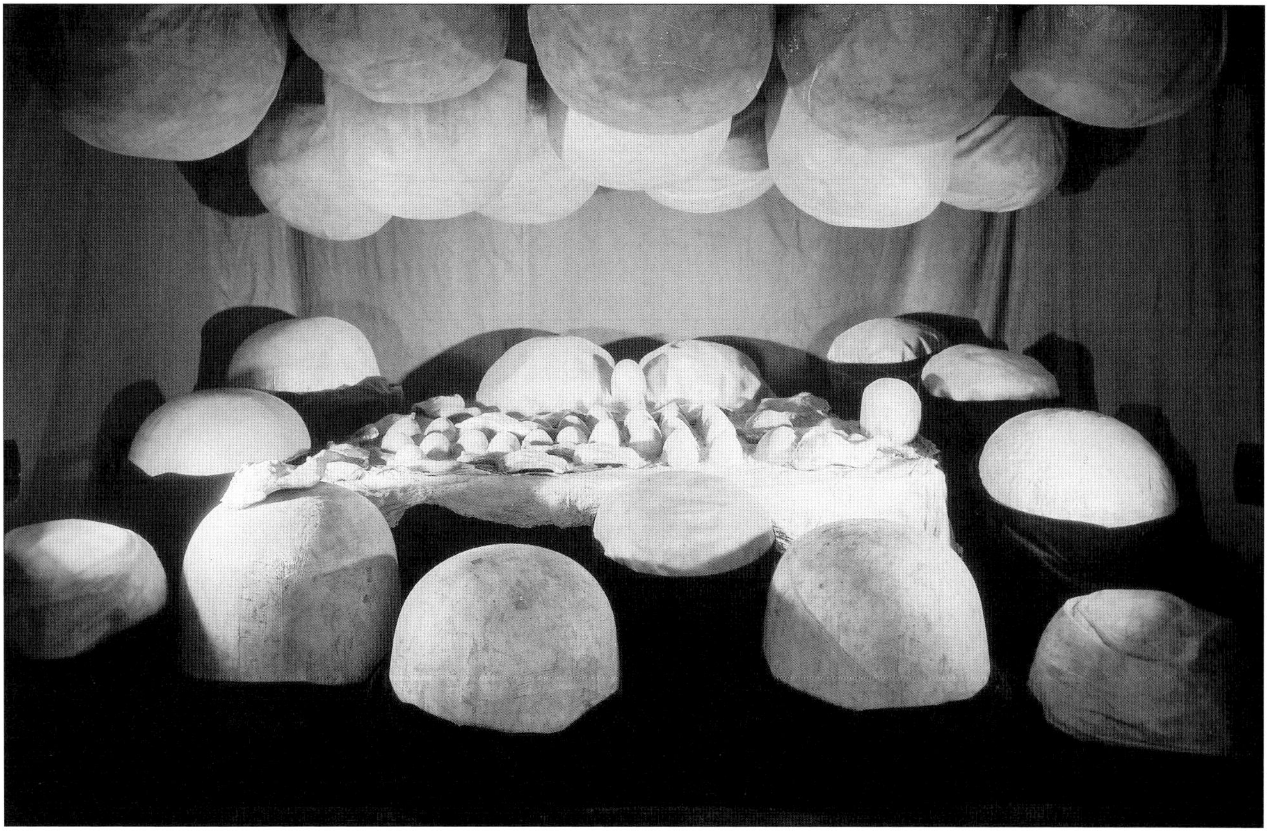

62 *The Destruction of the Father*, 1974
Latex, plaster, wood, fabric and red light
93 5/8 x 142 5/8 x 97 7/8
Photo © by Peter Moore

63 *The Destruction of the Father*, 1974.
Photo © by Peter Moore

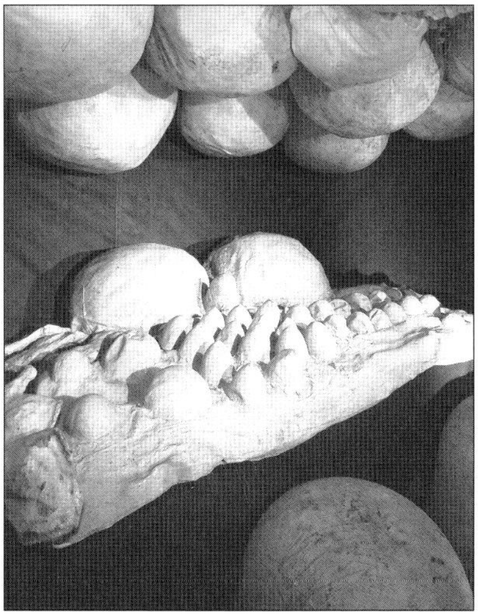

Turenne was alluding to precisely this situation when he cried to his horse: "You trembling carcass beneath me, how much more would you tremble if you knew where now I shall lead thee." In Louise's own estimation, she emerged as a changed person from the exhibitions of this work. She had subjected her fear to her own personal exorcism by forcing form on that fear. And this, in her view, is one of the reasons why artists go on — not that they get better and better, but because they can stand more.[40] "I'm afraid of power," admits Louise, "it makes me nervous. In real life, I identify with the victim, that is why I went into art. In my art, I am the murderer. I feel for the ordeal of the murderer, the man who has to live with his conscience. [...] As an artist I am a powerful person. In real life, I feel like the mouse behind the radiator. [...] By withdrawing, by recognizing you have no power, you become more than yourself. You get ideas which never would have occurred to you. In my art, I live in a world of my own making. I make decisions. I have power. In the real world, I don't want power."[41]

In 1974 Louise Bourgeois received numerous academic honors and fulfilled various appointments: she participated in *Seminars with Artists and Critics* at the Whitney Museum, and taught at the School of Visual Arts, the Pratt Institute, Cooper Union, and the New York Studio School. In addition she was engaged to teach as Visiting Artist at the Philadelphia College of Arts, Rutgers University in New Brunswick, Columbia University, Yale University, and the Woodstock Artists' Association. In 1976 she participated very successfully in the exhibition *200 Years of American Sculpture* in the Whitney Museum and in 1977 she received an honorary doctorate from Yale University. Her diploma records her achievement: "The precision of [your] craftsmanship, the range of your imagination, and your fearless independence have been exemplary."[42]

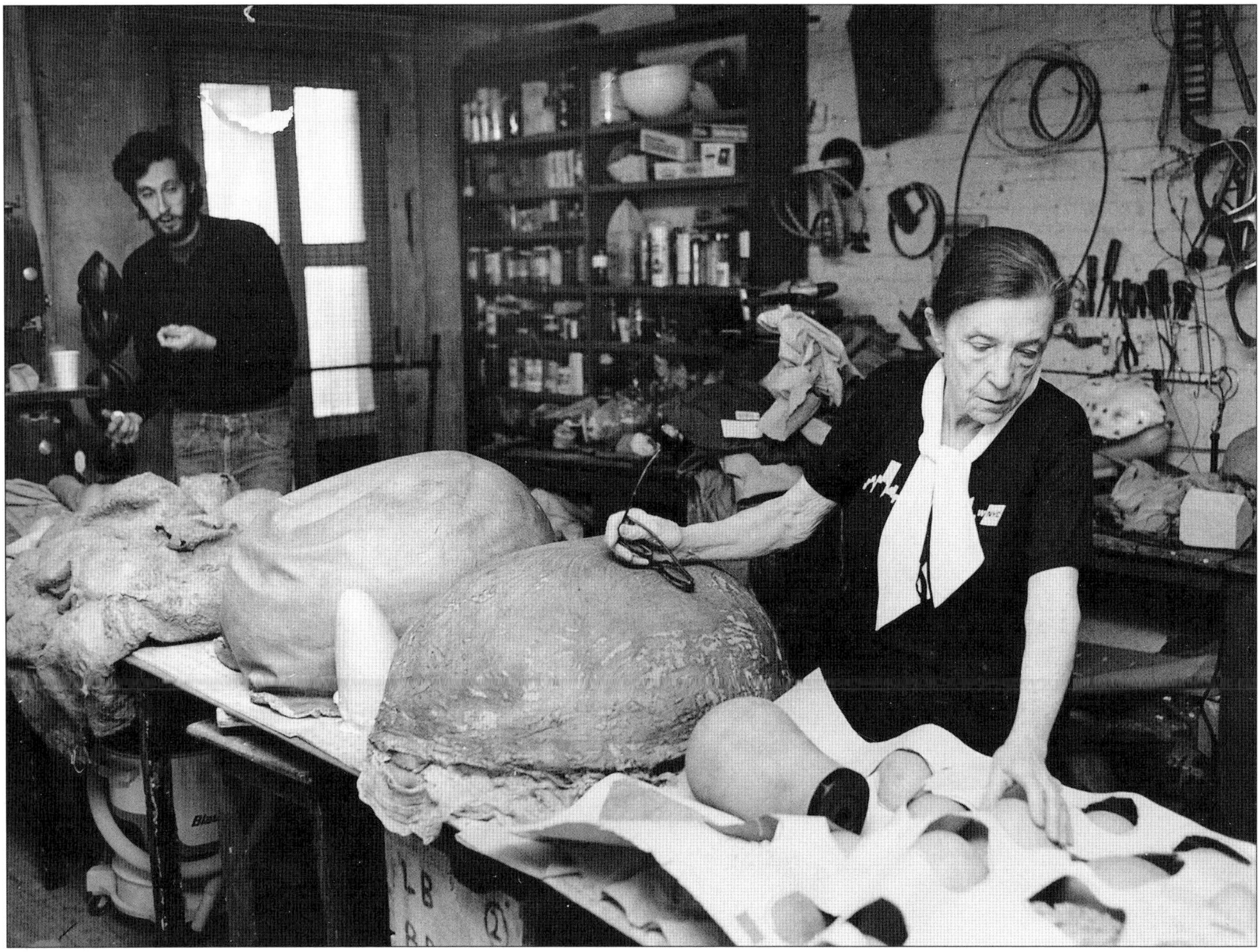

In 1982 the Museum of Modern Art mounted the great solo exhibition of Louise Bourgeois's work which set the tone for the steady rise of her reputation since then. Ten years later, in 1992, Louise Bourgeois was again in the public eye as a participant at *documenta 9* in Kassel.

In 1978, at the age of sixty-seven, Louise Bourgeois invited friends and aquaintances to appear in a living installation, expressed in a choreography which she wrote. *The Confrontation* (Ills 64, 65): whitewashed boards of various heights are arranged as an oval roughly 36 x 20 feet. The back walls face outwards, the bottom lies on the floor and the sides are fixed at various angles by triangular boards. The box with the virgin sawn in two — the running saw makes a screeching noise poised above the wood, ready to cut from one corner to the other, to create two halves, which, up-ended, are big enough for one person. The boxes, or 'coffins' as the artist calls them, are open towards the center of the room. In the center of the space there is a long, table-like construction that is covered with little latex mounds of different sizes. Two large, somewhat deflated latex domes take up the center of the table. This work, *The Confrontation*, is the setting for the performance, *A Banquet/A Fashion Show of Body Parts*, that took place one time only on October 21, 1978, in the Hamilton Gallery of Contemporary Art in Soho, New York. The performers were lay people, there were no rehearsals, and there was no script to speak of.

We are in a narrow room in a New York brownstone house in Chelsea where the artist

64 Louise with Jerry Gorovoy preparing for the retrospective exhibition at the Museum of Modern Art, New York, 1982, with *The Confrontation* (1978)

has lived for many years. Despite the fact that it is morning, the light from outside is fitful and the room is lit by a single lamp. It is surely only this city that hides objects of this kind behind its windows and doors. A video of that famous performance *A Banquet/A Fashion Show of Body Parts* starts up, images flicker across the screen and pulsating music fills the little living room where we are sitting almost twenty years later with Louise and Jerry, in order to look at the videotape of that performance.

Audience and performers are evidently on the same level, no stage for protection: the public becomes the cast and *vice versa*. The audience leans in boxes and crowds around the elliptical arena. The walls of the gallery are bare and white. A bearded man walks in through the chest-high wooden swing door. His face is substantially covered by his beard, his chest and stomach are bare, below this his private parts are covered by a latex semi-sphere. The top half of his buttocks is similarly covered, but below this

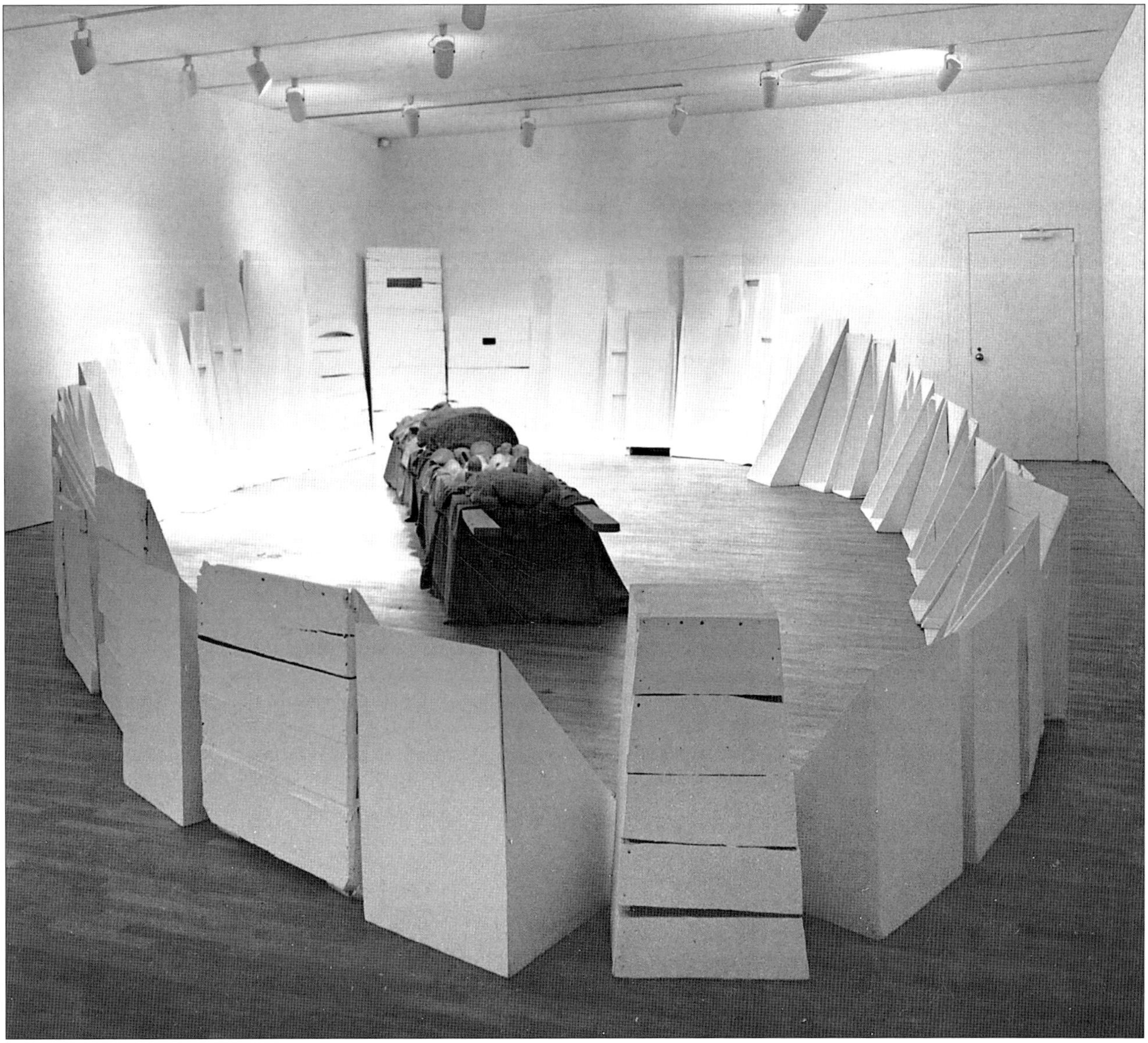

65 *The Confrontation* (1978) at the retrospective exhibition at the Museum of Modern Art, New York, 1982. Photo © by Peter Moore

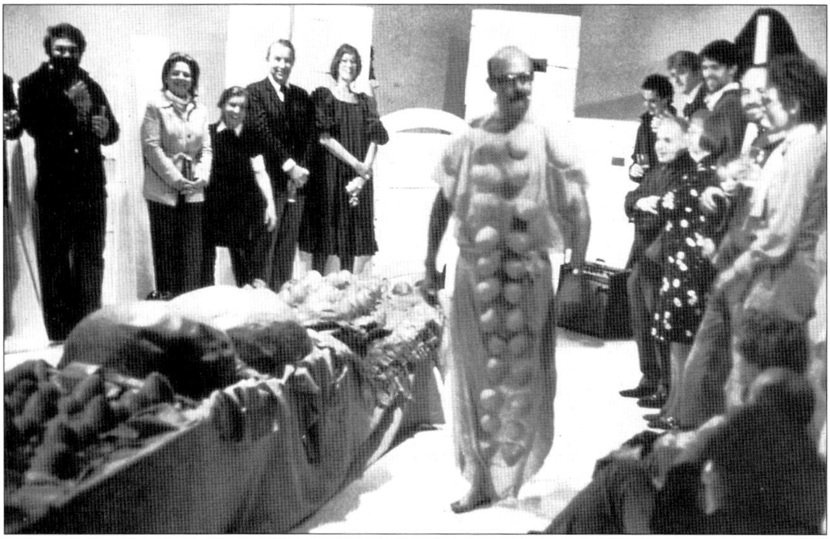

66 The art historian Gert Schiff performing in *A Banquet/A Fashion Show of Body Parts*, Hamilton Gallery of Contemporary Art, New York, October 21, 1978. Photo by Peter Moore © Estate of Peter Moore / VAGA, NYC

they are visible and look rather helpless, not quite sure of their purpose any more. This virile figure does the rounds, turns a circle, and makes body movements that caricature a bold hip-swing. With his hands on his hips he smiles down at the audience, who are squating in the wooden alcoves around the arena. With the self-confidence of a Roman legionary in toga and sandals who feels the emperor's gaze rest upon him, he completes his display and disappears through the door. Next a female figure enters whose upper body is covered with a cascade of rounded objects — it would not be quite right to call them phallic; they might perhaps best be described as sexual protuberances (Ill. 69). Under this, next to her skin, she is wearing a floor-length transparent latex dress. The viewer's gaze moves to the long table in the middle of the arena, covered in a cloth and stretching the length of the room. Two narrow, wooden poles stick out from the short ends causing us now to perceive the structure as two biers, end-to-end, under the bluish cloth. Large latex domes in a color that is somewhere between faded parchment and the pale light that might filter through a vellum window pane are placed at each end of the figure on the bier. On the one side they are shrunken and wrinkled, having collapsed in on themselves, while on the other side they are firm, smooth, solid, and rounded. There is a confrontation here, a confrontation between young and old. In the two centers of the ellipse the hearts of the young person and the old person are beating, leaving the question open as to which is the more desirable, which offers fulfillment, and whether new life is hidden in decay. The music continues and a man with spectacles and a bald patch steps out onto the stage. He is smoking and has two rows of latex breasts under

67 *A Banquet/A Fashion Show of Body Parts*, Hamilton Gallery of Contemporary Art, New York, 1978. Photo by Peter Moore © Estate of Peter Moore / VAGA, NYC

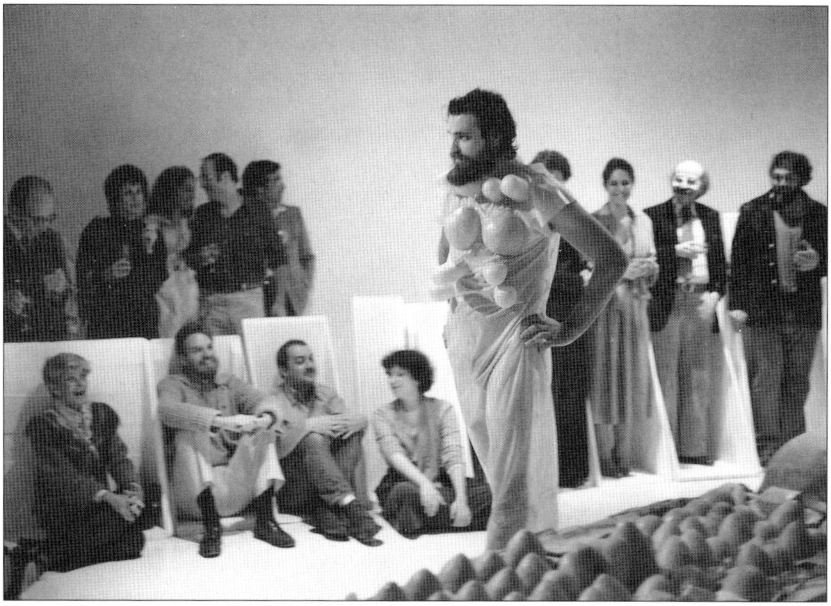

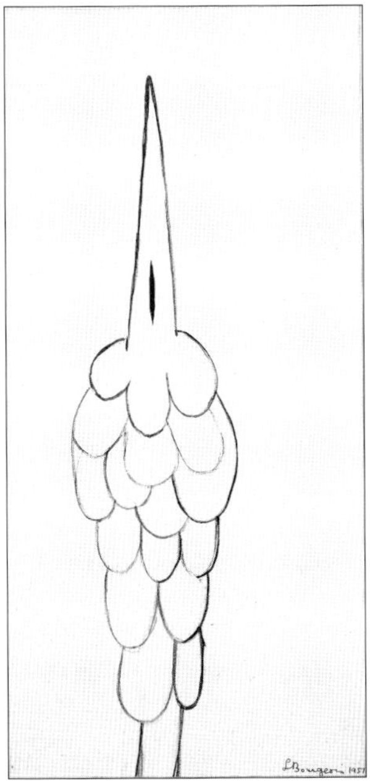

68 Untitled, ink and charcoal on paper, 1951, 12 1/4 x 6 in.

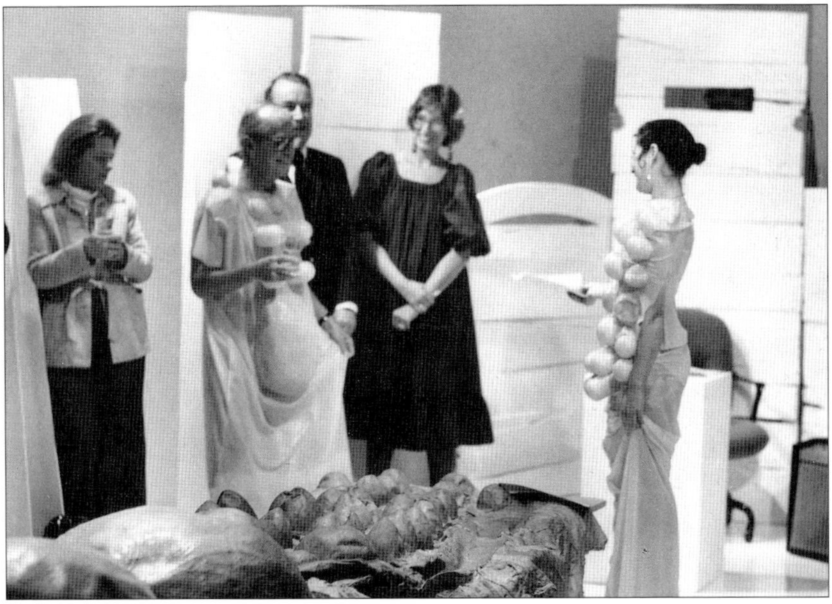

Above right:
69 *A Banquet/A Fashion Show of Body Parts*, Hamilton Gallery of Contemporary Art, New York, 1978. Photo by Peter Moore © Estate of Peter Moore / VAGA, NYC

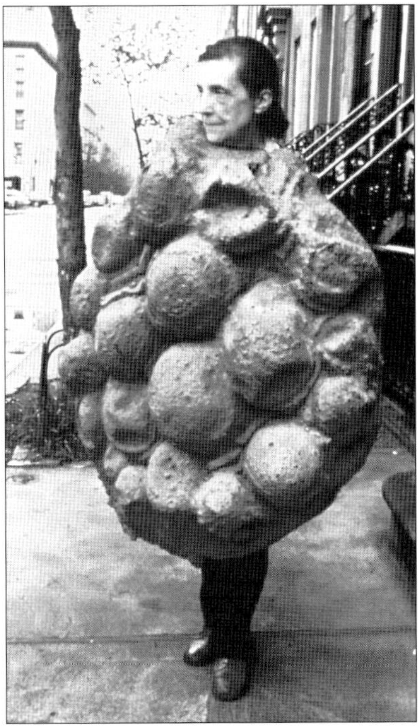

70 Louise in front of her NYC home in 1975 wearing the latex sculpture *Avenza* which became part of *Confrontation* (1978).
Photo by Peter Moore © Estate of Peter Moore / VAGA, NYC

his floor-length robe (Ill. 66). Obviously happy with his role and the costume he is wearing, he parades once around the arena. With a gentle laugh, Louise reveals the performer's identity as that of the art historian Gert Schiff, a university professor, whom she proudly casts and presents here as the artist's victim.

Meanwhile, a young man by the swing door has got up: he starts to play a violin with studied grace, drawing from it elegiac tones which then lure a woman out of the white wooden alcoves. Her no longer youthful figure is clad in a close-fitting, transparent dress. She starts to sing "She abandoned me [...]," crescendoes and writhes in invisible pain, cries out "MOTHER!" and in a dark, feminine voice repeats with a rising and falling intonation, "She abandoned me [...]"

"Astonishing — the music, the sounds and the language all wear out over the years", Louise comments when our visit is over, "but the images remain and the visual loses none of its power."

In 1996, amongst the vehicles which make their way daily between Manhattan and Brooklyn, there is also one belonging to Louise Bourgeois. Carefully driven by Jerry, Louise, the eighty-six-

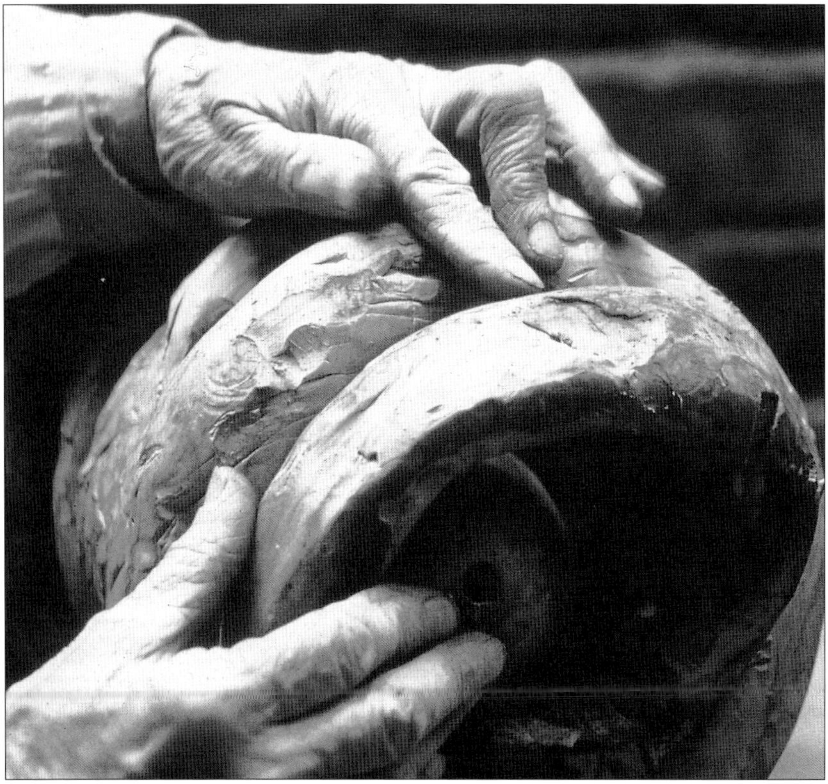

71 In the studio, c. 1985

year-old artist, goes to her studio every day. As the car crosses Brooklyn Bridge it begins to sway slightly. The mighty construction has its own rhythm. One's gaze rests on the steel supports; the skyline of Manhattan arises along with images of the artist at work; the gentle strength in the way she handles a chisel, notches and smooths the wood, following the grain until the slender form is complete. Then there is the sight of her hand grasping and kneading malleable clay until the rounded form elicits in the viewer a desire for contact and sets his thoughts in motion. Large, suspended plaster forms take shape in her hands, petrify as monumental droplets, develop labyrinthine passages inside, overturn vessels, and demand that the viewer should not relax his or her attention for one moment. Latex, pink and red rubber, glass, bronze, steel, flax, and wax — the materials of our own world are tested, exposed, and melded at the sculptor's behest and imbued with expressive meaning. Blocks of marble from Pietrasanta and Carrara become fragile light-traps, develop waves like petrified

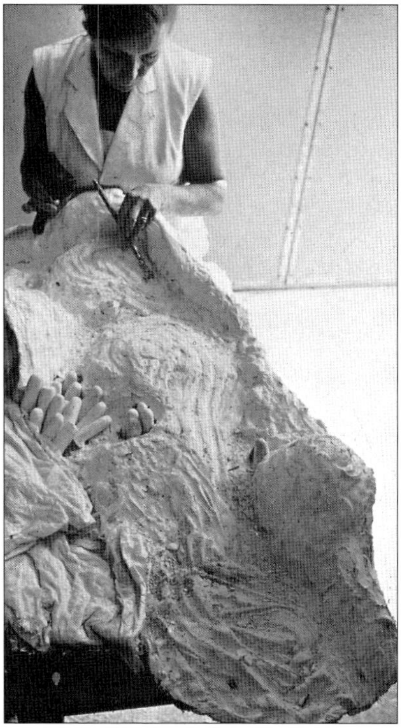

72 Louise working on one of her sculptures in Quercata, Tuscany, 1967

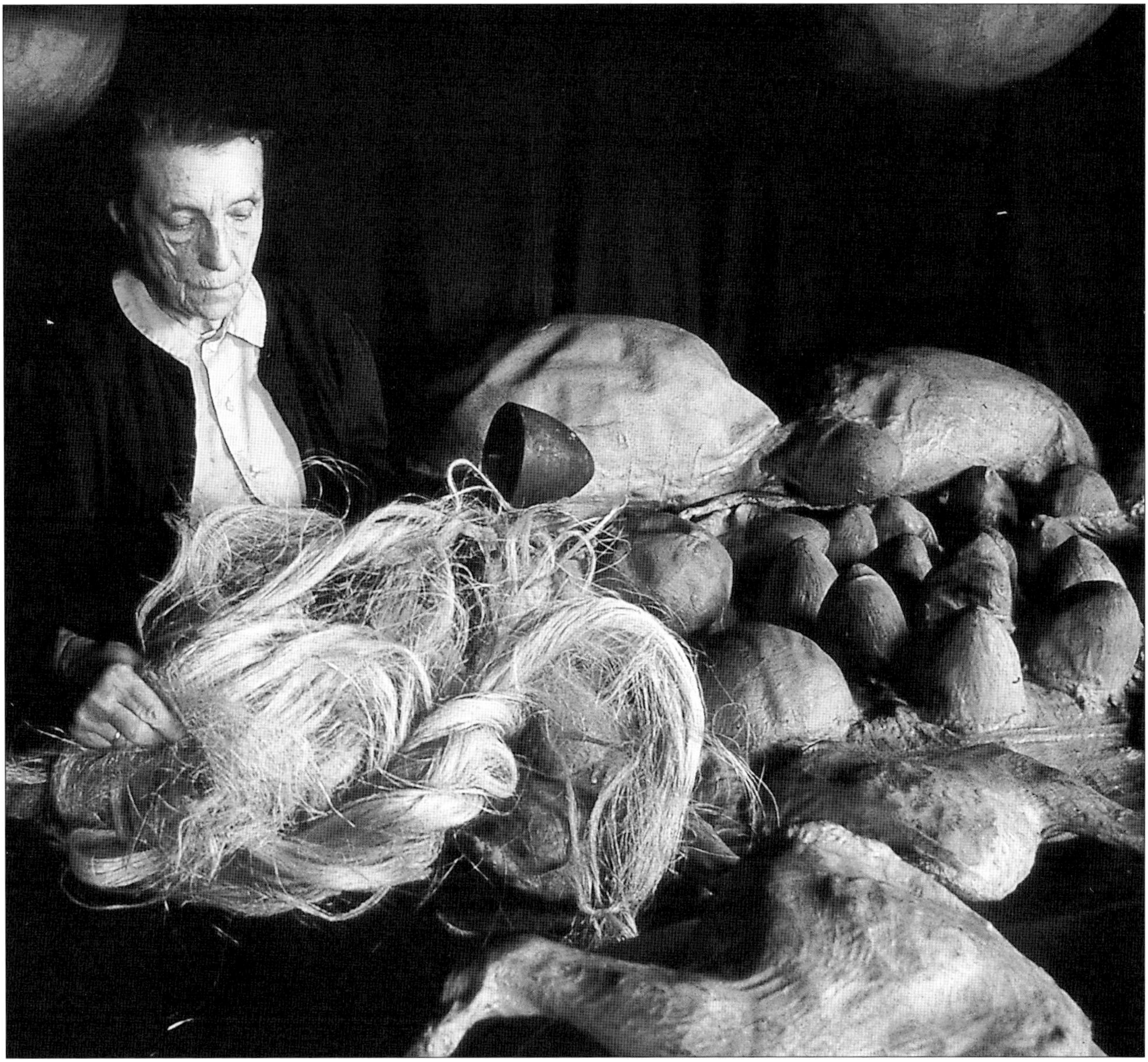

73 Louise working on *The Destruction of the Father*, 1974.

streams of lava, shimmer rosily like the skin of a voluptuous Rubens figure, and appear as tender as a baby's foot. Weight, mass, volume, and density become the physical expression of a material world that exists in space and which as a rule is generally only to be described in three-dimensional terms. The tool in the artist's hands gives off a sense of energy that she then uses for those creations which constitute a kind of life after life and which are not ultimately subject to temporal limitations, neither those of the past nor the future, and which become meaningful only in the presence of our perception. Louise Bourgeois's own life is at an advanced stage and yet the spark in her eyes can still bring color to a youthful visitor's cheek, the sound of her voice can still bring one's thoughts to a halt, when her hands wander over the table, the wise fingers turn the pages of the diaries of her childhood and another pebble goes into her father's box.

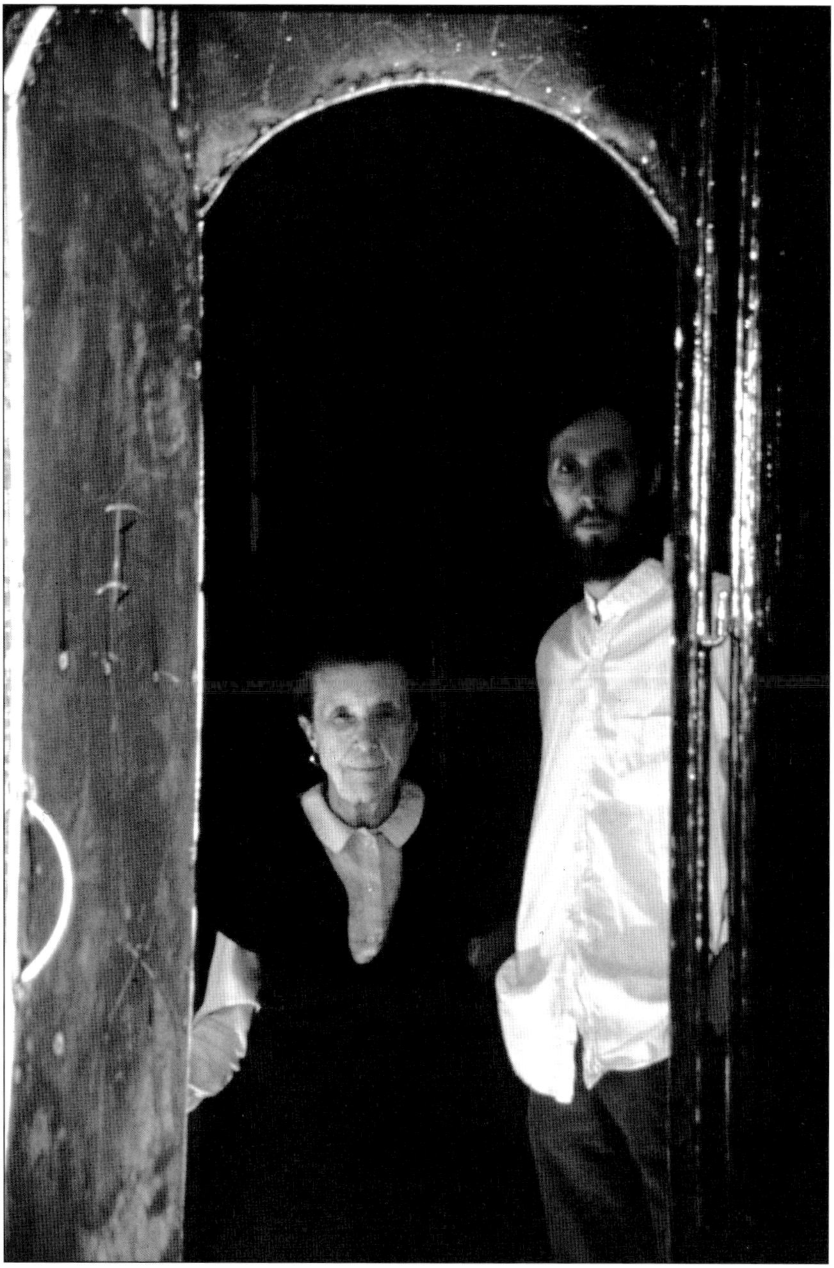

74 Louise with Jerry Gorovoy in *Articulated Lair*, 1986

Let us take our leave here with a glance through the door of the *Cell* that opens up another world to us, that requires us to be in a state of constant departure and, as we go, let us acknowledge our grateful thanks to Louise and Jerry.

III. MARBLE, CLAY, AND WOOD: IMAGES OF MAN

From *Pass* to *Femme volage*

I have many stylistic possibilities — the most multifarious art of style that has ever been at the disposal of one man.

Friedrich Nietzsche, *Ecce homo*, 1888

The people I like most are interested in portraiture, the symbolic and recognizable unique essence of a person. I, on the other hand, am interested in the portraiture of a relationship, how a relationship can be twisted, the effect people have on another.[43]

Louise Bourgeois, 1992

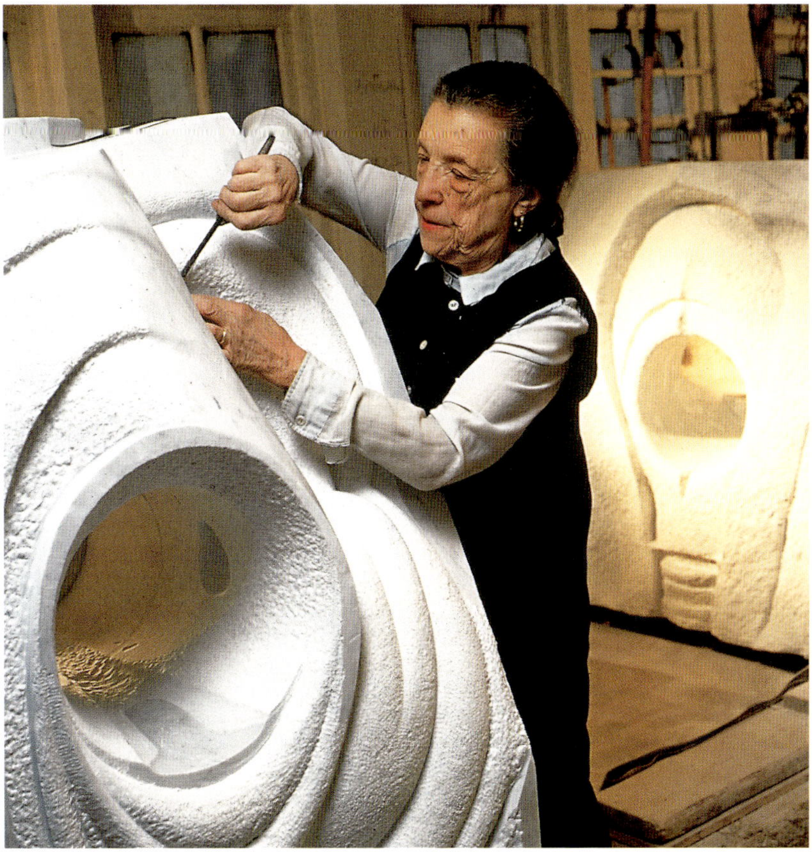

75 Louise working on *The Sail*, 1988

Articulated Lair, a strangely intimate work of art that offers the viewer an active experience, seems to have little to do with the monumental, stunningly weighty marble block, *Pass*, of 1988–89 (Ills 76, 77, 79, 80). Both works were created at roughly the same time by the same elderly lady who taciturnly flung her arms

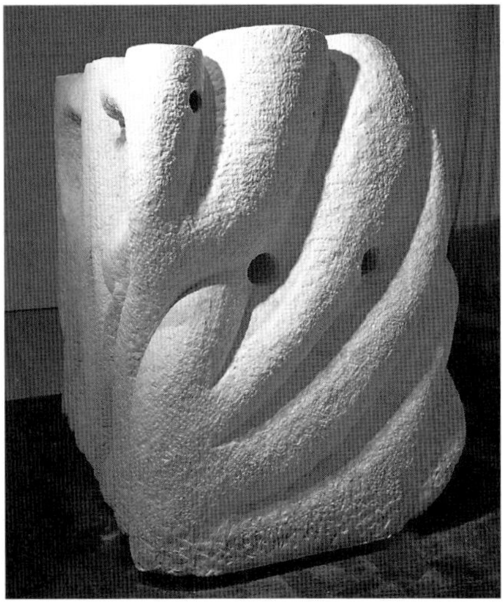

76 *Pass*, 1988–89
white marble, 50½ × 48 × 37 in.

Right:
77 *Pass*, 1988–89

up into the air in a telling response to her own 'articulated lair.' Moreover, this was barely finished when the seventy-seven-year-old artist started out on a new, major project and set to work with chisel and hammer on a block of marble (Ill. 77) considerably larger than herself. "I see the cube as a problem", as Louise Bourgeois commented when she started on this piece. "I see it as a physical cube, not as a symbolic cube or as a concept. My problem is to penetrate the physicality of the cube. Modern technology allows you to do that. [...] I take great pride in the solitary cube, and great pride in the fact that I can penetrate it. My work with the cube is very modern. It does not repeat former work."[44]

Plate-sized, conical hollows like an owl's eyes gaze menacingly at the viewer. Thickly swelling bands run around the marble block. Round, carefully-hewn marble stems with rough surfaces rise upwards. Blindingly bright light streams out from inside. Cracks are filled with deep black shadow lines. Bodies seem to merge into faces as on a totem pole, bird-like gods rub beaks. Licentious fantasies that might find sexual elements in this piece are quickly repressed as they are overlaid with other — defused — images and associations; and the now slightly more relaxed viewer, although not quite recovered from the shock of the power of the images conjured up in his imagination, may be reminded of a crab's claw.

Using precious marble from the renowned quarries at Carrara and Pietrasanta in Italy, which she had by then been visiting for more than twenty years, Louise Bourgeois has fashioned a mysterious, vital and yet corpse-like body that seems to unite all organic creatures and yet does not try to conceal its own lifeless, rocky origins. After all, are those not the tendrils of some tropical, flesh-eating plant — and are those not lianas twisting around its trunk? And is this not the mocking image of an empty skull, the mighty bone structure of the head of some prehistoric animal with the roof of the cranium removed so that we can look down into it and see the cleanly polished interior of this monster?

The dark, terrifying grimace of *Pass* conjures up wild, richly associative images, only to reject them and remain puzzlingly incomprehensible, because its forms do not establish any kind of link between our troubled imaginations and the reality of our daily lives. Taken one step further it becomes utterly baffling if we try to identify its figuration and expressive qualities in terms of other well-known works in marble. Michelangelo and Canova themselves chose to use marble from Carrara for their Heroes and Graces, because marble from that particular quarry was and still is famous for its purity and it contains practically no trace of glittering quartz or fine veins of graphite, which artists do not necessarily want to have to deal with in designing their work. The choice of the unbroken, pure white of Carrara marble, with a surface that reflects the full range of light from the sharpest and brightest to the deepest inner shadows, is a unique challenge to the sculptor's talent as an artist and craftsman, from the choosing of the block — seeing the form already embodied in it — through the design stages and on through to the completion of the physical task.

Marble — even in its unworked, unformed state — carries the resonances of the immensely long, richly fruitful history of sculpture in the Western world. From Antiquity, many of the most outstanding visual works in Western culture have been sculpted in marble. Magnificent works created in Greece at the dawn of our own age have been substantially lost in the mists of time, and all that survives of the legendary sculptor Phidias are some Roman copies, some doubtful fragments, and glowing written praise of his works: and thus the high artistic ideals by which sculpture is measured have been passed down through the generations. In the mid-eighteenth century, in his *Gedanken über die Nachahmung der griechischen Werke in der Malerei und Bildhauerkunst*, Johann J. Winckelmann described *Laocoon*, one of the most important pieces from that period. This sculpture, and its reception, were instrumental in the revival of interest in Classical sculpture which in turn led to Neo-classicism, particularly since Winckelmann's text was immediately translated into several languages. Yet Winckelmann, known through his *History of the Art of Antiquity* as the father of descriptive writing in modern art history, knew the Greek masterpieces only through much later Hellenic works or Roman copies, and he was never to see with his own eyes the land of Greece, which in his imagination occupied some ideal

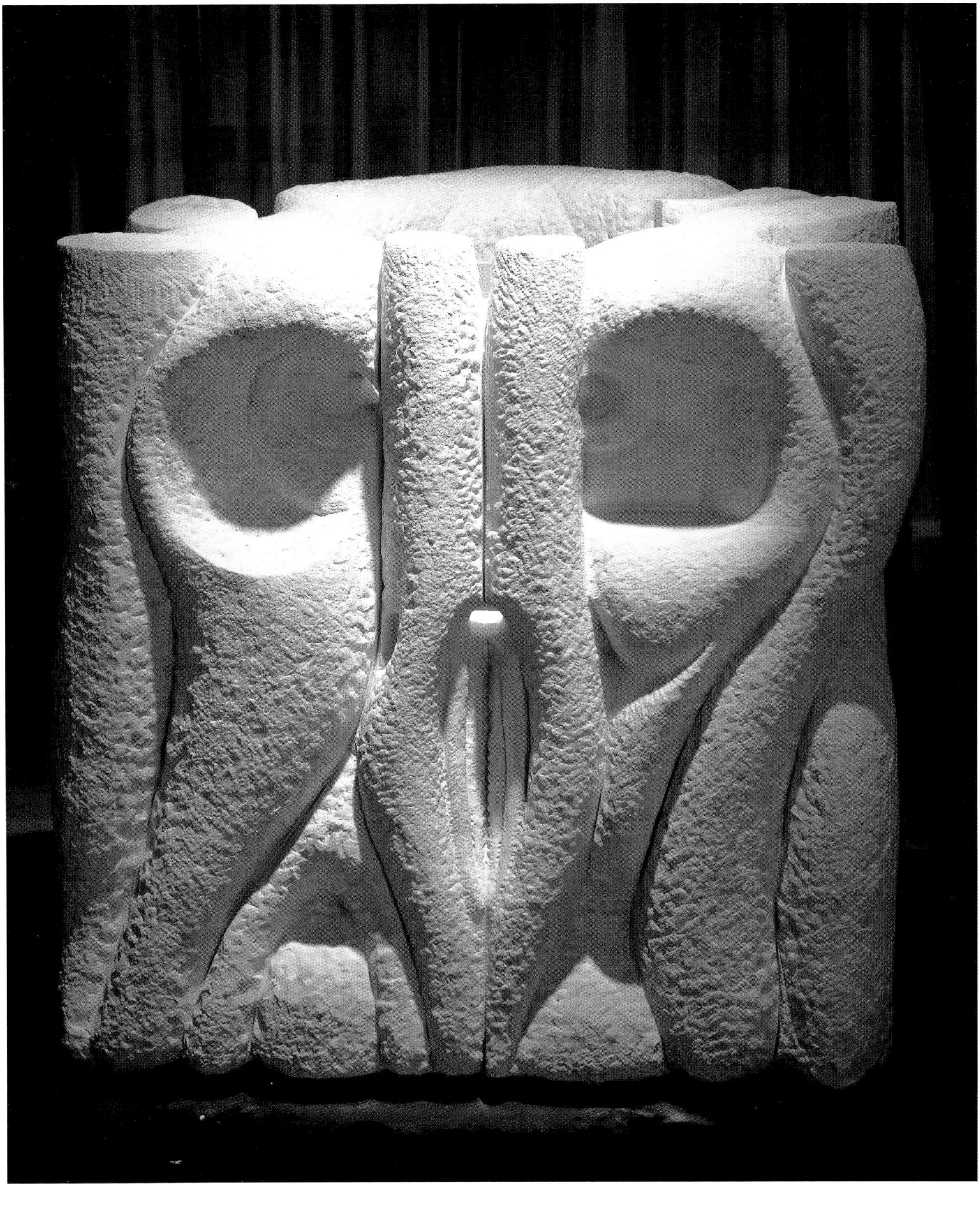

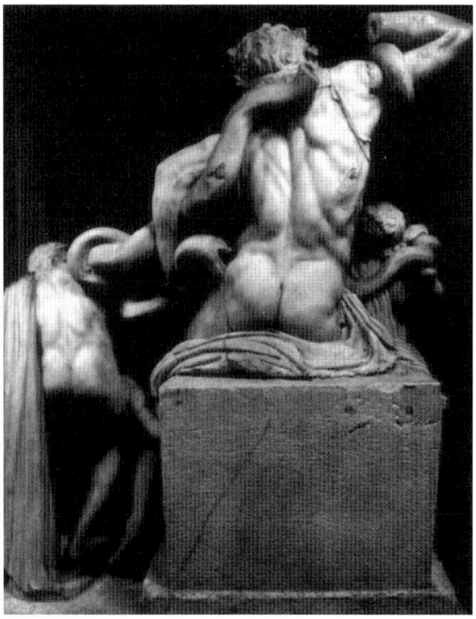

78 *Laocoon*, Roman copy (1st century B.C.), after the Greek original by Agesander, Athanadorus and Polydorus

79 *Pass*, 1988–89

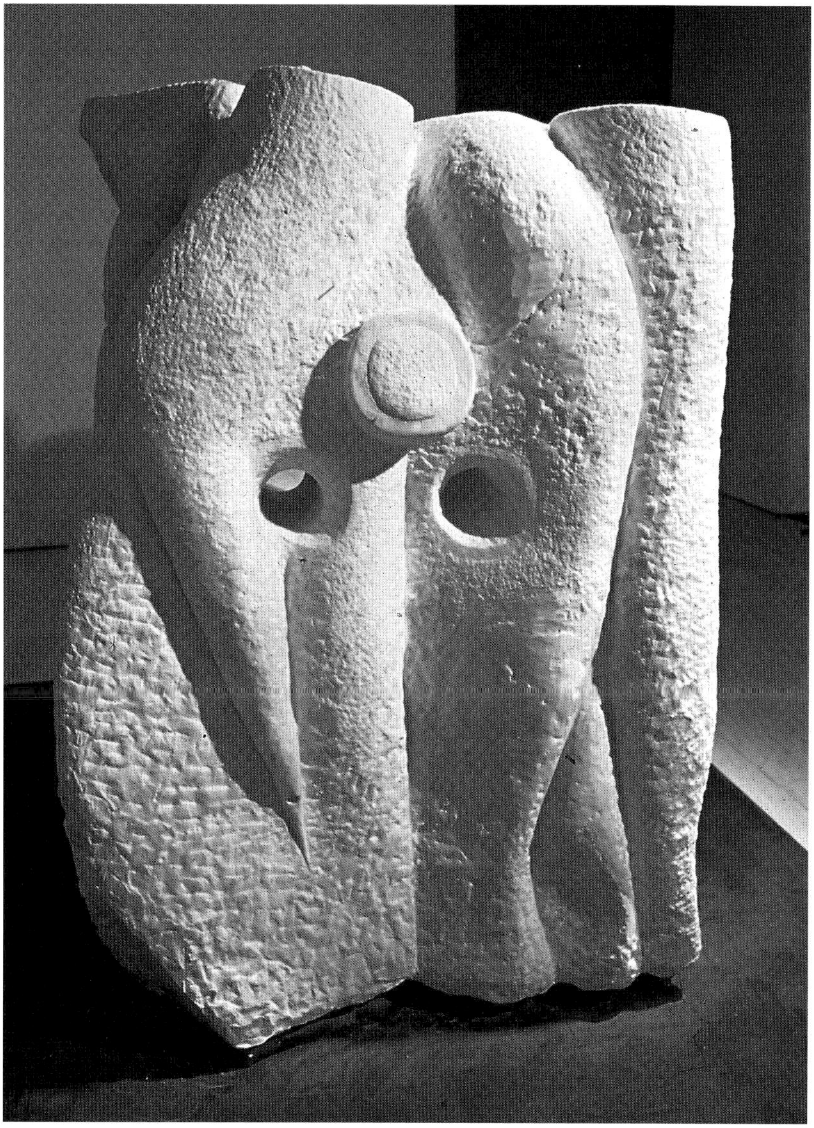

sphere albeit with some distinct similarities to the reality of the eighteenth century as he knew it. Only slightly adapting the Aristotelian dictum that had held good since the Renaissance — *ars imitatur naturam* (Art imitates Nature) — Winckelmann's artistic ideal was grounded in the most complete and harmonious representation of the human body: "The only way for us to become great, and, yes indeed, if possible, inimitable, is through the imitation of the Ancients."[45] With that he opened the doors to a form of art that measured itself against its own concept of Greek art and set itself the aim of creating an idealized image of man, of perfectly recreating the actual appearance of the human body: but all too often the results were simply figures caught in stiff poses, gesturing hollowly and meaninglessly into nothingness. It was not until the turn of the twentieth century that Auguste Rodin, with his unique genius, breathed new life into sculpture.

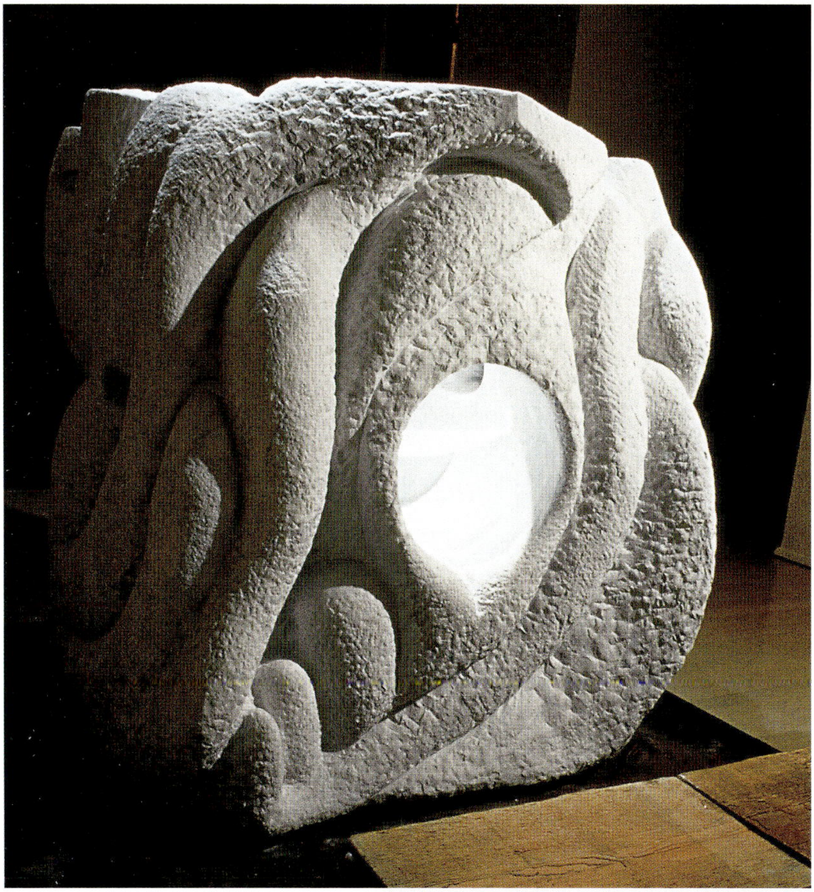

80 *Pass*, 1988–89

Laocoön with his two sons, entwined by snakes and struggling desperately, whom Winckelmann had described with such feeling — even sentimentality, as the taste of the day dictated — takes up a theme from mythology already endorsed as noble and honorable in poetic works such as the *Iliad*. *Laocöon* illustrates this theme according to all the artistic rules of the time, with anatomical exactitude, a harmonious balance in the relationship of the parts to the whole, and with a surface that, on close examination, gives the viewer the impression of being able to make out each individual pore on the skin. Beyond this, it embodies the mood of the time, when the aim above all was to escape human frailty, to find fulfillment, and to attain an ideal state through divine power.

In 1990 Louise Bourgeois wrote a rare theoretical essay, 'Freud's Toys',[46] in response to an exhibition of Sigmund Freud's collection of antiques. She describes the figurines and fragments as "socially meaningless" artifacts and uses them as a framework to put forward her own views on art:

> *"There is also a big difference between an artifact and art. An artifact is first of all useful, and does not relate to anything more vitally than to its use. It is not isolated in its momentary meaning, and is easily reproduced. It is not an original. So much contemporary art should really be seen as artifact; but then, so should some of the objects in Freud's collection. Is a little Tanagra*[47] *statuette from the Greek period a real embodiment of that civilization? [...]* **Art is**

reality. *The artifact is a manufactured object;* **a work of art is a language**. *The artifact has only an educational or sentimental value. The work of art has an absolute value."*[48]

[Bold script: L. B.]

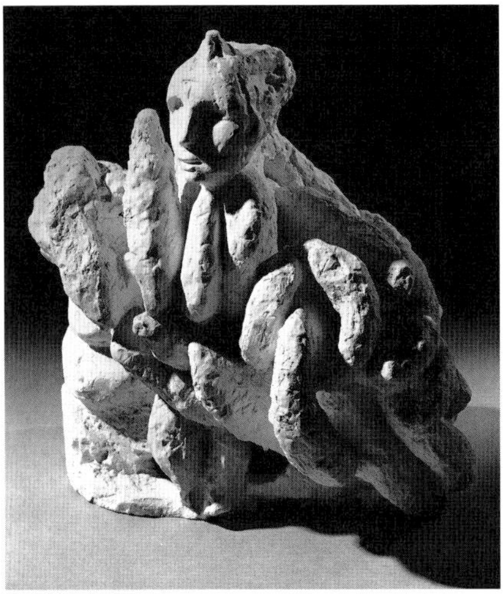

81 Portrait of Robert, 1969
bronze, white patina, 13 × 12½ × 10 in.

Right:
82 *Female Portrait*, 1982
marble, 22 × 17 × 11½ in.

These radically explicit statements by Louise Bourgeois point clearly towards a schism, a break, an unbridgeable gap between the art of this century and that of the previous century. This approach, linking an artwork with its social context and equating its artistic form with language, marks a paradigmatic change in what was now understood as the function of a work of art in comparison with the aesthetic codes that had held sway until the turn of the century. In this passage Louise Bourgeois no longer sees art as representation, as the imitation of some externally perceptible reality, but instead as an expression of reality, indeed as a specifically created reality, "a real embodiment of that civilization."

When we looked at *Pass* we were led by the understandable desire to identify figurative references and — if we had indeed made out a strict, illustrative representation of some familiar object — we would in effect have been setting limits on the meaning of the work. Are there not in fact entwined snakes encircling the round aperture in the rear of *Pass*? Is Louise Bourgeois's sculpture not taking up an honorable sculptural tradition going back to the unforgettable fascination of *Laocöon*? However, the left side of *Pass* (Ill. 79) raises the difficult question of whether the attempt to link scraps of memory with things from the real world in fact brings us one iota closer to discovering the meaning of this sculpture. What we actually see is simply a lump of marble consisting of flowing, swelling forms that come together in a point, with circular incisions and equally precisely formed protuberances. In this context the term 'organic' could be used to refer less to representational animal or plant allusions than to the work's formally rich, linked, ordered structure. Rejecting figurative references and their narrative tendencies, at the end of the twentieth century Louise Bourgeois has developed an artistic language that — in contrast to what has gone before — draws on the sculptural repertoire of the multiplicity of abstract forms that make up the formal grammar of non-representational art.

And yet we are persistently followed by mercilessly staring eyes and the chilling, slit-like, saw-toothed, vertical incision in the front. Walking around the sculpture immediately dispels these projections of our own feelings; and the very name of the work again emphasizes its inextricably complex range of meanings, which seems suspended between total abstraction and potential figuration, with discordant echoes of tradition and modernity, of convention and revolution, locked at one and the same time into the perfection of sublime beauty and abysmally ugly horror. *Pass* is a dividing line, a threshold, an awkward stage somewhere between holding out and giving up, the pass that grants the traveler safe-conduct, a difficult saddle in the mountains, but it also implies attempted intimacy and a critical state: refering to "making a pass at someone." *Pass* must be grasped if one is to comprehend Louise Bourgeois's work as a whole. What could we read in its forms and shapes? "The work may be subject to many interpretations", as we have already cited Louise Bourgeois on this topic. Is she here perhaps formulating an image with the pictorial capacity to transcend traditional formal criteria for 'likenesses'?

In fact, in the same year that she created this major sculpture, Louise Bourgeois allowed us to share the thoughts that governed the formal aspect of this work:

"I contemplated the penetrated cube for a long time. [...] I tried to translate **my** *problem into the stone. The drilling begins the process by negating the stone. [...] The cube no longer exists as a pure form for contemplation; it becomes an image. I take it over with my fantasy, my life force [...]."*

Convincingly she explains how this marble cube, in its overwhelming physicality, presents "a problem" for her:

"It is [after penetrating the cube] now the problem of the voyage. It is the voyage inside the cube. After the penetration by the technicians comes the voyage. That is the art."[49]

83 *Spiral*, 1960
plaster, height 20 in.

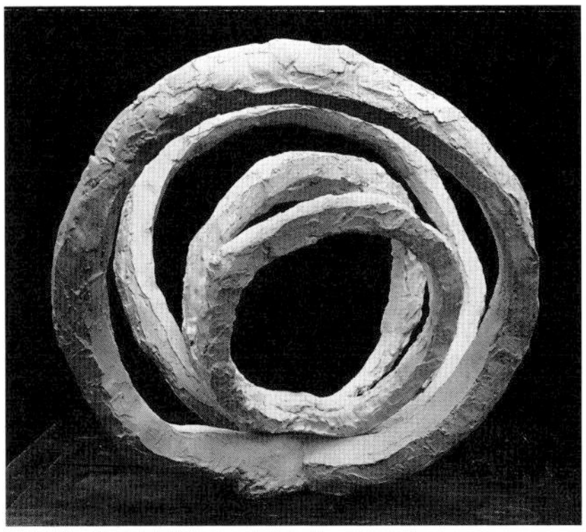

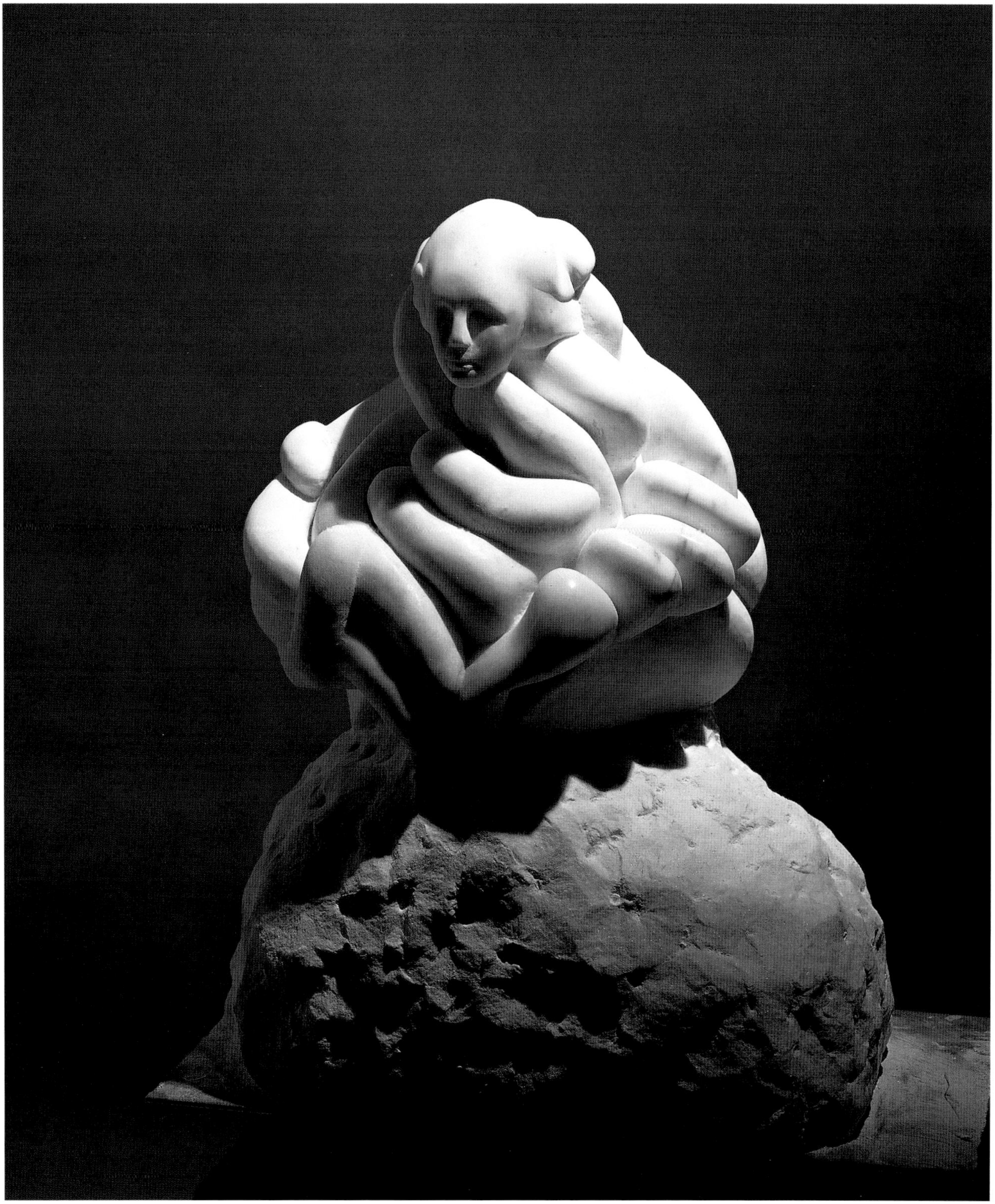

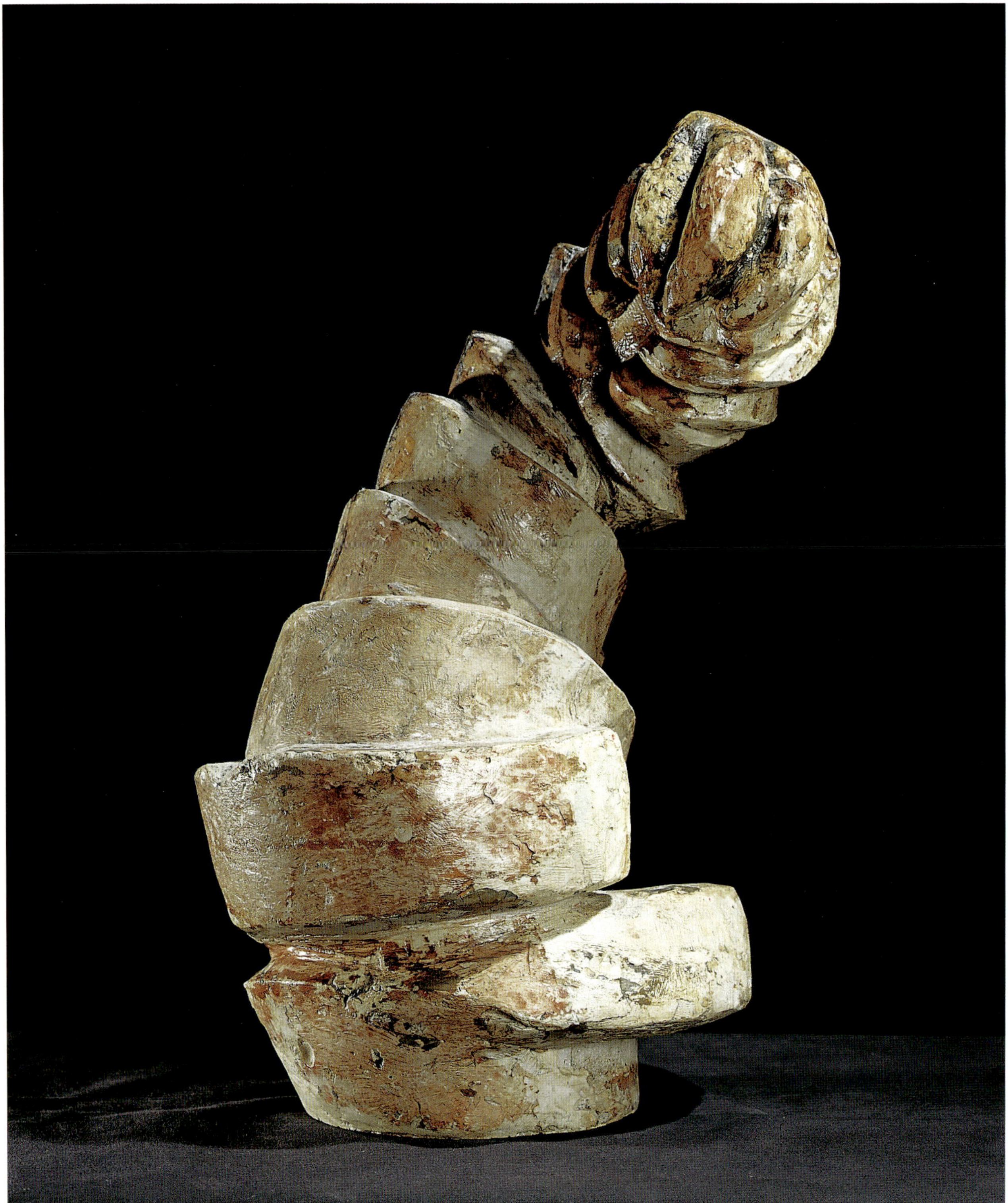

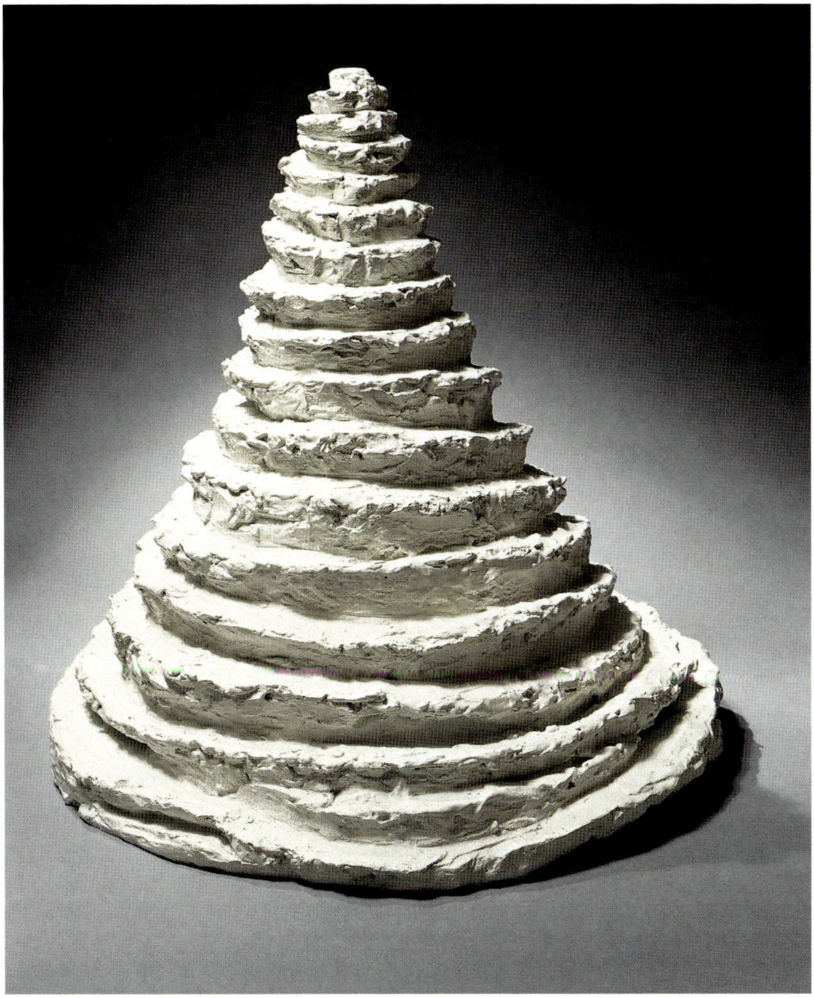

Opposite page:
84 *Labyrinthine Tower*, 1962
plaster, 18 x 12 x 10$^{1}/_{2}$ in.

85 *Lair*, 1962
bronze, white patina, 22 x 22 x 22 in.

86 Louise in her studio with *Life Flower I* in plaster, 1960

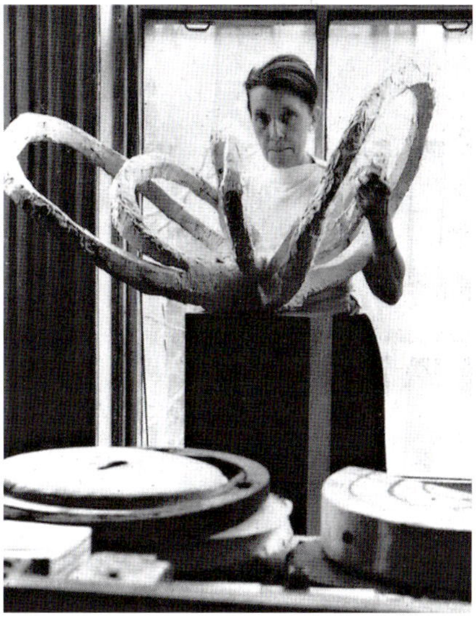

With these words the artist manifests all too clearly her creative thought processes and not just anyone's whimsically subjective interpretation — in this case by the sculptor herself: "I am just going on with this investigation, this voyage by myself. Inside the cube I am on my own."[50]

Only a few years before *Pass*, Louise Bourgeois designed a human face, a portrait, an image of man; that idiosyncratic yet beautiful and formally satisfying structure demands closer examination. A small, tender face looks trustingly out into the world and a gentle smile plays round the lips of the *Female Portrait* of 1982 (Ill. 82). Its curled-up marble body with fine, gray veins balances precariously on a spherical, roughly hewn, plinth-like pedestal. A narrow little head looking enquiringly out into the world emerges from a labyrinthine, arabesque-like, intertwined, and inextricably entangled mesh that seems to hold the hidden body in the iron grip of a thousand-fingered fist. The whole figure on its clumsy base threatens to lose balance and topple forwards at any moment, yet it also seems that the rump of the slight figure is in fact made up of the snake-like mesh. The rough, hard outer surface of the marble which kept harm at bay has been broken open, knocked away, worked on, and formed,

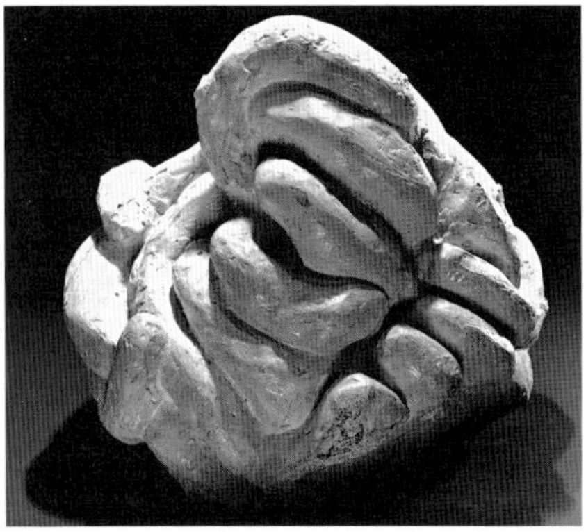

87 *Clutching*, 1962
plaster, 12 x 13 x 12 in.

revealing a small head, freed from the weight of its load and looking with amazement out into the world, with its soft, warm interior now laid bare and unprotected: a newly-born, vulnerable, confused tangle that is waiting to unfold and develop. No divine Aphrodite stepping from the sea's billowing foam, no image steeped in myth, but rather the symbol of an utterly human being, belonging to this world and at the mercy of this world — yet not reflecting **our** reality but creating a reality all of **its own**.

This work constituted an immensely daring step: not a sublime portrait of an individual human face, aiming to capture the innate character of that person, but an open-ended, non-specific formulation that successfully uses abstract forms to integrate figurative images into a complex unified whole, thereby breaking through the hitherto unresolved dichotomy of figuration and abstraction. As Jerry Gorovoy has rightly put it: "Bourgeois knew the risks that the greater the abstraction, the greater the artificiality that style signifies, and the greater the distance from her original ideas."[51] Completely non-representational forms like *Spiral*, made in 1960, (Ill. 83) prove in retrospect to be forerunners, aesthetic precursors, a stage in the development of a wholly individual language. They resemble illustrations of mathematical

88 *Baroque*, 1970
marble, $37\frac{1}{4} \times 25\frac{1}{4} \times 25\frac{7}{8}$ in.

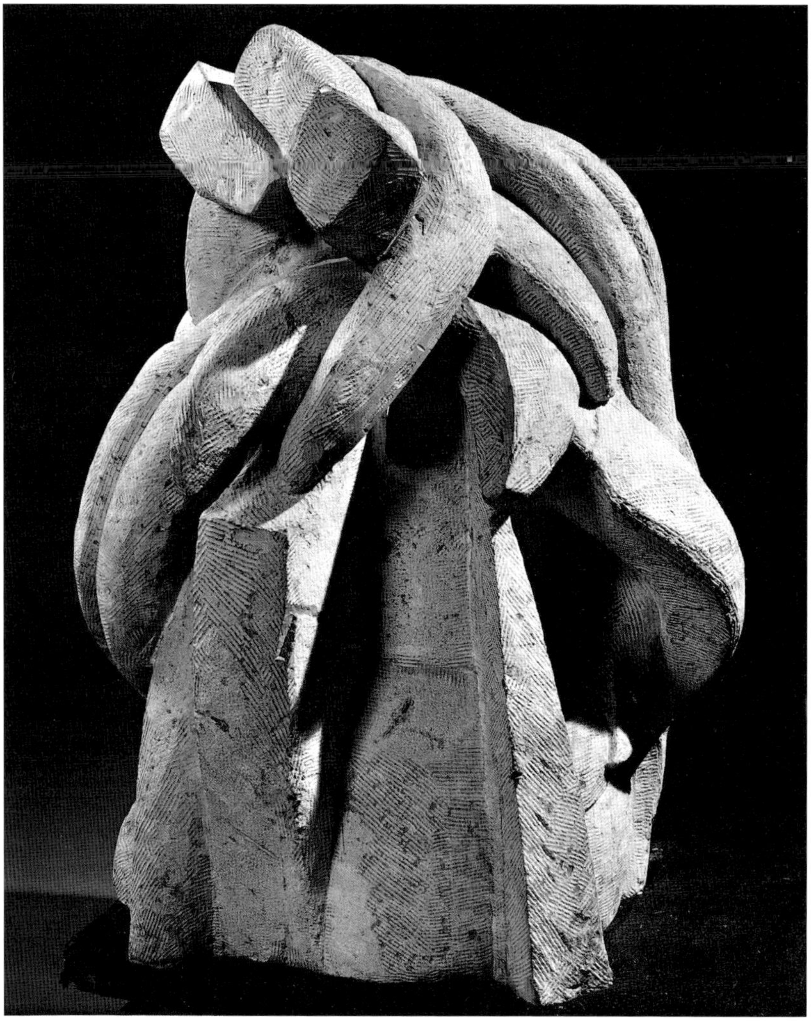

calculations dealing with complex spatial forms, or highly complicated biological structures like the helix (Ill. 86). Nevertheless, they are also formally independent plastic solutions to the problem of creating a sculpture as a completely open spatial structure, where the body itself is formed as much by the structure as by its empty interstices. The designation of this little sculpture, the title *Spiral*, emphasizes its simplicity and directness, in which the simple, plaster form and the significant name are as one. In this work we find structural laws similar to those behind the spiral in the sculptures *Lair* (Ill. 85) and *Labyrinthine Tower* (Ill. 84) with their classical rigor and beauty — both made in 1962.

Similarly, the marble sculpture, *Baroque*, of ten years later, with its utterly non-referential interplay of sharp edges and architectural and rope-like organic forms, may be seen as part of the striving in Bourgeois's work from the mid-1950s onwards to develop a new grammar of sculpture, which — as we saw in *Pass* and *Articulated Lair* — had by the 1980s become a fully developed, innately rigorous language of forms which must certainly stand as a typological paradigm. The bronze versions of the female portrait discussed above (Ill. 90) which were made in the early 1960s, bear significant witness to the transition from non-representational sculptures such as *Spiral* or *Lair* to later corporeal, more figurative structures. But their real significance is only evident when they are seen together with the *Nature Studies* from the mid-1980s. *Clutching* (Ill. 87), for example, is admittedly a metonymic representation in formal terms of the notion of grasping, seizing and pressing. Yet in the concrete images of heads emerging (Ill. 82) in the images of hands (Ill. 89) freeing themselves, of arms reaching out and as parts of the series *Nature Studies* — in all of these bulbous forms we recognize a powerful symbolic figure that shatters us on an existential level.

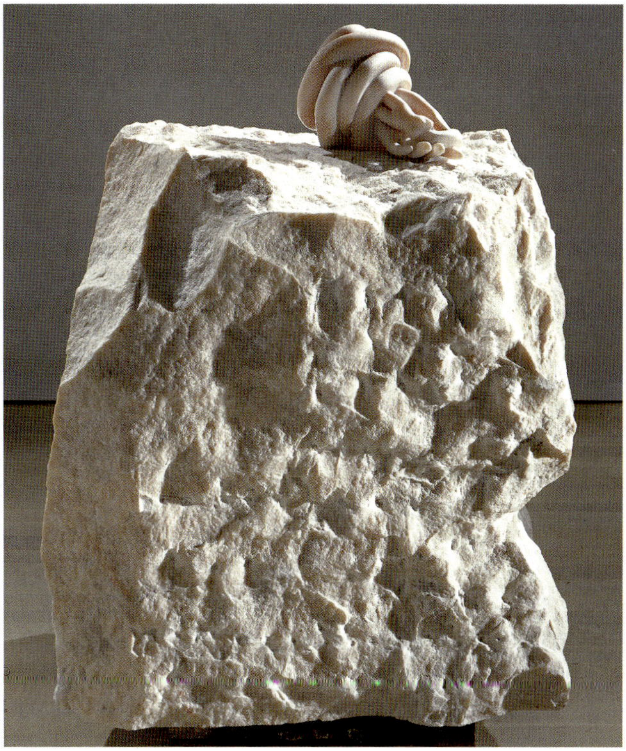

89 *Nature Study*, 1986
marble, 33 × 28 × 21½ in.

Seen in context of the New York School in the 1950s and 1960s, *Female Portrait* (Ill. 82), this formally idiosyncratic, yet sensational, humble sculpture, becomes even more meaningful. In its structural simplicity and direct, uncomplicated beauty, its significance within Louise Bourgeois's oeuvre — particularly in conjunction with *Lair* (Ill. 85) — can scarcely be overestimated.

90 *Female Portrait*, 1962
bronze, 15⅝ × 13¼ × 11½ in.

91 *Nature Study*, 1986
marble, 35 × 61 × 29 in.

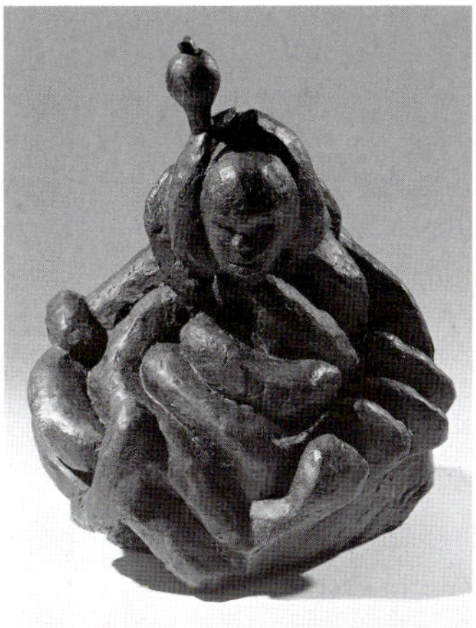

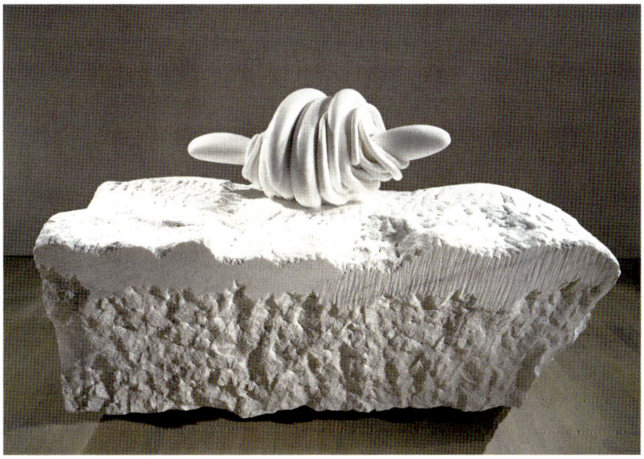

The question which concerns us here is, what moved Louise Bourgeois to create these works, what fundamental insights about man´s image lies behind them? Even if *Female Portrait* includes the word 'portrait' in its title, we cannot perceive any identifying features in the delicate head; instead, its formal structure would appear to be made up of generic elements. *Female Portrait* does not portray a specifically female anatomy but presents 'the female' *per se*: a metaphor — without representational restrictions — of what Louise Bourgeois sees as intrinsically female.

This portrait is determined in its content by the confluence of two opposed, formal strands: abstract, non-referential forms as in *Clutching*, and the figurative head of a woman. This marble piece, which has been discussed in some detail here, was made in 1982, but its artistic inception must date as far back as 1962, to the version in plaster. In these years less modeled bronzes were made than *Female Portraits*.

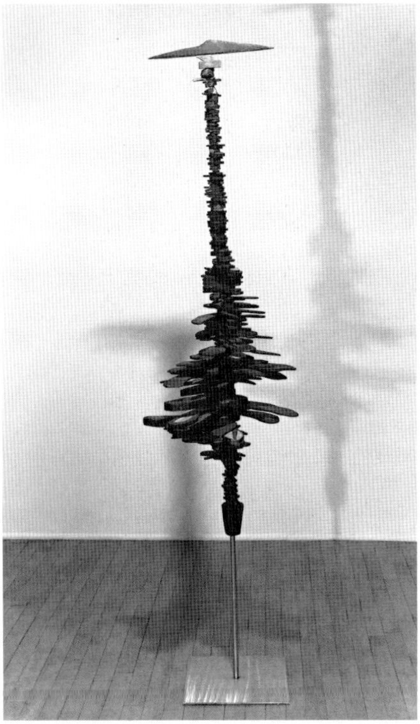

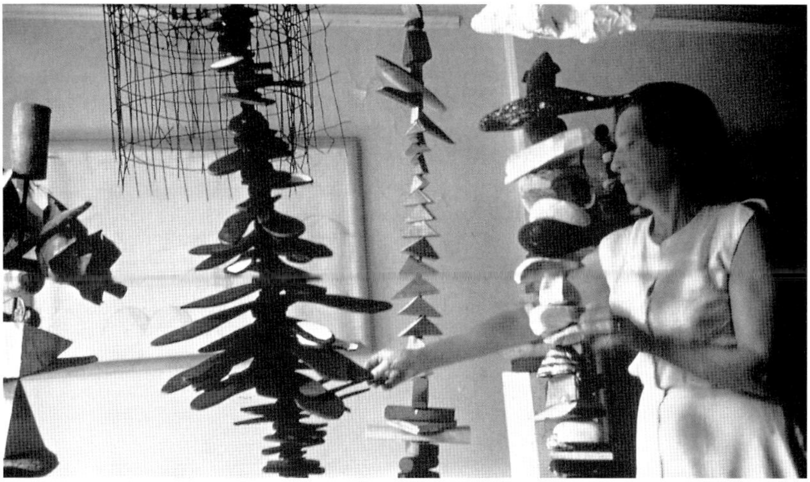

92 *Femme volage*, 1951, painted wood and stainless steel, 72 x $17^1/_2$ x 13 in.
93 Louise with *Femme volage*, photo: c. 1965
94 Memling Dawn, 1951, bronze and stainless steel, 64 × 15 × 18 in.

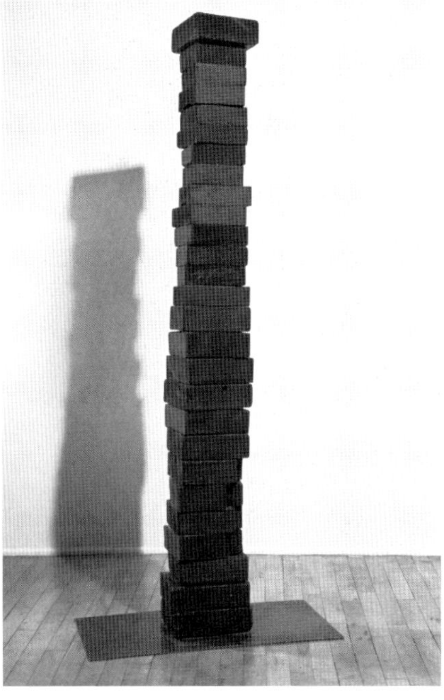

Louise Bourgeois's inception of man´s image — in this case, by virtue of its figurative form and unmistakable title, clearly that of a woman — may seem distinctly singular both in its form and in its content. Yet the artist's images do present us with a clearly defined, socially and culturally relevant concept of oneself which should be pursued further here. In order to lay a firm basis for our understanding of the sculptures of Louise Bourgeois, we must first examine and view two further female portraits, images of man.

The artist at the age of forty, in this photograph with one of her works, is touching it tenderly, checking it, and here and there correcting it. She is placing the stele-like objects in such a manner in the space (Ill. 97) that they relate to each other — nestling together, whispering mundane banalities and commonplaces to each other and, purely by their positioning in the space, creating a communicative situation. In the sculpture, entitled *Femme volage*, of 1959, she adjusts one of the spatially extensive elements along the central axis of the sculpture, which creates the impression that the whole piece is rotating and spiraling elegantly upwards. Many minute pieces of painted wood laid one on top of the other create a multitude of different forms, delicate and fragile: while they are dependent on each other, they nevertheless strain in all directions and, in doing so, form the sculptural, biomorphic body of this object. The title takes up the formal innovation and gives to the pictorial object a human character trait: *Femme volage* — flighty, capricious, fickle woman. In her early work Louise Bourgeois created a whole number of variations on this basic formal idea. Cut from a piece of wood the same height as the sculptor herself, and then colored red, white, or black, they stand up straight and upright, pared down to their skeletons and reduced to pure function as silent, abstract witnesses of a world inhabited by 'people' (Ill. 96) and dependent on the social interaction of individuals.

In *Memling Dawn* (Ill. 94) and in the close-up of *Spiral Woman*, from the same period, we see the remarkable similarity of the structure of the elemental forms of this sculpture, vaguely reminiscent of forms of Russian Constructivism and its traditions, as in Kurt Schwitters. Small, identical, horse-shoe shaped pieces of wood, turned slightly in on each other, create the screw-like effect of a rotating inversion. However, a view of the whole sculpture reveals other broad and narrow spiral structures running upwards counter to this in interrupted rhythms, either with breathtaking speed or smoothly and slowly, depending on the position of the viewer. Louise Bourgeois's intended set-up of this work, whereby the steles were to be forced right into the floor without plinths or bases, was only possible with the help of more or less hidden small iron plates. As she herself described it: "Instead of displaying pieces, the space became part of the piece. Peridot worried about his floors. I explained that these pieces had to come without any kind of bases, coming directly to the floor on one point."[52]

Despite their formal diversity, all the sculptures discussed here from the 1950s to the early 1960s, like those from the 1980s, have one aspect in common: they represent a notion of an authentic human uniqueness and the concept of an utterly humane society — expressed through sculpture — through their formal criteria, and also by the revealing way her installations are arranged. These works bear witness to a clear understanding of man's image, highly innovative in both its form and content, which Louise Bourgeois had developed in the decade after the Second World War, barely noticed and scarcely appreciated by her fellow-artists. The photograph of her second solo exhibition at the Peridot Gallery in 1950 shows the cautious and carefully worked out positioning of her steles, which, without proper reflection, could all too easily be understood,inadvertently and misleadingly, in terms of so-called 'primitive' African or Oceanic tribal art.

But, at this point, Louise Bourgeois, mother of three children, had lived for ten years in New York — an artistic center no less exciting than Paris in the pre-war years with its abundance of invention and

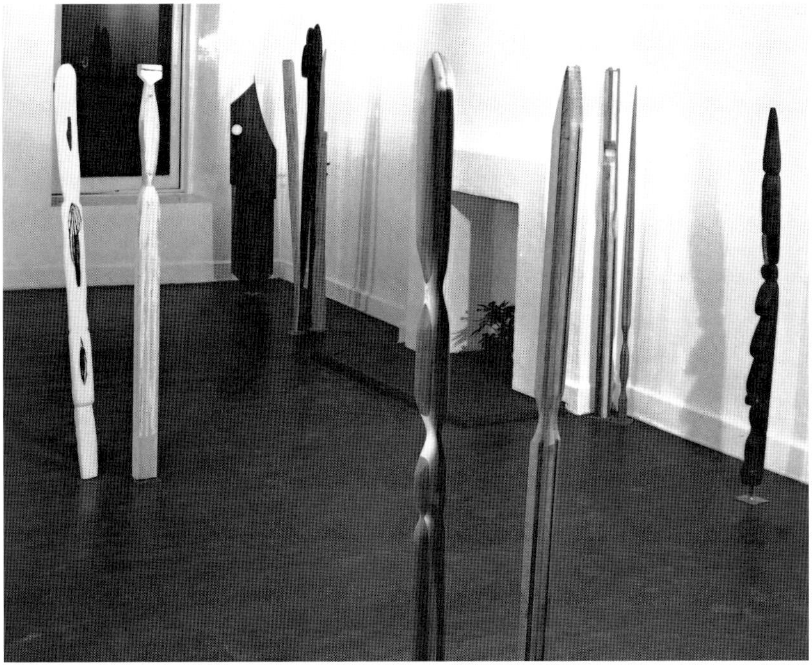

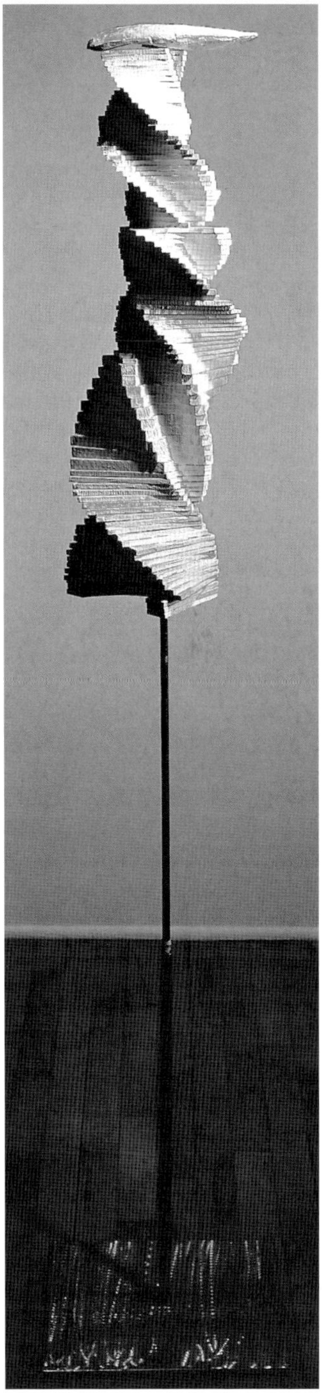

95 *Spiral Woman*, 1951–52, painted wood and stainless steel, $62^1/_2$ x 12 x 12 in.

96 View of the installation in the Peridot Gallery, New York; solo exhibition, 1950

97 Segmented wood personages from the early 1950s in the artist studio. Photo © by Peter Moore

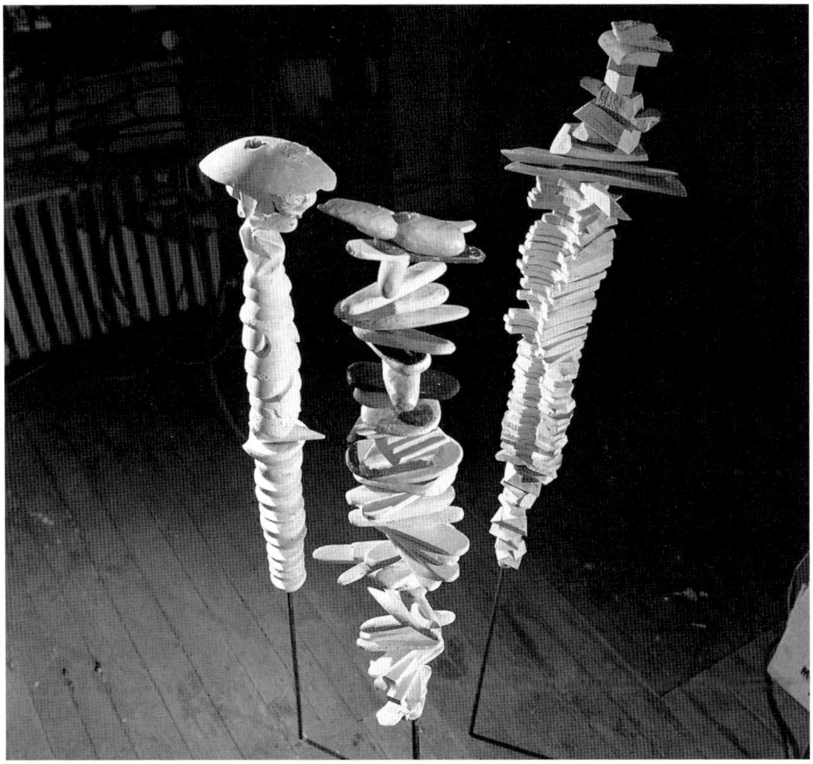

98 *Portrait of Jean-Louis*, 1947–49
bronze, height 35 in.

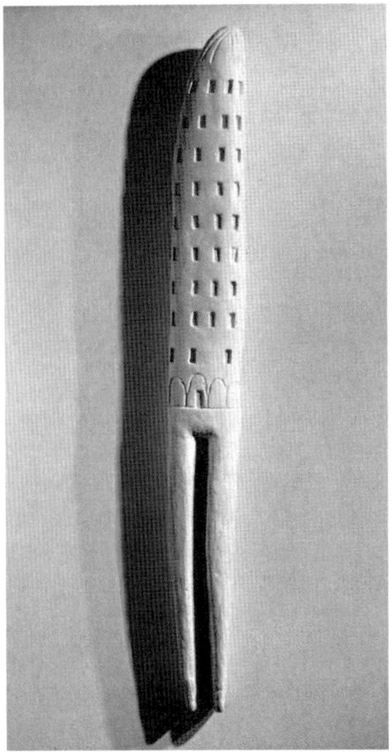

rapid succession of art movements. What then can have induced her to create artworks of this kind, which the artist understood as pictorial representations of those close to her?

> *"It was a re-creation of people I missed. They were presences, and they occupied the whole room. They represented the people I had left behind — that is to say, my father, my brother, and their family, my cousins, all the people I had left in France. I had to come to this country alone. It was a kind of memorial, you might say. I must have felt guilty to have abandoned my family in France."*[53]

Given these circumstances, what kind of a world view underpinned these works? What notion of human existence led Louise Bourgeois — married to an art historian and having come through the monstrous events of and following the Second World War — to create sculptures of this kind with such original, singular images of humanity as those manifested in the portrait of her first-born son, *Portrait of Jean-Louis*? Was it, as the critics persistently claimed, that this highly original, authentic artist was simply creating wholly singular, even eccentric works of art as a response to the art treasures and exhibitions to be seen in a metropolis like New York? Or is it possible to reconstruct a socio-cultural and anthropological background to these works from her early years that would cast new light on them and on the various levels of their meaning?

"This theme of symbolic abstraction through the creation of forms that suggest both the structure of geometry and human individuality has been a consistent preoccupation of my work", Louise Bourgeois stated retrospectively in the late 1960s. "I was concerned with the relation of the individual to his surroundings and the wish to translate this concern into simple, elemental compositions and visual structures, always the very opposite of sentimental."[54]

IV. NEW INQUIRIES INTO TRADITIONAL THEORIES OF REPRESENTATION.

New York in the 1940s.

A lot of people are so obsessed by the past, they die of it. This is the attitude of the poet who never finds the lost heaven, and it is really the situation of artists who work for a reason that nobody can quite grasp. Except that they might want to reconstruct something of the past. It is that the past for certain people has such a hold and such a beauty. [...]
You cannot arrest the present. You just have to abandon every day your past. And accept it. And if you can't accept it, then you have to recreate it. Which is exactly what I have been doing. I am not a surrealist; I am an existentialist.

Louise Bourgeois, 1997

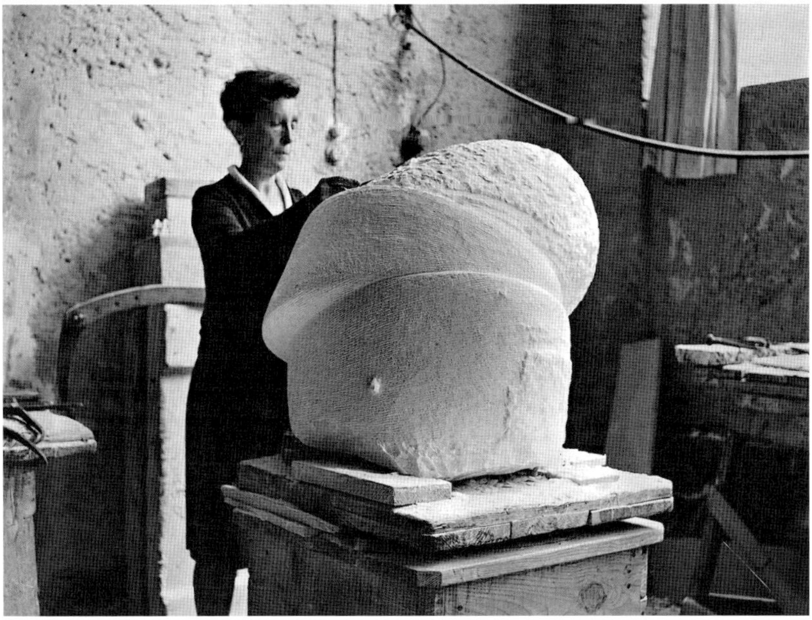

99 Louise working on *Sleep II* in in the Pietrasanta workshops, 1967

The profound insights that we have gained through close examination of selected sculptures from Louise Bourgeois's early period lead, in the context of her later work, at least to the conclusion that there is, despite the wealth of formal invention in her work, an astonishingly consistent *leitmotif* running through it continuing up to the *Cells*: a vision of man's image using a hitherto unknown formal language of Modernism. In order to gain a clearer picture of the power of formal innovation in the *Personages*, most of which were created in the period 1945–55, we must analyze the conceptual parameters of these early works, which — even today — display a high degree of aesthetic rigor, and were to have a decisive effect on the artist's later work. The umbrella title *Personages* does clearly refer to their contents, defining the steles as personalities, characters, or some similar role. Their formal qualities are initially

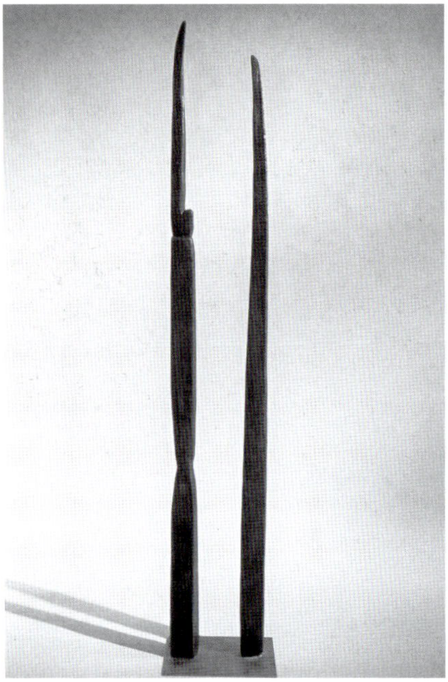

100 *Knife Couple*, 1949
bronze and stainless steel, $67^{1}/_{2} \times 12 \times 12$ in.

101 Unknown artist (Totonacan culture), head, post-classical (900–1521)

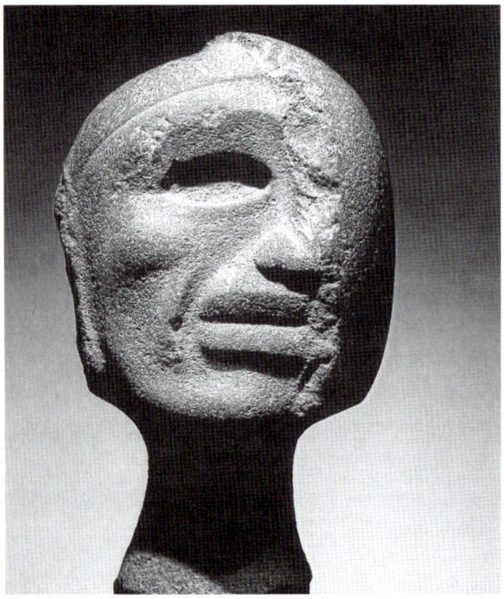

impenetrable, since they use an abstract, reductionist, curtailed sculptural language with only minimal variations, to which we are unable to find real access in that our knowledge is limited to conventional figurative images (Ill. 100).

In these rigorous structures, which are so expressive although restricted to a stringently limited vocabulary, we certainly find more than one-sided, formalistic, and purely perception-oriented links with schemes of artistic production in non-Western, non-European, primal, perhaps African, Oceanic, or pre-Columbian cultures. At the same time, however, the general tenor of exhibitions and the discourse this initiated among artists in New York in the 1940s demonstrate clearly how these exhibitions were received in a variety of ways that tell us a great deal about the history of sculpture in the twentieth century — at a time, that is, before the Abstract Expressionists (including Willem de Kooning, Jackson Pollock, Clyfford Still, Mark Rothko, Robert Motherwell, Franz Kline, and Barnett Newman) had come to dominate the scene in New York as they did in the late 1940s and early 1950s.

The catastrophic events of two World Wars, and the unimaginable horrors unleashed by the Holocaust, shattered any faith one might have had in 'high civilization' and confirmed the shadows of doubt in European art traditions that had been seen as late as 1944 in the magnificent Fifteenth Jubilee exhibition at the Museum of Modern Art. Only two years later, in spring 1946, what proved to be a highly influential major exhibition at the Museum of Modern Art presented the cross-fertilization of Modern art and that of non-Western cultures. *Art of the South Seas*, an exhibition of Oceanic art, was to be the most comprehensive of its kind and gained international recognition. It was debated and discussed in leading art circles. Oceanic, African, and pre-Columbian cultures recalled the origins and the roots of the visual arts, particularly as far as sculpture was concerned. It shed a new light on European and Western art which had in any case already lost some degree of its erstwhile relevance.

Barnett Newman, eminent painter and eloquent essayist, was to become the leading spokesman in the hotly debated discussion on a form of art that owed little to European traditions, and on the redefinition of aesthetic standards. Exceptionally cultured and widely read in philosophy, science, and art, Barnett Newman was blessed with the rare talent of being able not only to express himself in theoretical terms, but to articulate — understandably, logically, and persuasively — the complex problems that were exercising himself and his artist friends and to which, as yet, even art critics had no ready access. Many years before the tremendously important subject of 'Abstraction' became the overriding focus of attention of the New York School in the late 1940s and, for over a decade, dominated artistic expression until Pop Art once again took up figuration — before all of this, Barnett Newman was formulating its artistic premises and the foundations of its basic concept. At this time, besides many short, succinct critiques and reviews, he also published what must be considered his most famous and influential essay, *The Sublime is Now* (1948). He also conceived and organized two exhibitions of — as he called it — 'primitive' art.

In his two essays for these exhibitions, we find articulated his views on the aesthetics of modern art, after the second World War, of the *New York School* — ideas which have to be understood as being of major importance for our context here. The role of art, as Newman argues, has altered man's image and the contemporary artist´s understanding of the concept of his own self in his overall social responsibility. In 1944, in the avant-garde Wakefield Gallery that was run by one of the most committed modern art enthusiasts, Betty Parson, Barnett Newman mounted an exhibition of pre-Columbian stone sculpture. In the text for the catalog he convincingly elucidates his objective in putting on — specifically in a gallery of modern art — an exhibition of such stone sculptures:

> *"The growing aesthetic appreciation of pre-Columbian art is one of the satisfying results of our inter-American consciousness. It is by looking at them as works of art rather than as the artifacts of history or ethnology that we can grasp their inner significance. [...] While we transcend time and place to participate in the spiritual life of a forgotten people, their art by the same magic illuminates the work of our time."*[55]

As a witness to humanity's need, after the upheavals of the Second World War, for a new self-awareness, sense of value and identity, Newman turns to pre-Columbian sculptures — torn from their scarcely reconstructible historical context — and, intending to free them from their delimitation as artifacts, reveals their aesthetic potential and the artistic possibilities that they manifest:

> *"Here the sculpture was to be enjoyed — as sculpture. What is there in this sculpture that means so much to the modern mind? We have to come to realize that these sculptors were interested in the elemental mystery of life, not in the flippant facts of the transitory life round them. We today are still concerned with the same problem. When the pre-Columbian sculptor handled stone, he sought to capture the meaning of life."*[56]

In his exposition of the concept of this exhibition, Barnett Newman expands his argument on the meaning of the stone sculpture's formal qualities in relation to what he saw as the deeply epistemological relevance of the exhibits:

> *"We already see that abstract quality of formal relationships which tells us more of man's nature than a realistic representation of man's physical contours."*[57]

Barnett Newman's introduction offers a clear, convincing description of the development of concepts in Western art over the past forty years, explaining the transition from illusionistic-mimetic, illustrative, and narrative representation to abstract, increasingly non-representational, pictorial solutions — a development of pictorial concepts that from its beginnings in the work of Pablo Picasso, Henri Matisse, Paul Klee, Kazimir Malevich, Vassily Kandinsky, and Piet Mondrian, was borne up by a strict ethos of humanity, if not pathos. The New York public responded with immense enthusiasm to this exhibition — as Barnett Newman tells us — and he was able to arrange for it to be followed in the post-war years by a number of equally important exhibitions, which must considerably have sharpened general critical awareness amongst New York artists. For, in Newman's eyes, these sculptures embodied the notion of the sublime which, four years later, he was to unveil in his influential essay 'The Sublime' as an artistic program to establish a responsible and thoughtful form of painting. For him, this determination was part of a clearly defined value system to be set against empty, meaningless aesthetic conventions:

> *"The sense of dignity, the high seriousness of purpose, the sublime plane of 'moral state' evident in this sculpture, makes clearer to us why our modern sculptors were compelled to discard the mock heroic, the voluptuous, the superficial realism, the exercise of virtuosity that inhibited the medium for so many European centuries."*[58]

In his consistently lucid style, Newman — for the first time in the North American context — points to the innate reality of aesthetic objects, to the hitherto unrealized metaphysical dignity of artworks. In questioning the principle of mimesis, the attempt at an illusionistic imitation of reality, and the idea of simple narrative illustration (Ills 102, 103), these sculptures — as Barnett Newman put it — constitute a new notion of reality that pertains to a second world, based on the values and criteria of the artworks themselves. Ultimately the formal proof of reality is in the art itself, rather than in a more or less disrupted connection with Nature, or in the attempt at an illusionistic *imitatio* of Nature (as Surrealism tried to do), or in its material content.

In his brilliant review of *Art of the South Seas*, that comprehensive, internationally-acclaimed exhibition in the Museum of Modern Art in Spring 1946, Barnett Newman points out the references between the great European artists at the beginning of this century and so-called 'primitive' art: Pablo Picasso's fascination for "l'art nègre", as the artist himself called it, Henri Matisse's interest in the

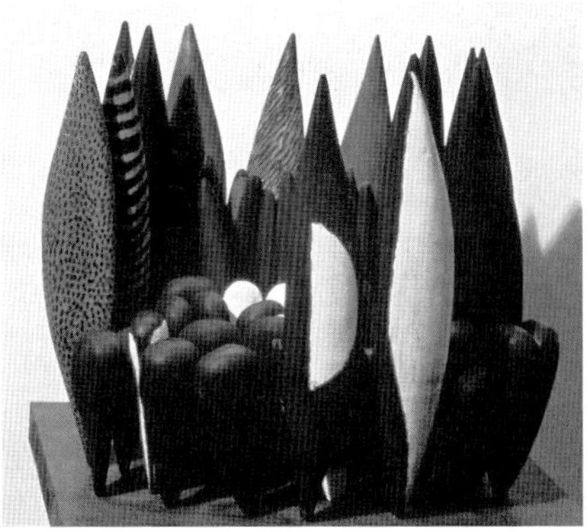

102 *One and Others*, 1955
painted wood, 18 1/4 × 20 × 16 3/4 in.

103 *Untitled*, 1949
black ink on graph paper, 11 × 8 1/2 in.

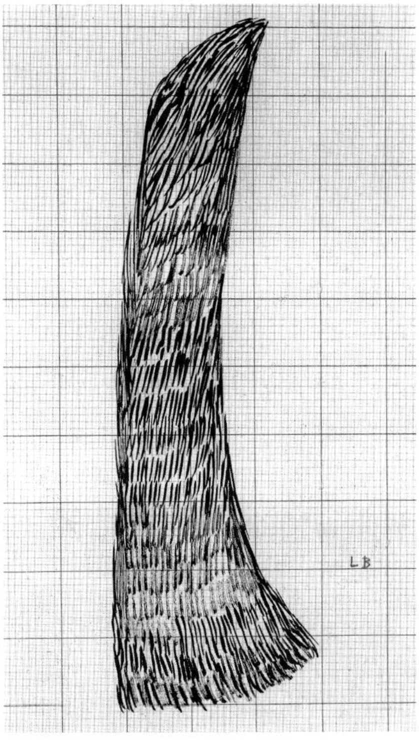

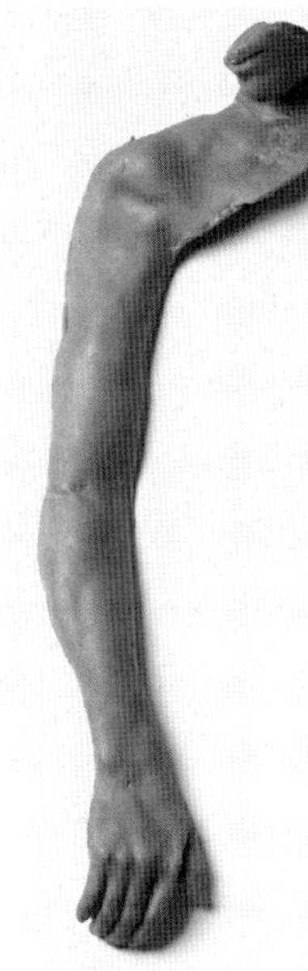

104 Bruce Nauman, *From Hand to Mouth*, 1967
wax over cloth, 28 × 10 3/8 × 4 3/8 in.

105 Eva Hesse, *Laocoön*, 1966
acrylic paint, cloth-covered cord, wire, and papier-mâché over plastic pipe, 120 × 24 × 24 in.

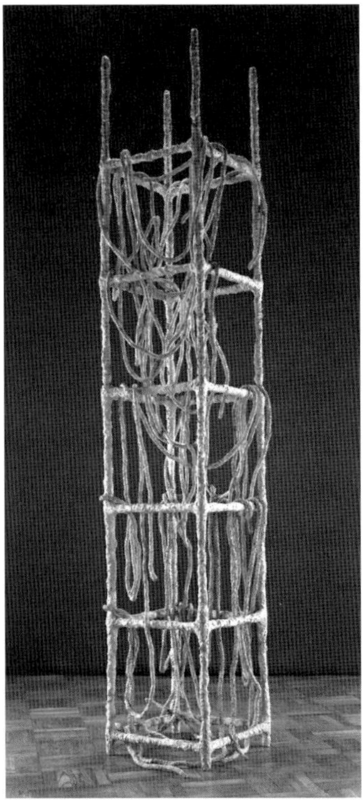

"decorative tradition of primitive Persia," Henry Moore's interest in "pre-Columbian sculpture," and Constantin Brancusi's in "the prehistoric". For our purposes the most important aspect in Newman's reception of non-Western, 'primitive' art becomes evident in his writings as early as 1946, when, as a visual artist, he argued for a geographical distinction between various examples on the basis of their meaning and their 'primitive' qualities: according to Newman, black African art "... is an art of terror, terror before Nature as the idea of Nature made itself manifest to them in terms of the jungle."[59] In the case of Oceanic art, on the other hand, Newman saw this art as having a "sense of magic. It is magic based on terror; but unlike the African terror before Nature, this is a terror before Nature's **meaning** [...]".[60] Leaving aside the ethnological validity of these statements, their anthropological meaning becomes the central issue here. For it seems right that we should understand Newman's perspective on these artworks in his desire to set up a new aesthetic system for himself and his artistic colleagues. In the wake of the shattering existential effect of Gulag, Holocaust, and Hiroshima — the form of modern terror 'before mankind and mankind's meaning' — which unquestionably engendered a major epistemological crisis for humanity, he proposed for the first time in Western art an aesthetic system that would include these existential experiences, man's conditions of being and this concept of reality:

> *"The reason primitive art is so close to the modern mind is that we, living in times of the greatest terror the world has known, are in a position to appreciate the acute sensibility primitive man had for it. Yet though all men live in terror, it is the objects of terror that contain within themselves those elements of cultural interpretation that permit the differentiation of its various subjective expressions. Modern man is his own terror. To the African and to the Mexican, it was the jungle. [...] In Oceania, terror is indefinable flux rather than tangible image. The sea and the wind, unlike the static forest and the jungle, approach metaphysical acts. Whether benign or catastrophic, they arise out of the mystery of space. The terror they engender is not, then, a terror before an inscrutable nature but one that arises before abstract forces. The Oceanic artist, in his attempt at an explanation of his world, found himself involved in an epistemology of intangibles. By coping with them, he developed a pictorial art that contained an extravagant drama — one might say a theater — of magic [...] it was an expression of the artist's being rather than his beliefs. Without any attempts at illusion, working directly, using the plastic means per se, the primitive artist gives us his vision, complete and with candor."*[61]

Looking prophetically into the distant future, Barnett Newman was here formulating the fundamental aesthetic positions that were to underpin the development of the New York School and the defining criteria that were to remain valid up to Bruce Nauman and Eva Hesse. Abstract forms generated in conjunction with emotionally-generated expressions articulate the limits of the existentialist indifference which confronted the modern artist for many years as, in the second half of the twentieth century, he is being released from ideological false promises and misconceptions. The fact that art aims to replace the chaos, arbitrariness and confusion of life with a coherent structure generates at the same time its own reality with its own laws. So — in competing with an imaginary, virtual world — art has to measure itself against the characteristics of a living world.

In 1946, the year of *Art of the South Seas*, Barnett Newman arranged a further exhibition of 'primitive' art. At the inaugural exhibition in Betty Parson's new gallery on East 57th Street, which was later also to put on group shows with works by Louise Bourgeois, Newman put on *North-West Coast Indian Painting* — an art concerned with the cultural heritage of North America itself. He made it abundantly clear that any attempt to understand Modern art must be preceded by a proper appreciation of 'primitive' art, for Modern art was itself an island of rebellion in the current of West European aesthetics. His main interest in the art of the North American Indians was, however, in the dominant aesthetic traditions of those cultures that were abstract and non-representational and that portrayed their 'other' world in abstract symbols and organic forms without consideration for the contours of their actual appearance (Ill. 109).

It is clear not only from numerous exhibitions but from the heated debate among various institutions and representatives of the visual arts, the museums and leading galleries, the artists themselves that 'primitive' art was playing as important a role in the development of modern art in New York and the United States in the mid-1940s as it had previously done in Europe, particularly in Paris, in the early years of the century.

In the 1939 exhibition *Picasso: Forty Years of his Art* in the Museum of Modern Art — Louise Bourgeois was then already resident in New York city — a very special picture took on a central role: Pablo Picasso's *Les Demoiselles d'Avignon* of 1907 marks the beginning of modern art in the twentieth century.[62] For, in order to free European painting from the device of illusionistic mimetic representation, a cul-de-sac, to which it had been confined for centuries, and in order to subvert the absolute law of pure pictorial modalities, Picasso magnificently integrated the formal characteristics of African and Oceanic tribal art into his own work. Important as *Les Demoiselles d'Avignon* was to be for Cubism, indeed for the art world in Paris in general and for Picasso himself, it was just as influential and stimulating for New York and the artists of the New York School. In the exhibition catalog, the then Director of the Museum of Modern Art, Alfred H. Barr, compared certain formal aspects of this picture with those of African masks (Ill. 107) from the Etoumbi region (then known as the French Congo). The formal correspondences between African art and Picasso's outstanding painting — the picture of the century — are undeniable and evident for all to see. Yet, in view of our overriding *sujet* — man's image — the relevant issues in Picasso's picture cannot be seen in a formalistic, morphological, or perceptual relation to 'primitive' culture as elaborated by Alfred H. Barr in the 1940s and later by William Rubin and Kirk Varnedoe in the epoch-making exhibition *'Primitivism' in Twentieth Century Art* in 1984. Instead, Picasso's concern, just as much as that of Louise Bourgeois and Barnett Newman, refers to a conceptual, if not epistemological, dimension that non-Western creative practices bring to the pictorial and sculptural tradition of the West. Thus, for example, as early as 1912, in his essay, 'Conception et Vision', the young French critic Maurice Raynal, a friend of Picasso and the Cubists, puts forward the decisive paradigm of modern painting: "Painting based solely on external perception is, therefore, clearly inadequate." This insight stems from the recognition that we can never perceive an object simultaneously from in front, from the side and from behind, and yet are nonetheless capable of imagining a three-dimensional form (Ills 108, 111), and it is only our "conception" that "even makes us aware of objects we are not able to see." It has replaced "the idea of art for art's sake, which the principle of conception involved, by an idea of practical efficiency [...]."[63]

In 1947, in the foreword to the catalog from Barnett Newman's organized exhibition, *The Ideographic Picture*, with pictures by artists (including himself) represented by Betty Parson, all his earlier thoughts and ideas crystallize and come together to show how an analysis of 'primitive' art from the standpoint of the modern artist can bear fruit for the development of a contemporary aesthetic. In Newman's view, form had been a living component in the work of 'primitive' artists:

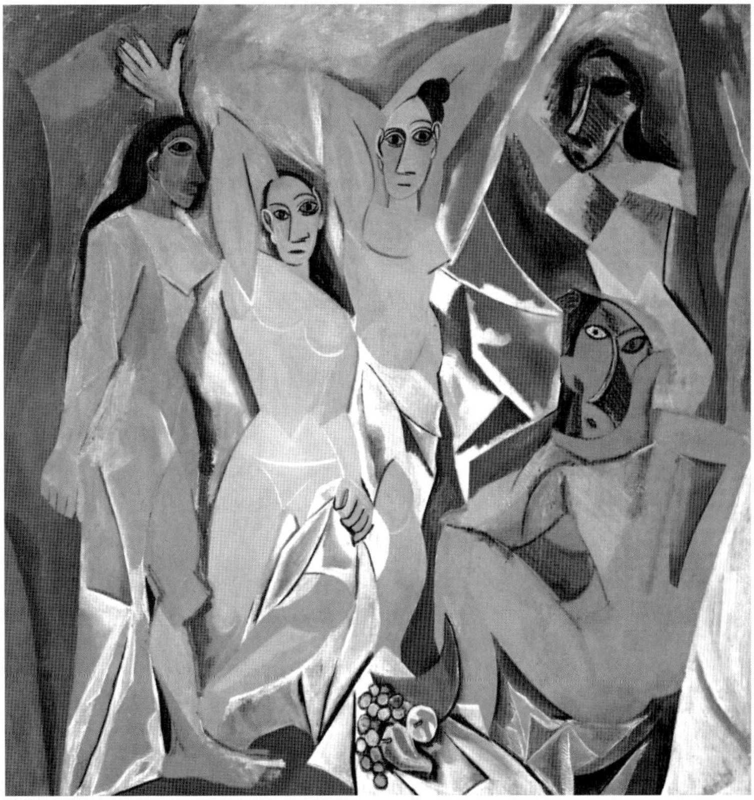

106 Pablo Picasso, *Les Demoiselles d'Avignon*, 1907
oil on canvas, 95 1/5 × 92 4/5 in.

107 Unknown artist (Mahongwe or Ngare tribe, Rep. of Congo), face mask, wood, height 13 4/5 in.

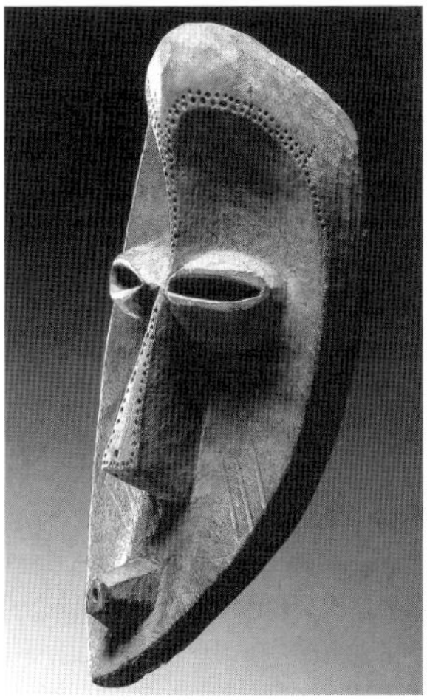

"a vehicle for an abstract thought-complex, a carrier of the awesome feelings he felt before the terror of the unknowable. The abstract shape was, therefore, real rather than formal 'abstraction' of a visual fact, with its overtone of an already-known nature. The basis of an aesthetic act then is the pure idea. But the pure idea is, of necessity, an aesthetic act. Here then is the epistemological paradox that is the artist's problem ... For it is only the pure idea that has meaning."[64]

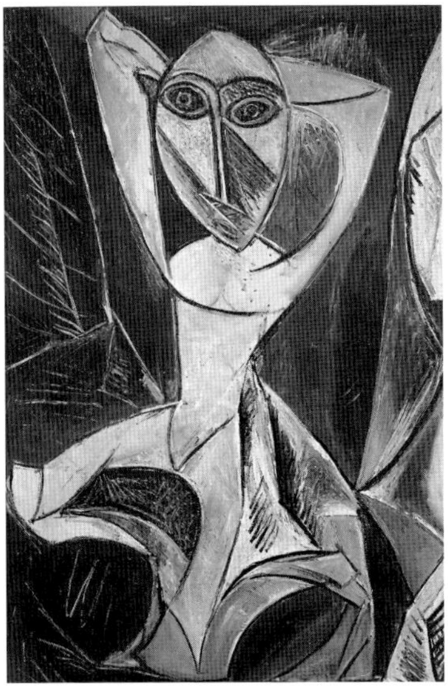

108 Pablo Picasso, *Nude with Raised Arms – The Dancer from Avignon*, 1907, oil on canvas, 59 × $39^1/_2$ in.

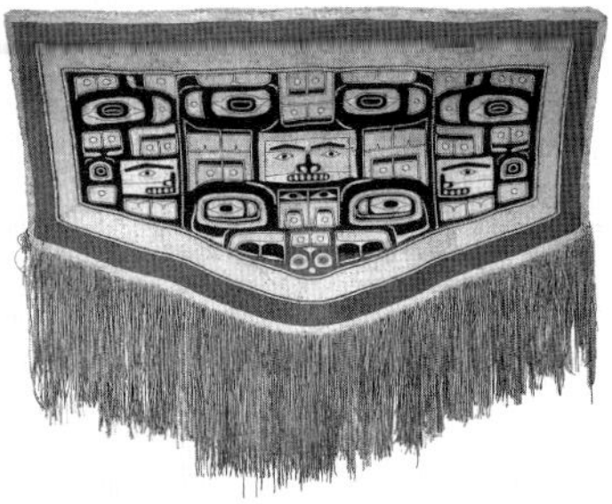

109 Blanket, Tlingit, Alaska
dyed wool and cedar-bark fibres, height 22 in.

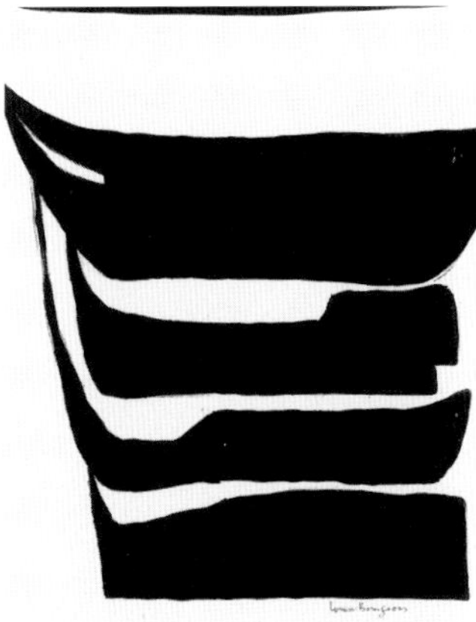

110 Untitled, 1950
ink on paper, $13^1/_2 \times 10^1/_2$ in.

It would be wrong to imagine that Picasso and his fellow-artists such as Matisse, Brancusi, and Lipchitz had been inspired by 'primitive' art on a purely visual, formal level. For Picasso's fascination with 'primitive' art was based — if not theoretically well-founded as in Barnett Newman's case — first and foremost on the wholly different, even revolutionary, concept and representation of man in non-European cultures, which offered a positive contribution to the desired redefinition of formal-aesthetic criteria at the time. All at once the underlying principles of the hitherto absolute dictum of European art that above all demanded a likeness to the given reality were called into question; and doubt was cast on them by objects such as African sculptures and the growing awareness of non-Western representations of man from 'primitive' cultures as in Africa and Oceania. The centuries-old, restrictive tradition of illustrative representation (*ars imitatur naturam*) had been abandoned in favor of a completely new concept of reality: the newly emerging idea of a *second world*, in competition with Nature, that implied both limitation and intensification at one and the same time. The striving for colors and forms — in painting as in sculpture — that were as close to reality as possible, was simply never an issue in 'primitive' cultures. A picture was not intended as an illustration of some reality (Ill. 110) but was conceived, in Newman's words, as a "metaphysical act", as "an extravagant drama of magic." What mattered was that this was "an expression of the artist's being rather than his beliefs."

In *Femme volage* and in the *Spiral Women*, but particularly in her two inspired installations of 1949 and 1950 in the Peridot Gallery, Louise Bourgeois gave form to the artistic visions and ideas that Newman had been formulating so powerfully since 1943. In the tradition of Picasso and Brancusi (as we will later see), Newman had identified the twin heart of the paradigm of modern art: the picture as a metaphysical design and as an extravagant drama of the magical. In respect of this argument, we must conclude that Louise Bourgeois's early work and her later installations tell no stories and render no anecdotes: in an apparently structured world descriptive of stories, they do not set up narrative structures; instead they represent the artist's struggle to create a fusion of identity between the artistic self and the work it produces. Now, for the first time in the history of Western art, viewers are thrown back on their own resources, left to their own personal experiences and memories, while the artwork does not of its own accord enter into dialogue: the viewers are forced to initiate their own discourse with the work. No longer presented with a fine story, vouched for by history, theology, or mythology, the audience itself is being forced into an individual response to the artwork. Just as the audience was challenged by some of Auguste Rodin's early twentieth-century sculptures, such as his *Iris* of 1903 (Ill. 103), a fragment from a once-whole figure (as we will point out in the next chapter) apparently unfinished or destroyed, so now in those early years of Abstract Expressionism in America the viewer was equally asked by the avant-garde artists to identify with a fragmented, non-representational concept of a reality true to life, true to the existential questioning of the artists who were becoming self-aware in the years after the Second World War.

The aesthetic conception that was clearly emerging in the works of Clyfford Still, Mark Rothko, Jackson Pollock, Willem de Kooning and above all Barnett Newman in the 1940s and 1950s determined the compelling conditions of being, art and artists in those years of global existential threat. This thinking characterized the situation of the artistic avant-garde.

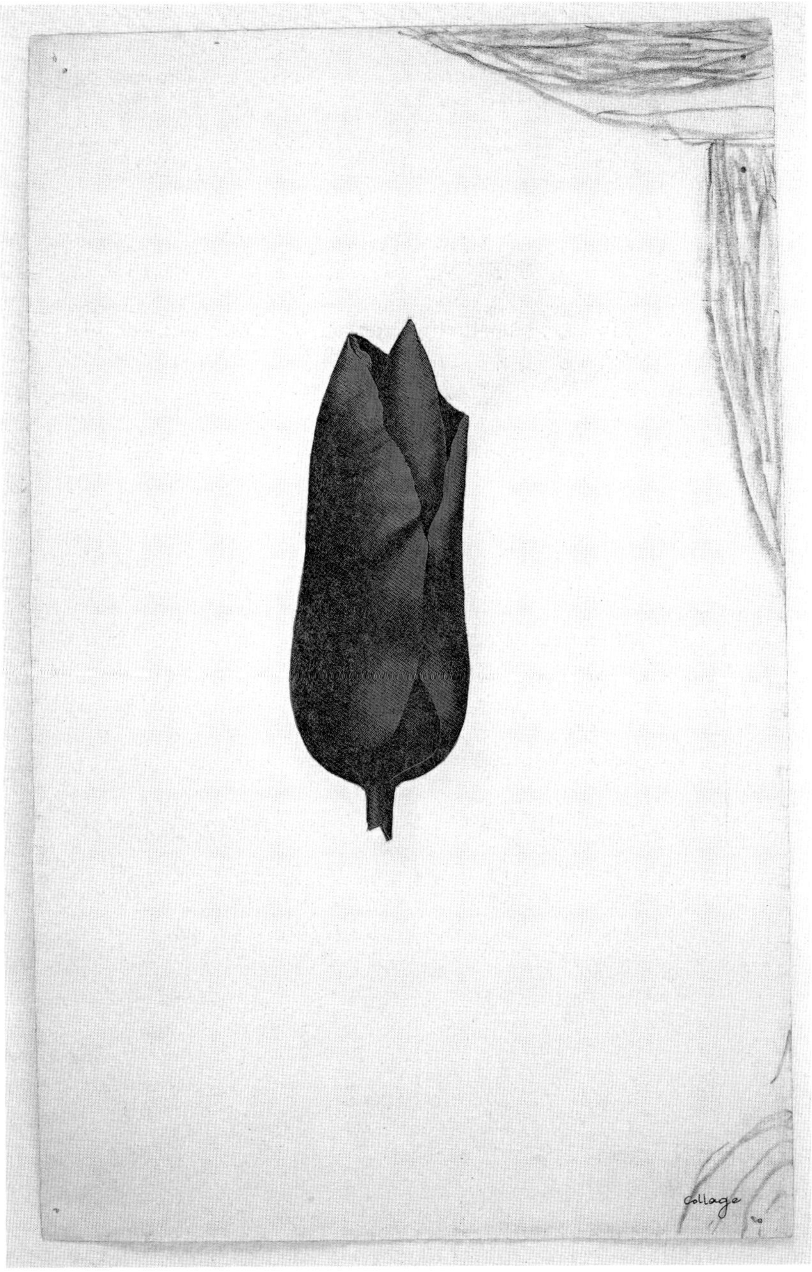

111 *Collage*, 1949
paper collage and charcoal, $11\frac{1}{2} \times 7\frac{1}{4}$ in.

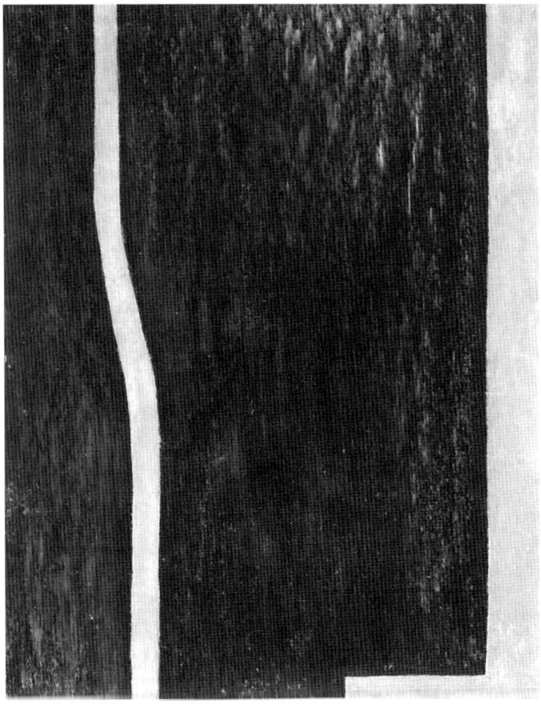

112 Barnett Newman, *Euclidian Abyss*, 1946–47
gouache on canvas, 28 × 22 in.

"I made friends with American artists", as Louise confirmed, "who were my age and I showed with them at the Peridot Gallery from 1949 to 1953, at Norlyst and at Egan, which was one of the key galleries for the Abstract Expressionists. And Alfred Barr was a supporter from the beginning. He included me in an early panel discussion along with De Kooning and the rest, and he bought a piece in 1951 which has been shown at the museum ever since."[65]

If the reader turns his attention to the small gouache by Barnett Newman, *Euclidean Abyss* of 1946–47, he cannot help but be aware of the huge artistic potential, the significance this picture holds for our understanding of a reality true to life. For the concept of a non-illustrative epistemology, that employs forms and numbers for the sake of their relationship to things or the connections between these things, presumes a metaphysical support in an entirely **new** premise: what is seen as a satisfactory degree of identity between a given reality and its objects is now understood in **functional** rather than in **material** terms. The **notion of an image**, of a picture that even in its most abstract form, as at the beginning of the century (Malevich, Kandinsky, Mondrian, *et al.*), is still employing symbols or signs to convey things and their conditions, has now been released from the hitherto indissoluble interlocking with an archetypal image of given reality and its representation. *Adaequatio*, the degree to which an artwork conveys a likeness to the real object, thus becomes simply what someone has created for his or her own self, which is therefore complete for that person but may exist without symbolic import. This, ultimately, is the great metaphysical quality that Picasso, Matisse and many of their contemporaries believed they had found in non-European art; and it was not until the middle of this century that this non-material, metaphysical quality of the pictorial was formulated as a new 'linguistic' version of visual art by Still, Pollock, and Newman in painting and by Louise Bourgeois in sculpture.

113 Auguste Rodin, *Iris*, 1903
plaster, 62 2/5 × 37 × 23 3/5 in.

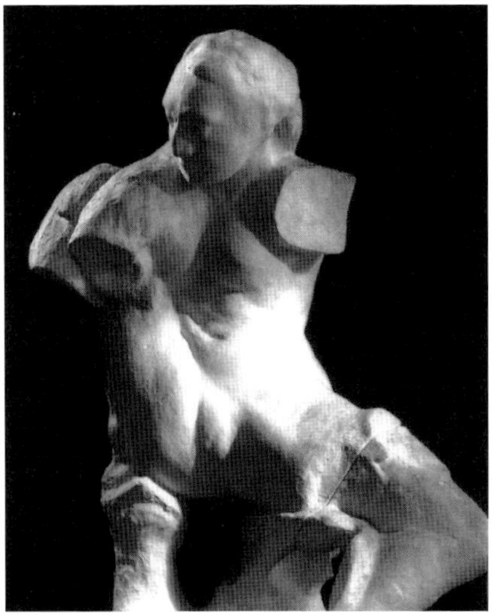

V. AUGUSTE RODIN: SPRING'S AWAKENING

We are unknown to ourselves, we men of knowledge — and with good reason. We have never sought ourselves — how could it happen that we should ever find ourselves? [...] — so we are necessarily strangers to ourselves, we do not comprehend ourselves, we have to misunderstand ourselves, for us the law 'Each is furthest from himself' applies to all eternity — we are not 'men of knowledge' with respect to ourselves.

Friedrich Nietzsche, *On the Genealogy of Morals. A Polemic*, 1887

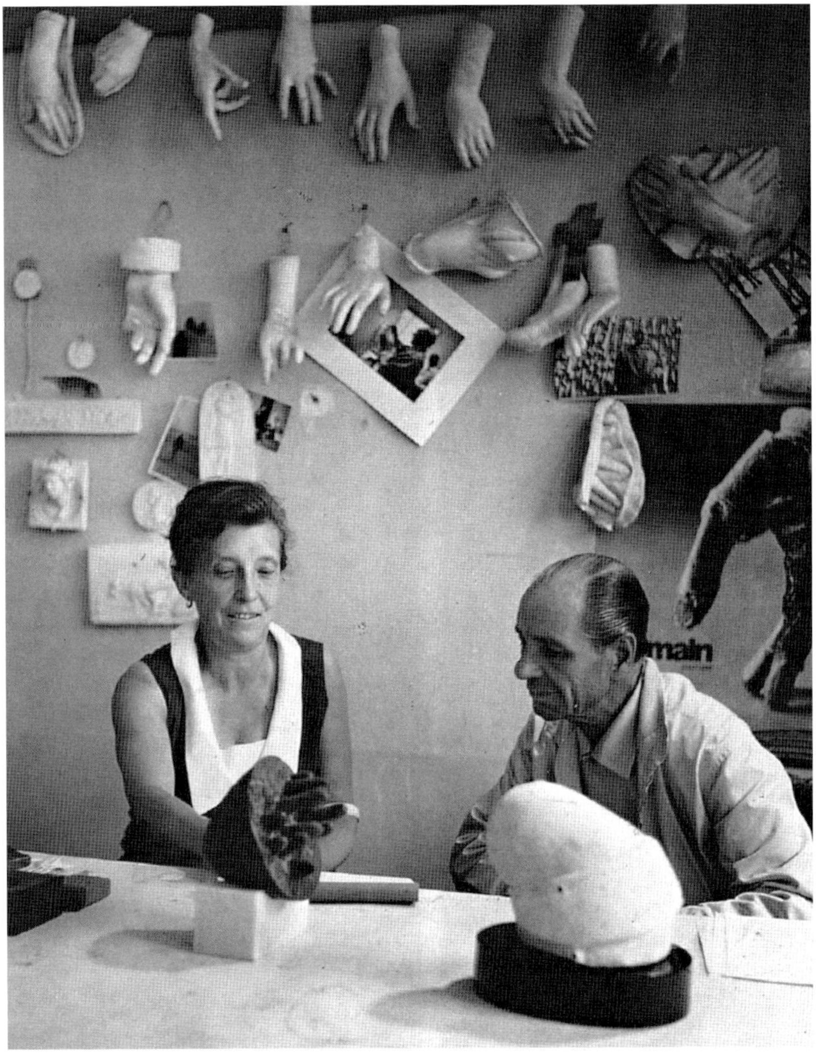

114 Louise in Italy, 1967

These thoughts reveal Nietzsche's precarious questioning of the potential and the conditions of his own creativity as writer and thinker; they open up a completely new horizon as regards the ultimately epistemological and existentialist implications, discussed in the previous chapters, of the essays of

Barnett Newman. For Nietzsche's thoughts are rendering something non-tangible, expressing in words the expanding effect of self-knowledge on creativity. They tend to express this in a way which clearly indicates that his thinking — or more generally his creativity — does not rely on successfully reaching its final objective in order to fulfill its purpose. In fact, the opposite is the case. For the man of knowledge, to know himself would render him incapable of his task of inspiring the creative mind. It would remove the compelling absence of desire that drives him forward, pushes the mind past the boundaries where it possesses no further option than that which itself desires. "Each is furthest from himself," a dictum that applies for all eternity, denominates for us the foundation form which a discourse can arise. The premium is placed upon disclosing other knowledge.

Nietzsche's ideas on creativity contain characteristics of a notion of human creativity that we also find in the work of the great sculptor, Auguste Rodin. We can detect similar thoughts in the numerous interviews given by Louise Bourgeois. Nietzsche's aphorisms on the striving of the thinker and of the artist reflect late nineteenth-century views on the nature of artistic creativity and on the creative realization of the unattainable.

These thoughts on creativity may be seen in Rodin's first major work, *The Age of Bronze* (or *Spring's Awakening*) of 1875–76. In keeping with its subtle ambiguity, Rodin's first, life-sized sculpture was given a number of titles. Each of them has its own claims to validity: *Conquered, Early Man, The Golden Age*, and, lastly, *The Awakening of Man*. However surprising their number and variety, these titles could be seen as a reflex of the thematic richness and ambiguity with which the artist has imbued this figure.

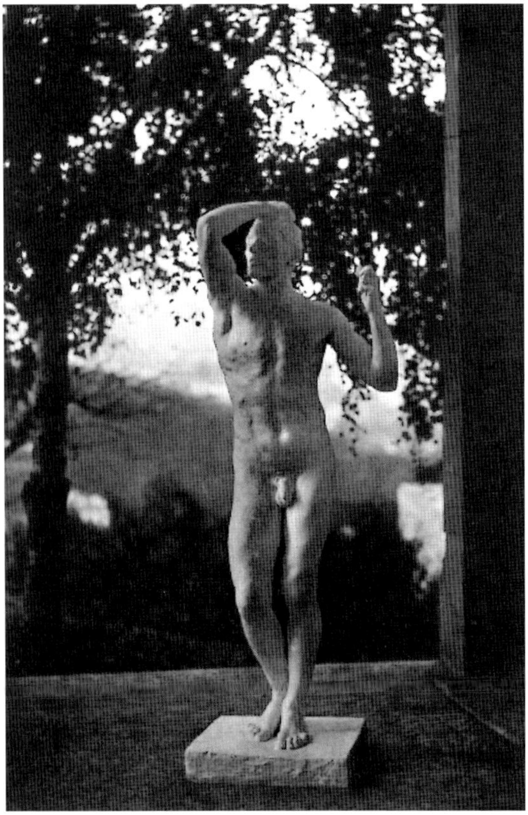

115 Auguste Rodin, *The Age of Bronze*, 1875–76, plaster, height c. 71 in. in the park at the 'Atelier Meudon'

The youth's appearance has a timeless resonance all its own. We feel that a distant stage far back in the history of evolution has been given form here. Our gaze is inexorably drawn by the vulnerability of this human being. We look at his body in our own individual ways, possibly even sharing Rodin's own feeling about the work. The person embodied in this sculpture does not simply bend to our will — on the contrary, the figure's vulnerability forcibly imposes on us an obligation that we cannot reject. The observer is required to respond to the sculpture with his own imagination, for it offers no readily available narrative. What kind of a man might this be?

"In its unblemished nudity," Rodin commented, "it bears the sign of no one epoch; it is the eternal man touched in his innermost sensibility by something of which he knows not the cause. Is it his soul, his flesh that trembles? One does not know. No knowledge comes without suffering."[66] When the sculpture was shown for the first time in the Paris Salon of 1877, it unleashed an indignant storm of controversy. Struck by the enigma of this male figure, displayed in all its evident complexity, critics sought to denigrate it with the accusation that Rodin, still largely unknown at the age of thirty-seven, had merely taken an impression from Nature, a casting from life. For, as a breathtaking portrayal of fleeting resolve, *The Age of Bronze* surprised and impressed connoisseurs and lay-people alike as a work that could not be categorized in any conventional sense. The figure was utterly non-formulaic and, far from delivering familiar narrative patterns, was only faintly suggestive of earlier precendents in art history. It also lacked attributes or identifying features that might give a hint of its social, historical or even mythological role or background.

116 Auguste Rodin among plaster works in his studio, 1902

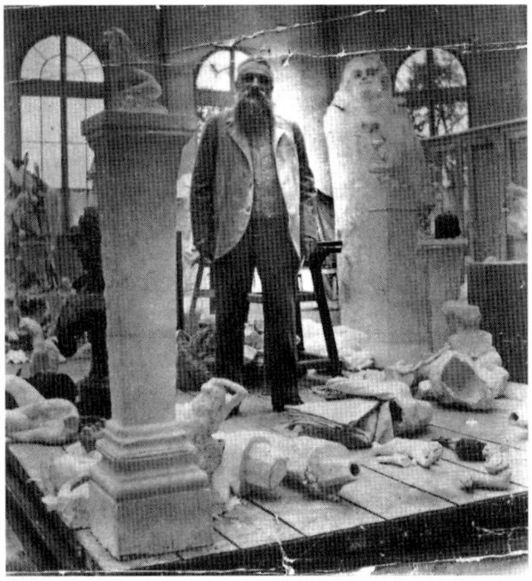

Rodin was relying entirely on the expressive power of the naked human body — a manifestation of the erotic: it alone was the carrier of his artistic concept. However, the prevalent response to the work — then as now — mistakenly and persistently focused on what was regarded, in terms of Antiquity, as its 'realistic' naturalism, its closeness to reality, being faithful to real life. On the contrary, this body invites our gaze to glide over sensual shadows and highlights, over dips and curves, exploring the

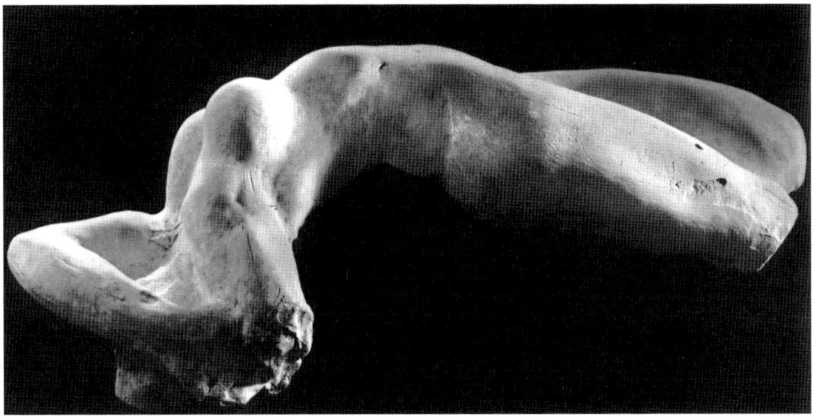

117 Auguste Rodin, *Torso of Adèle*, 1882
plaster, $6\frac{1}{5} \times 19\frac{1}{2} \times 7\frac{2}{5}$ in.

musculature in the context of the figure's delicate resignation; and, as we apprehend the naked anatomy, we begin to understand the figure's abandon and hesitation, that this sculpture signaled a new beginning in art that no longer depended upon the primacy of subject matter, narration, or mimesis. This wholly beguiling visual experience in fact derives from a concept of art that is no longer beholden to specific anecdotal representation: a concept of art that has freed itself and is thus no longer clutching at the centuries-old Aristotelian principle of mimesis, of imitating Nature as truthfully and faithfully as possible.

Similarly, Rodin's *Jean de Fiennes*, made about ten years later in 1885 — monumental in effect even though not life-sized — shows how intensely the artist was working on non-narrative concepts like the erotic, how he had released art from its hitherto primarily descriptive and narrative function. Now he was entrusting it entirely to the genuinely artistic realms of free, creative imagination.

In his first major works with conventional subjects (the unidentified, life-sized male nude) Rodin was already testing this form of creative license, but in some other later works from this period, namely the mid-1880s, he took it to excess. For the artist developed a unique and radical concept, previously unknown to the visual arts — the fragment or the intentionally incompleted work. By this means he tried primarily to undermine the widespread false perceptions of his sculptures as being cast from life — a misapprehension that arose primarily as a result of his immense sculptural skills. Consequently, he created a female torso without arms or only partially sculpted legs (Ill. 121). Literary aphorisms — Nietzsche's, for example — can express an entire idea in a succinct, reduced, rudimentary form. By the provocative use of similarly fragmentary forms, the now forty-five-year-old Rodin was able to refocus the audience's attention on the essence of sculpture and its need for reformulation. Whereas the literary aphorism raises questions about the relationship between language and thinking, from the mid-1880s onwards Rodin uses fragments to work towards a new model of visual perception and comprehension. Fragmented sculpture presents a complex idea in an abbreviated form, including both the thinking that has led to it and the conclusions that may be drawn from it. This conceptual approach illuminates Rodin's use of fragments which — as we will later see — has particular relevance for Louise Bourgeois's *Cells*. Fragments have a significance all their own in artistic terms, as much for Rodin as for Nietzsche.

Confronted with a fragment such as Rodin's marble *La Pensée* of the mid-1880s (Ill. 119), the viewer— rather than having to follow a descriptive narrative — is challenged to make his own independent, intuitive contribution to the ensuing dialogue with the artwork. A small, delicate head is resting on an otherwise roughly-hewn, solid marble block: the face has neither any intentional nor identifiable similarity to a particular face, even if art historians occasionally favor the possibility that this is a

118 Auguste Rodin, *Jean de Fiennes*, 1885
plaster, $27\frac{3}{5} \times 17\frac{2}{5} \times 17\frac{2}{5}$ in.

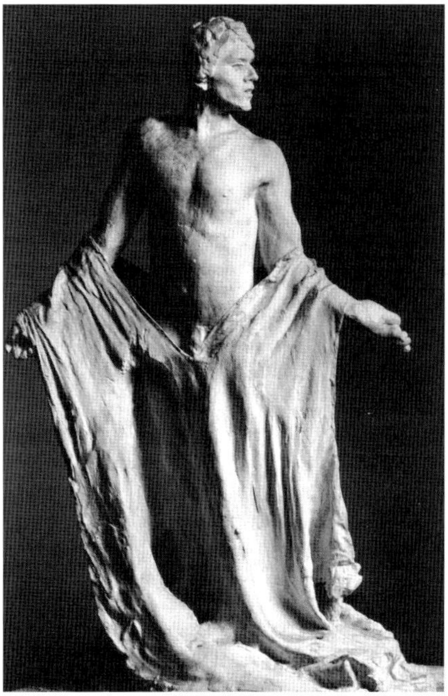

119 Auguste Rodin, *La Pensée*, 1886
marble, height 29 in.

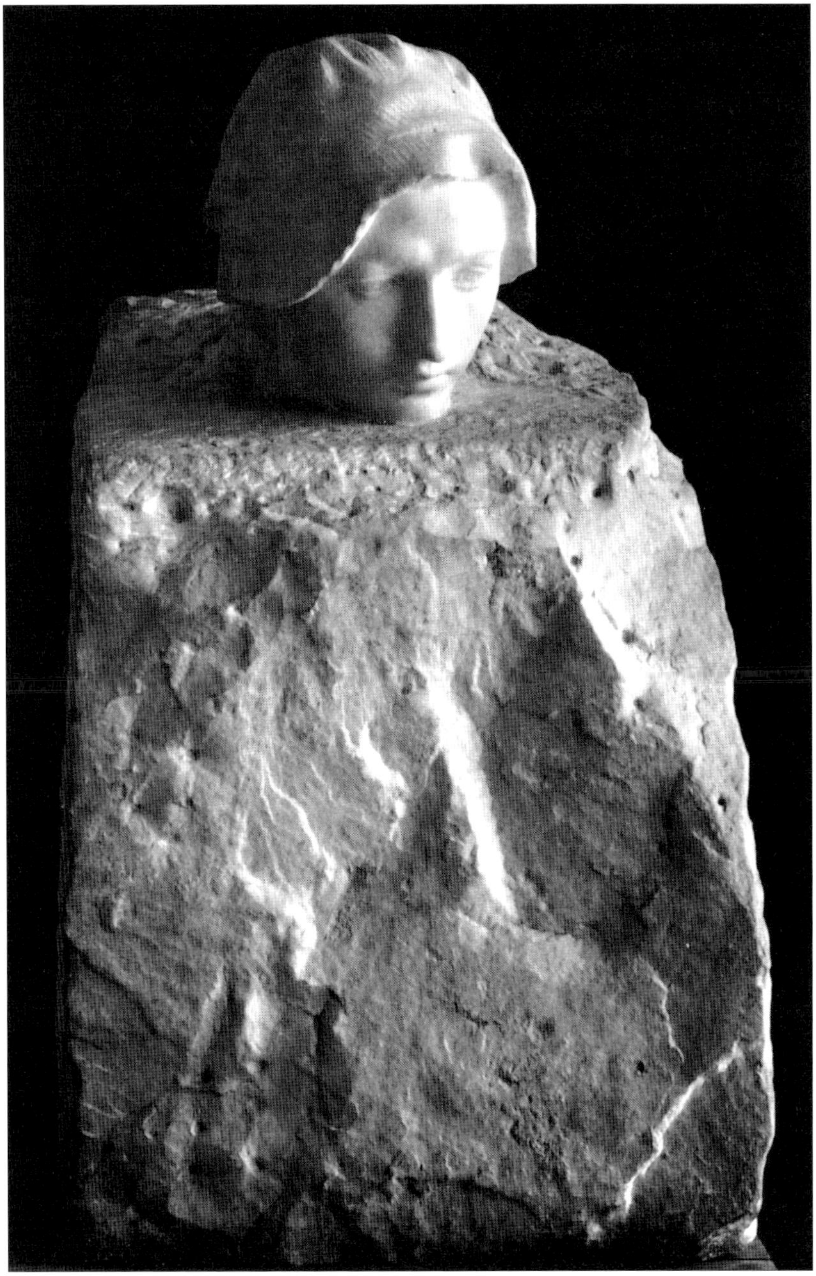

120 Auguste Rodin, *Assemblage of the Head of Pierre de Wissant and Female Nude*, post 1900
plaster, $9 \times 6^{3}/_{5} \times 5$ in.

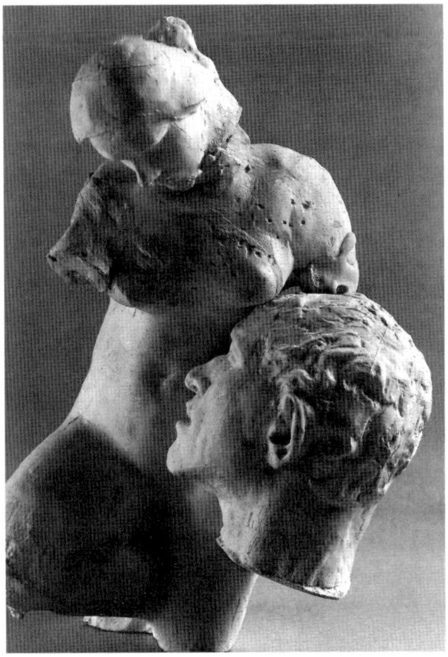

portrait of his then lover Camille Claudel, who was twenty-two years old at the time. The woman's head has a sense of profundity, of introversion born of deep meditation — the materialization of a thought! Paying homage here to the realization of creative inspiration, Rodin is at the same time also portraying the pain of self-denial and the heavy burden that this entails. The woman's head with a sensitively chiseled countenance, lies pensively on a roughly sculpted marble block which is quite out of proportion with her face. From the enormous piece of marble the head has been wrought with great effort — an image of a woman that hardly could be more suitably designed at the end of the last century. Or, is 'the thought' here transcending itself, more sublime than the physical form it has taken on? Or, did a stream of thought break off like a sudden inspiration, immortalized in stone before it could be formulated in linguistic terms? This sculptural image can be seen as a paradigm for an exchange of thoughts: an object dedicated to the muse.

This newly developed concept of the fragment in Rodin's sculptural work allows us — even requires us — to conjure up disjointed narratives and complete them with meaningful allusions. (Ill. 120) Setting our imagination free, the concept of the fragmentary opens up an entire new realm of subjective and highly intimate interpretative possibilities that lie far beyond dogma and convention. As a result, the observer is impelled to give up his otherwise simply receptive status for an approach usually geared towards an overall comprehension and evaluation of the artwork. By this process he is now inspired to abandon all value judgments and to sound out for himself the possible ideas and multiplicities of meaning in a given work. Thus, in both an artistic and aesthetic sense, these results privilege the fragmentary as an artistic device over any other artistic-technical aspects of the artwork. Ultimately the fragment becomes an autonomous carrier of meaning, fulfilling a function similar to that of the literary aphorism from Novalis and the Romantics up to Nietzsche.

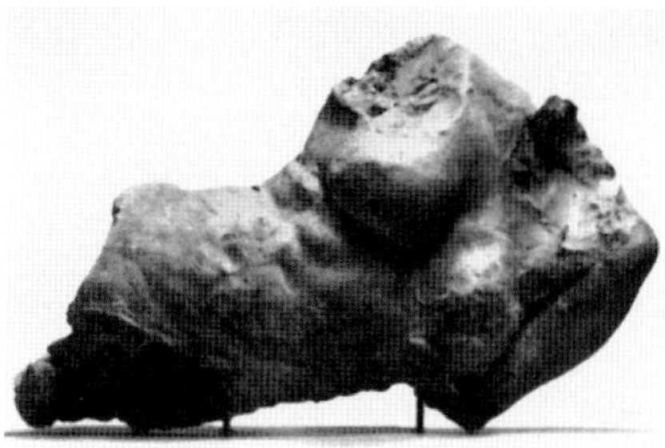

121 Auguste Rodin, Torso, ca. 1880–89
terra-cotta, height 9 1/5 in.

In avoiding the typical misreadings of, and bringing a deeper understanding to, the late twentieth-century sculptures that are the subject of this study, in particular Louise Bourgeois's *Cells*, it is necessary to examine in some depth the notion of the fragment as evidenced in Rodin's work. His fragments *per se* have rarely been analyzed or even recognized as such, because the academic view has often misinterpreted them as 'unfinished' rather than seeing in them a purposefully developed and applied artistic concept. The new, immense creative potential that the fragmented torso offered to Rodin inspired him to experiment even more with fragments, which he began subsequently to work on intentionally and in a wholly planned manner. Rodin's unique reflections on a sculptural whole which constitutes itself through fewer parts than necessary for its conventional completion, have to be understood as a result of his concept of the fragmentary that came to him after studying sculptures of Antiquity which had survived the passage of time — broken, cracked, weathered, and partially destroyed. This in turn then gave him the courage to present hands, feet, heads, sections of torsos, and proto-limbs in various stages of completion (Ill. 123).

122 Auguste Rodin, *The Inner Voice (Without Arms)*, 1896–97
bronze, 53 × 23 × 17 1/2 in.

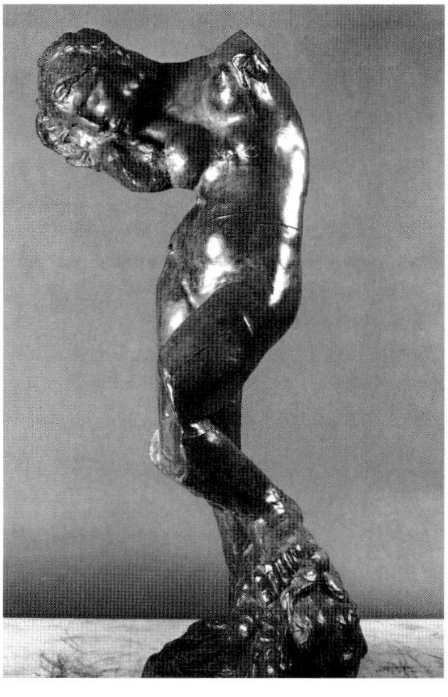

In 1896, at the age of forty-five, Rodin made *Méditation sans bras*, now in the Metropolitan Museum of Art in a bronze version known as *The Inner Voice*. A work such as this has no need of figurative completeness in order to convey Rodin's vision of creativity and aesthetic form. In fact, the fragmented figure positively and forcefully inspires the observer to complete the sculpture for himself, that is to say, to involve himself in visualizing the intact figure. Faced with this work, we must initially address the unworked, or largely unformed, mass of bronze on which the head rests. The excess of material conceals potential forming; it substitutes and replaces the conventional expectations of formal perfection.

In the terracotta *Torso*, Rodin fulfills his promise of independent artistic creation freed from external constraints. It demonstrates the thoroughness with which he cleansed and freed his sculptures from all superfluous elements. Rodin cut the limbs away and equally spontaneously tore the head from the body, as we are able still to observe with admiration a hundred years later, for when the Metropolitan Museum of Art in New York purchased his *Triton and Nereid* (Ill. 124), Rodin included this terracotta *Torso* as a gift. All these sculptures and a later, almost life-sized, bronze casting (made in 1983) of *The Inner Voice* may be seen today in the Metropolitan Museum.

With these radical gestures Rodin thus affirms his artistic conviction that fragmentation can serve to give greater emphasis and more effective meaning to the physical. For the imagination of the artist and viewer alike, each of these individual body parts has the capacity to evoke the image of the whole figure, intensifying the dialogue between artistic creativity and its reception by the viewer.

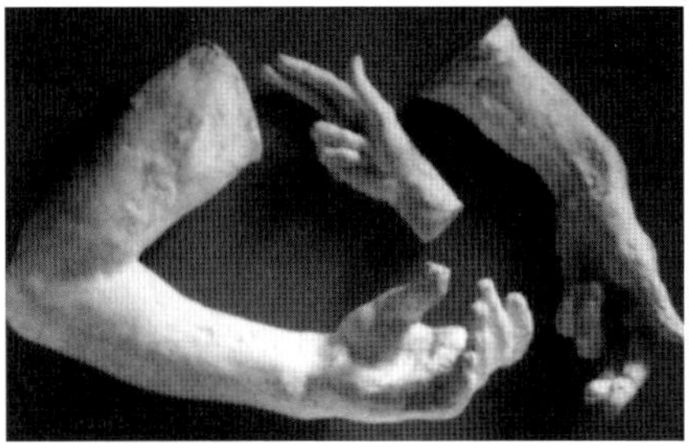

123 Auguste Rodin, plaster fragments, 1912
length of arm ca. $8\frac{1}{2}$ in.

In these sculptures pictorial language is blazing a new trail that no longer has anything to do with the tradition of mimetic representation. The artistic idea has distanced itself from motif and has entered into that transient, fluid sphere where talent, idea, and genius collide. Free and untrammeled by the cumbersome accouterments and supposedly indispensable detail of figurative sculpture, the fragment — by virtue of its succinctness — demonstrates its capacity to convey and to give a voice to something much greater than itself: a notion that encompasses a whole new area of meaning for sculpture, a new realm of artistic thinking. *Méditation sans bras* and *Torso* alter the human form, its body, so radically that they imbue it with completely new expressive potential, not communicable by gesture or mime. In these works Rodin has developed a constantly changing and reinvigorated concept of comprehending the body: the recognition of what a human body is able to act as and to mediate. In the end, these fragmentary sculptures provide insights into the energies and strengths that direct and determine human behavior vis-à-vis the human being.

"Thoughts" writes Nietzsche in one of his aphorisms, "thoughts are the shadows of our feelings — always darker, emptier, and simpler."[67] Are thoughts indeed the darker shadows of our emotions, or does a thought become rationalized in its dual role with feeling and stop being what it originally was, namely a reasoned response to a moment of emotion? The activities of the mind are geared towards reducing things to their essence. The mind is aiming at form that still allows the emotions to resonate, but at the same time to be consistent within itself; it must, above all, be precise, that is to say, poignant. The fragment is the process and the product of what happens during meditation itself. In its very form it sustains and contains the essence of the present moment — a concluding unification of plan and result.

In realizing this, the dream of creativity is being constituted. The concept of fragmentation is Rodin's major stylistic and conceptual achievement and leads us to the heart of his artistic endeavor. The fragment emphasizes both the craft aspect and the conceptual side of an artist's work. The narrative, once only apprehended as a constituent part, now appears merely as one possible aspect of a fully defined but not fully portrayed sculptural whole. In addressing so deliberately the concept of fragmentation, Rodin is opening up new domains of creativity, and laying the foundations for an artistic approach that will continue to nurture future creative talents. His artistic work embodies a major paradigmatic change in the history of early Modernity. Artistic style can no longer serve as a means to frame the substance, becoming instead the substance itself. For the first time, motifs merge with the personal; plurality of narrative themes is channeled into a single, stringent essential, and the conceptual gives way to the material. And all this comprises, in an albeit rudimentary — fragmentary — form, the beginnings of a seminal network of ideas that will concern the artists of the late twentieth century for many decades to come.

124 Auguste Rodin, *Triton and Nereid*, ca. 1893, terra-cotta, $3\frac{3}{4}$ x $13\frac{1}{2}$ $3\frac{3}{4}$ in.

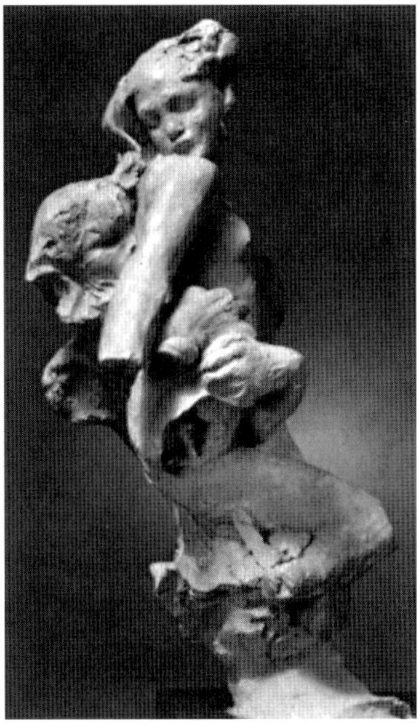

VI. CONSTANTIN BRANCUSI: THE SPIRIT OF NATURE

Here sculpture was enjoyed — as sculpture. What is there in this sculpture that means so much to the modern mind? We have come to realize that these sculptors were interested in the elemental mystery of life, not in the flippant facts of the transitory life round them. We today are still concerned with the same problem. When the pre-Columbian sculptor handled stone, he sought to capture the meaning of life.

They were the sublime creation of highly sophisticated artists with the same doubts, the same wonderings, and the same searching for salvation, that same indomitable courage which activates men of spirit today.[68]

Barnett Newman, *Pre-Columbian Stone Sculptures*, 1944

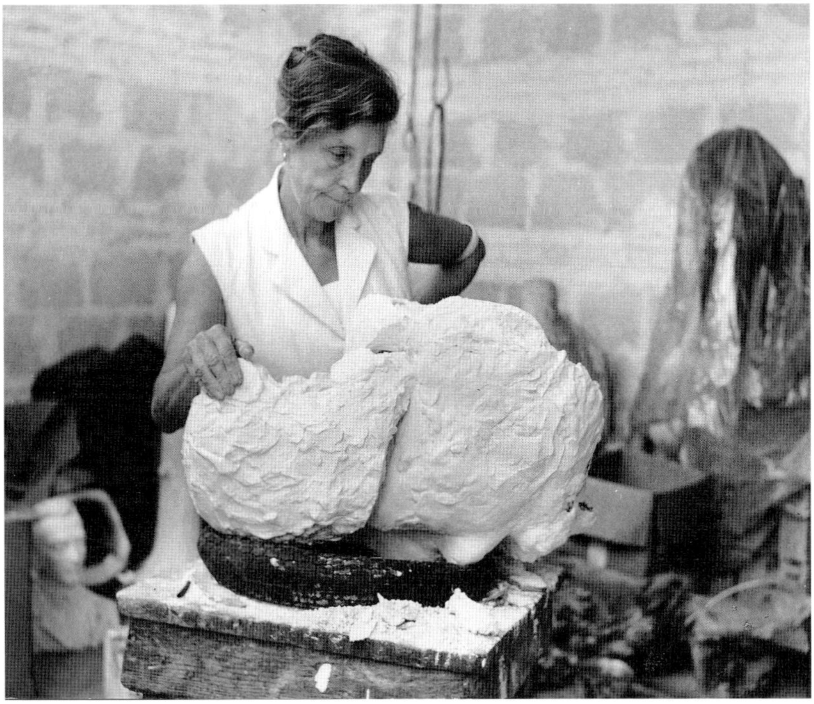

125 Louise working on a plaster sculpture in Quercata, Tuscany, 1967

In the early summer of 1907, in response to the revelatory shock of a visit to the collections of African and Oceanic art in the Museum Trocadéro in Paris, Picasso abandoned at a stroke any sense of allegiance to the pictorial conventions of representation in a world of referential perception. In the following years, in Cubism, he worked, step by step, through the formal ramifications of this change in the nature of reality for painting. The new kind of 'reality' that Picasso and Braque were trying to achieve (as were Matisse and Derain, albeit from a different angle) also necessitated a redefinition of the functional value of their artistic output. Picasso's first monumental, life-sized realization of the new concept, *Les Demoiselles d'Avignon* (Ill. 106), was in the artist's own opinion so revolutionary that he initially refused to put the picture on public display and kept it in his studio, showing it only to his closest friends.

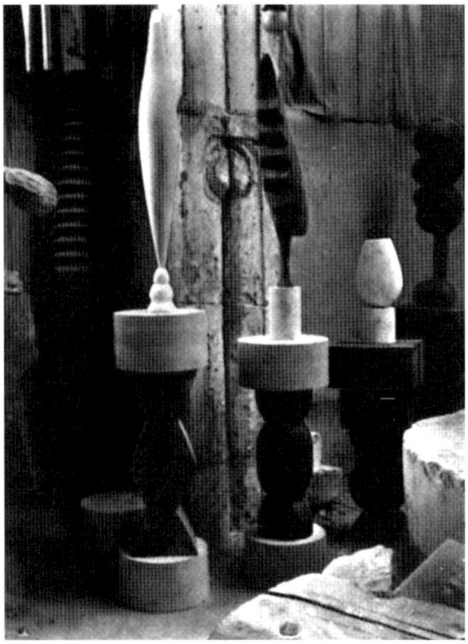

126 Constantin Brancusi's studio, ca. 1923, with *L'Oiseau dans l'espace* (1923), *Le Coq gaulois* (1922), *Torse de jeune fille* (1922), *Adam et Eve* (1921)

By contrast, Rodin was working gradually towards liberation from the dictates of a by now meaningless tradition. Through his bold stylistic technique of fragmentation, Rodin unleashed his vast creative potential from the chains of *imitatio*, from narrative "artistic realism" and "the practice of virtuosity" (Barnett Newman). Furthermore, he consistently intensified his own formal innovations and their conceptual implications, by combining fragmented parts of various sculptures which connected neither thematically nor as a narrative. But Rodin did not abandon representational imagery abruptly and completely: instead he incorporated it into a formal puzzle of a thousand different combinations, for he was undoubtedly still interested in the formal impact of 'reality' for sculptural images. His artistic discourse concerned a world that defined itself according to its physical and phenomenological experience and imitation of Nature — above all in that of the human body — rather than any imaginary notion of reality. Creating an imaginary contextual reality, Rodin arranged illustrative representational fragments in startlingly new constellations that measured themselves against and in opposition to a given reality. Ultimately he undertook this endeavor to evoke the idea of an infinite context tapping into the viewer's imagination as a creative tool.

In cedar wood and cement, in plaster and onyx, from gold-gleaming bronze to deeply black marble, chiseled from Carrara marble and fashioned from cherry-wood, placed on a mirror or presented on basalt: the artworks of Constantin Brancusi are endlessly fascinating. As the other outstanding sculptor in the first half of this century, inspired by the enthusiasm for Gauguin, Picasso and Matisse, for tribal art and prehistoric artworks, Brancusi sought to carve out a path all his own. Feeling the need to escape from Rodin, his spiritual father and teacher, he reduced the observed morphological forms of real objects to their absolute minimum of signifying sign. The body of a crane, for example, might become a slender, upright conical form coming to a point at the top — a process comparable with that found in many African works (Ill. 129). This concept, which Brancusi practiced from 1913, could be described as a process of abstracting from the given constituents in Nature. Ultimately, this led him from illustrative mimetic representation to the intrinsic reality of aesthetic objects, whose relation to their initial context of 'Nature' — their *adaequatio* to reality — has been pared down to its barest essence. To the extent that Brancusi indicated the degree to which the sign bore similarity to the original subject, the resulting artistic object itself takes on the substantiality of that original.

127 Armory Show, New York 1913

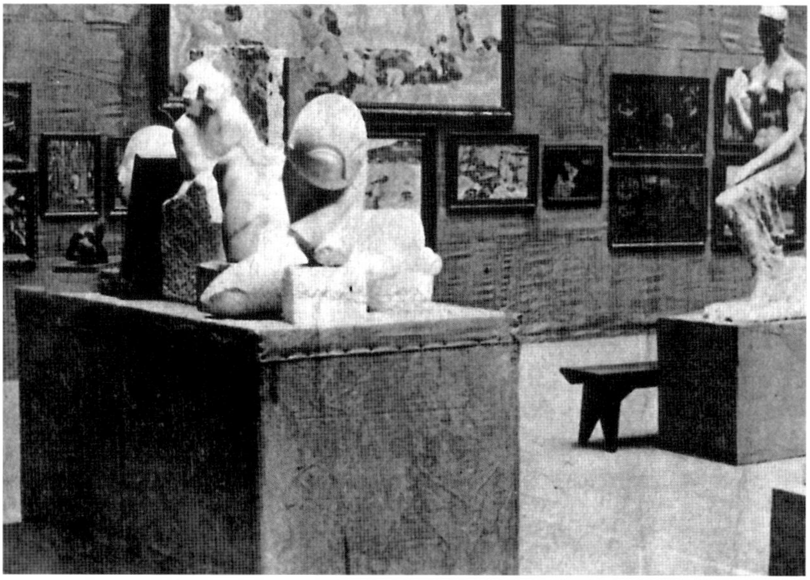

Brancusi's artistic concept was directed towards the final object as a coherent, tangible form. Apart from his well-known early works of 1912 and 1913, which were included in the famous *Armory Show* in New York, two of Brancusi's sculptures manifest this stylistic device quite clearly, namely *Le Premier Cri* of 1917 (Ill. 128) and *Torso de jeune fille* of 1922 (Ill. 130).

The birth of sculpture out of the spirit of Nature was realized in its most basic, abbreviated form in *Le Premier Cri*. Facial features have been reduced to a shorthand of three almost geometrical signs, and stand in contrast with the coarse, wooden pedestal in a form which is wholly abstract and non-representational. The oval sculpture, made from grayish-black cement, creates — in its modern, well-crafted materiality and its artistically transformed reference — its own self-referential reality. Nevertheless, it still draws on given reality in that the head rests on a wooden plinth that was once living and growing, falling back on its own abstract schemeta — Nature as its own notion. In the reciprocal correlation of art and Nature, between the organic and the synthetic, between the grown and the sculpted, between abstract reduction and symbolic figuration, we see an alternative creative method to the artistic processes that Eastern European artists such as Vladimir Tatlin and Naum Gabo were pursuing in sculpture and that Picasso and Matisse were also to follow.

In another work, *Torso de jeune fille*, Brancusi articulated more radically this artistic method and reduced the representation of the human body to its absolute minimum: young, bud-like, almost untouched innocence in the form of gently gleaming, tender pink, perfectly polished precious stone. It portrays neither more nor less than the chaste purity of temperate balance — formed, timeless beauty — and is all the more captivating for being placed on a rough piece of basalt. The title of this standing figure reflects the formal origins of the sculptor's craft, which in this sculpture represents itself — content tautologically, expressed the embodiment of endless self-presentation, a truthful 'sign' of an 'asemantic' loss of function. There is a remnant of erstwhile meaning in the title: Rodin's conceptual aesthetic strategies of broken bodily fragments as the spark that fires the viewer's imagination. Nevertheless, the title cannot conceal the fact that the bipolarity of being and meaning, of a thing and a symbol, of an object and a sign, has been destroyed by an image which is self-reflecting and thrown back on its own resources. Brancusi has subverted the whole range of correspondences and congruities that traditionally governed our differentiation of truth and reality.

Similar thoughts on the truth and reliability of our powers of observation and of our linguistic and visual depiction of material objects had already been raised by the great philosopher Friedrich Nietzsche in the second half of the nineteenth century, and were to become a *leitmotif* in literature and the visual arts throughout the whole of the twentieth century. As Nietzsche wrote in 1873 in his essay 'On Truth and Lying in an Ultra-Moral Sense':

> *"Is language the adequate expression of all realities? [...] What is a word? The* **image** *of a nerve stimulus in sounds. But to infer from the nerve stimulus a cause outside us, that is already the result of a false and unjustified application of the principle of reason. How — had truth alone been the determining factor in the genesis of language, the viewpoint of certainty in terminology — how might we say: the stone is hard, as though 'hard' were otherwise known to us, and not merely as a purely subjective stimulation. [...] The different languages, set side by side, show that what matters with words is never the truth, never an adequate expression; else there would not be so many languages. The 'thing in itself' is quite incomprehensible to the* **creators of language**, *and not at all worth aiming for."*[69]

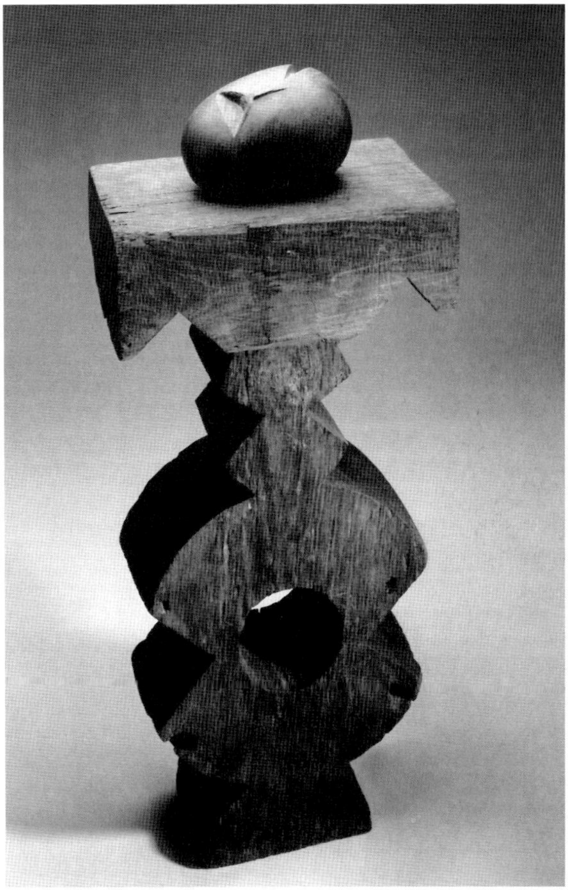

128 Constantin Brancusi,
Le Premier Cri, 1917
cement, $6\frac{1}{2} \times 10\frac{1}{8}$ in.,
on wooden plinth

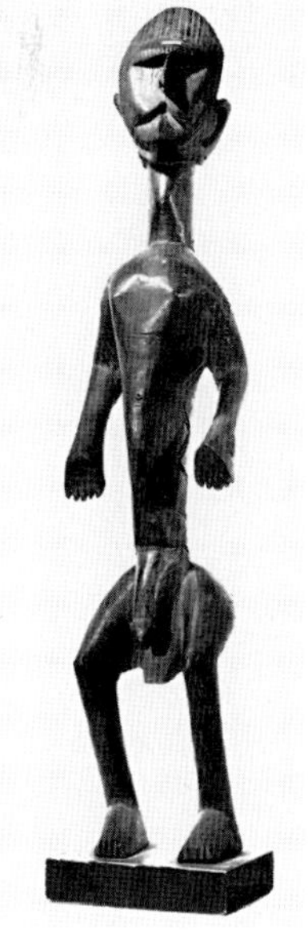

129 Unknown artist
(Bambara tribe, Mali),
wooden figure,
height $25\frac{5}{8}$ in.

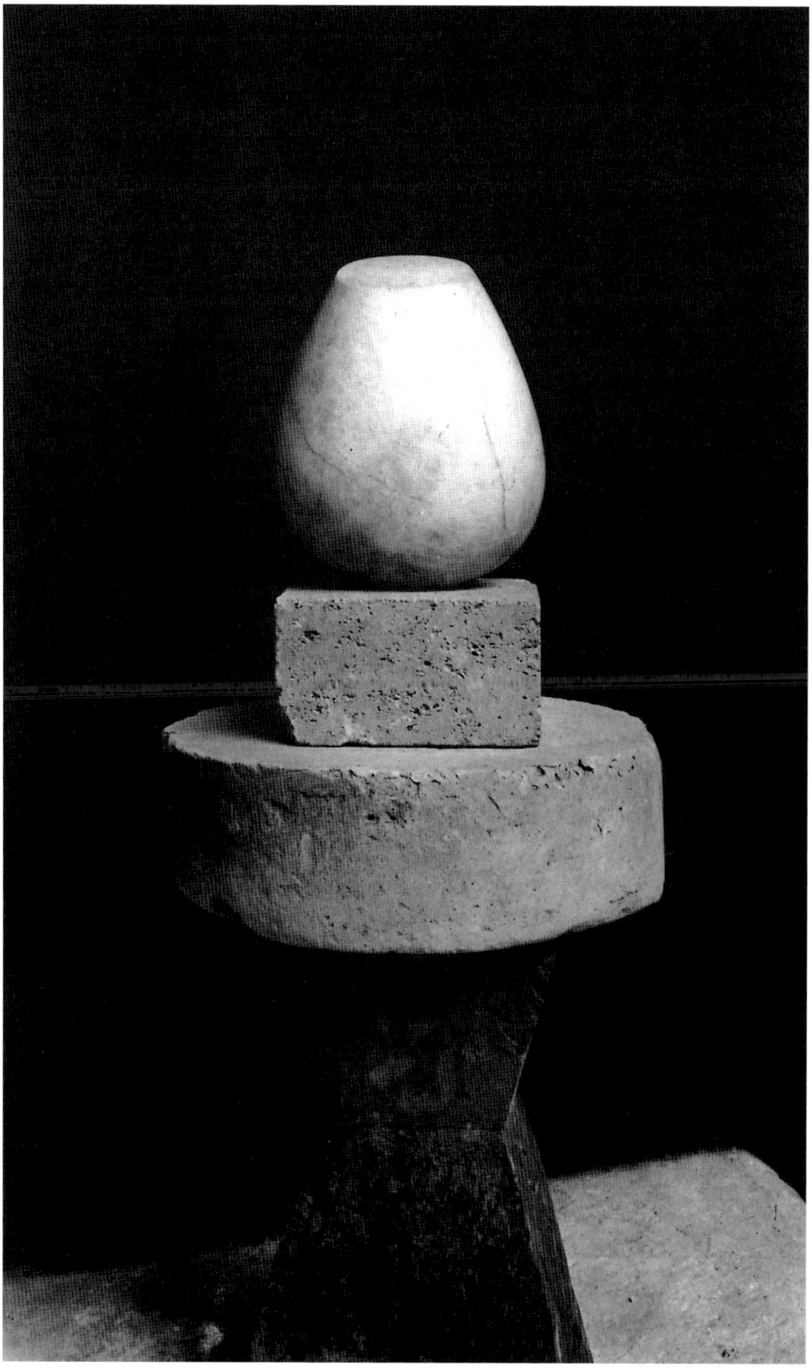

130 Constantin Brancusi, *Torse de jeune fille*, 1922
onyx, height 12 7/8 in.

Released into autonomy, the sign of a thing — without direct reference to the real thing — ultimately takes on the substance of that thing itself (noble, pure, white, smooth and so on). It now seems to correspond absolutely to reality and its meaning becomes increasingly fluid; the thing develops the same metaphysical dignity that Barnett Newman was to credit two decades later to pre-Columbian objects.

VII. TRACING THE SECRET OF THE *CELLS*

The subject of pain is the business I am in. To give meaning and shape to frustration and suffering. What happens to my body has to be given a formal abstract shape. So you might say, pain is a ransom of formalism.
The existence of pains cannot be denied. I propose no remedies or excuses. I simply want to look at them and talk about them. I know I can't do anything to eliminate or suppress them. I can't make them disappear; they're here to stay.
The Cells represent different types of pain: the physical, the emotional and psychological, and the mental and intellectual. When does the emotional become physical? When does the physical become emotional: It's a circle going around and around. Pain can begin at any point and turn in either direction.
Each Cell deals with fear. Fear is pain. Often it is not perceived as pain, because it is always disguising itself.
Each Cell deals with the pleasure of the voyeur, the thrill of looking and being looked at. The Cells either attract of repulse each other. There is this urge to integrate, merge, or disintegrate.[70]

Louise Bourgeois, 1991

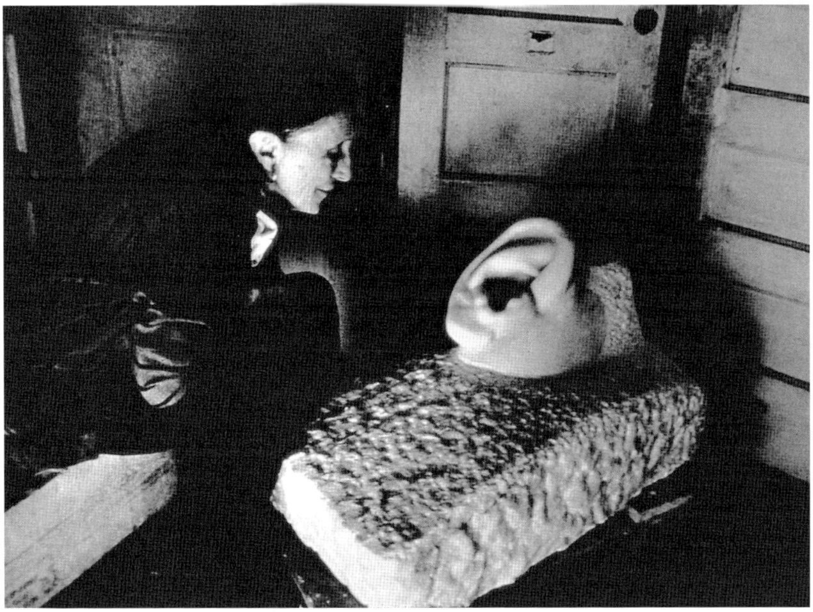

131 Louise in *Cell IV*, 1991

Our sketchy review of the erratic and by no means rigorous development of sculpture in the twentieth century has laid the ground for an examination of some of the most crucial and significant aspects of Louise Bourgeois's stylistically seemingly heterogeneous work (Ills 136, 137). It will also, it is hoped, throw light on the local context of its origins. The works that we have discussed so far were created during the forty years from 1945 until 1985 — before Louise Bourgeois decided to challenge her public with a series of elusive, unexpected installations in space, to which she gave the title of *Cells*.

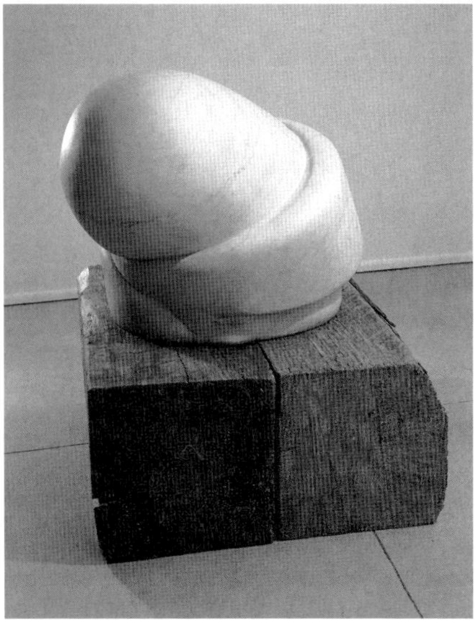

132 *Sleep II*, 1967
marble and steel, $23^{3}/_{8} \times 30^{1}/_{4} \times 23^{3}/_{4}$ in.

In view of the far-reaching conceptualization of modern art and of the diametrically opposed possibilities of figurative representation, with particular reference to the image of man in the work of Rodin, Picasso, Brancusi and (in the post-war period) Barnett Newman, we intend to demonstrate that Louise Bourgeois's creative output may be seen as an integral part of the Western European tradition, while fitting equally into a genuinely all-American context. Before her famously acclaimed retrospective of 1982 at the Museum of Modern Art in New York, this extraordinarily innovative artist was known only to a relatively limited group of insiders. Since then, with her wealth of stylistic invention and the amazing variety of aesthetics in her production values, Louise Bourgeois has proved to be an artist, a pioneer who has added hugely, if not predominantly, to the development of sculpture in the post-war years and has spurred it on in a number of often indefinable ways.

Louise Bourgeois has never succumbed to the seductive dogma of a given stylistic approach, which — while not entirely releasing her — might at least have relaxed the bonds of her responsibilities as creative artist. Instead she continued to develop new concepts in a state of restless energy, working constantly on new formal solutions to fundamental ideas. However, the scintillating interaction in her work of figuration and abstraction did not lead her lightly down the path of formalistic invention. On the contrary, it lends her sculpture significance in that it draws the viewer's imagination into an apparently endless stream of visual images that serve to stimulate the viewer's own visionary insights (Ills 132, 133). Her use of endlessly unfamiliar aesthetics in materials such as rubber or latex endows her sculptures with an artistic concept free of the inherent baggage of traditional materials such as Carrara marble. Louise Bourgeois's sculptural work concentrates on and is oriented towards the various forms that one single object can take on, firing our perceptive faculties as they scour the work for hidden hints of reality and allusion.

Amongst other things we find hermaphroditic, erotic references at their most provocative in the sphinx-like *Nature Study* (Ill. 168) and its companion piece, *The She-Fox* (Ill. 134). While the physical presence of their formal structure is, if not negated, at least called into question by their contextual independence and their material composition, these references make up a fully-fledged system of sexual aesthetics (Ill. 135). Which constitutes an unparalleled high-point in later twentieth-century sculpture and, in terms of both content and form, pushes the tactile, tangible aspects of sculpture to their lim-

133 *Cumul III*, Avenza, 1969
with *Sleep II*, 1967, in the background

Opposite page:
134 *The She-Fox*, 1985
marble and steel, $70^{1}/_{2} \times 27 \times 32$ in.

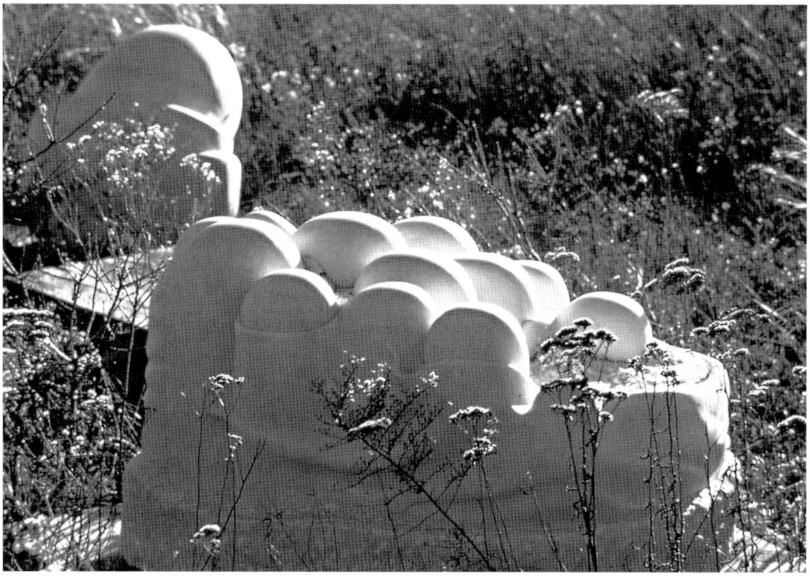

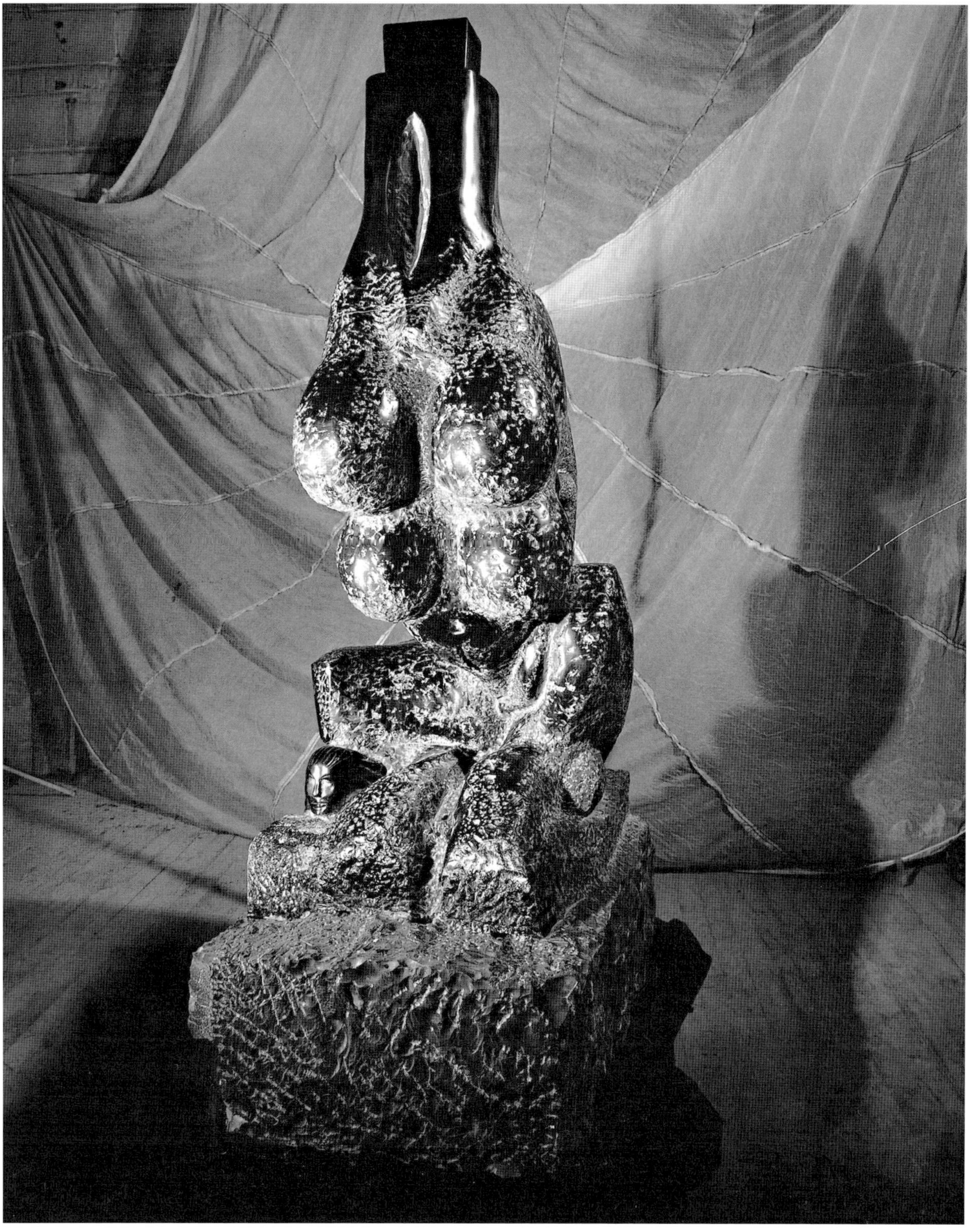

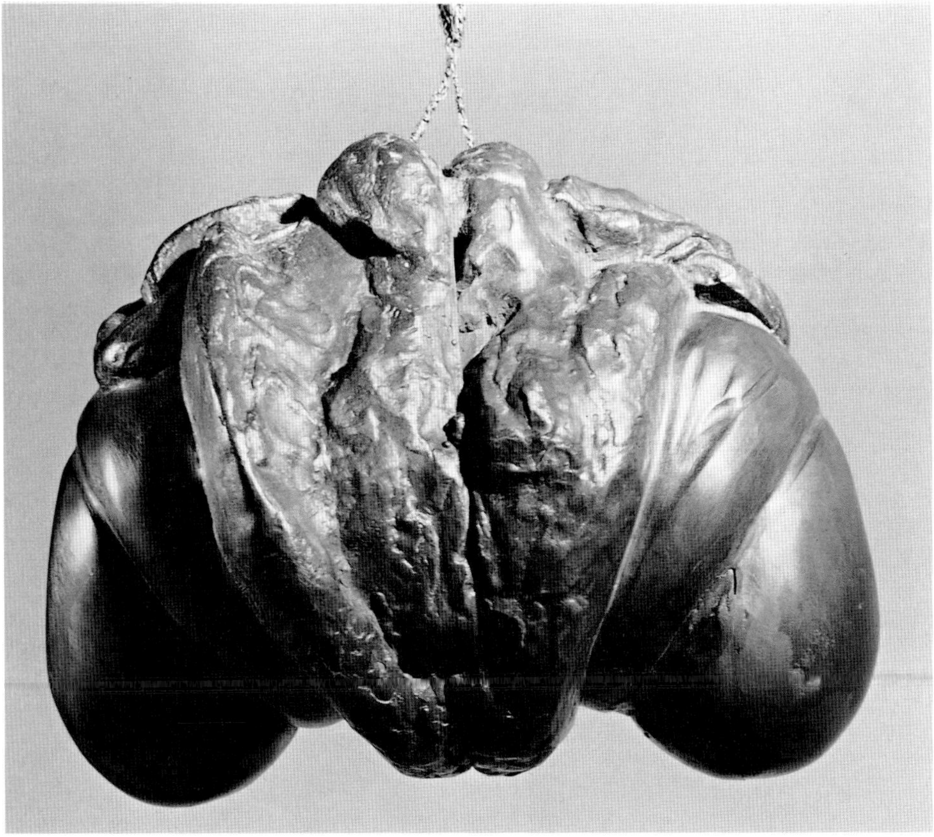

135 *Janus fleuri*, 1968
bronze, $10\,^1/_8 \times 12\,^1/_2 \times 8\,^3/_8$ in.

Below:
136 *Fallen Woman*, 1982
black marble, $3\,^3/_4 \times 13\,^1/_2\ 3\,^3/_4$ in.

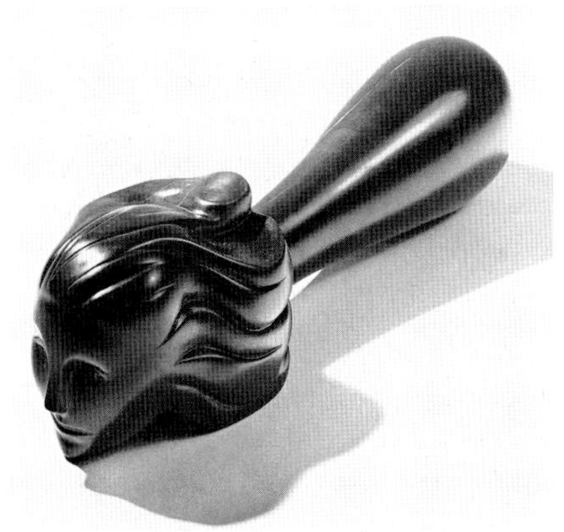

its. Louise Bourgeois's comprehensive criticism of the system is not restricted to redefining aesthetic norms: it extends beyond this to quite disparate, socially acceptable, regulatory mechanisms such as the art market, political allegiances, and her own resistance to appropriation by the Feminist movement.

An incorporation of the exhibition space itself as part of the installation and creatively formal process in Louise Bourgeois's first two solo exhibitions in 1949 and 1950 in the Peridot Gallery in New York de-emphasized the objecthood of sculptures for the first time in the history of Western sculpture. The viewer was thus cast in an active role and became an intrinsic part of the interacting dynamics of a sculptural program, experiencing essentially different sculpture in a completely new way. According to the viewer's freely chosen physical position in the exhibition space, the artist's life-sized objects, which are there to be walked around, not only display different new aspects of one and the same piece, but the relational structures of the objects both internally and in relation to the viewer take on new meaning.

Whereas artists and indeed easel painting itself since Giotto, since the Renaissance have tried to escape from the chains binding them to the two-dimensional surface by employing a variety of illusionistic and 'mannerist' techniques, the three-dimensional medium of sculpture has always seemed closer to reality. The sculptor's most urgent task was to set sculpture against everyday notions of reality and to surpass these with ideal, god-like figures. But Rodin shattered the illusion of an unattainable higher world; his male nude, *The Golden Age* (1877), scandalized his contemporaries whose reactions seem to us to spring from cynicism and ignorance. By means of the fragmentary, Rodin restored to sculpture the innocence of its own innate materiality, enlightened it as to its own revealing indifference and left it to the viewer's imagination to complete his inspired idea: "It is the eternal man touched in his innermost sensibility by something of which he knows not the cause. Is it his soul, his flesh that trembles? One does not know. No knowledge comes without suffering." (Rodin)

In 1991 at the Carnegie International Exhibition in Pittsburgh, Louise Bourgeois, by now over eighty years old, exhibited a series of six *Cells,* as she called her utterly new, positively revolutionary version of 'environmental sculpture.' In so doing, she presented the artworld with an incomparable, challenging, cataclysmic notion of sculpture. Each of the *Cells I–VI* is a space enclosed by simple doors and there is a steady decrease in the number of objects placed in them. At the same time it is possible to do justice to these objects only by paying them intense, even meditative attention. In *Cell II* it is as though a gentle perfume pervades our imagination, while in *Cell IV* the listening ear (Ill. 131) is met by the resounding silence of a huge gong. In *Cell V* we yield to a rounded duality of wooden spheres and in *Cell VI* we are left entirely to our own resources. Just a year later, at *documenta IX* in 1992, Louise Bourgeois presented another stunning work, *Precious Liquids.* With its strangely arranged glass shapes, its mysteriously empty bed and its little alabaster sculpture *Trani Episode*[71] (Ill. 138), it overwhelmed the viewers who walked through this huge, former New York water tank squeezed into a corridor in the exhibition hall. This baffling installation left visitors speechless with admiration and amazement.

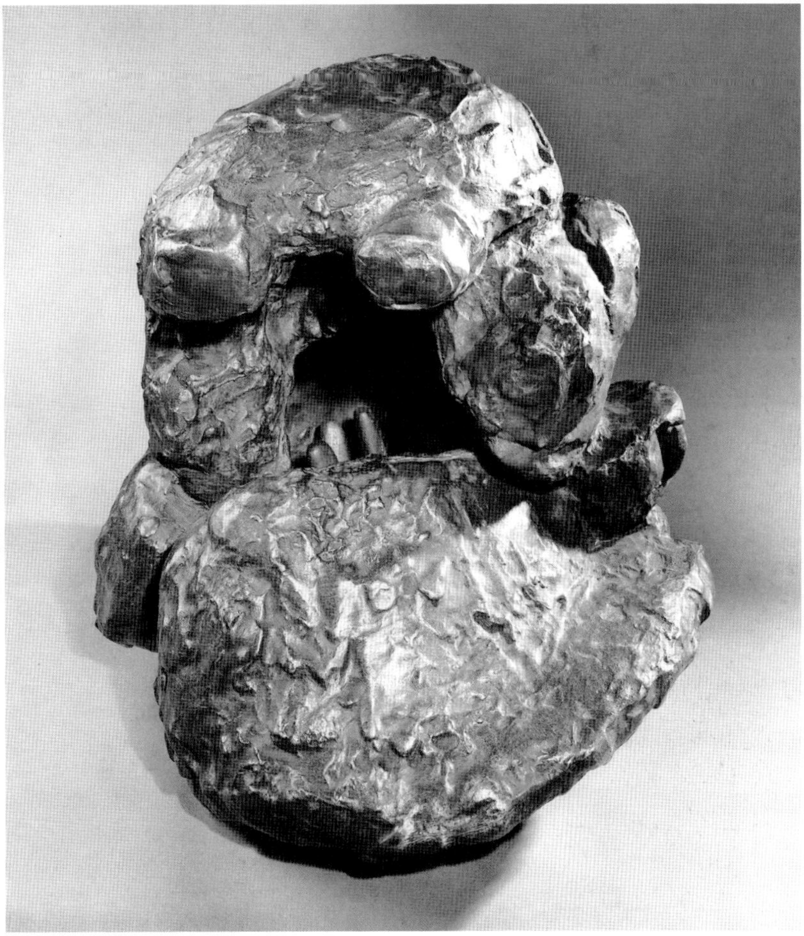

137 *Homage to Bernini,* 1967
bronze, 21 1/2 × 20 × 23 in.

Beyond their specifically generated individual meaning, the *Cells* demand a thorough, categoric examination of the notion of sculptural work. Sense and meaning, form and structure, function and effect — the reception and perception of sculpture — are all open to comprehensive reassessment and redefinition through the medium of these spaces of situative empathy where time and location have given way to a wholly altered thematic and aesthetic position.

As mentioned above, Louise Bourgeois chose the name *Cells* for this entirely new category of sculpture. In view of the *Cells'* significant mode of construction, this designation, intentionally chosen by the artist for its multiplicity of interpretations, evokes in the viewer meanings and ideas of the most complex kind. These can range from simple, even childlike notions of a friendly or hostile living space right through to deeply psychological implications (involving voyeurism, intimately personal feeling and things of that nature). We would like here to peel back the many-layered interconnections that the term *'cell'* evokes in the reader or viewer almost in spite of themselves, with particular reference to the rich spectrum of metaphorical associations elicited by Louise Bourgeois's *Cells.* We will begin with the scientific connotations of the term in the hope of revealing something of the deep, gleaming realms of meaning of these sculptures from the last decade of the twentieth century.

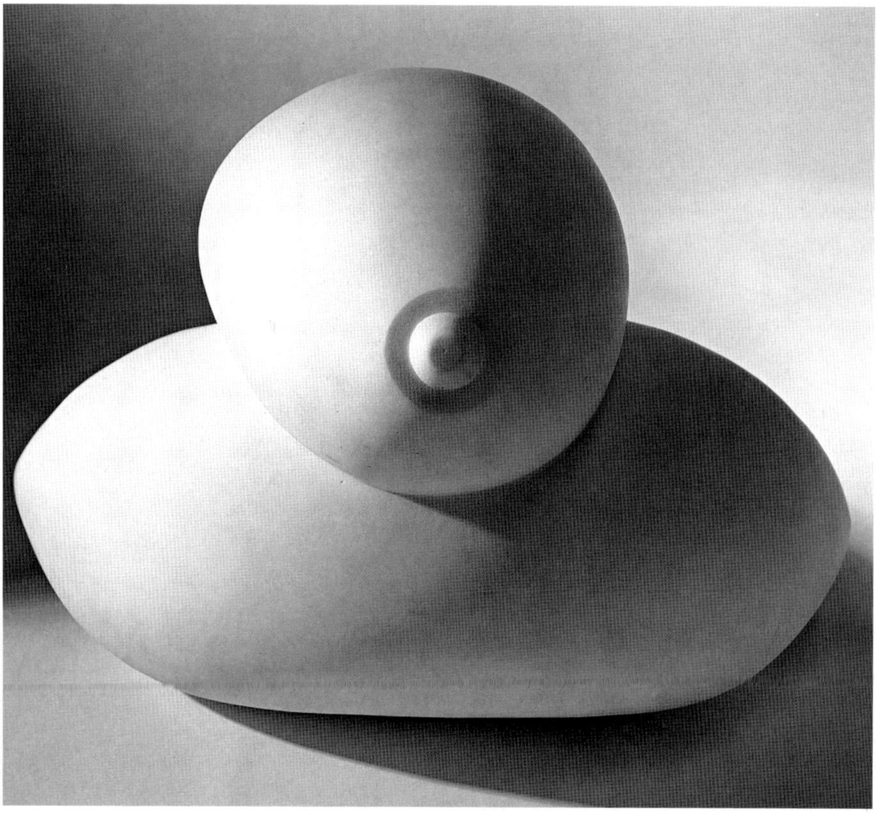

138 *Le Trani Episode*, 1971
marble, 17 x 22 x 23 in.

139 *Untitled (St Sebastienne)*, 1987
ink, watercolor, pencil on paper, 24 7/8 × 19 in.

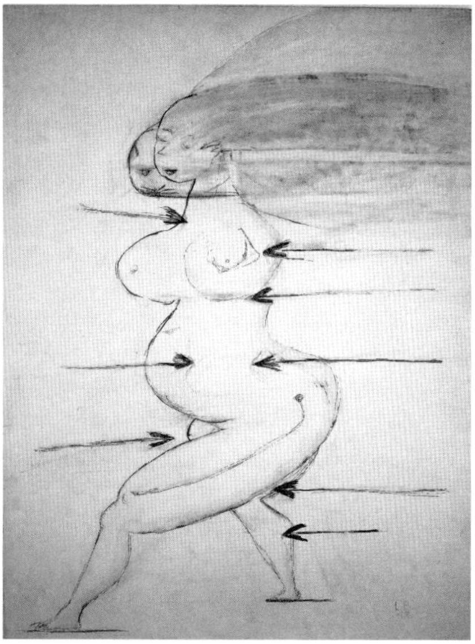

In fact the epistemological explosiveness of the *Cell* as an image is due not only to its obvious spatial analogy but even more to the theories and concepts surrounding biogenetic and biochemical discoveries of the last thirty years in the now immensely important field of the '*cell*' in a world spellbound by the successes of genetic engineering. Louise Bourgeois's *Cells* present a complex of interwoven metaphor and morphology, where the web of associations conjures up real architectonic features (honeycombs, prisons, cloisters) (Ills 141, 142) and abstract models (biological and physical elements). It is only by following up the multifarious connotations of the term '*cell*,' by pursuing its subtle ramifications which are drawn together as a single idea, concentrated into a prototype of life itself, that one can do justice to the deep levels of meaning contained in these works.

In the earlier chapters of this study we traced the changing image of man as it progressed through the work of Rodin, Picasso, and Brancusi to that of Barnett Newman and Louise Bourgeois (Ill. 140). There can be absolutely no doubt that the formal invention and sculptural concepts — including video and multimedia works — of artists such as Bruce Naumann, Joseph Beuys, and Eva Hesse (the leading sculptors in the second half of the twentieth century), also follow in the same tradition. Taking into account the fascination for non-Western, 'primitive' tribal art with its morphological human imagery, we have also endeavored to demonstrate its radical and decisive influence on the aesthetics of the human image in the art, and particularly in the sculpture, of the twentieth century. Now, at the end of this century — in the face of changing paradigms — we are again witnesses to a unique creative spirit which, inextricably bound up in the social context, is sculpturally transforming the notion of **life** with its many forms and structures.

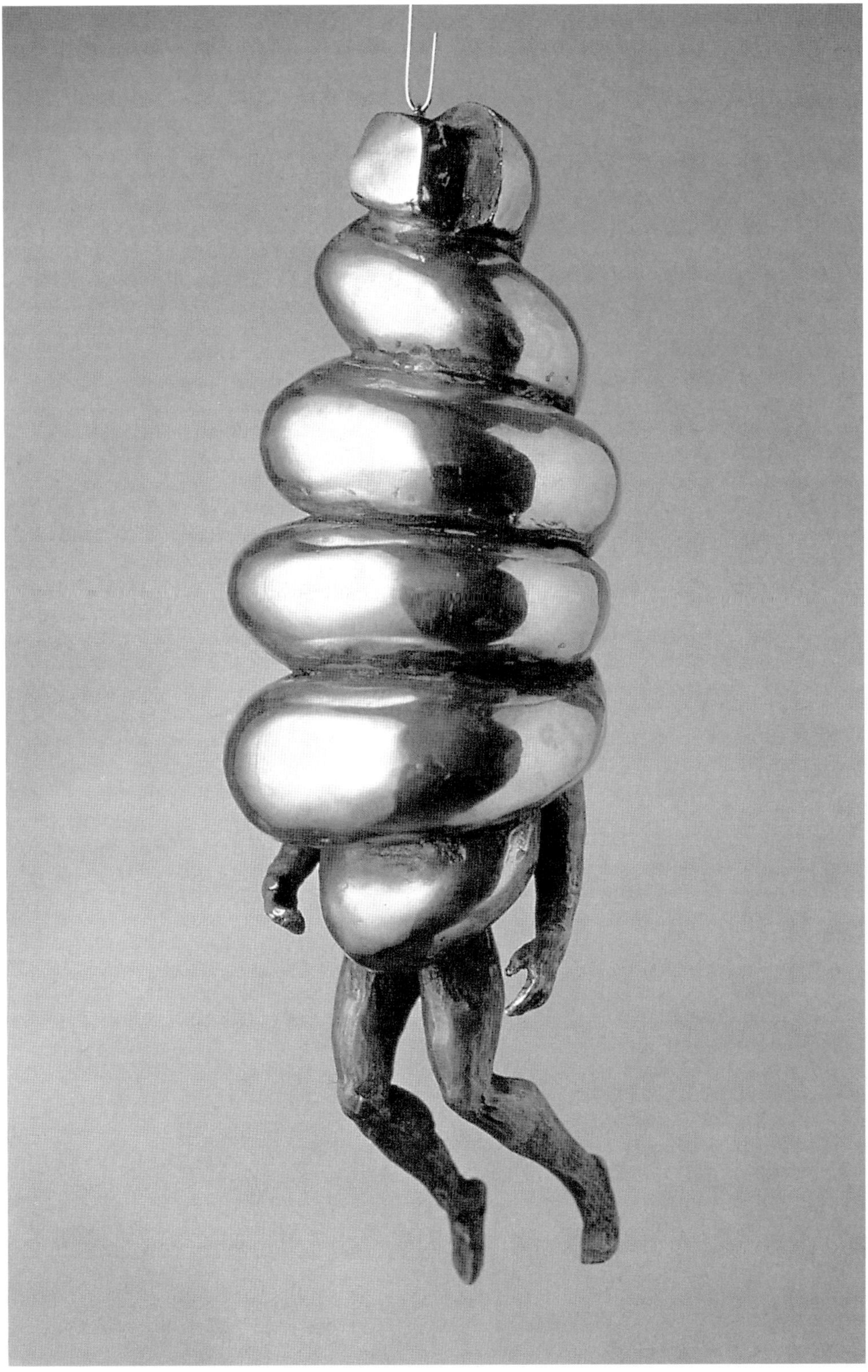

140 *Spiral Woman*, 1984
bronze, 14 × 4½ × 5½ in.

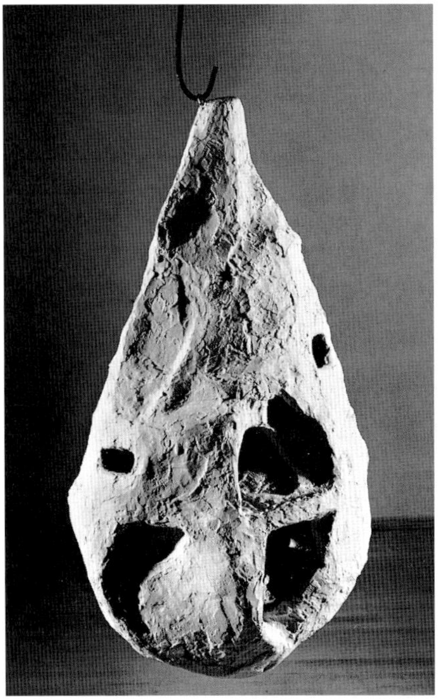

141 *Fée couturière*, 1963
plaster, 39½ × 22½ in., Photo © by Peter Moore

142 *Fée couturière* (detail), 1963, Photo © by Peter Moore

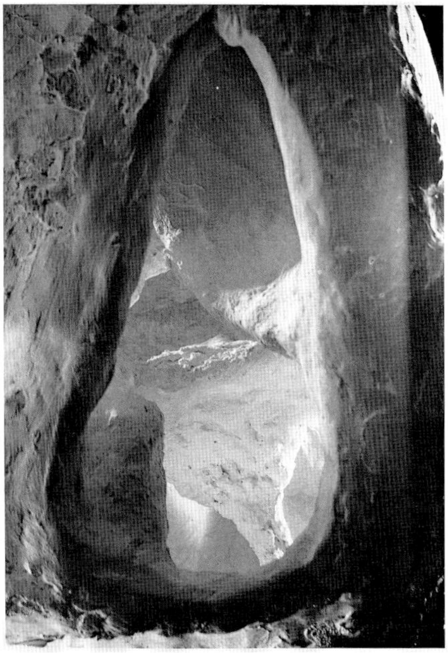

"Science is truth. Art is pleasure, but, in the end, science has the last word. Life comes to an end and so do art and pleasure. Science is unerring, in the same way that we are born and that we die. If any of this is conveyed in my works, then I am satisfied. If we think about our own survival, science is more important than art."[72]

Louise Bourgeois, 1997

A synthesis of the results of two scientific approaches — systematic observation and methodically-structured experiment — has shown that life would be impossible without properly functioning, intact cells. Thus the cell may, by definition, be understood as the seed, the basic element, in some senses the tangible **visualization of all life**. The cell has proved to be the simplest and most basic biological structure, yet it contains all the characteristic features of life. The structure and function of **all** cells — both in animals and in plants — display fundamental similarities, although they are constantly modified by evolution and may manifest themselves as the most diverse of life forms. "A cell and even some of its isolated parts," as we are told, "are capable of growth and reproduction as a result of the assimilation of substances drawn from the environment." However, "an intact cell is the simplest structure that displays all the characteristics of life."[73] Under the heading of cell theory and classification, biochemists have shown that the structure of a cell, while dependent on its environment, nevertheless has all its own life features.

The discovery of the microscope in the seventeenth century gave a tremendous boost to the hectic search for hidden realms. Yet, although scientists were able to identify a myriad of single cells and cell types, these early observers had no knowledge of the function, structure, and reproductive methods of these tiny life forms. It was only in the eighteenth century when microscope techniques had improved and the stubborn traditional notion of one original **life-giving** unit had been discarded, that the make-up of the cell, with its nucleus, plasma, and membrane, was discovered. Now, for the first time, scientists began to understand cells as elemental, crucial, constituent parts of larger organisms. However, it was not until the nineteenth century when microbiologists grew cells in artificial cultures that researchers, led by the Frenchman Louis Pasteur, confirmed their long-held suspicion that the cell is the basis of all life and that organisms are only formed through the reproduction of oth-

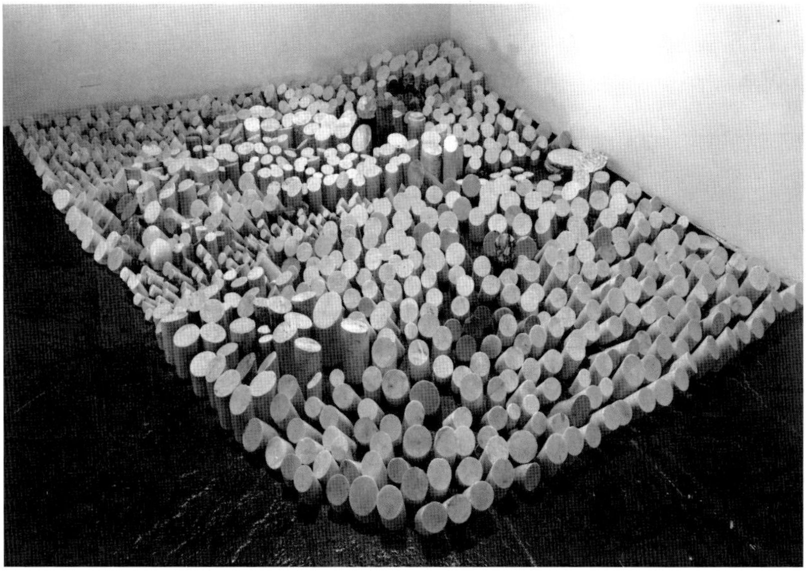

143 *Number Seventy-two (The No March)*, 1972
marble, 20 × 120 × 108 in., in the Whitney Museum of American Art, 1973
Photo © by Peter Moore

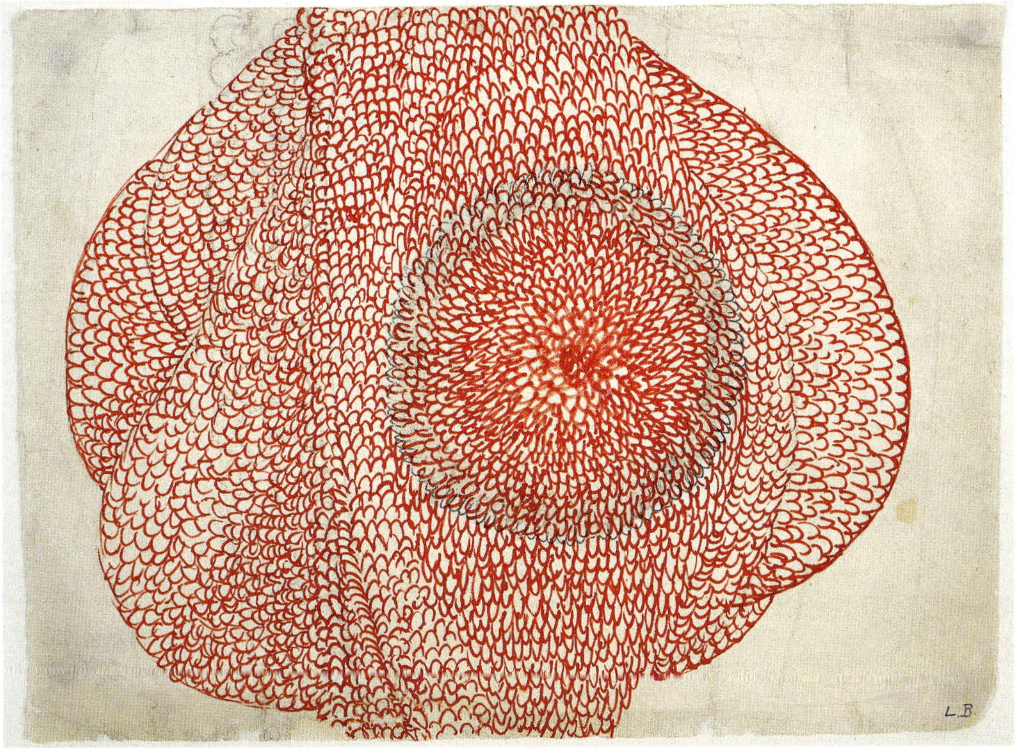

144 *Eccentric Growth*, 1960
red ink on paper, 9 1/2 × 13 in.

er organisms. In the end a combination of different scientific approaches, namely microscopic observation and experimental proof, showed that biochemical processes are largely identical in all cells. Molecular biologists, studying the contents of cells, have shown not only that important features such as genetic codes are similar and comparable in all life systems, but also that the same patterns of chromosomes, ribosomes, and the like constantly recur.

Although the most modern instruments of observation such as the electron microscope, have revealed many significant characteristics of cell structures, scientists working on cell theories were still faced with the enormous difficulty of finding an explanation for the development and coherence of multicellular organisms. A cell is not necessarily an independently operating unit: an individual, a plant, or an animal is more than just a conglomeration of separate cells. This in itself is an observation that could be taken almost literally as a description of Louise Bourgeois's own *Cells*, as we will later make abundantly clear.

Since 1960, interest has centered on the interaction and communication between cells: the exchange of materials between cells, contacts, and interconnections have all become major topics in the field of cell research. A cell's environment had hitherto not always been seen as crucial, but it now seems increasingly clear that recognition, union, and co-operation between cells is not only vital for the functioning of the cells themselves but also for the overall structure of conglomerations of cells, i.e., organisms. Research into cells both as single structures and as groups properly reflects their nature. For the overall organism must be viewed as a community of cells, where — although each bears the same genetic code — each must ultimately adhere to the rules of its own function within that organism. Any departure from the prescribed guidelines can have catastrophic consequences for the organism, as demonstrated in the spread of cancerous cells. And when scientists, commenting on cell unity, remark

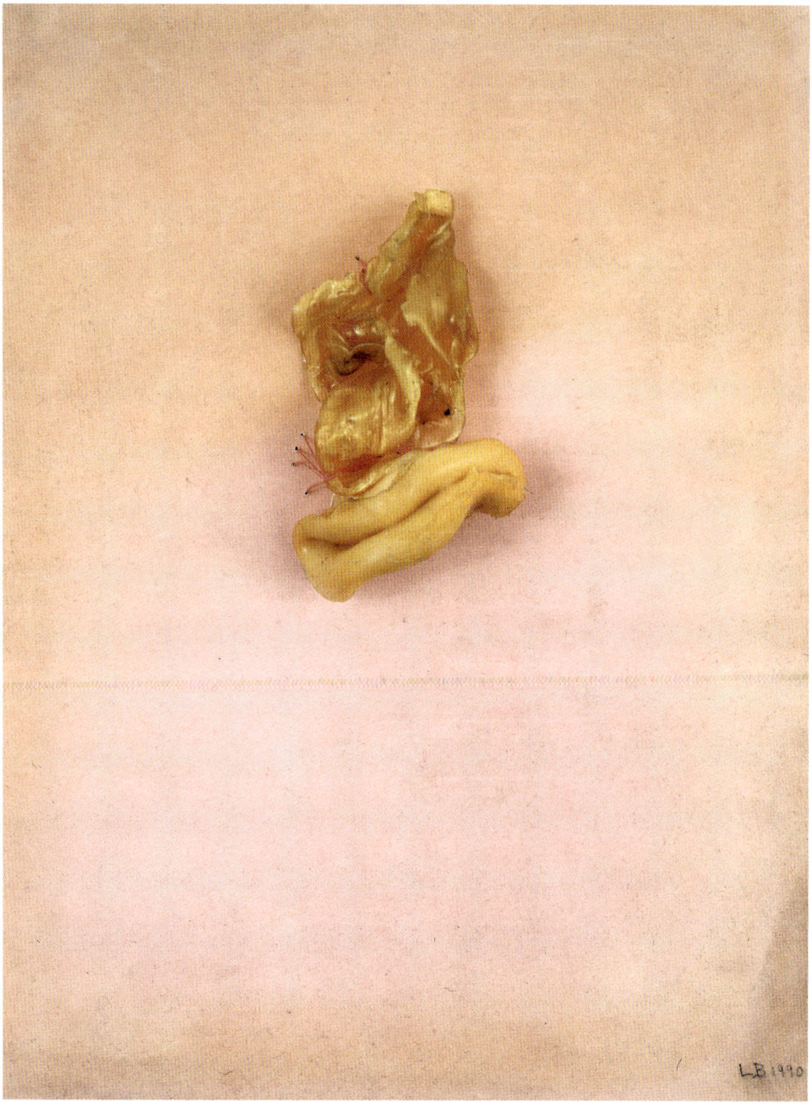

145 Untitled, 1990
Latex sewn on pink paper, 13 × 10 × 1 $^1/_2$ in.

that "the evolution of multicellular life requires the extension of the cell concept to include means by which cells can combine, communicate, contribute to the survival of the collective society"[74] then they are presenting an imaginative model of a complex situation as a vivid image — thereby putting us in the picture.

Language provides us with compliant metaphors to elucidate deep thought-processes. But it is the essence of this imagery, its vivid communication, in sum, the functioning of these metaphors, that we would like to examine here after having looked in more detail at the parts and the sum of Louise Bourgeois's *Cells*, which are in themselves the very embodiment of metaphorical thinking.

VIII. SIGHT AND INSIGHT: *CELL I* (1991)

Andy Warhol collected cookie jars; these are only valuable in that they represent Warhol's choice. They meant something to him, but they are not socially significant. A toy is fine, but it is only a toy. It's not a reality. **Art is a reality**. *The artifact is a manufactured object: a* **work of art is a language**.[75]

Louise Bourgeois, 'Freud's Toys', 1990

Several years ago I called a sculpture One and Others [Ill. 102]. *This might be the title of many since then: the relation of one person to his surroundings is a continuing preoccupation. It can be casual or close, simple or involved, subtle or blunt. It can be painful or pleasant. Most of all it can be real or imaginary. This is the soil from which all my work grows. The problems of realization — technical, and even formal or aesthetic — are secondary; they came afterwards and they can be solved.*[76]

Louise Bourgeois, 1992

People feel each other, perceive each other, turn toward or away from each other [...] fated to work together as part of an ongoing phenomenon [...] always perceiving others and adjusting to them.[77]

Louise Bourgeois, 1997

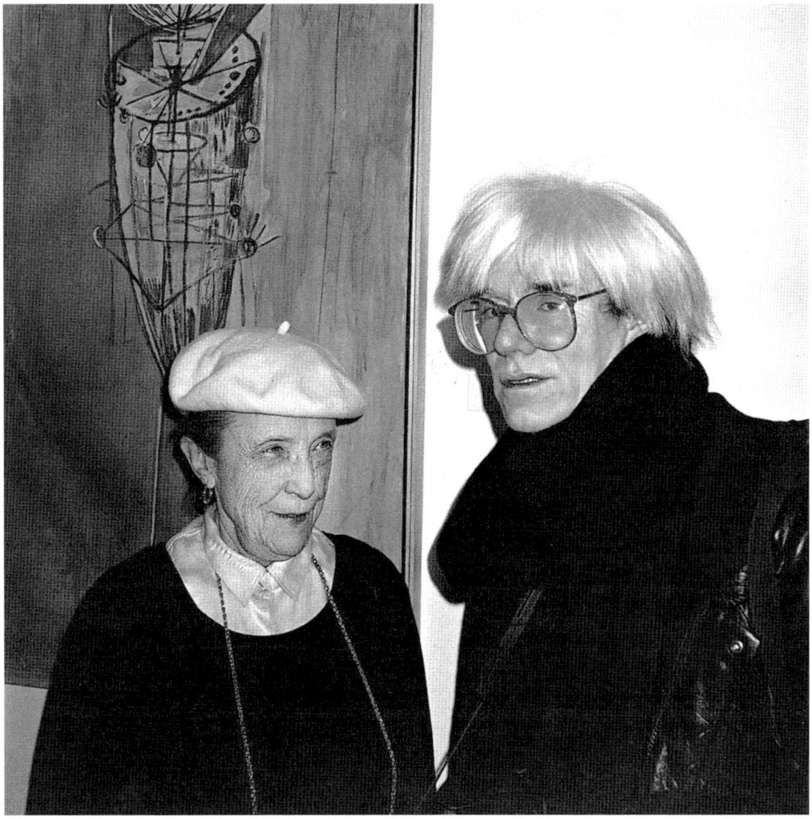

146 Louise Bourgeois with Andy Warhol, 1987

Tense with anticipation we approach a mysterious, spiral-shaped space bounded by old, used doors, and called a *Cell* (Ills 147–50). What will be revealed inside? Could there be a person hiding behind this barricade, curled up with pain in the bed — as Louise Bourgeois herself suggested — terrified of the viewers, of voyeurs who want to poke their noses into his private life; gripped with the fear of having no friends or losing the few friends he does have, and then festering away in there, all alone and starved of the touch of human kindness?[78]

Doors simply standing there, linked together by hinges, colored pale blue and white, serve as makeshift walls enclosing the interior of *Cell I*. Walls?

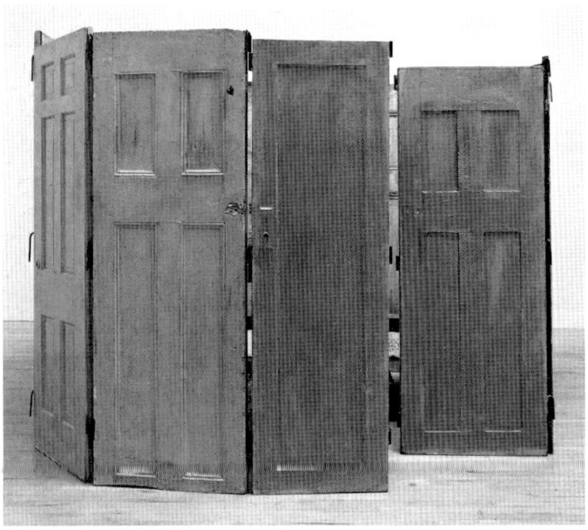

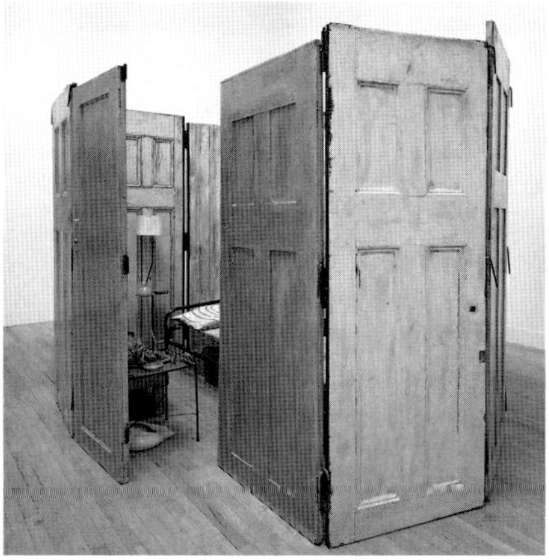

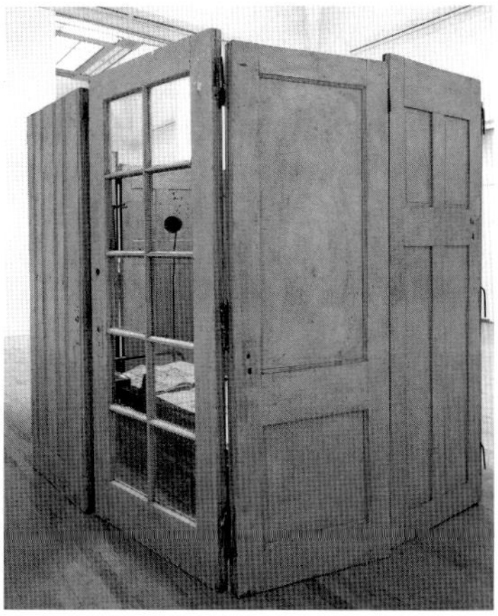

147–149 *Cell I*, 1991
glass, fabric, wood, metal, 83 × 96 × 108 in.

More like hastily painted doors, retrieved from somewhere, *objets trouvés*, flotsam, junk — the worse for wear, in a bad state, unusable, covered in thick layers of paint flaking off in places with even older layers of paint showing through: these doors lay bare their own history. One tells of a family of immigrants that had found refuge behind it in a new world; the trepidation of a mother, anxious about whether she could still protect her children in this new country; the burden a father had to bear — poorly paid work, a difficult language, exile. These doors also bear witness to high expectations and bitter disappointments: the loss of friends, the first night of love, misunderstandings born of unfamiliarity. These doors have endured outbursts of rage, have stood open as mediators, been pushed shut to create division, been locked to keep secrets, have kept out prying eyes.

The doors, standing upright, have neither locks nor handles — they have been stripped of the indispensable prerequisites for locking, locking out, and keeping out. A bolt triggers a person's instinct for indiscretion, its absence robs the door of its dual role as a refuge or a route to a break-in. Without bolts, the doors take on a different status as mediators, the interlocked hinges dynamize the structure, whose form remains 'unlocked,' movable.

Through the gaps between the doors we can see inside, where we discover an iron bedstead and a clothes stand. This interior is evidently a habitable homestead. Although there is a shoulder-width gap between two of the doors, it is not possible to enter the *Cell* because a roughly-welded metal chair is barring the way. Disappointment spurs our desire to find out more about the room, and we try to get a view of the artwork by going from gap to gap. Gradually a mental picture emerges: broken, fragmentary impressions come together and the view from each different angle reveals more objects, even though — for the moment — we are persistently denied an overview of the whole room.

Unexpectedly we find ourselves in front of a glass door, and our curiousity is satisfied by the sight of the whole interior of the *Cell* (Ill. 149). A few of the glass panes are missing, others are whitish

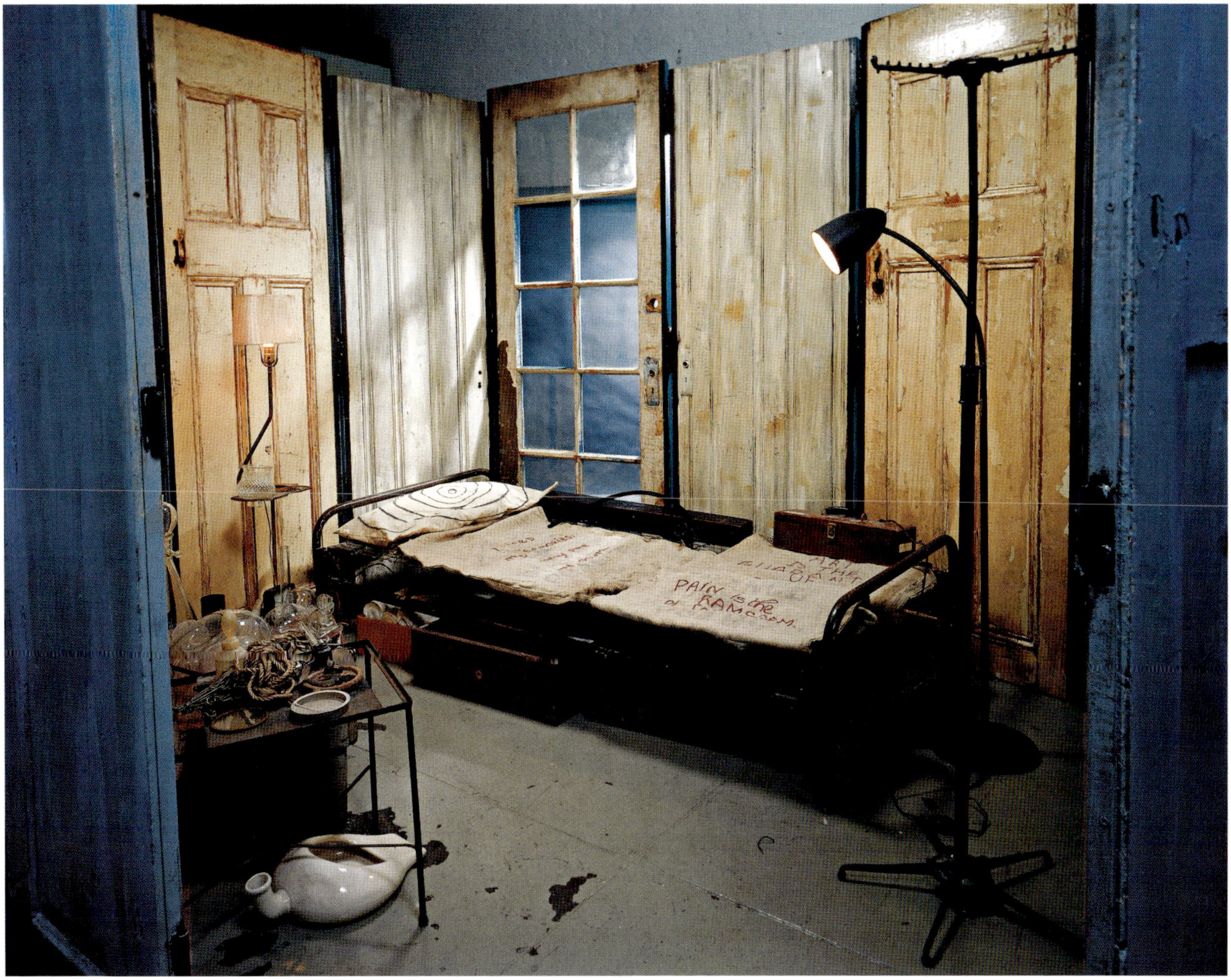

150 *Cell I*, 1991

and covered with dirt. We are still prevented from entering the *Cell* itself, from making physical contact with the space, 'getting close to it' in the literal and metaphorical sense. The fragile, useless window glass completely loses its function-dependent usefulness; thin, wooden poles by the blocked-up opening between two doors seem to be yet another, subtle barrier preventing us from entering the *Cell*.

Yet, one window frame without glass invites us to indulge our curiosity: to stick our head inside and to examine every corner, giving space to our imagination in the art space within the exhibition space. The imagination leaves the body, abandons the text, spreads its wings, takes off, and, circling round, descends as though from a great height towards this experience in spatial form:

> *"No trace of life, you say, pah, no difficulty there, imagination not dead yet, yes, dead, good, imagination dead imagine."*[79] *(Samuel Beckett)*

A *mise-en-scène* of a state of mind — stage: plain hall, depository, undemanding. Completely white, sacred gloss, unconsecrated secularized cult, neutral place of encounter with images. Absolute autonomy? A white cube: serving, not talking, expressionless. Sometimes a little whimsical, sometimes not quite hiding remnants from the past. Uneven, pale light, four sides, doorless doorways, short of thresholds. Here and there the flickering of a yellowish neon light — glass sections revealing Nature outside. The visitor's gaze turns from the show indoors and roams freely through the outside world: green meadows, weeping willows, red maple, a broad expanse of blue, a lily pond perhaps, a splashing stream. No ebb no flow. Meditatively murmuring whispering from inside, no echo to speak of, restraint required. Unlocated space, faceless, petrified mime: **in a museum**. The viewer's imagination its own curiosity cabinet of curiosities. An idealized vision, an atmosphere conveyed. The tone struck here will resonate far and wide.

Shafts of white light penetrate the dirty, shabby panes in the glass door, striking the interior of the Cell like the last rays of the departing evening sun (Ill. 150). The warm, muted light illuminates a seemingly desolate scenario. A plain, iron bed with a rusting black frame is pushed up against the hinged doors, which from the inside of the Cell seem like protective, sheltering walls. Objects crowd together in the narrow space. What secret is hidden in the wooden case between the bed and the partition wall? Is this not the kind of case that was used for instruments of scientific curiosity like dissecting kits and microscopes, or instruments for measuring the blood pressure and for letting blood? Perhaps we might also find documents, hand written, best of all a will, the first page of a novel, business papers. But this briefcase forced in between the bed and the wall is not destined to leave the room, it is not going anywhere.

An improvised coat-stand constructed from metal tubes is flexing its claws. At the head of the bed — suspiciously enough, as though to assist voyeurs, the bed is right by the glass door, which allows one to look out and positively demands that one should look in — there is a large, only moderately thick pillow, caught in the persistent rays of the penetrating light. The artist has painted black, concentric circles on the linen pillowcase (Ill. 152). They focus on an ideal middle point, the center of its being. The exhausted or sick sleeper, the daydreamer and picture-maker, lays his weary head down here to rest, seeking refuge from the strains of the day. Following a circular path, he makes his way down the memories and experiences of his life; the doors of the Cell take up this spiraling motion, loosely interlocking; the thinker entangled in his own thoughts, his imagination caught inside his head (Ill. 151). Lamps shedding a pale light keep watch by the bed. They illuminate, they see. The lamp is the room's eye and through it the room takes on a melancholy human air.

151 *Insomnia (in progress)*, 1995
ink on paper, 9 × 12 in.

Like a poor substitute for a comfortable mattress, there are some carefully folded sacks from POSTES FRANCE, the French mail service, lying directly on the bedsprings. Now torn and partly patched, these sacks once crossed the Atlantic filled with letters of hope, anxiety, trust, dreams, congratulations, and bereavement. These mailbags conveyed and delivered manifestations of life. Louise Bourgeois has carefully embroidered short sentences onto them with striking red thread. As in a child's first attempts at writing, there is no obvious logic to the distribution of large and small letters, as though Louise Bourgeois wanted to avoid any particular handwriting which might have implicated her in these statements on too obvious a personal level. Just below the pillow we can read: "I need my memories: they are my documents." As the artist herself has said of her memories:

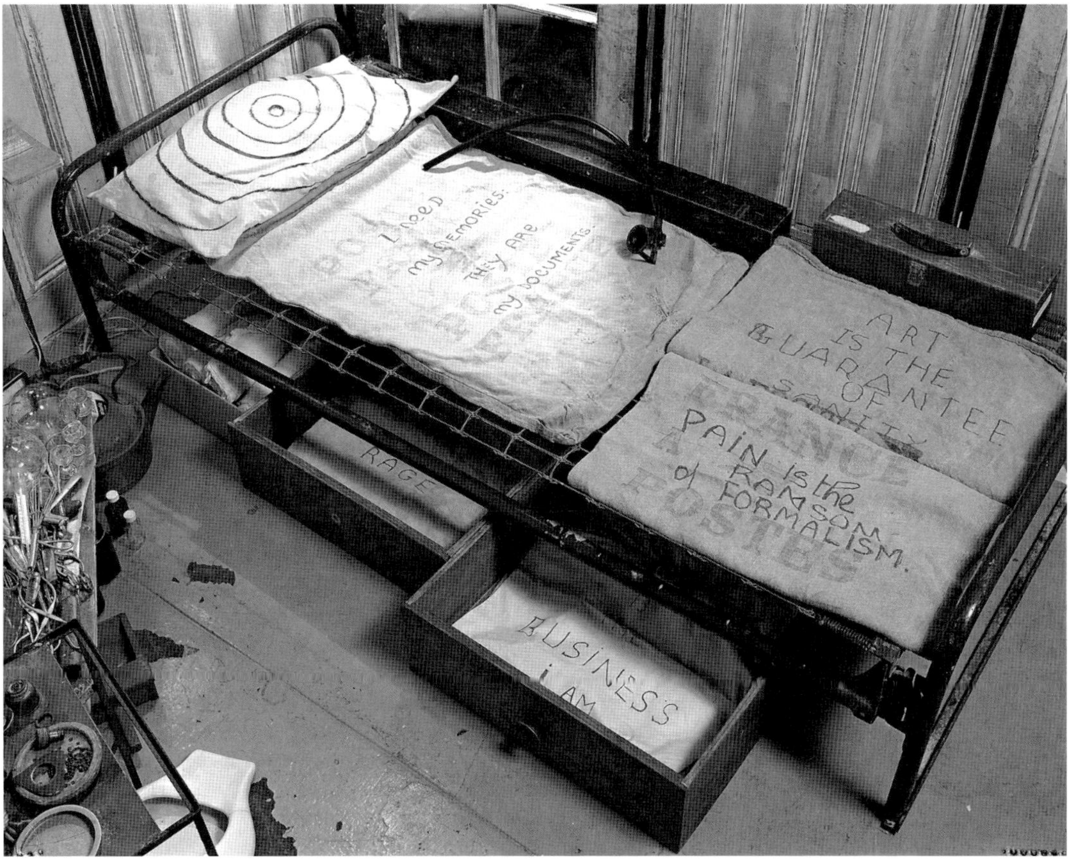

152 *Cell I*, 1991

"I need my memories. They are my documents. I keep watch over them. They are my privacy and I am intensely jealous of them. Cézanne said: 'I am jealous of my little sensations.' To reminisce and woolgather is negative. You have to differentiate between memories. Are you going to them or are they coming to you here? If you are going to them you are wasting time you are wasting time. Nostalgia is not productive. If they come to you, they are the seeds for sculpture."[80]

At the foot of the bed there are two more folded-up mailbags (Ills 152, 153). The artist has embroidered the top one with large writing that reads "Art is the guarantee of sanity." The lower one bears the words: "Pain is the ransom of formalism." In the drawers under the bed we can make out fragments of words, including "rage" and "is the business I am." In order to fulfill the promise of art, peace, shelter, security, and spiritual well-being, one must keep company with rage and unavoidable suffering — suffering that does not seek a comfortable life, but that both exhausts itself and finds fulfillment in its constant search for the intrinsic meaning of life.

By the bed, which in fact dominates the space, there is a chair being misused as a storage space (Ills 154, 155). A simple steel plate serves as the seat. On it are arranged bits of metal, screws and fittings, that neither fit each other nor belong together, and an unusable, frayed rope. Unscrewed, stored, and forgotten. Under the chair, put there for no apparent reason, we find a gleaming white chamber pot, with a rounded, sweeping form that is strangely compelling. Glass bottles, bulbous retorts and long-necked phials; pliers, a machete, and a whisk are clustered together on a low table. At one time, life-bringing and life-destroying solutions bubbled in these instruments of chemical analysis and synthesis. They may even have been used to distill *l'eau de vie* — the precious, burning elixir of life.

But gradually an uneasy suspicion creeps up on us: the odor of illness, of suffering, and of frailty, clings to the hot-water bottle. The red, white, and blue BAND AID box in the dusty kettle, the measuring stick, the dust-pan, the alarm clock, the moldy rope, all the easily broken, fragile glass objects, the book with the word "tuberculosis" on the bedside table: all attributes of transience, mortality, everyday objects yet moribund and somehow tainted. Life is short. Time runs out inexorably, leaving a sign where it has been.

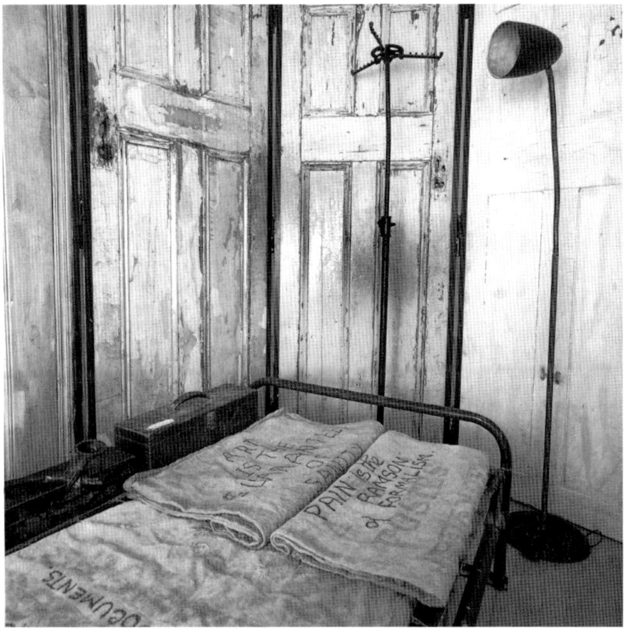

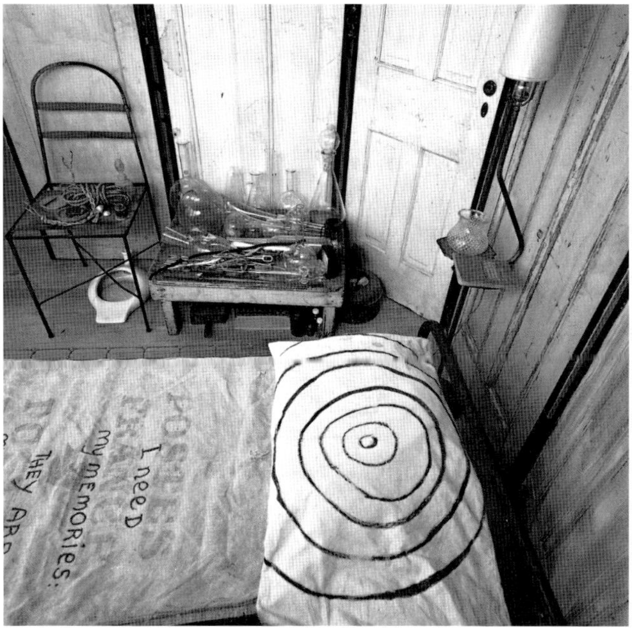

153, 154 *Cell I*, 1991

The viewer holds still and at the same time runs through an endless chain of his own memories: images of his mother, his first home, the drawer with the toys, rooting about in the attic.

The individual objects in the Cell, such as the rope, the lamp, and the book, are entangled in a web of connections that becomes all the denser as the viewer's input increases and ever greater demands are made of his imagination. Responsibility for the constitution of an artwork is handed over to the viewer's active imagination. The individual objects in the *Cells*, the glass hot-water bottle, the wooden case, require an effort to unfold the imagination. Ludwig Wittgenstein pointed out the difference between the following observations:

> *"'Aspiring to see something' and 'aspiring to form an image of something.' In the first case one says: 'Look, just over there!', in the second, 'Shut your eyes!' Because forming images is a willful activity, it does not instruct us about the outside world. What is imagined is not in the same* **space** *as what is seen."*[81]

Despite the fact that the objects in the *Cells* are all evidently borrowed from a seemingly familiar real world, they systematically resist being slotted into any of the perceptual experiences that we have on hand as knowledge. The deconstruction or, if you with, the defunctionalization of all these objects is

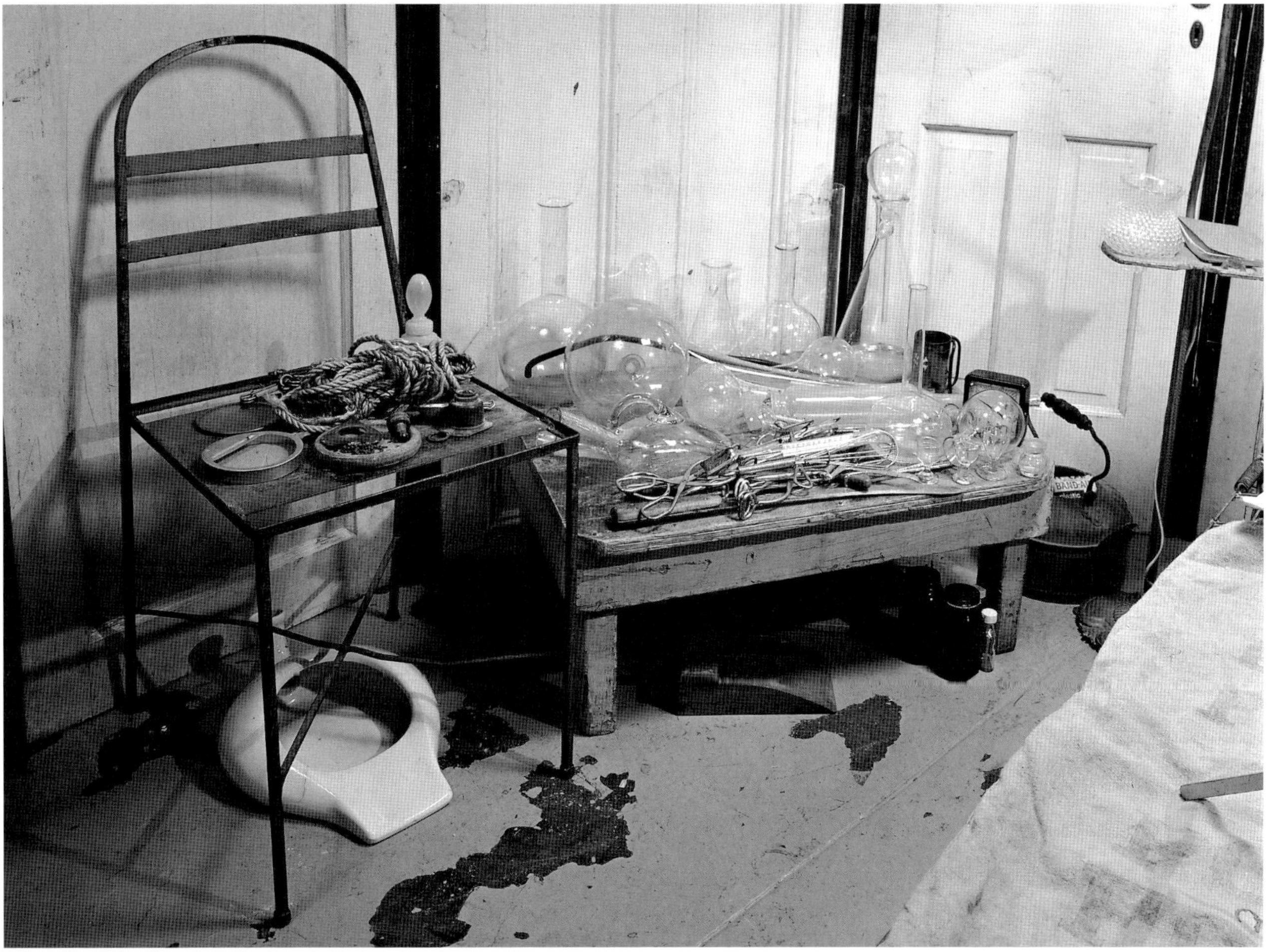

155 *Cell I*, 1991

effected by an extremely subtle shift of meaning — they increase reality without yielding to the dictates of truth, just as Nietzsche had found fifty years earlier in the case of language, where words themselves may not be an adequate expression of reality. The philosopher uses this to account for the existence of so many different languages: "The thing *per se* is also wholly unattainable for the wordsmith and indeed absolutely not worth striving for." One can detect this shift of meaning in each individual object, even though they all clearly refer back to their original purpose. The timeless, styleless appearance of lamp, chair, bed, and coat stand allows for separation, between the imagined and the world round us. The non-hierarchical, serial arrangement of similar objects as the adding of test tubes, retorts, and phials in successive order prevents our gaze from fixing the attention on any individual object, and it invalidates the attempt — taking place in our own heads — to create some kind of logical structure. As it is not possible to distinguish any fully worked-out composition, the chaos that we are to experience must not be structured — the form must be such that it admits of chaos, a form that is compatible with disorder:

> *"To me the spiral is a form of arranging chaos. The spiral is completely continuous, predictable or infinite. It is a form of disorientation: you don't know whether its direction comes from the right or the left, but not in a political sense. [...] The references that man needs to live in an orderly way disappear."*[82]

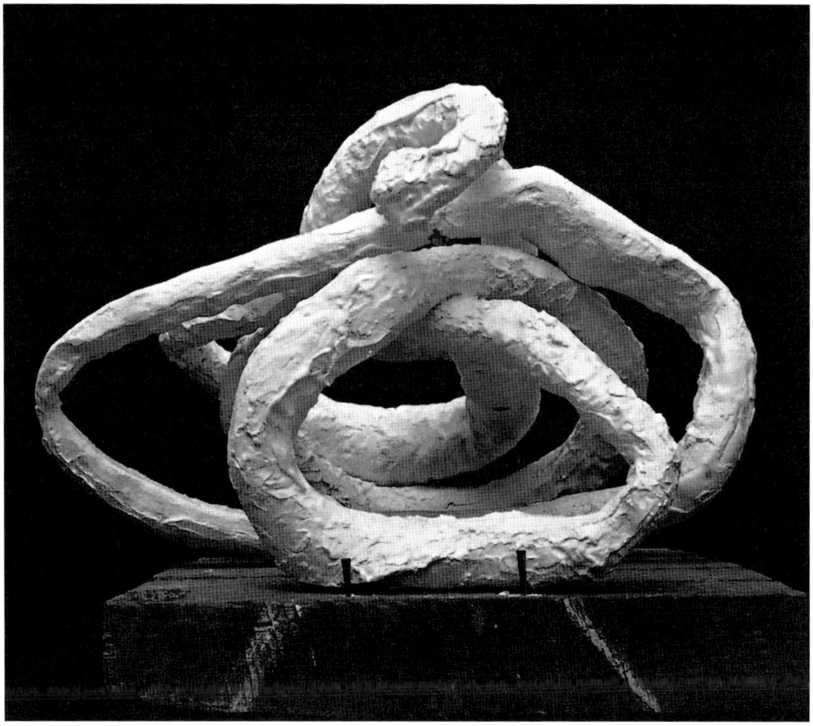

156 *Spiral / Summer*, 1960
plaster, 14 × 21 in.
Photo © by Peter Moore

Since the space of the *Cell* may not be located in any situation and may not be assigned to any particular time, it seems to have an echo of emptiness about it: the viewer's melancholy gaze alights on a disappearing world of objects. An apparently fragmentary, torso-like sight — as in the case of Rodin's identifiable, fragmented sculptural items and human forms — sparks the viewer's imagination into trying to complete what it is seeing. Even though this response is admittedly set in motion by the artist's choice and arrangement of objects, phantoms of the viewer's imagination — behind closed eyes and in the viewer's head alone — then vie with the formless, persistently evasive images located in the space itself. As a consequence, the viewer's imagination becomes a creative tool and, by constantly attempting to subject the objects to empirical verification and to bring his own experience to bear on the situation, the viewer comprehends the formative strength of fiction itself as an experience. The decisive insistence on fragments leads one to suspect that it is meant to redress the apparent disappearance of the 'real' world in the midst of these fragments of objects, connected neither in a time/space nor in a causal sense. Through the dissolution of formal perception, since no meaningful relationship exists any longer between figure and ground with each possessed of its own autonomous meaning, conditions are created whereby the imagination can progressively undermine perceivable reality. Close study of the objects and comparison between different elements do not yield clearly delineated results. The outcome is much more a kind of dispersion, a burgeoning of the imagined object. As connections slip and slide between objects, nonfixable connotations arise which appeal to our faculty of independent thought and encourage our imagination to take flight. The final consequence of this process is best summed up in the words of Samuel Beckett: "All is mental, figments."[83] For in this process the mind is introduced as the place where one encounters art.

IX. ENCOUNTERING *CELL (YOU BETTER GROW UP)* (1993).

In Entanglement with *Red Room (Parents)* and *Red Room (Child)* (1994)

All art comes from terrific failures and terrific needs that we have. It is about the difficulty of being a self because one is neglected. Everywhere in the modern world there is neglect, the need to be recognized, which is not satisfied. **Art is a way of recognizing oneself.**[84]

Louise Bourgeois, 1988

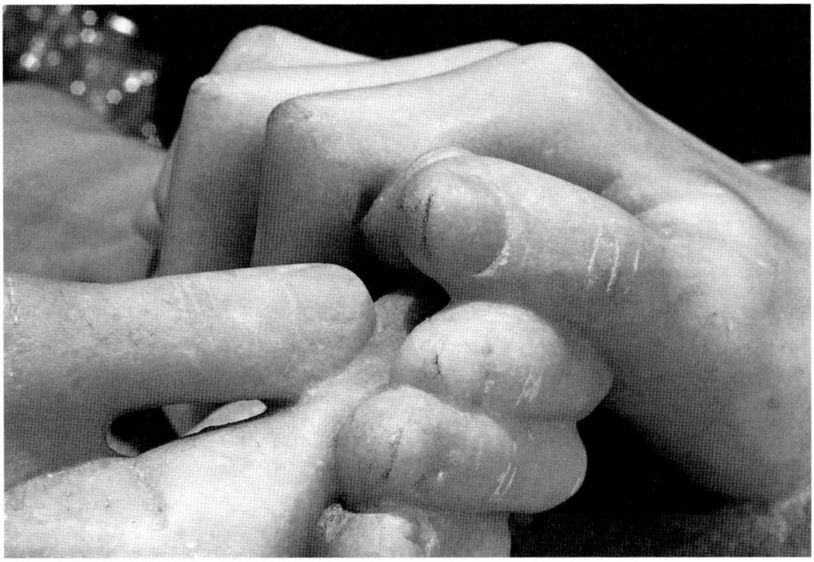

157 *Detail of Cell (You Better Grow Up)*, 1993

While, in *Cell I*, something mysterious and secretive behind a wall of doors compelled us to pry curiously inside in an attempt to unravel its enigma, *Cell (You Better Grow Up)* of 1993 reveals its entire scenario at first sight (Ill. 160). Yet at the same time the cage, for all its openness, is in fact to be seen as a straight figure without artifice, set up for disjunction without mediation; in a cage one appears to be naked, its transparency is irreversible and without perspective. Freedom inside the cage is no more than a sham. Characterized by its intrinsic unevenness, the objects locked inside the cage are always within reach of the bailiffs, while at the same time remaining untouchable. The cage puts forward power against powerlessness as inside knowledge triumphs over ignorance. A cage instrumentalizes the painfully exacting order of a precisely demarcated reality.

In keeping with the long traditions of sculpture, the few chosen objects are presented on slightly raised pedestals, yet their strange forms resist immediate comprehension. A barely perceptible gesture of soothing understanding, of unobtrusive liking and of friendly protection encompasses a whole world of the most intimate feelings human beings have for each other. This mild gesture is set against the resounding gesticulations of an artist like Rodin, who created an immense range of expressions through his ability to give powerfully tangible form to pathos, despair, superhuman strength, and passionate disintegration, drawing in his figuration on his titanic creative potential to capture the full extent of human misery and happiness.

But Louise Bourgeois's gesture does not rebel; instead it accords with its own time. It does not capitulate or shout out loud; it does not inveigh against the destiny of its own existence. Silent as the shadows, this gesture accedes to its fate, for it is cared for. It is silent because it *knows*. Two tiny hands lie folded, relaxed and composed, almost meditating, in their own lap. They activate no reference beyond themselves; they don't aspire to mean. Solemnly they receive the blessing of the large hand that tenderly touches the others and protects them; it shelters these lesser entities, giving them warmth and a safe refuge, and takes them into its keeping with a sense of benevolent understanding. Yet, for whom might the artist have created an unbreakable form, a ton-weight of pink marble resting on steel carriers that is apparently to last for all eternity — and what rests here so smoothly and evenly on a roughly-hewn base and so lovingly touches itself, while leaving somehow an impression of fragility?

Deceptive scents from perfume bottles seduce rather than persuade. (Ill. 158). Their concentrated essence is fleeting, short-lived, transient. The scent enfolds us like a veil and, with its evocative power, awakes in us the delusions of desire. Cunningly these scents lure in the unwitting victim, who in his innocence perceives only what is pure, and, suspecting nothing, allows himself to be drawn into the trap of sensual confusion. The invisible veil wraps him in the fine web that chance, haste, and shame have thrown over him. It floats malevolently in the air, dropping deceitfully and unexpectedly over him, flattering his vanity. Like a fading phantom its sweet scents arouse chimerical visions. Yet at the same time it remains locked and unapproachably closed like that transparent female torso that Louise Bourgeois has captured in a glass vessel consisting of three bulbous, stacked shapes (Ill. 159).

With an air of inviolability this glassy body evades importunate desire. The bewitched glance searches its transparency for graspable forms, but merely slips off its gleaming surfaces. The apotheosis of glass is seen in its most concentrated form in the glass tower, striving upwards with thousand-fold bands like a tropical growth, an exotic plant. Even this crystalline, clear substance must — for all its delicacy and fragility — submit to the artist's creative will, catch the glittering light and illuminate the limitless potential of the artifact.

In the superficial encounter, the smooth surface of the mirror refracts the clarity of the insights just gained. The rhythmic groupings of three — the hands, the three-sectioned glass vessel, the three perfume bottles, and the ceramic vase with three openings — are balanced by the interplay of the

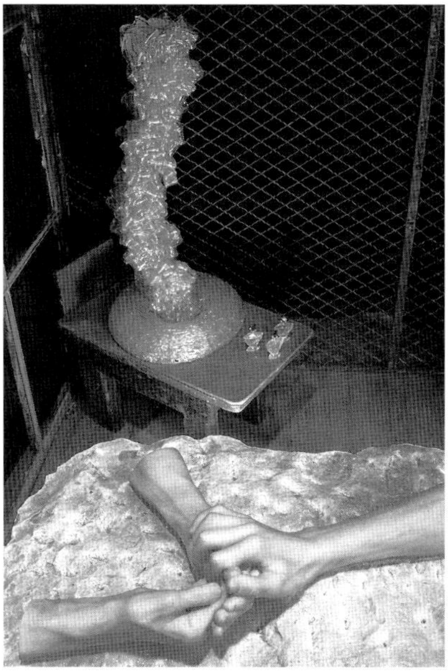

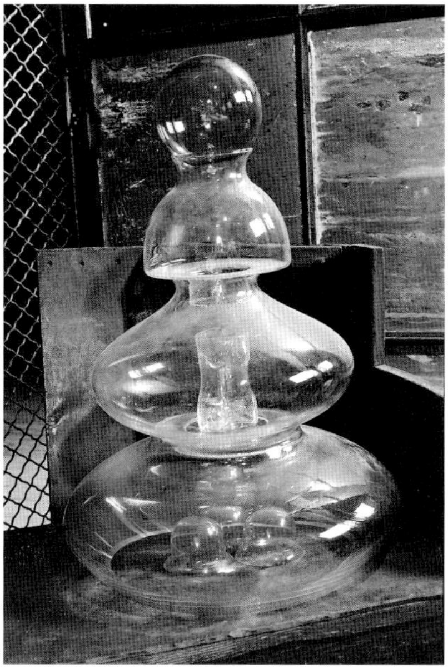

158, 159 *Detail of Cell (You Better Grow Up)*, 1993

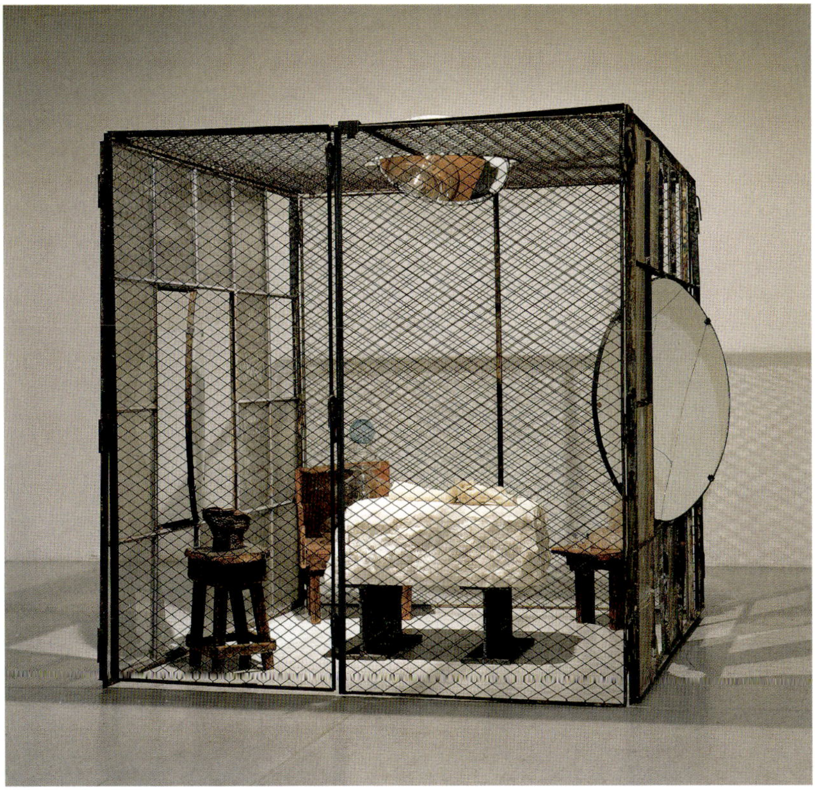

160 *Cell (You Better Grow Up)*, 1993
steel, glass, marble, ceramic, wood, 83 × 82 × 83 ½ in.

three adjustable mirrors. Yet this purely formal composition, satisfying our deep-rooted longing for harmony and symmetry, proves to be just as deceptive as the apparent insights in the mirror which reveal only what they are hiding. They create a multilayered, inconsistent picture of the world. A mirror is non-partisan; it reflects smug self-contemplation, it is open yet does not form its own impressions; it is thus the parodistic reversal of selective awareness. The mirror invites the closed extension of the spatial body to stretch itself infinitely into the depths, only to close its surface off again by taking up as little space as possible itself. In the mirror the invisible, imperceptible present super imposes itself on the sight of the Self recognizing himself.

Louise Bourgeois's prismatic refraction of the concept of reality not only shatters apparently secure, well-founded notions of pictoriality, but at the same time subverts the degree to which the world can be described and named or presented in pictorial terms. Only through a spiraling, infinitesimally gradual approach can a human being experience the Self, through constant, inevitable striving, that persists despite the certainty of its own fruitlessness and failure to clutch at any passing straw of revelatory insight. Wafer-thin interfaces reflect our worlds; they capture us and weave round us the wonderful game of the constant discovery and exposing of possible worlds, in which we become aware of glittering facets of our own existence and which release extremely personal, intimate, private associations. As the artist herself has said in a comment on this *Cell*:

> *"The tiny figure inside the stacked glass shapes is cut off from the world. That's me. The little hands are mine. They are self-portraits. I identify with the dependent one. The world that is described and realized is the frightening world of a child who doesn't like being dependent and who suffers from it. So the moral of this Cell is, you better grow up."*[85]

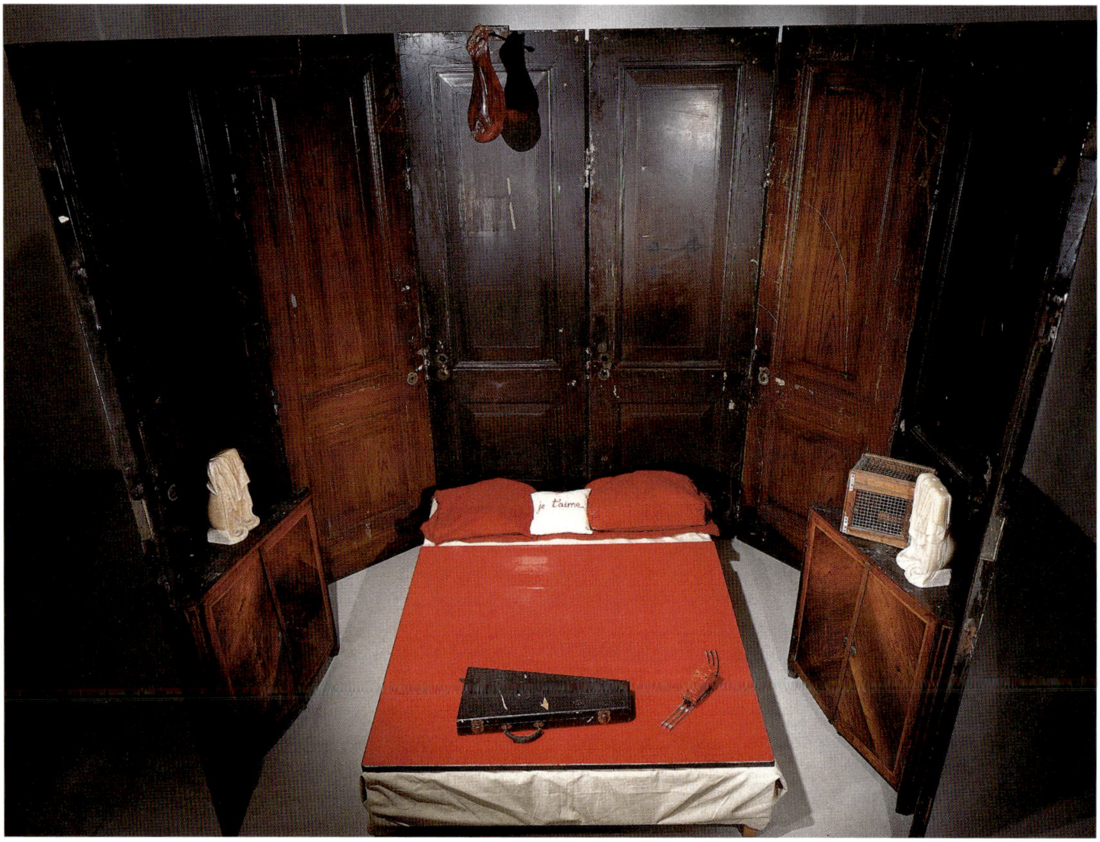

161, 162 *Red Room (Parents)*, 1994
wood, metal, fabric, mirror, 97½ x 168 x 167 in.

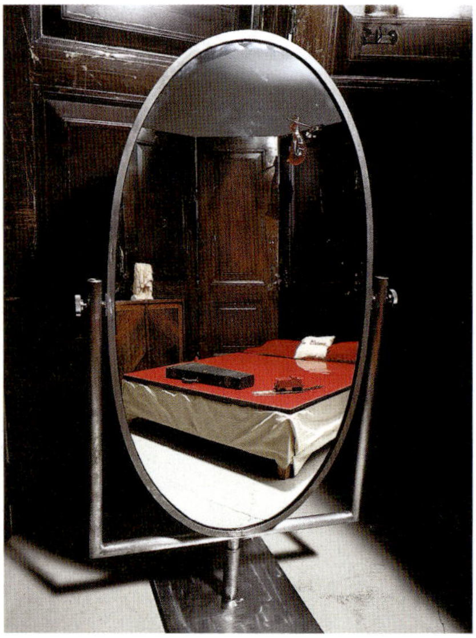

In *Cell (You Better Grow Up)*, Louise Bourgeois beguiles the viewer with an all-encompassing, all-pervasive transparence of sculptural elements, physical forms, and sensually appealing images; she creates a sense of well-being in the viewer through the beauty of perfectly crafted objects and the deeply significant, the world view and conceptually revealing design of this sculpture.

However, in *Red Room (Parents)* and *Red Room (Child)* — with the counterpoint of its dominant color, the screaming, garish, pulsatingly vital red scattered over it like a rash — Louise Bourgeois appeals unashamedly to our elemental, wild instincts, to the dumb, traumatic memories and involuntary feelings that shackle our mind and consign life to separate emotional sections. This red has taken us over. It is not persuasive, it does not connect meaningfully with any object but rather encloses it, envelopes it and autonomously pursues its single aim of capturing viewers and captivating them through its surface appearance.

As opposed to the manufactured perfection of something formed, complete, and flawless; we are confronted here with a definition of the arbitrary use of mastery, an unregulated, arcane creative process; a spontaneous departure into unknown regions; unfolding, changing, a step-by-step germination that has yet to acquire form and substance. Painstakingly balanced order and established reason are countered with the terror of unbridled imagination. As in Stanley Kubrick's film *The Shining* (1980), the secure world of a small family is suddenly invaded by the fearful reality of madness. Waves of blood wash out of a lift into a hotel lobby and, hoarsely, a boy monotonously chants "RED RUM, RED RUM" (pronounced: red ru:m) — an inversion of 'murder'; there are no longer any clear boundaries between hallucination and imagination, vision and reality.

In the parents' room (Ills 161, 162) everything is perfectly clear and completely harmonious. The bed is made and the pillows are plumped up. The perfect couple, whose identity is clear from the almost mirror-like similarity of the two sides, take up their predestined position. The densely interlocking weave of their relationship as partners, which culminates in this place of rest, is expressed not only by the material of the sheets and the pillowcase, but explicitly in the gently-flowing folds of the little marble sculptures corresponding to the drapery of the two 'Biedermeier' chests of drawers. These rudimentary items of historical furniture, redolent of a comfortable, ordered, middle-class world, are set against quasi-figurative visual works. These marble sculptures are no more than material shields for nude figures, to be seen only from the back. The flowing marble folds appear to be created, as if to conceal nothing and to reveal the transparent historicity of the former, showing them up as outdated objects that once implied status but are now faded and at best nostalgic.

The small white pillow, neatly embroidered with 'I love you' mocks this worthy, domestic world with its naive, faithfully trusting 'Je t'aime.' Art, albeit disciplined, enters this simple, ordered world in the form of childish games with train sets, early musical encounters with a xylophone, basic exercises in embroidering words; otherwise, it is domesticated and tamed in the form of crafted sculptural miniatures that illusionally master the material used.

163 *Red Room (Child)*, 1994
wood,metal, thread, glass, 83 × 139 × 108 in.

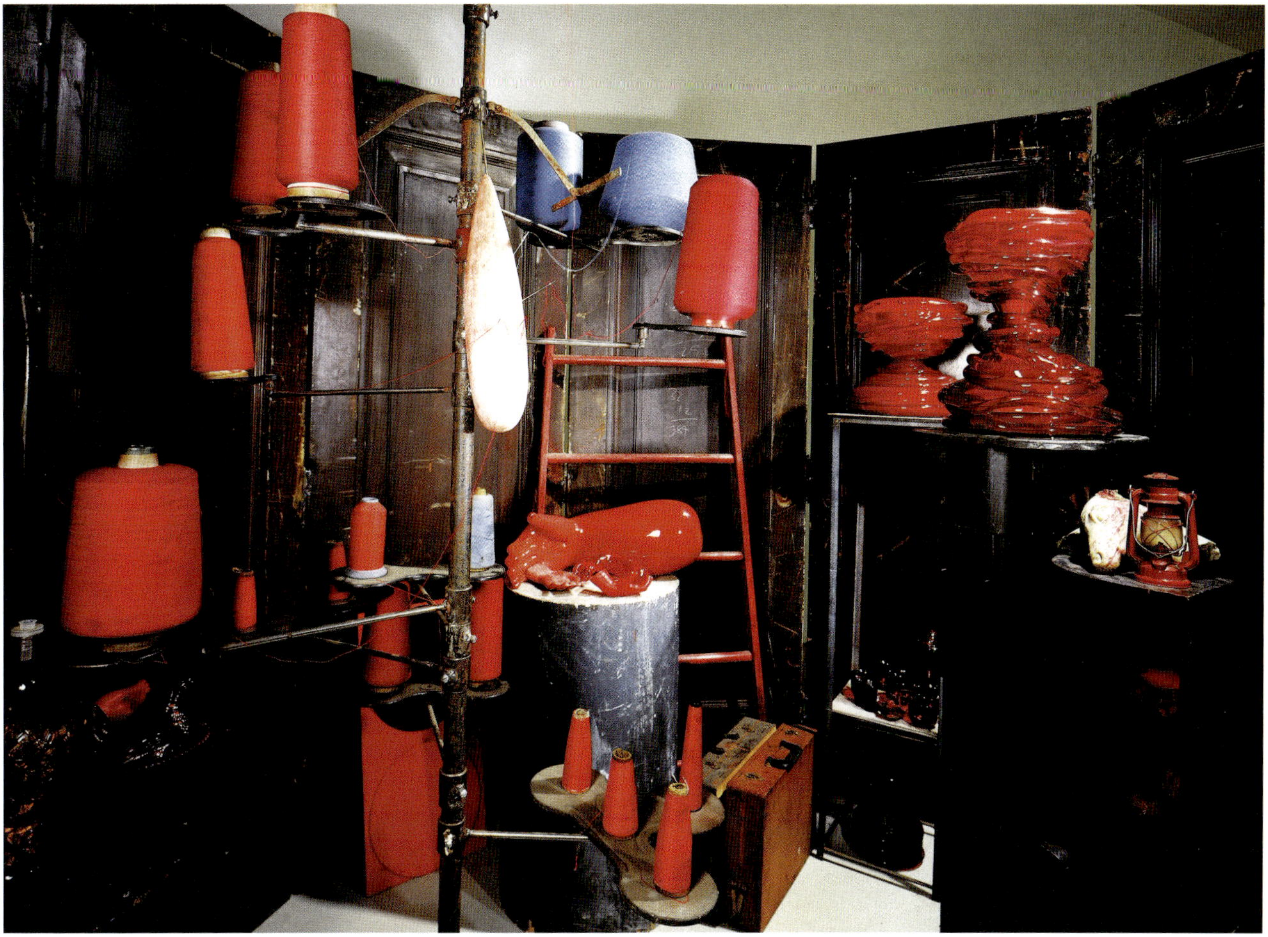

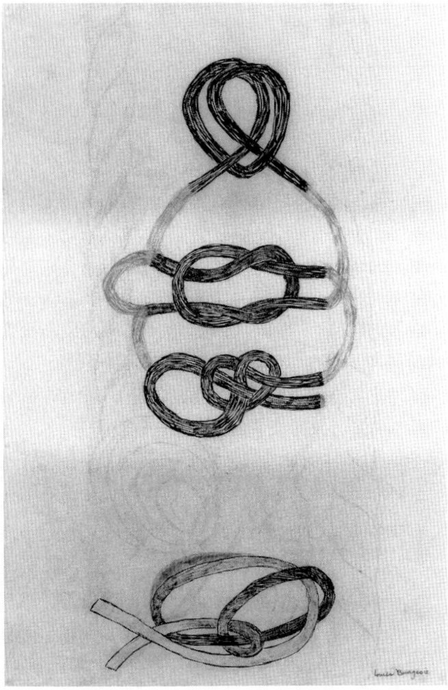

164 Untitled, 1950
ink and charcoal on paper, 22 × 15 in.

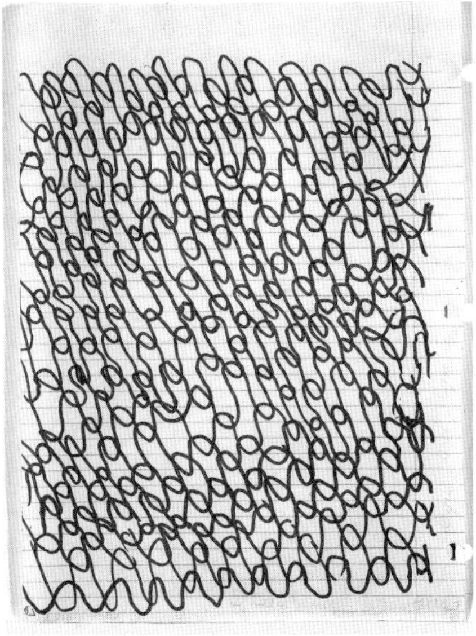

165 *Le Cauchemar de Hayter*, 1995
ink on lined paper, 11 × $8\frac{1}{4}$ in.

However, the glass 'Lair' is hanging like a species of threatening foreign body in the space. Its abstract form can accommodate every imaginable projection, desire, hope, idea or entertaining or unsettling fantasy. This figuratively unidentifiable object, which seems like an organic incarnation of wholly free, unrestricted creative intent, incubates unconventional artistic concepts and ideas. In the end, it reveals the mirror (Ill. 162) as an empty, merely illustrative, self-deceiving reflection of the drama of life, a *fata morgana* of knowledge laden with props, a feeble, an excerpted, simplistic, and arbitrary copy of reality.

If the smoothed-out sheet is concealing chimeras of hidden desire, lust, and sensual pleasure; if its dense weave is imbued with the complexities of an unrestrained, unbridled imagination; if a solid warp and weft of complicity knots together this sheltered world of conventional, traditional, acceptable sentiments; then the thin, breakable thread in the child's room reveals the unfinished process of creative construction, a loosely-structured world of possibilities.

The fine threads of life break away from over-large spools and are sewn onto unstructured, undeveloped, as yet unborn forms. Each spool may play its part in the endless process of forming. Thread or yarn has long been associated with one of the oldest metaphors in Western culture for the pattern of our lives (Ill. 164). Goddesses like the Roman Fates have spun, turned, and cut the thread, holding a person's predestined lifespan in their hands. In the thread-like structures in the biological cells that encode our lives and their genetic structure, the thread of life still holds its own as we move into the twenty-first century, and the yarn from which the tissue of narrative is woven will never break (Ill. 165).

X. VISIONS FOR A NON-CONCEPTUALIZED THINKING IN IMAGES

That impulse toward the formation of metaphors, that fundamental impulse of man, which we cannot reason away for one moment — for thereby we should reason away man himself — is in truth not defeated, nor even subdued by the fact that out of its evaporated products, the ideas, a regular and rigid new world has been built as a stronghold for it. This impulse seeks for itself a new realm of action and another riverbed, and finds it in Mythos and more generally in Art.

Friedrich Nietzsche, 'On Truth and Lying in an Ultra-moral Sense', 1873

[...] because of the symbolic quality of the thing. I worked with found objects, and I found a magic overtone in them.
What counts, our whole purpose, is to try to understand, what we are about, to scrutinize ourselves. Art is an aid to this.[86]

Louise Bourgeois, 1988

Biological evolution is a process of growing diversity. Cultural evolution is a process of collection.

Steven Jay Gould, palaeontologist, 1998

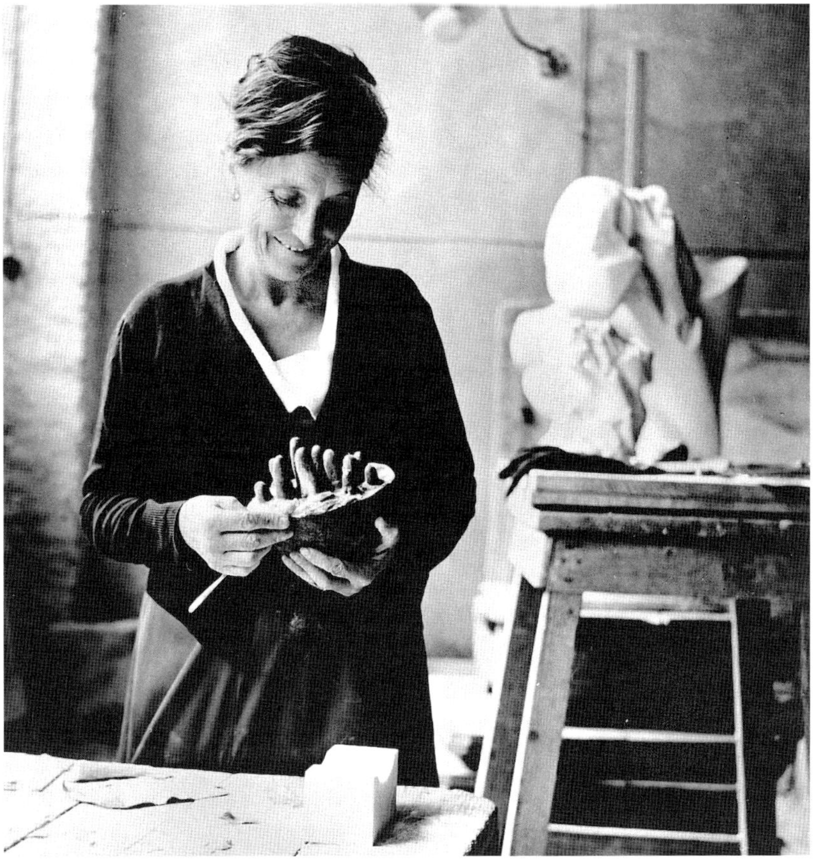

166 Louise looking at *Germinal*, 1967

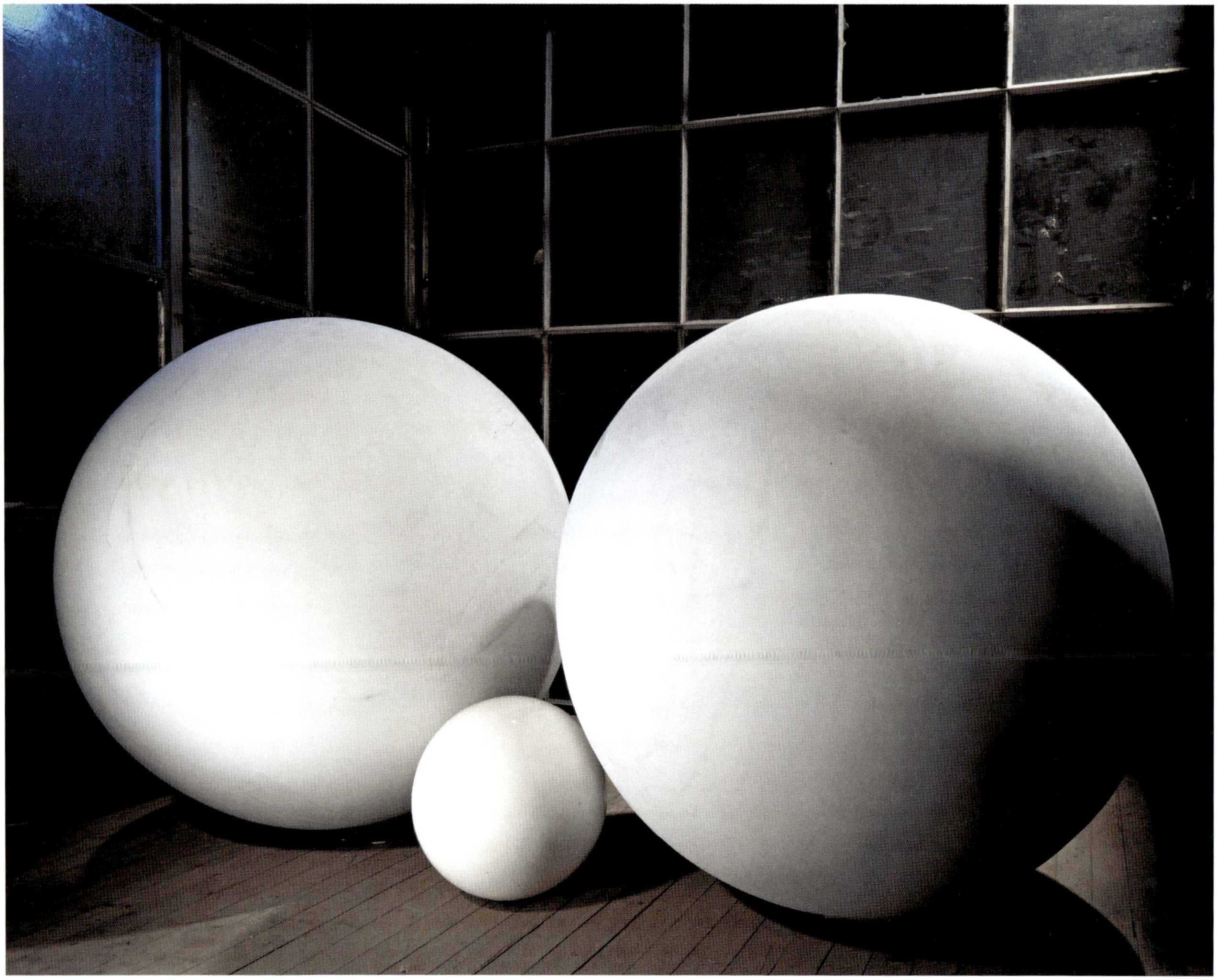

167 *Detail of Cell (Three White Marble Spheres)*, 1993
steel, glass, marble, mirror, 84 × 84 × 84 in.

After the profundity of *Pass*, the flightiness of *Femme volage*, the vulnerability of *Female Portrait*, and the rutting of *She-Fox*, after unintelligible and incomprehensible sculptural forms that resist definition and remain indeterminate, like the multiformed *Lairs*, *Spirals* and *Nature Studies*, in the last decade of the twentieth century Louise Bourgeois confronts us with works that point towards a wholly new sculptural approach. These works are characterized by an enormous stylistically disparate, often opposite, multiplicity and thematic diversity, which is not conducive to comparison of one with the other. Despite the artist's intention from the early days of her career to subvert the categorization of her works as figurative or abstract, it is possible to place her latest, self-contained, individual sculptural objects, the *Cells*, within the tradition of Western sculpture — the tradition which has produced works of the grandeur of *Laocöon*, Michelangelo's *David*, and Bernini's *The Ecstasy of St. Theresa*. However, in the *Cells*, Louise Bourgeois has also developed a sculptural system that combines the most modern narrative structures with a pictorial form of thinking in images, — a paradigmatic change — that, at the end of the twentieth century, generates effects which go far beyond the fine arts and are, these days, being developed and propagated with an appealing grandeur by the mass media. For example, popular commercially-produced

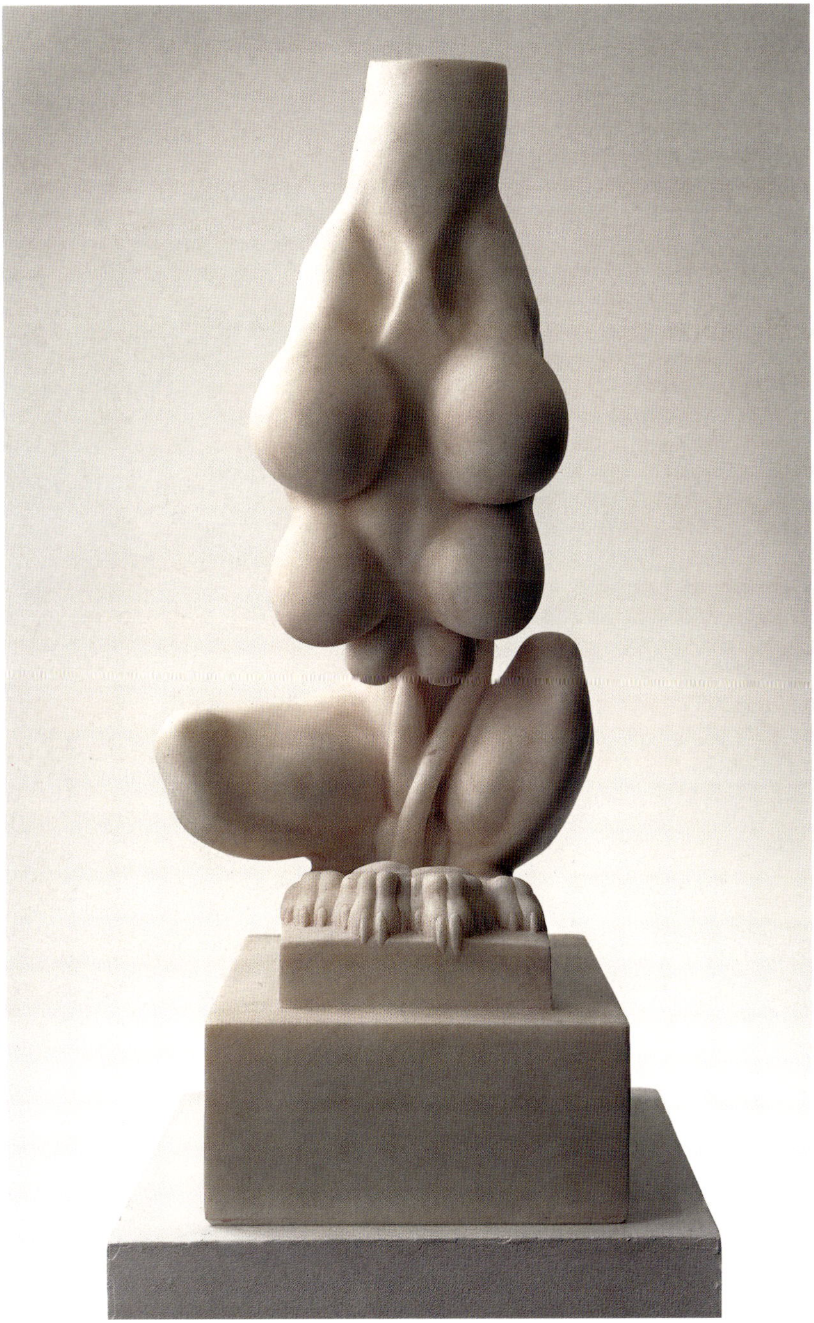

168 *Nature Study*, 1984–94
pink marble, 34 1/2 × 17 1/2 × 15 in.

feature films — particularly those made in Hollywood — represent new modes of pictography which are evidently inspired by highly conceptual and creative aspirations.

A constantly changing contextual reality — continuously stimulating new impressions, sentiments, hopes and desires — that is conveyed no longer by the text but through the image, raises the question of how ideas, values and concepts can today be mediated "rhetorically" (in a wholly metaphorical

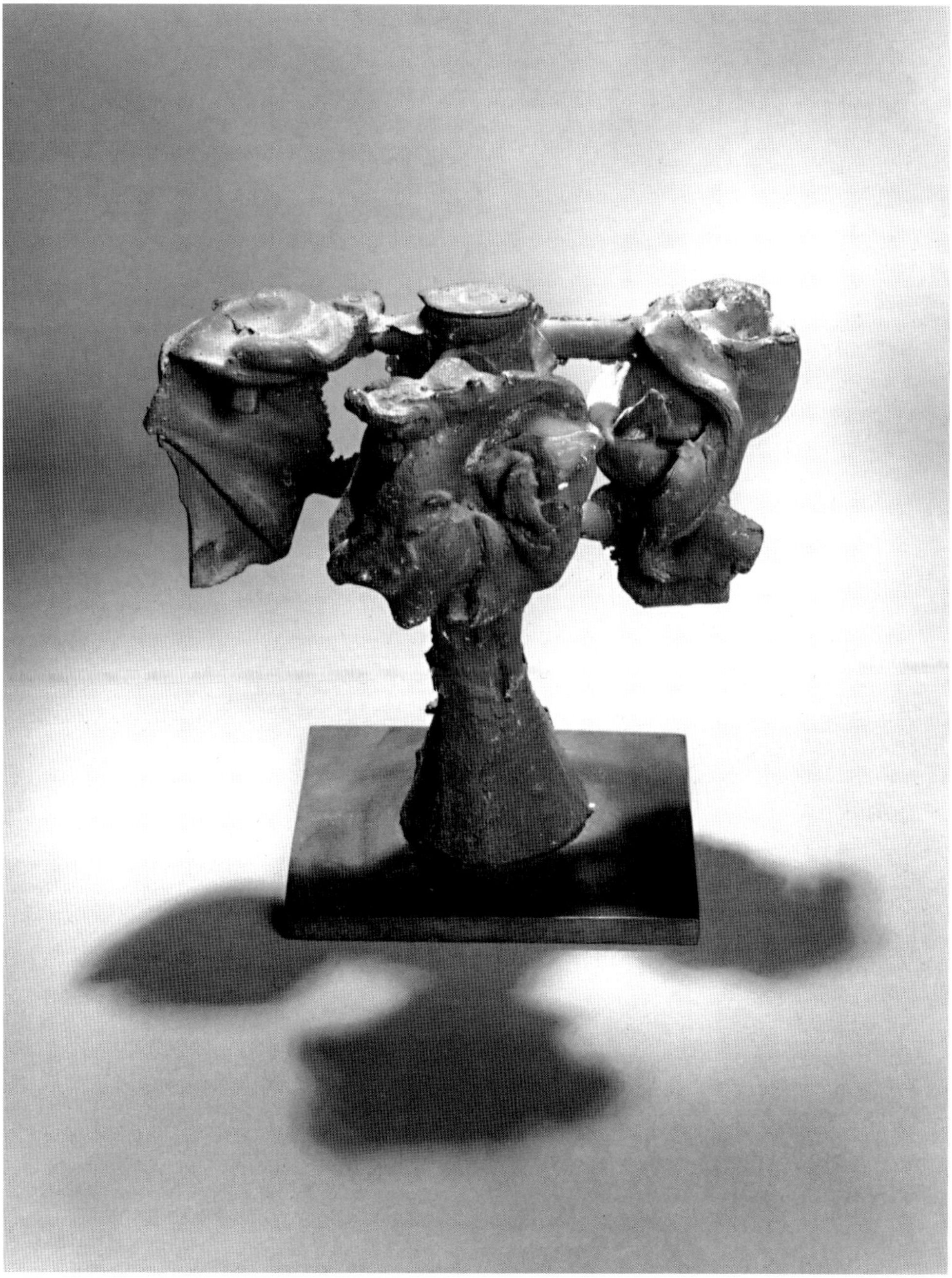

169 *Three Roses*, 1968
bronze, 7 × 5 × 7 in.

sense) to a creatively involved public. How is it possible today to tell stories cross-culturally and globally with conviction? Just how are events from the past recreated, and visions for the future developed?

The intellect today, already overtaxed by variety and fragmented reality, is being presented in the countless variety of media with actual links that in turn help to form opinions and to establish identities. Pictures and sequences of pictures from the living world around us assist the individual in search of his identity to unravel reality and not to fall victim to the illusoriness of imagination. In this pictorial world, where not only words or signs act as mediators but where 'things' themselves from the living world around us also take on their own meaning, visual metaphors supply a pictorial charge of fatally heterogeneous elements. Being placed in an everyday context these metaphors may become factors of interference and can shatter the customary equilibrium that unquestioningly accepts the mediated image effectively as the virtually unadorned fact. Since the metaphor not only pervades the world of poetic invention but is also — as our excursion into biological cell-theory has literally shown — rooted in the scientific and theoretical language, it can lay claim to a certain fundamental, unfettered emancipation.

The metaphor, nomadic and free, inhabits a niche in the no-man's land between image and concept. It does not feel comfortable in a disciplined, calculated world of digested experiences. Indeed it kicks against the traces of conceptual, clearly-defined world-view, and points towards the unsayable. The metaphor gives a face to what is otherwise indifferent and nameless. And it is the inexactitude of the metaphor, as Hans Blumenberg writes in one of his essays, 'Metaphorology,' that "corresponds to the frequently impressive highest levels of abstraction of notions such as 'existence,' 'history' and 'the world' which have not ceased to impress us. However, the metaphor preserves the riches of its origins which abstraction must disown." The power of the metaphor to touch and move us lies in its many-layered iridescence: 'you can't see the forest for the trees' has become an **absolute** metaphor for the world which, according to Blumenberg, "is as unable to separate into qualities and quantities as the aforementioned wood into trees. However, this is the same wood in which one, in accordance with Descartes's metaphor, loses one's way and must decide on a *morale par provision* (provisional moral), because one has no overview of the situation."[87]

The metaphor appropriates, refutes, and convinces by means of suggestion, and reveals, in its use of the context it exposes the deception of a clearly unattainable unambiguity; it virtually relieves the circumstantial context of its availability as a discursive argument. Louise Bourgeois understood and understands the emotional mechanisms by which the metaphor functions: "We talk about a need to express some very deep emotion. Then we talk about realization. Realization doesn't have to do with strategy. It has to do with a hit-or-miss process."[88] Pictorial thinking circumvents language directed towards objective unambiguity. The metaphor of the 'wood' becomes poetic suggestion if the aesthetic evidence is based on the fact that everyone has seen without being able to put it into words. In the inter-subjective agreement that derives from a well-chosen image, carrying it further although without being able to substantiate the source of its impact, the metaphor qualifies as aesthetic, and thus provides the ultimate, totally disinhibiting license for applied ambiguity.

The plea for a linguistically unambiguous hold on the world begins with the sentence: "The world is all that is the case." As early as 1912 Ludwig Wittgenstein, in his *Tractatus Logico-Philosophicus,* put forward the idea that there is a limit to the expression of thoughts through language and that transgressing this limit only leads to meaningless statements. All those cases whose size, extent, and content coincide with what may be experienced but may not be reported elude substantiation and definition through language. The *Cells* put Wittgenstein's case-law to the test and invert the dry claims of the statutory world, turning certainty into a glowing world of imaginative potential: 'All that is the case is the world.' (inversion by the authors). If, in the last sentence of the *Tractatus,* Wittgenstein draws the logical conclusion from his carefully constructed demonstration of the questionable nature of linguistic certainty — "What we cannot speak about we must pass over in silence" — then Louise Bourgeois imbues her own visual representations of existential experiences, such as suffering, being trapped, needing protection, tenderness, loneliness, sociability and the freedom of unleashed fantasy, with the justification of aesthetic evidence.

Wittgenstein himself took extralinguistic comprehension of situations into account when, shortly before the last line of the *Tractatus,* he admits: "There are, indeed, things that cannot be put into words. They *make themselves manifest.* They are what is mystical." Without wishing to ascribe to Louise

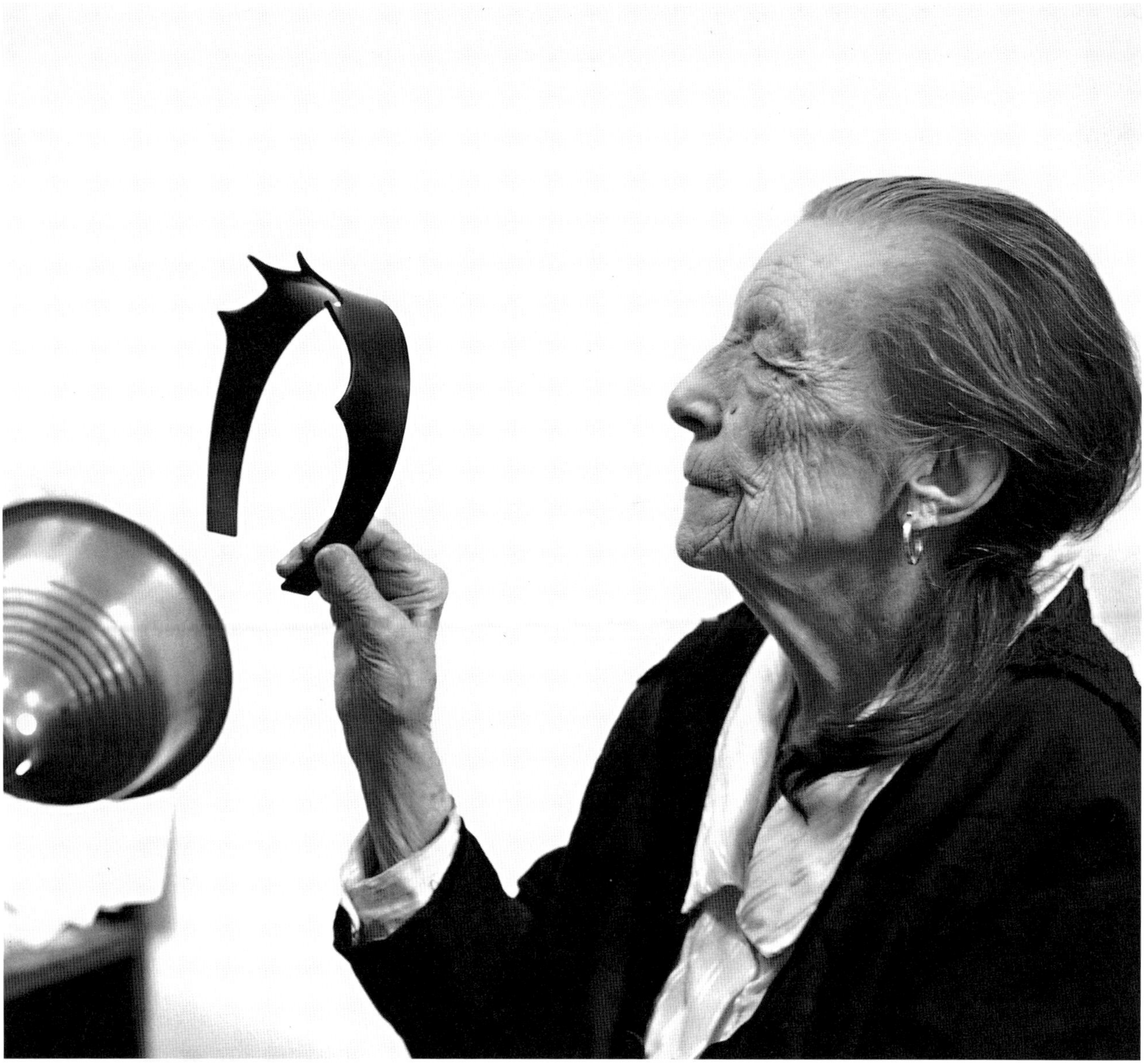

170 Louise Bourgeois, 1998

Bourgeois's utterly this-worldly creations of the late twentieth century a numinous otherworldliness and to categorize them with labels like 'mystical,' they nevertheless — silently — embody realms that resist exact definition, remaining paradoxical and ambiguous, mysterious and baffling, monstrous and dubious (Ill. 167).

Louise Bourgeois has seen artistic positions changing and developing for almost a century, and we owe her our thanks for giving us works that serve our critical understanding of the world. From an epistemological and artistic point of view these works strive towards a transformed, formed, reinterpreted actuality: not in an endeavor to duplicate the real world but in order to grasp the 'meaning of the world' — not merely to establish **that** the world is, but to explore **how** the world is.

CATALOGUE OF THE WORKS: THE *CELLS*, 1986–2008

Articulated Lair, 1986
Painted steel, rubber and stool
132 x 132 x 132 in.

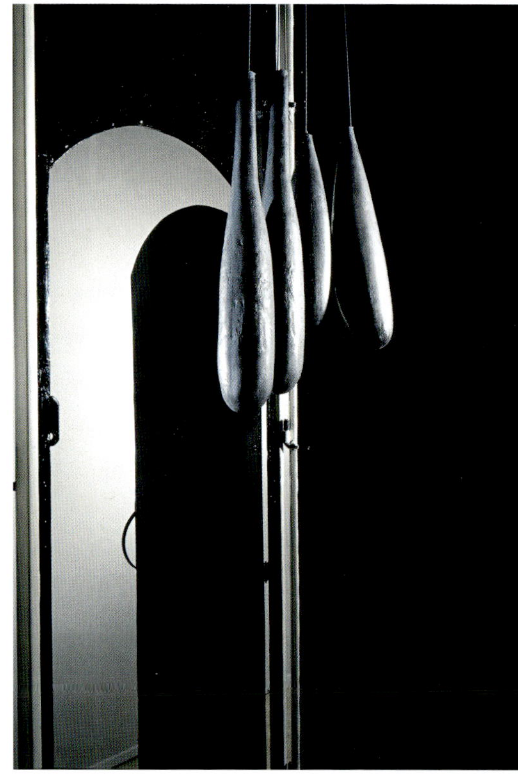

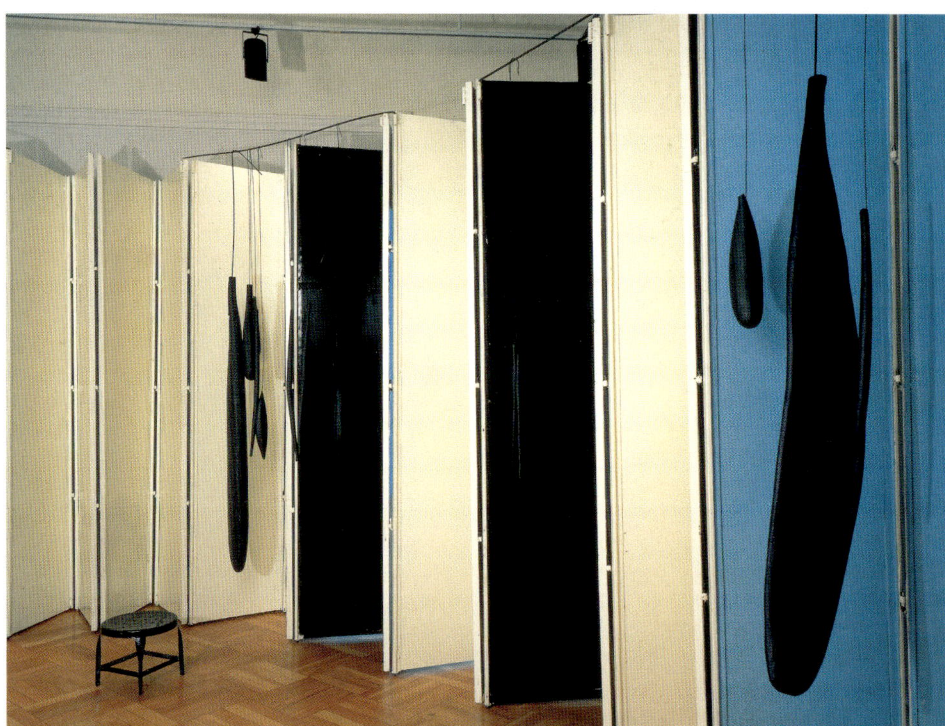

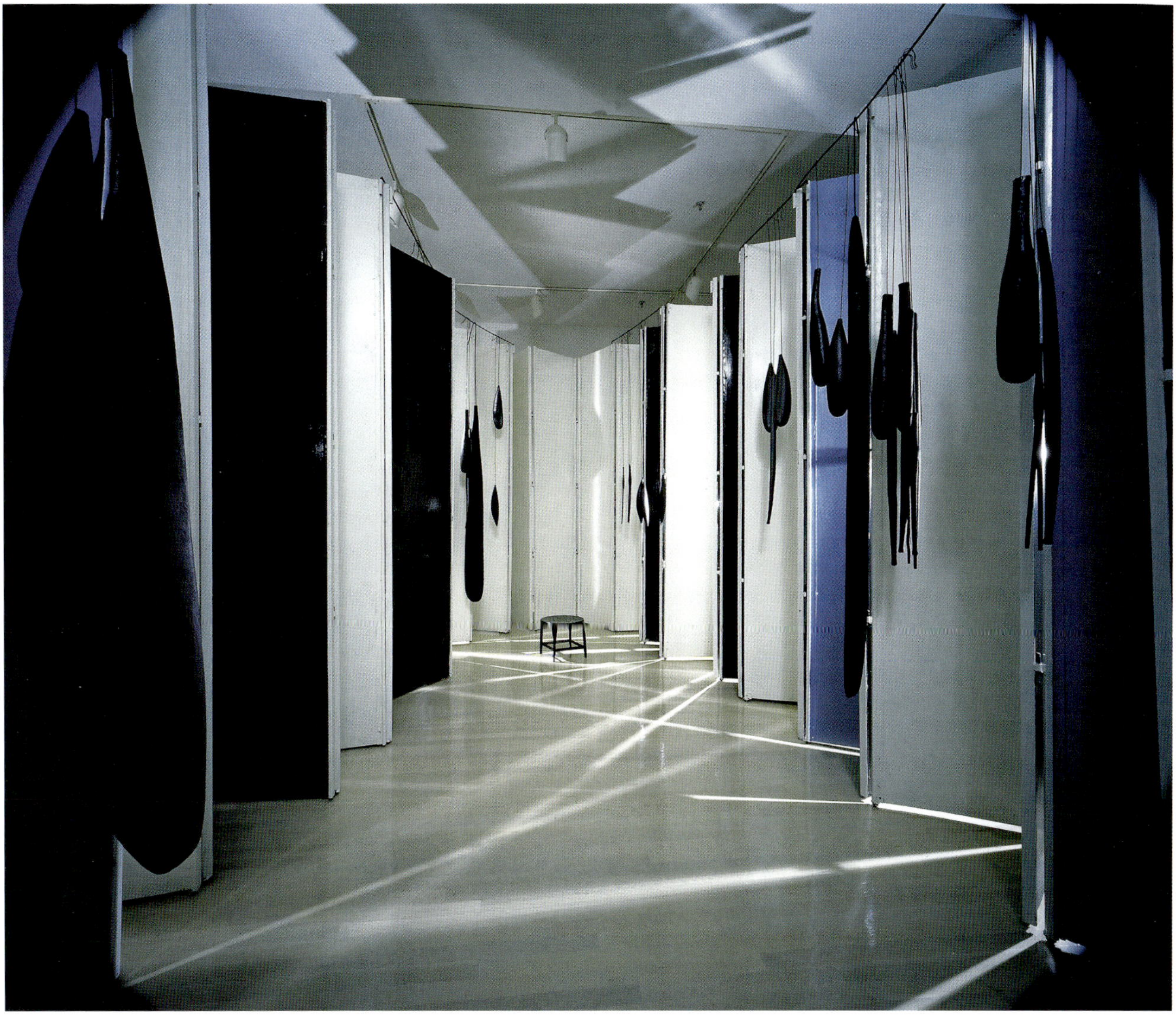

No Exit, 1989
Wood, painted metal and rubber
$82^{1}/_{2}$ x 84 x 96 in.

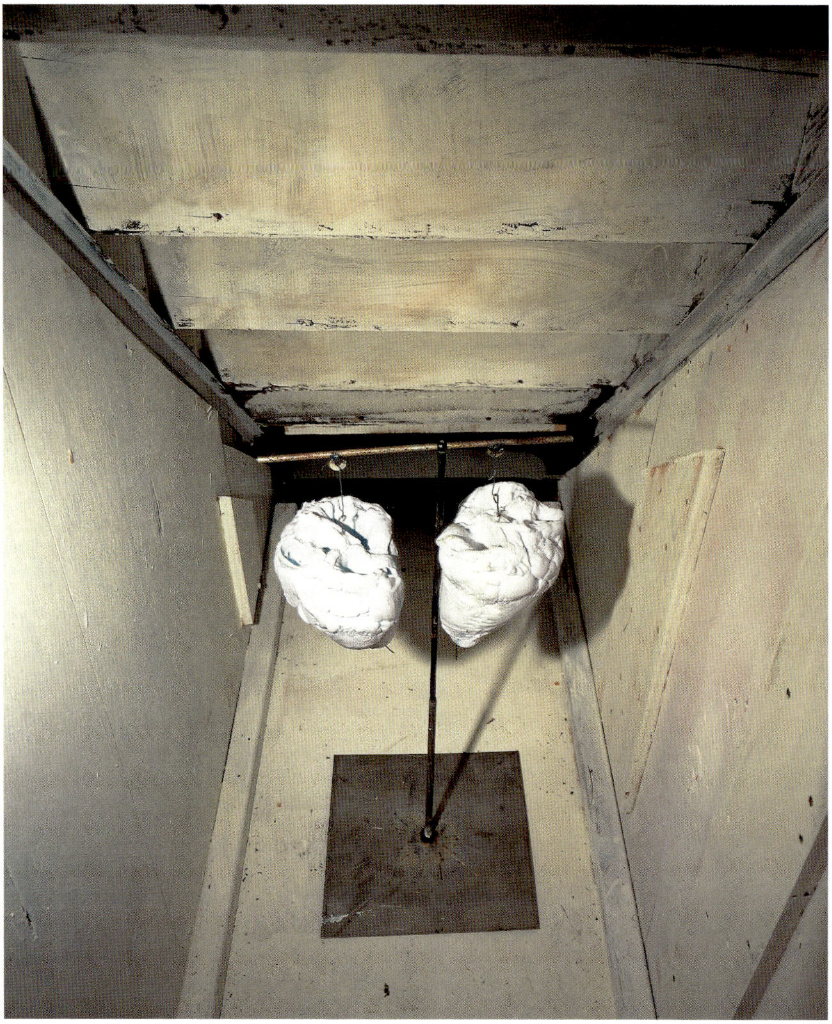

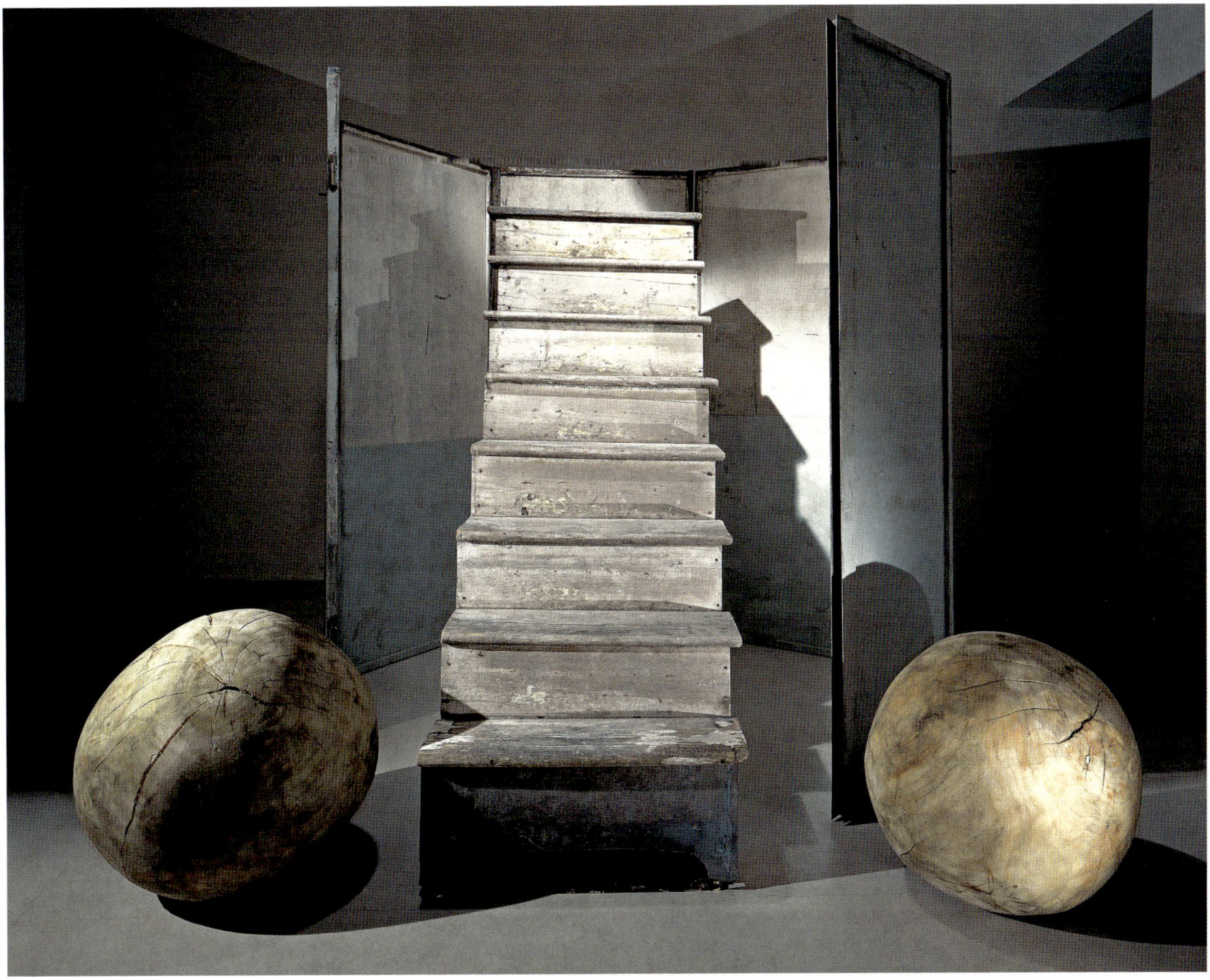

No Escape, 1989
Wood and metal
96 x 99 x 120 in.

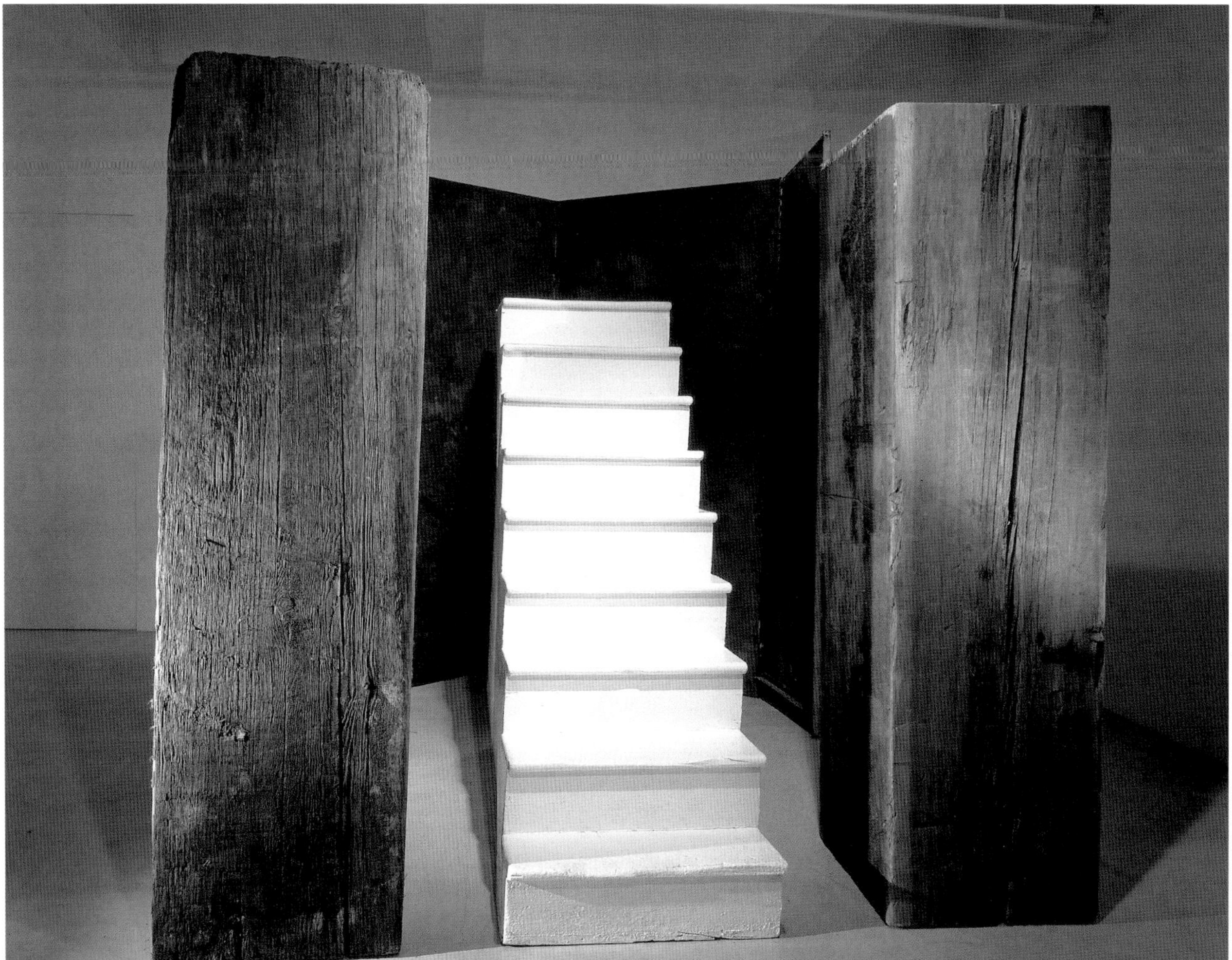

Gathering Wool, 1990
Metal, wood and mushrooms
96 x 156 x 180 in.

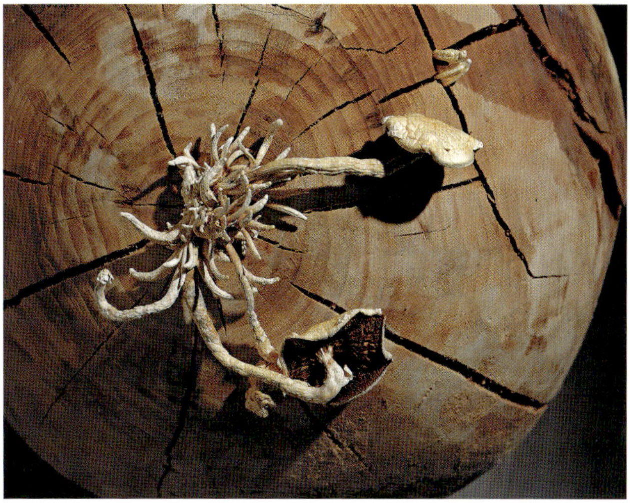

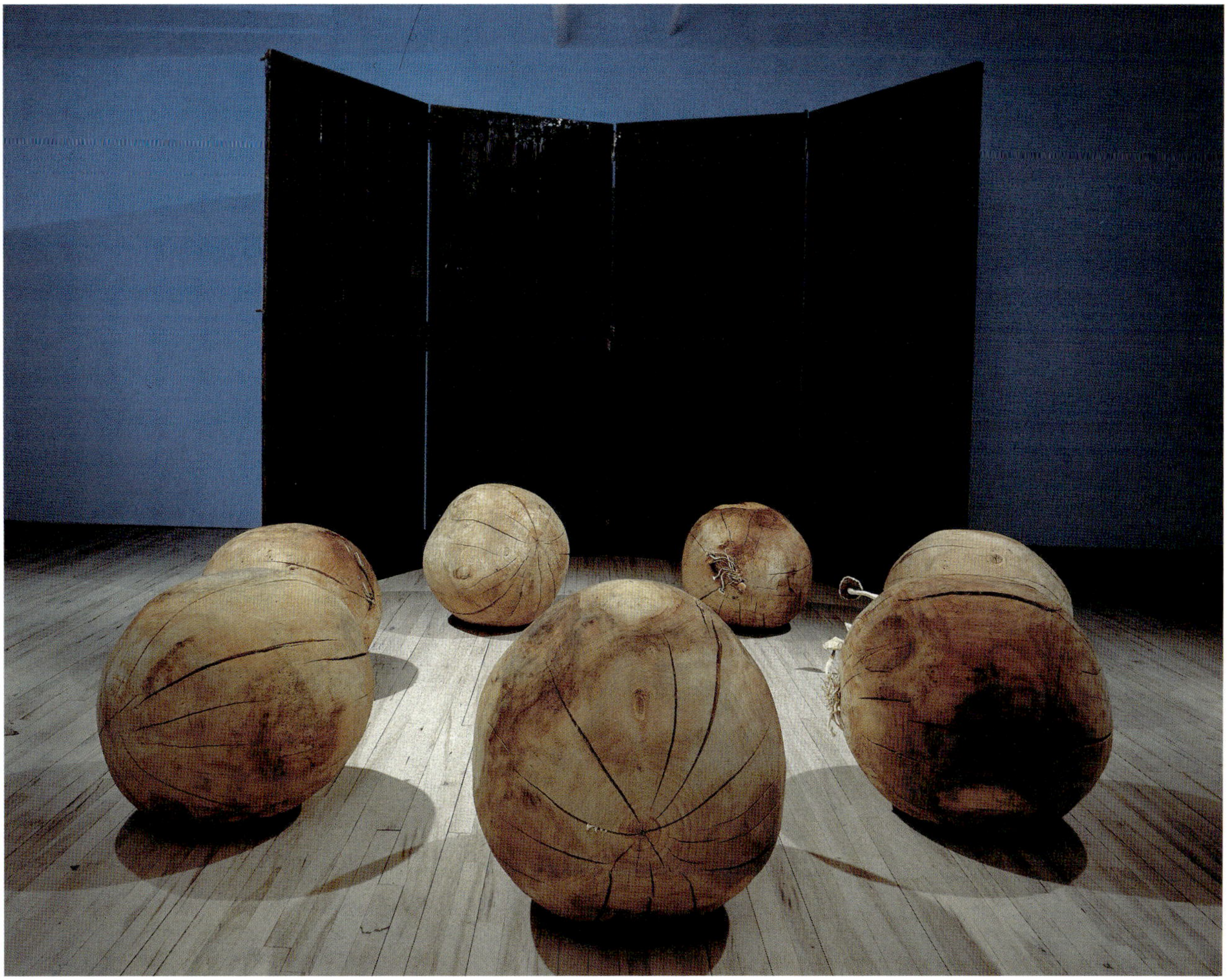

Cell (Eyes and Mirrors), 1989–93
Marble, mirrors, steel, glass
93 × 83 × 86 in.

Cell (Choisy), 1990–93
Marble, metal, glass
120½ × 67 × 95 in.

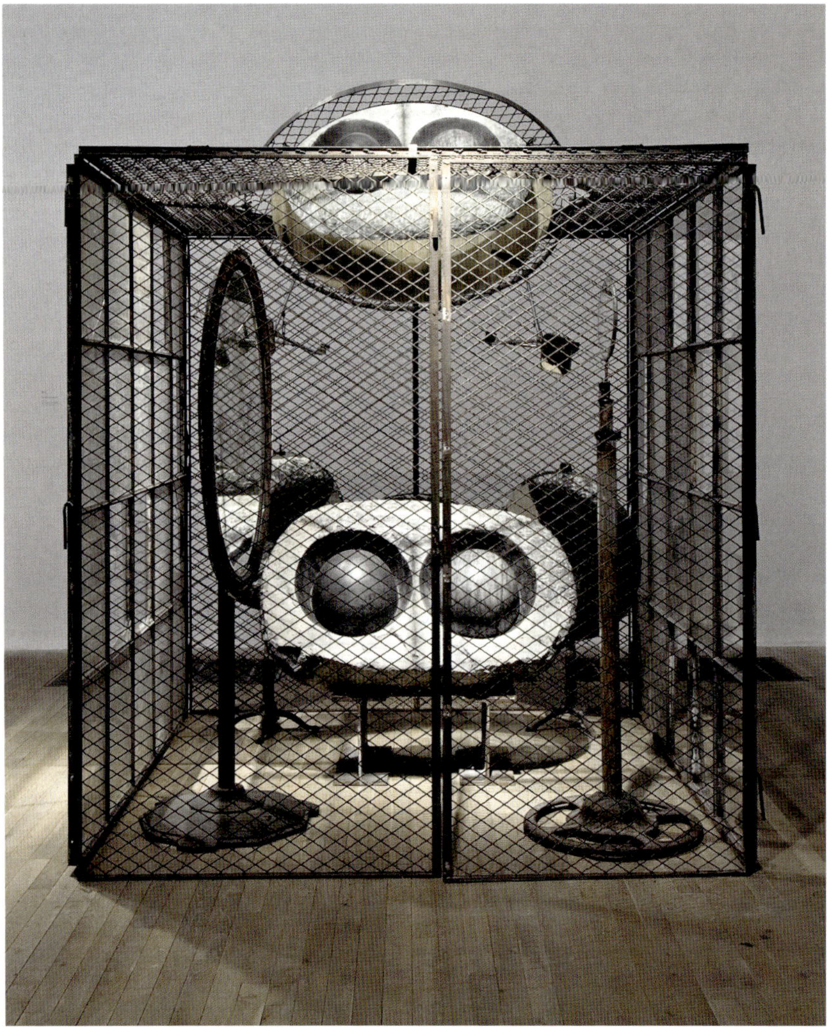

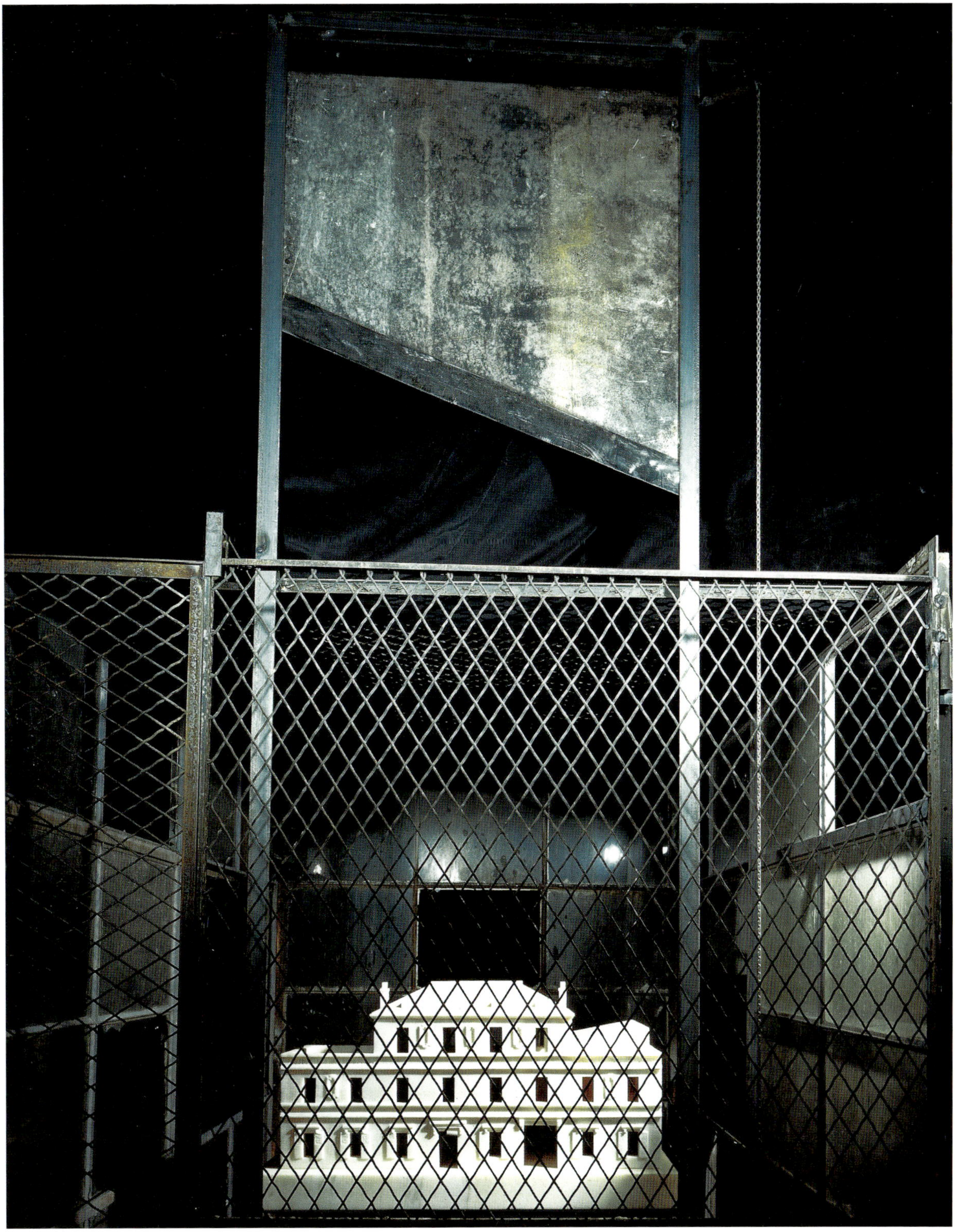

Cell (Choisy)

Cell (Glass Spheres and Hands), 1990–93
Glass, marble, wood, metal, fabric
86 × 86 × 83 in.

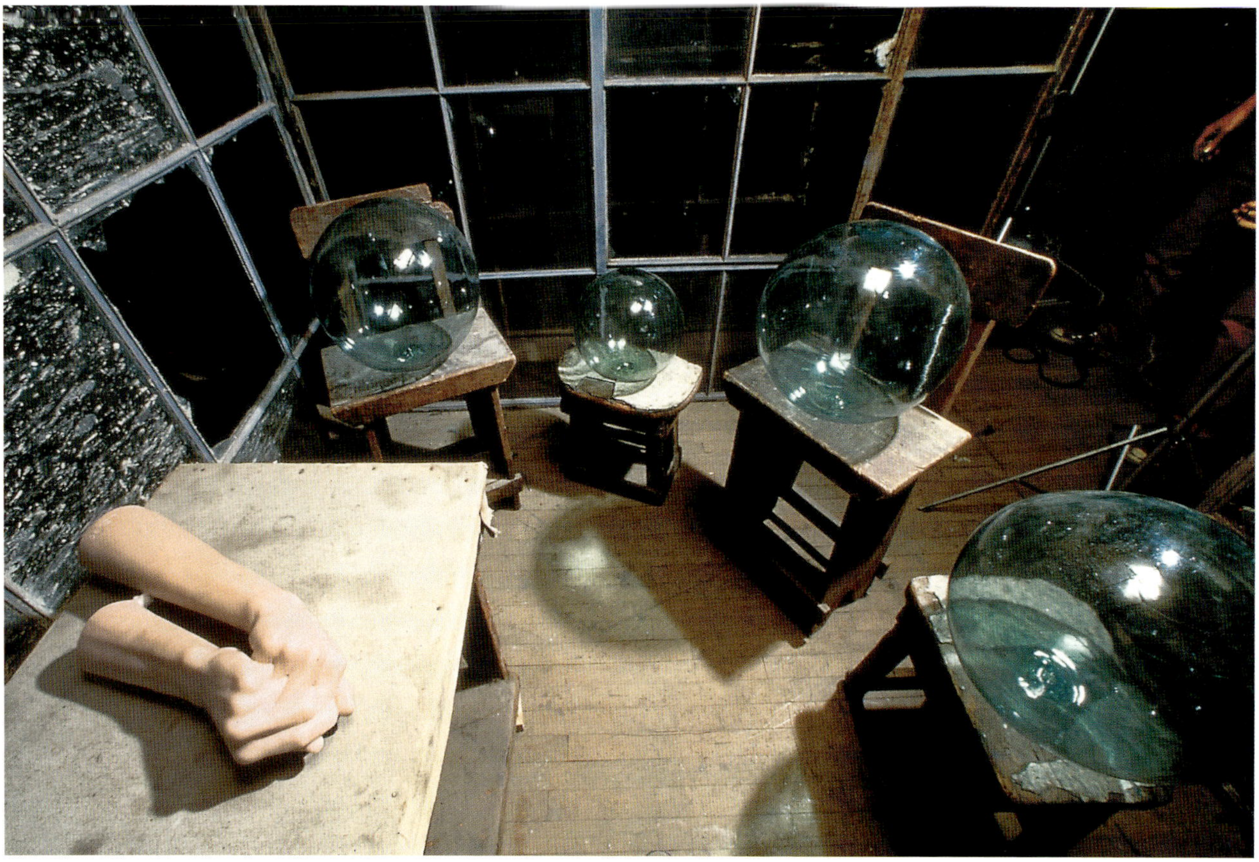

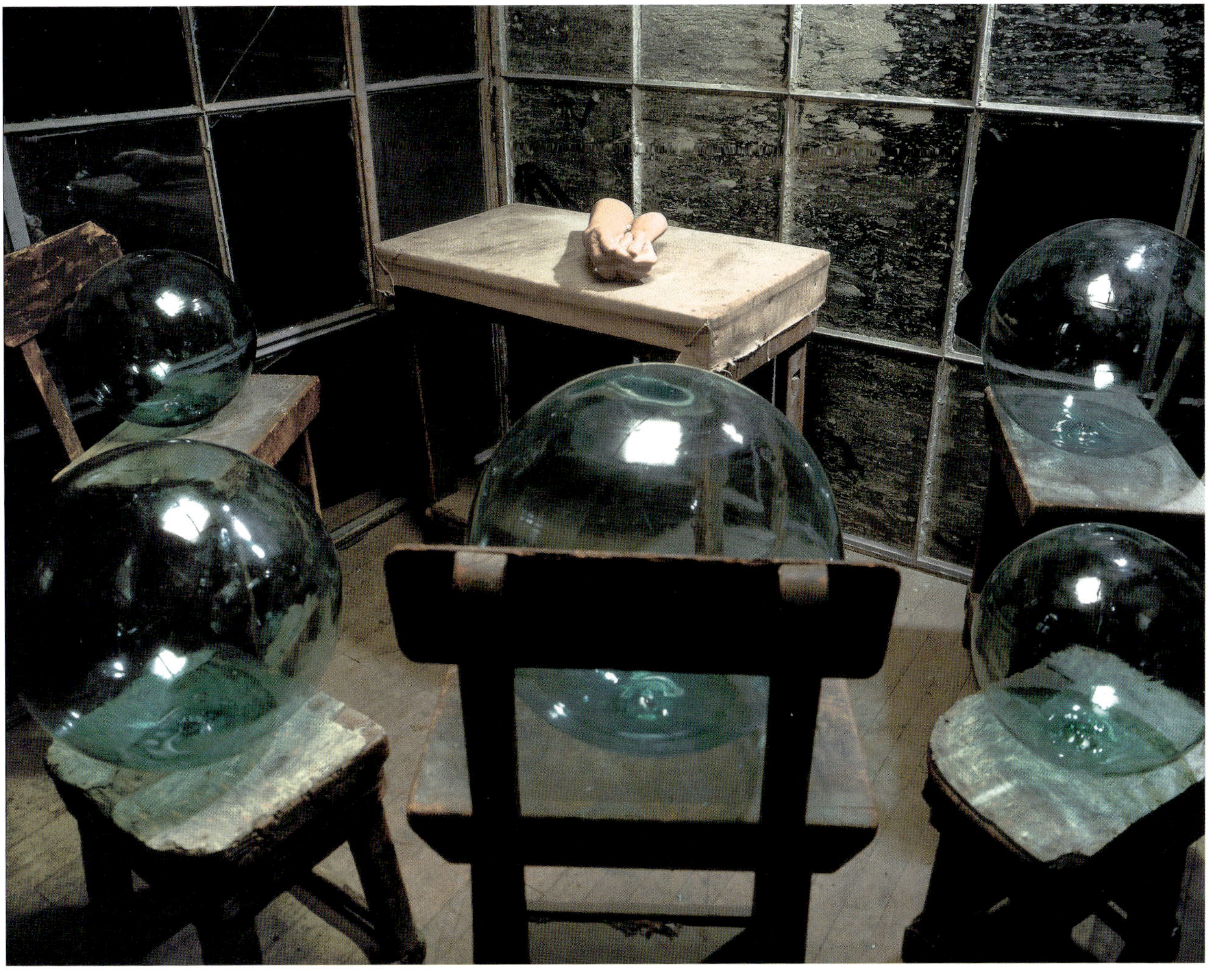

Cell (Glass Spheres and Hands)

Cell I, 1991
Painted wood, fabric, metal and glass
83 × 96 × 108 in.

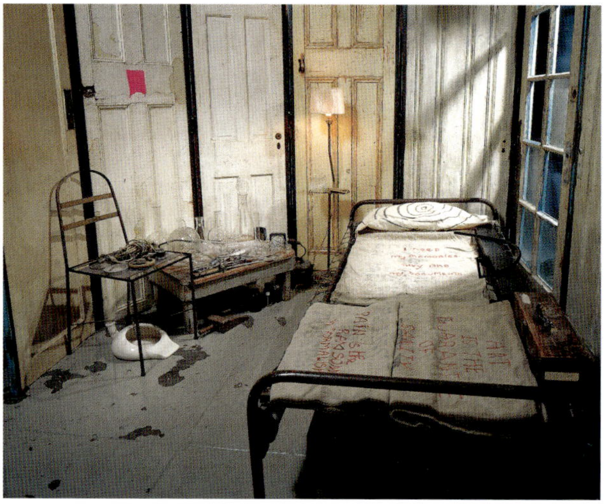

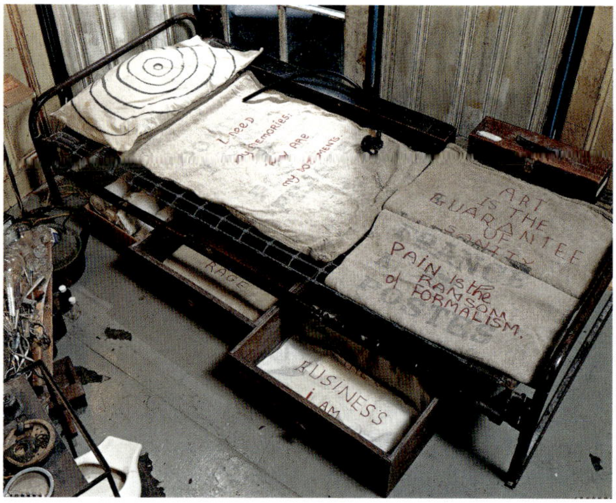

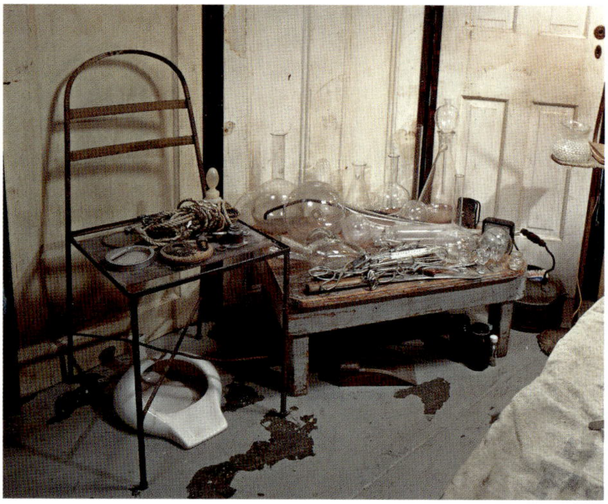

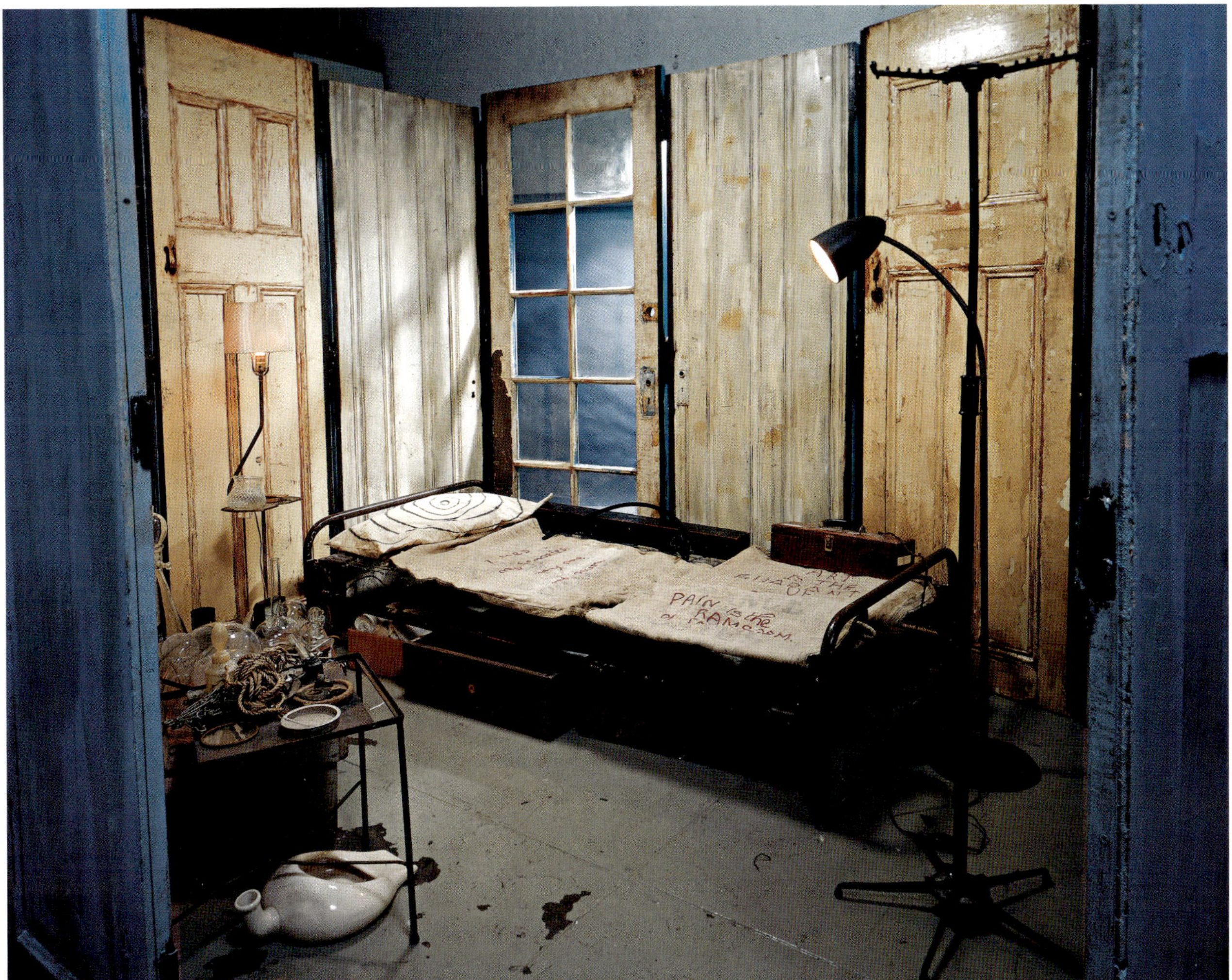

Cell I

Cell II, 1991
Painted wood, marble, steel, glass and mirror
83 × 60 × 60 in.

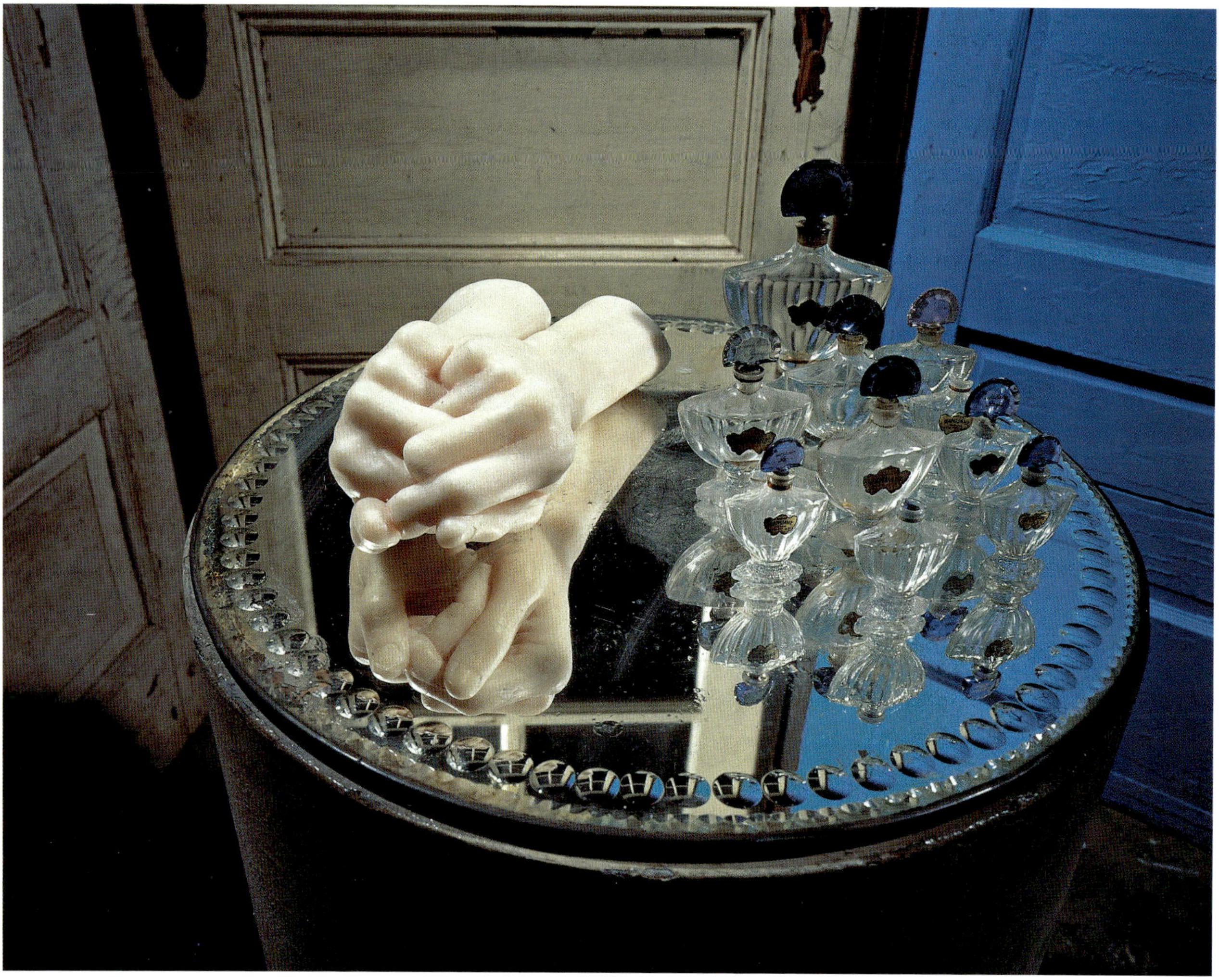

Cell IV, 1991
Painted wood, marble and steel
82 × 84 × 84 in.

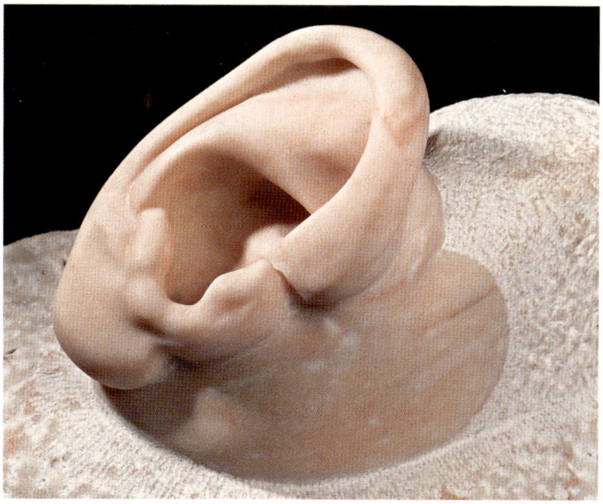

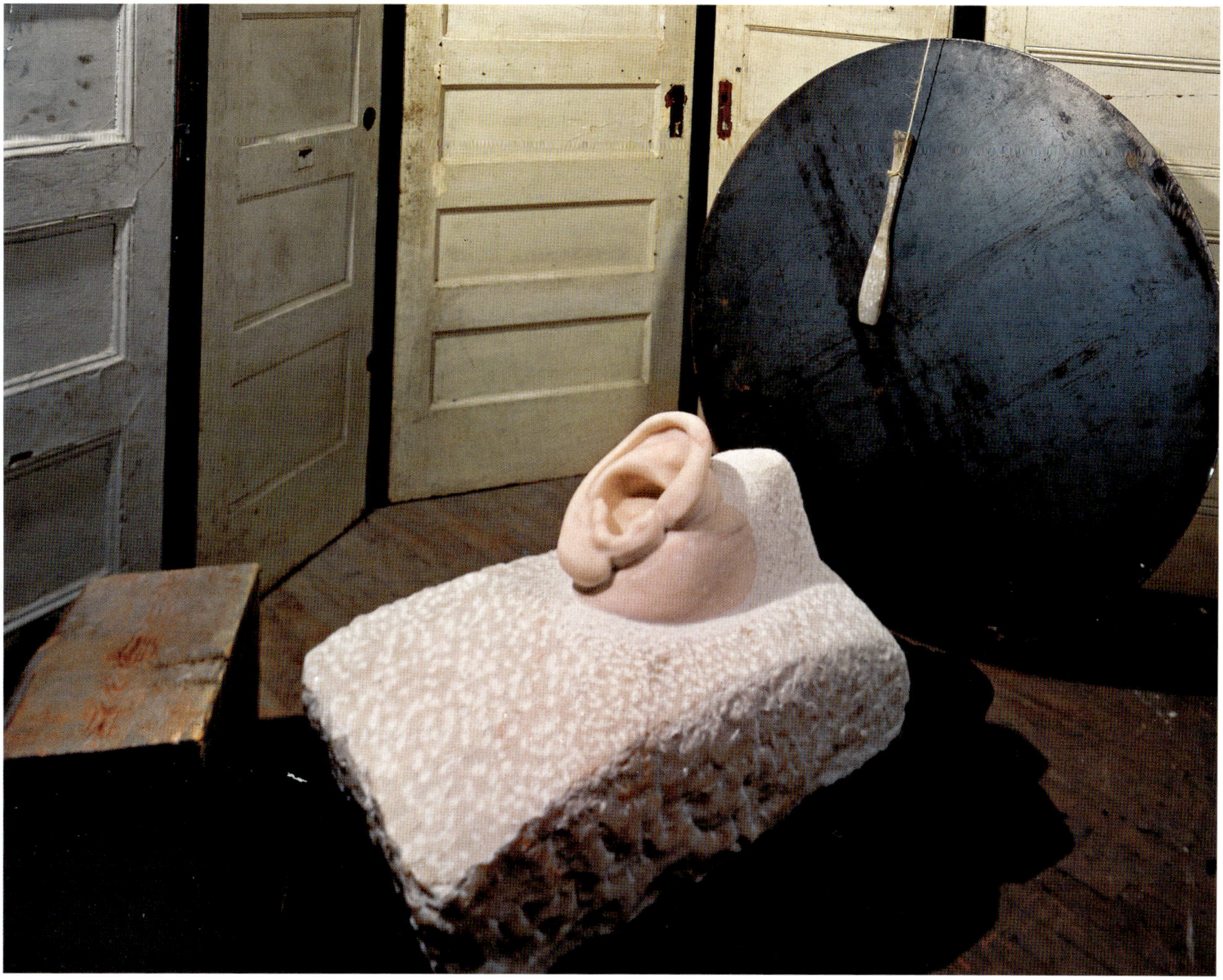

Cell III, 1991
Painted wood, painted metal, marble, steel and glass
111 × 130½ × 165⅛ in.

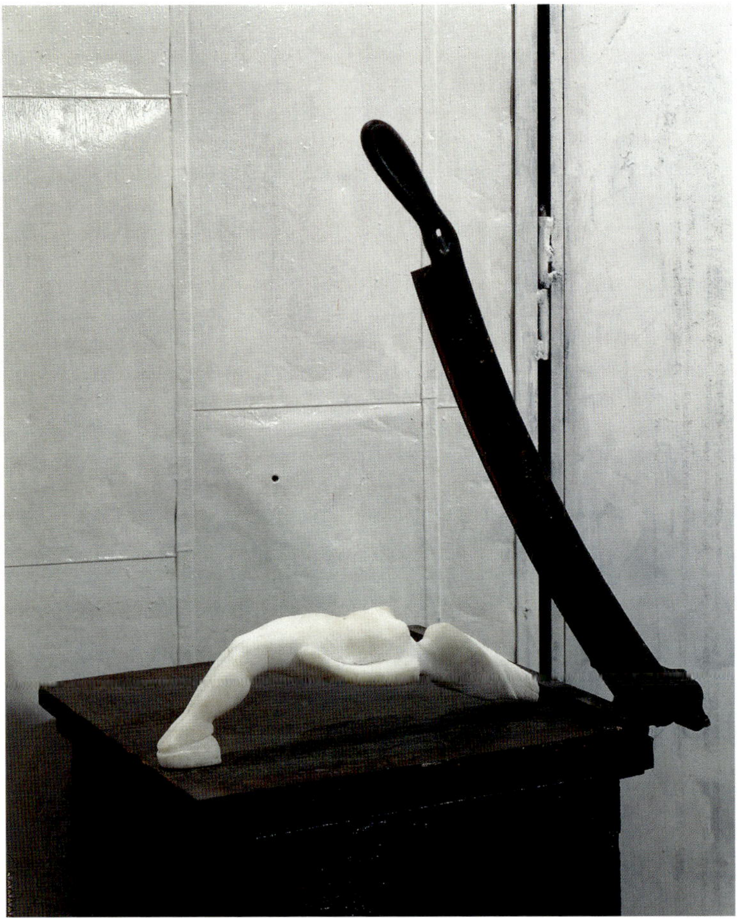

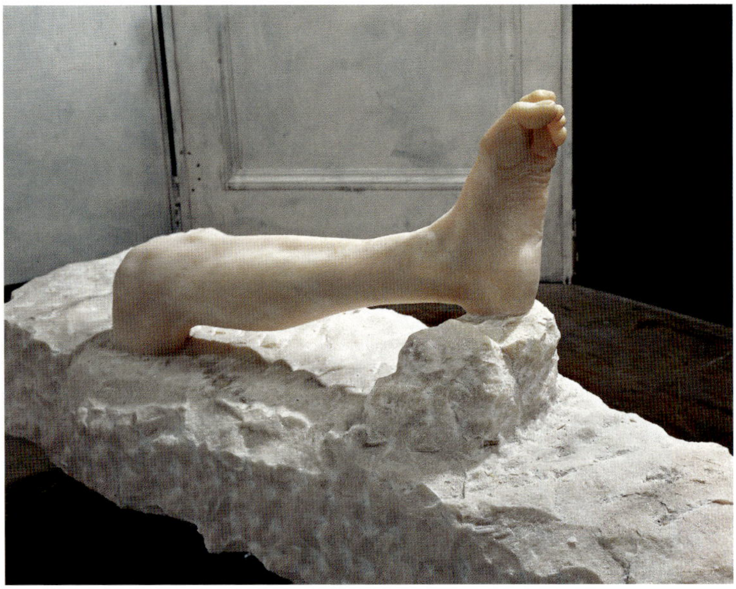

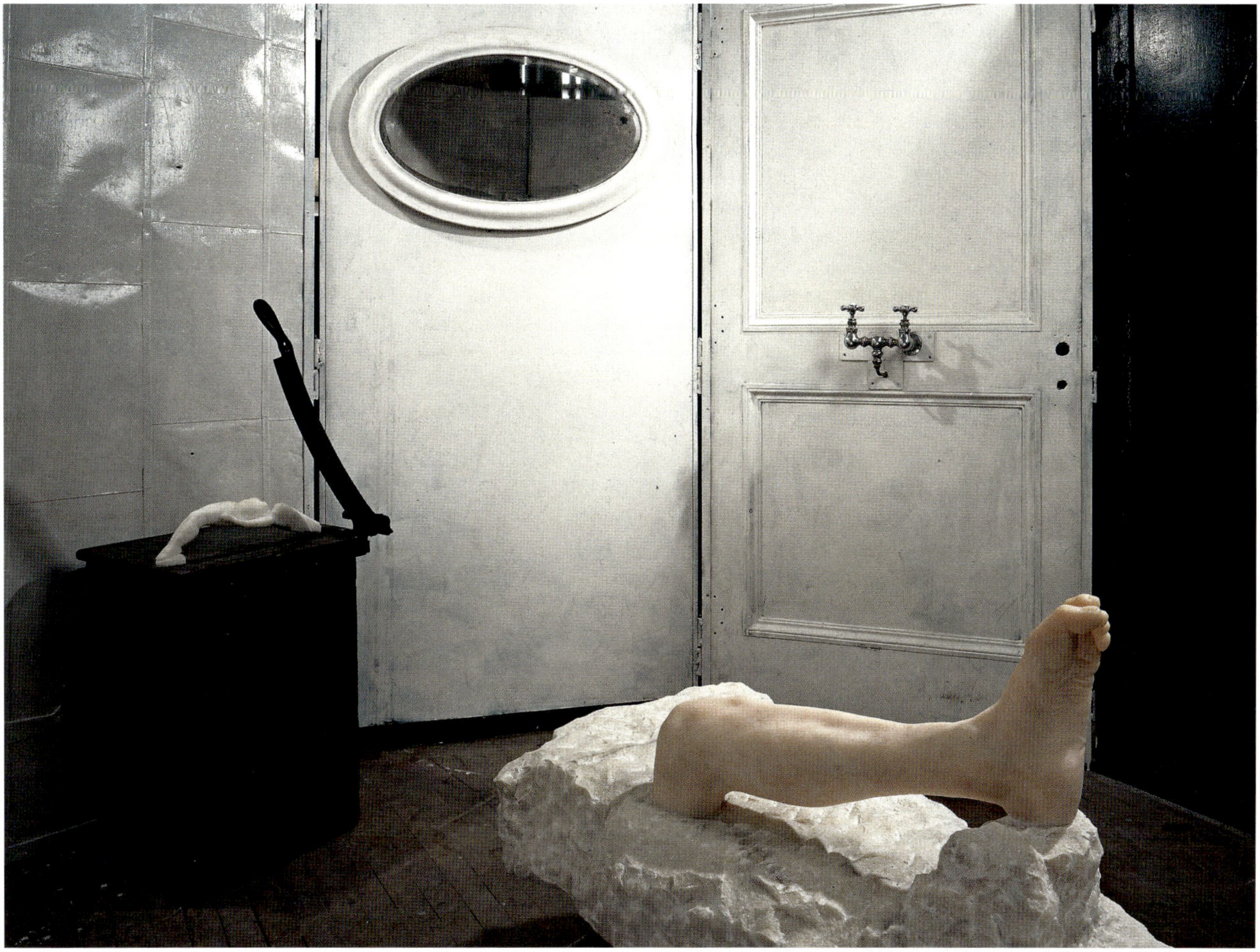

Cell V, 1991
Painted wood, wood, and glass
92 × 72 × 72 in.

Cell VI, 1991
Painted wood and metal
63 × 45 × 45 in.

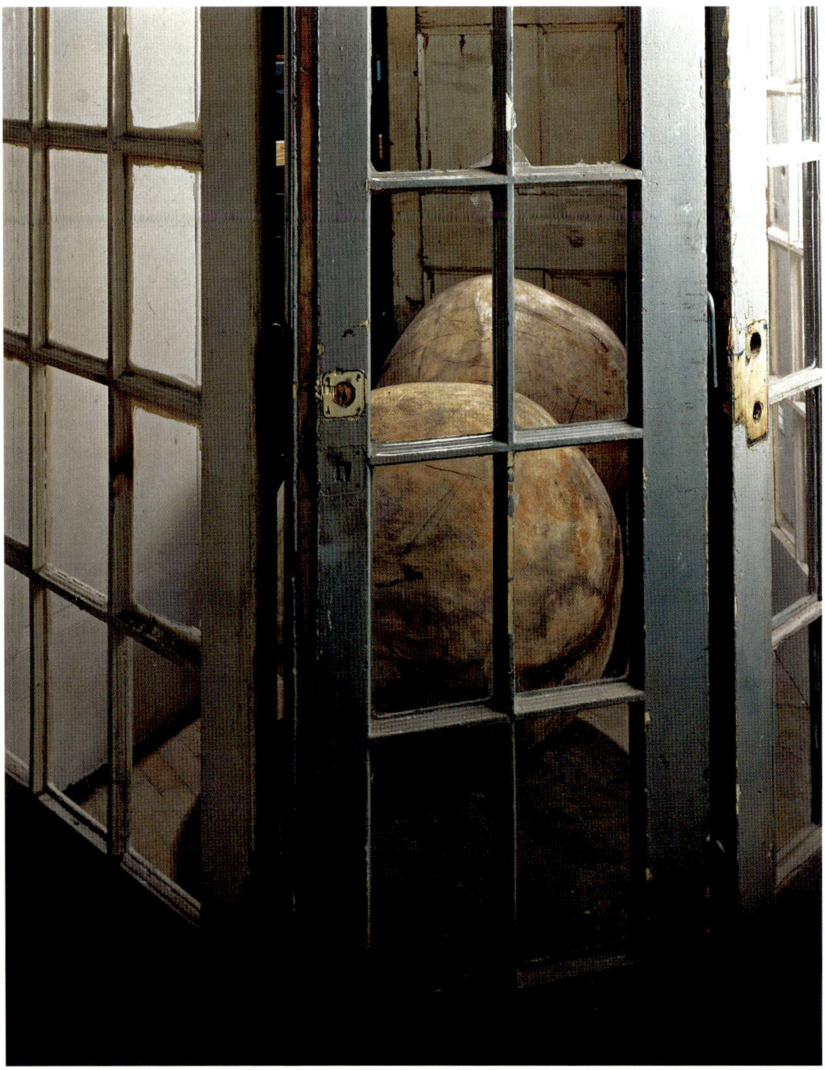

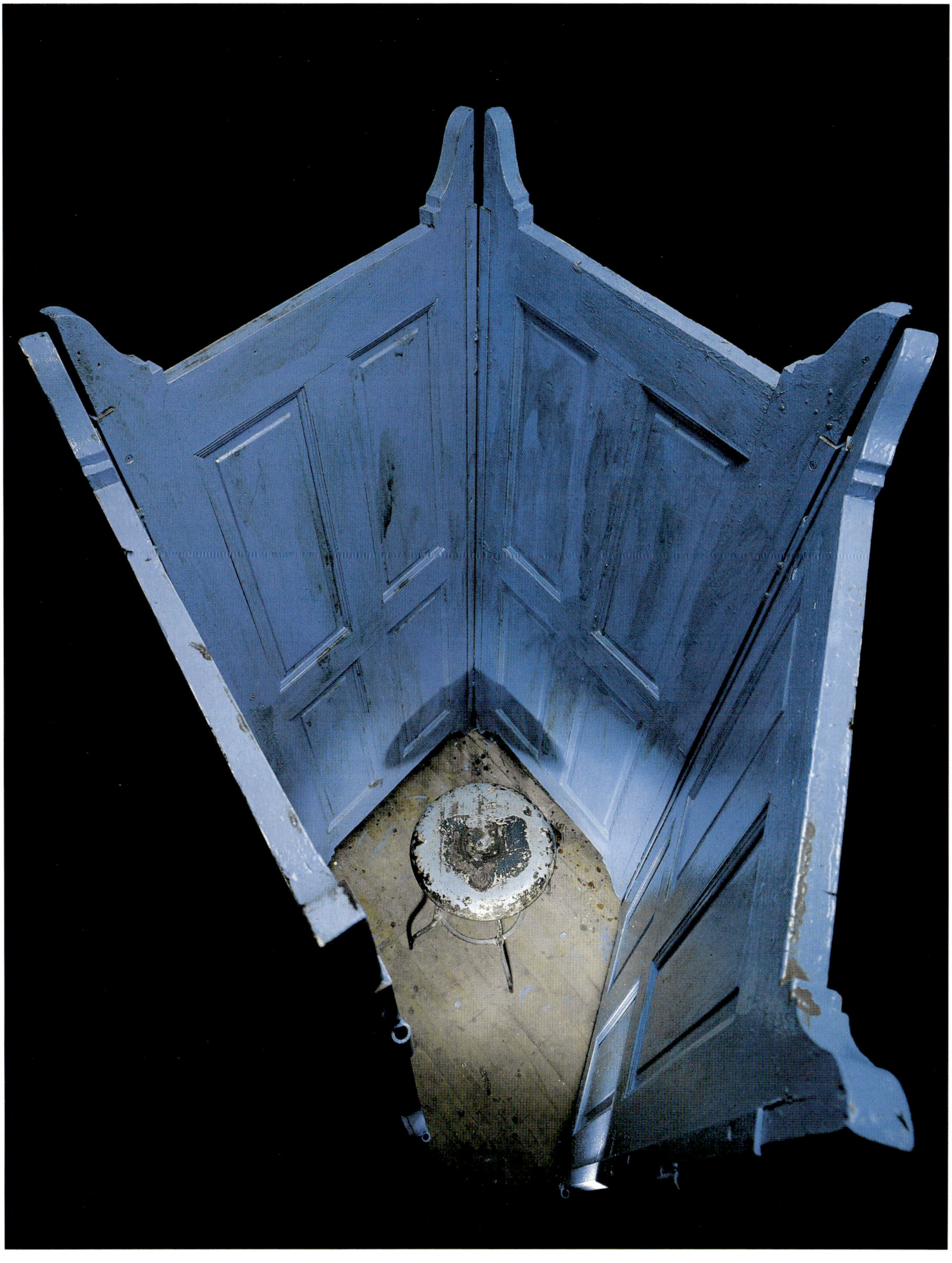

Cell VI

Precious Liquids, 1992
Wood, metal, glass, alabaster, rubber, cloth and water
Viewed from outside the installation at Documenta IX (1992)
Height 168 in. / diameter 175¼ in.

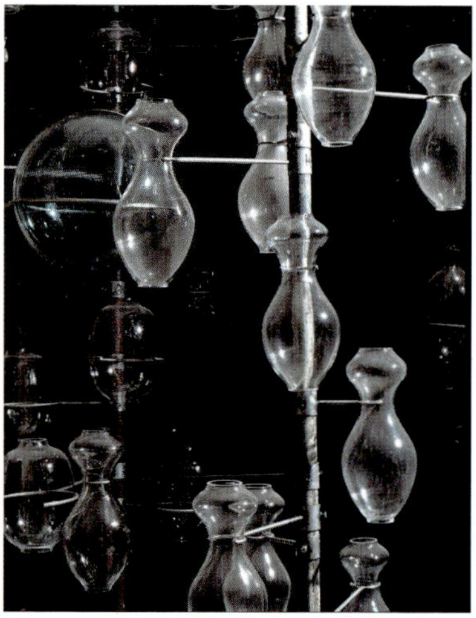

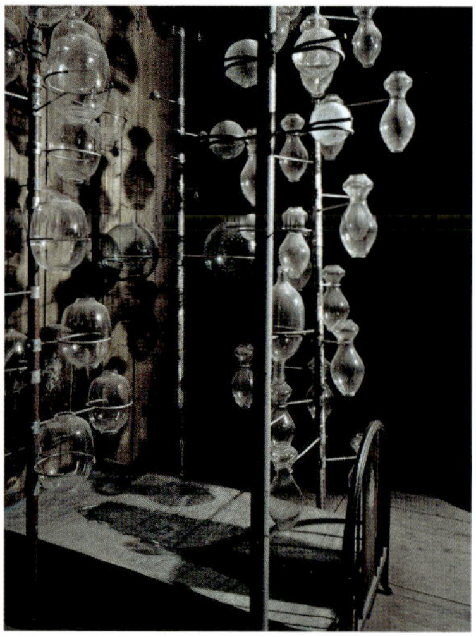

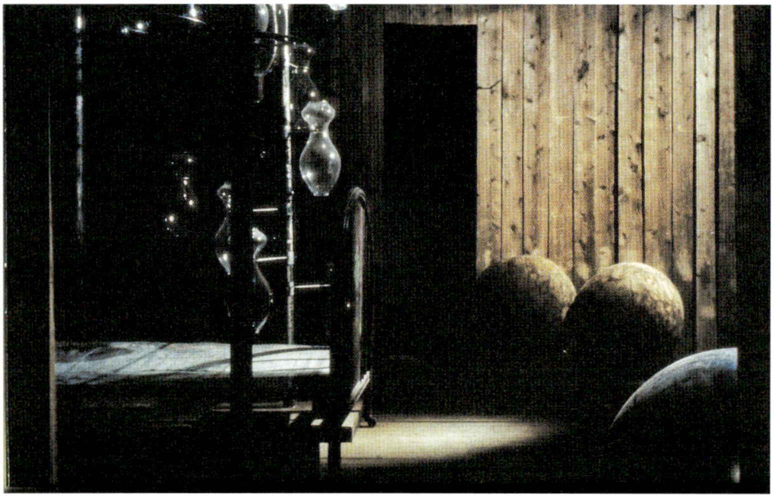

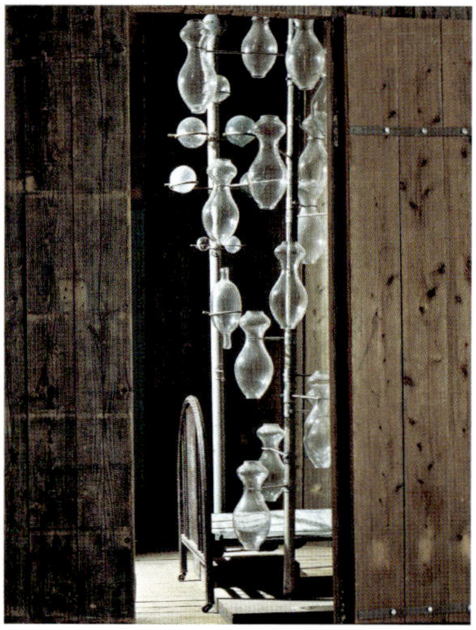

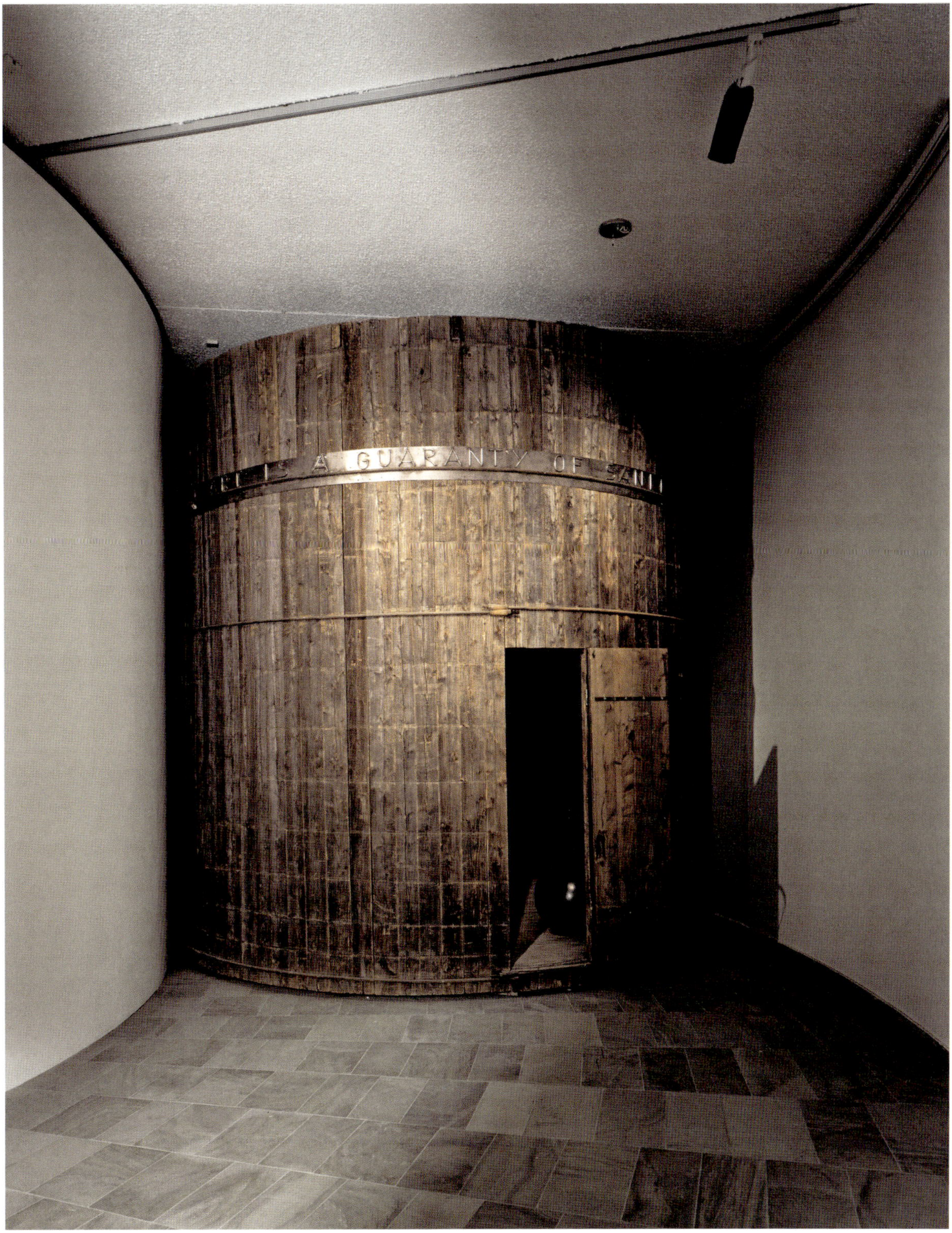
A GUARANTY OF

Bullet Hole, 1992
Steel, glass, iron and wood
90 × 102 × 71 in.

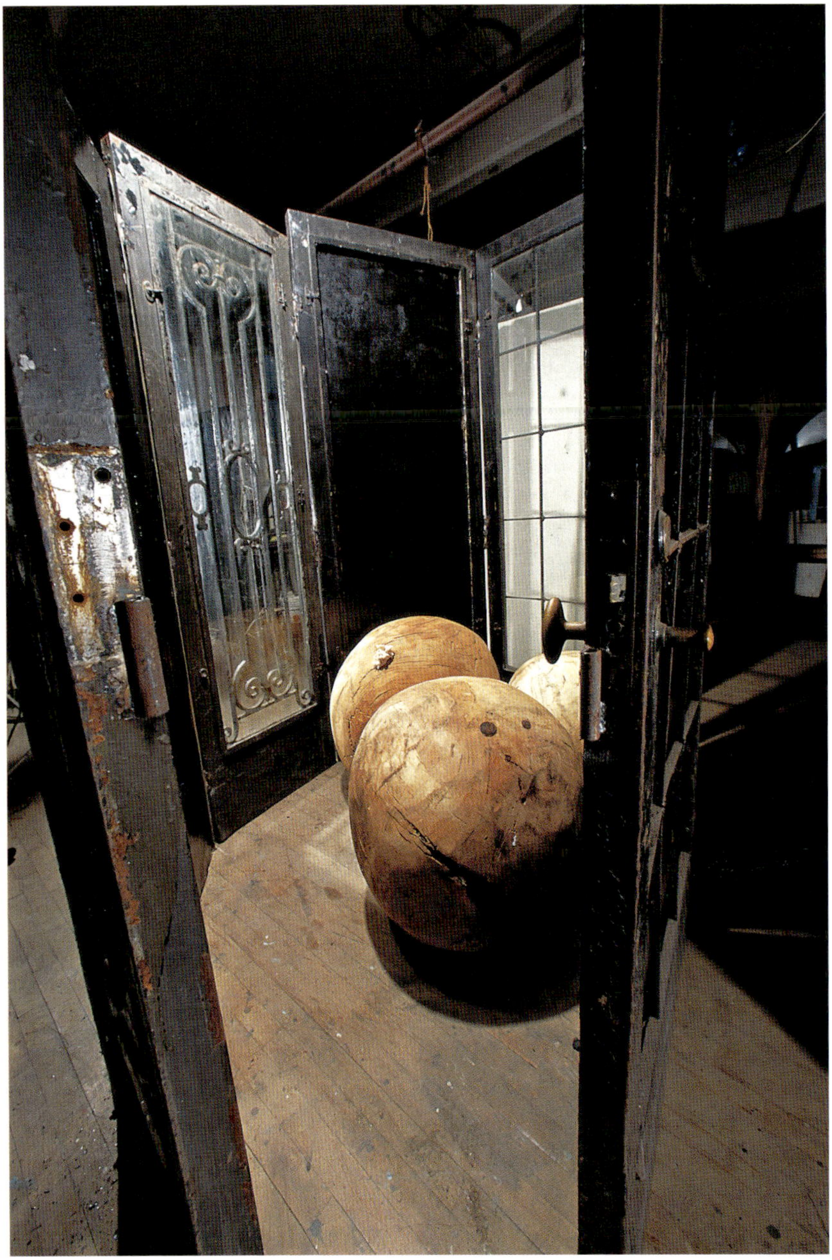

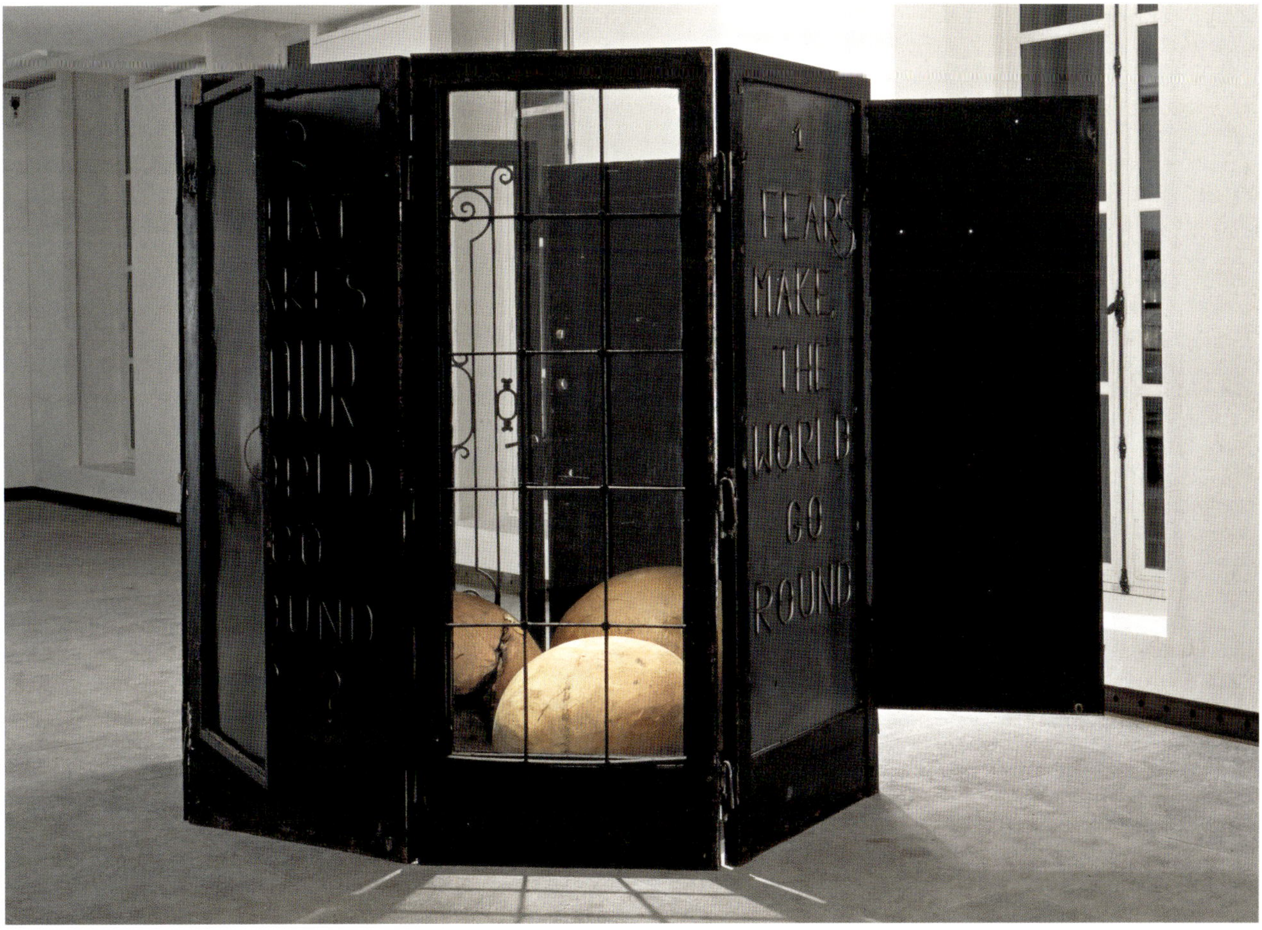
1
FEARS
MAKE
THE
WORLD
GO
ROUND

Cell (Arch of Hysteria), 1992–93
Steel, bronze, cast iron, fabric
119 × 145 × 120 in.

Cell (Three White Marble Spheres), 1993
Steel, glass, marble, mirror
84 × 84 × 84 in.

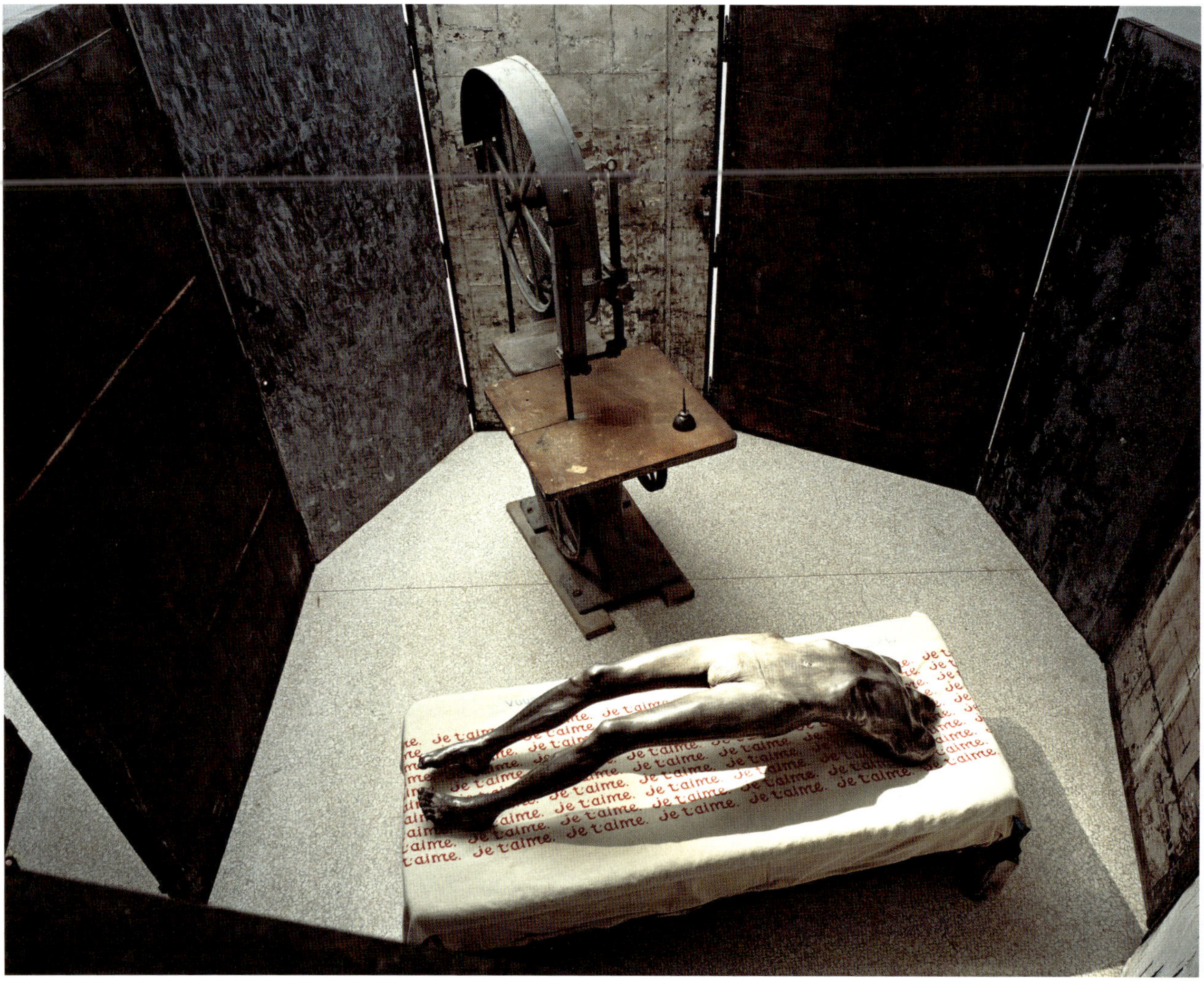

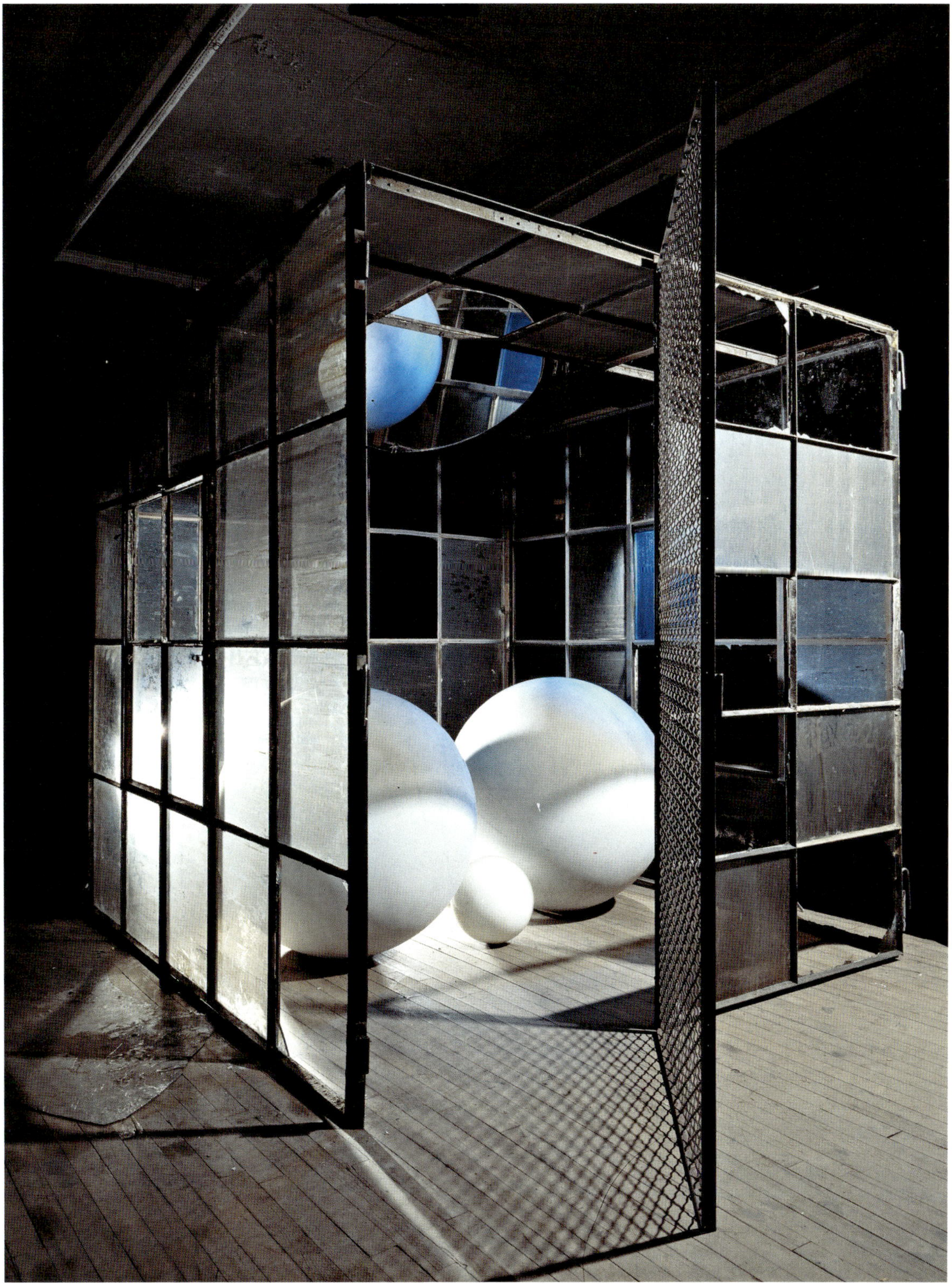

Cell (Three White Marble Spheres)

Cell (You Better Grow Up), 1993
Steel, glass, marble, ceramic, wood and mirror
83 × 82 × 83½ in.

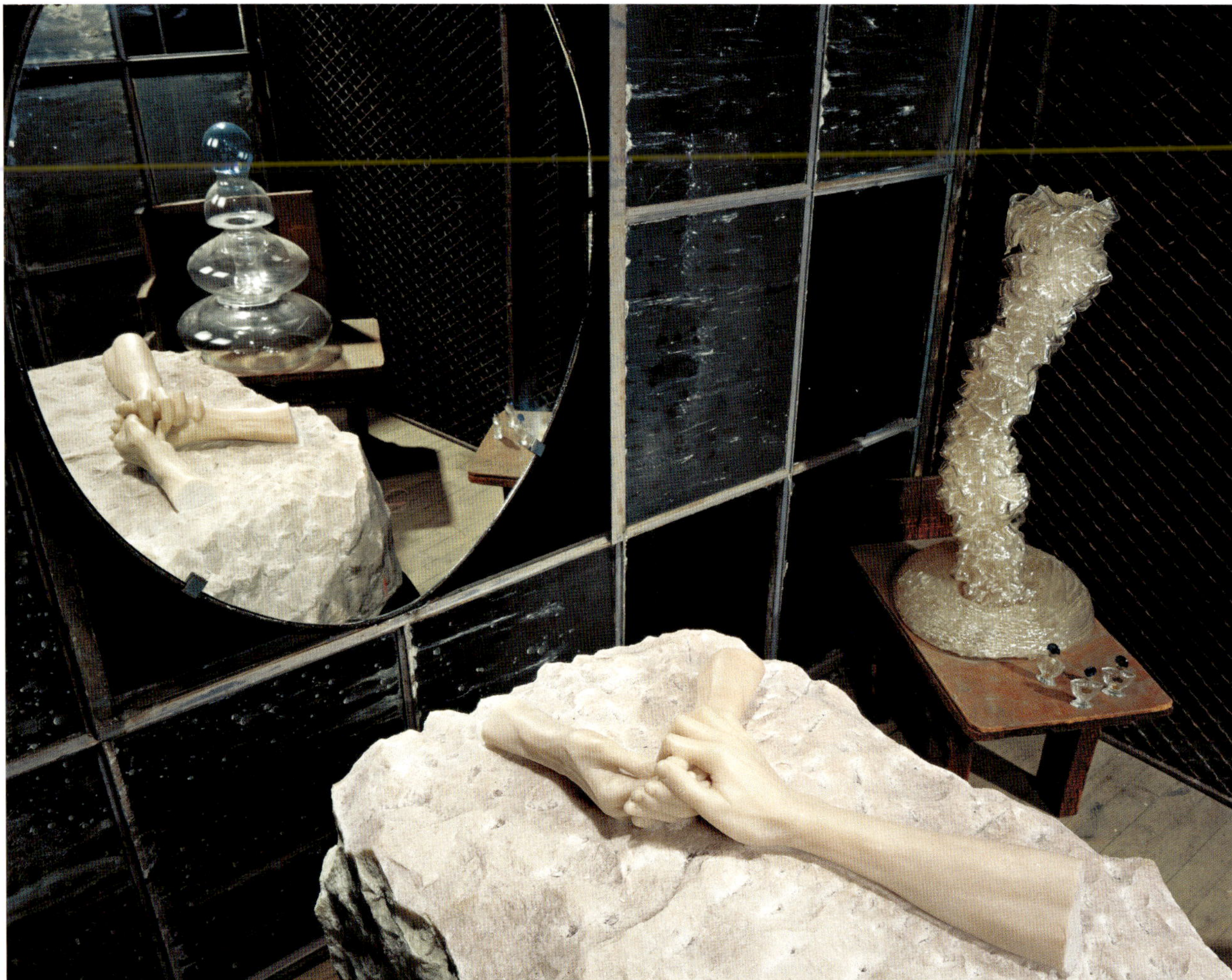

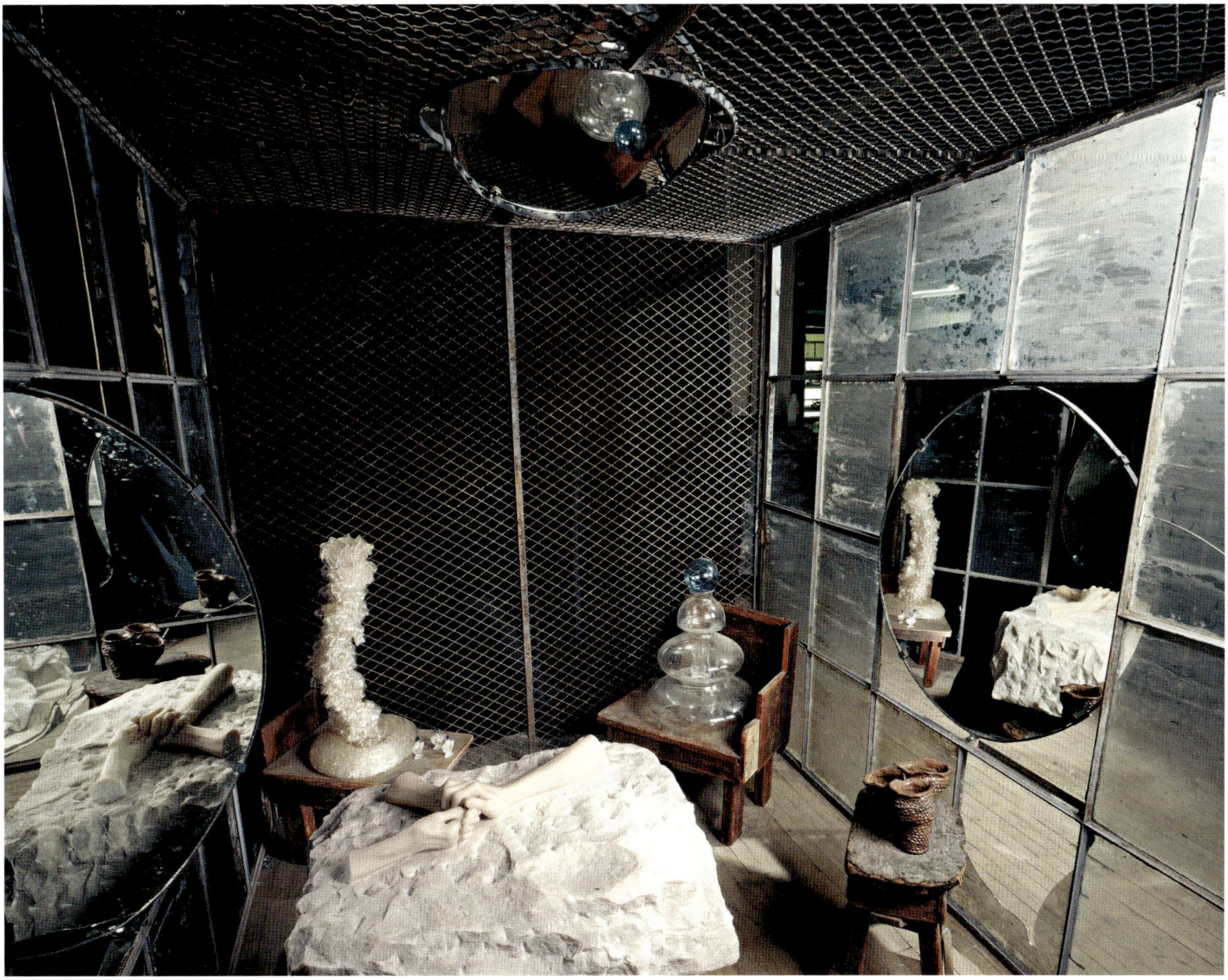

Red Room (Parents), 1994
Wood, metal, rubber, fabric, marble, glass
and mirror
$97^{1}/_{2}$ x 168 x 167 in.

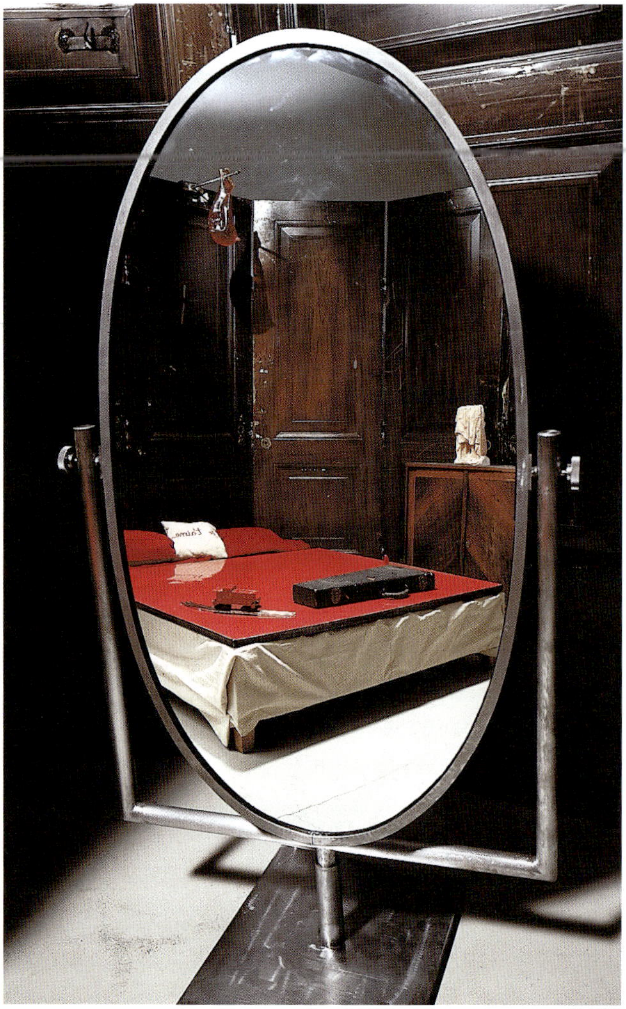

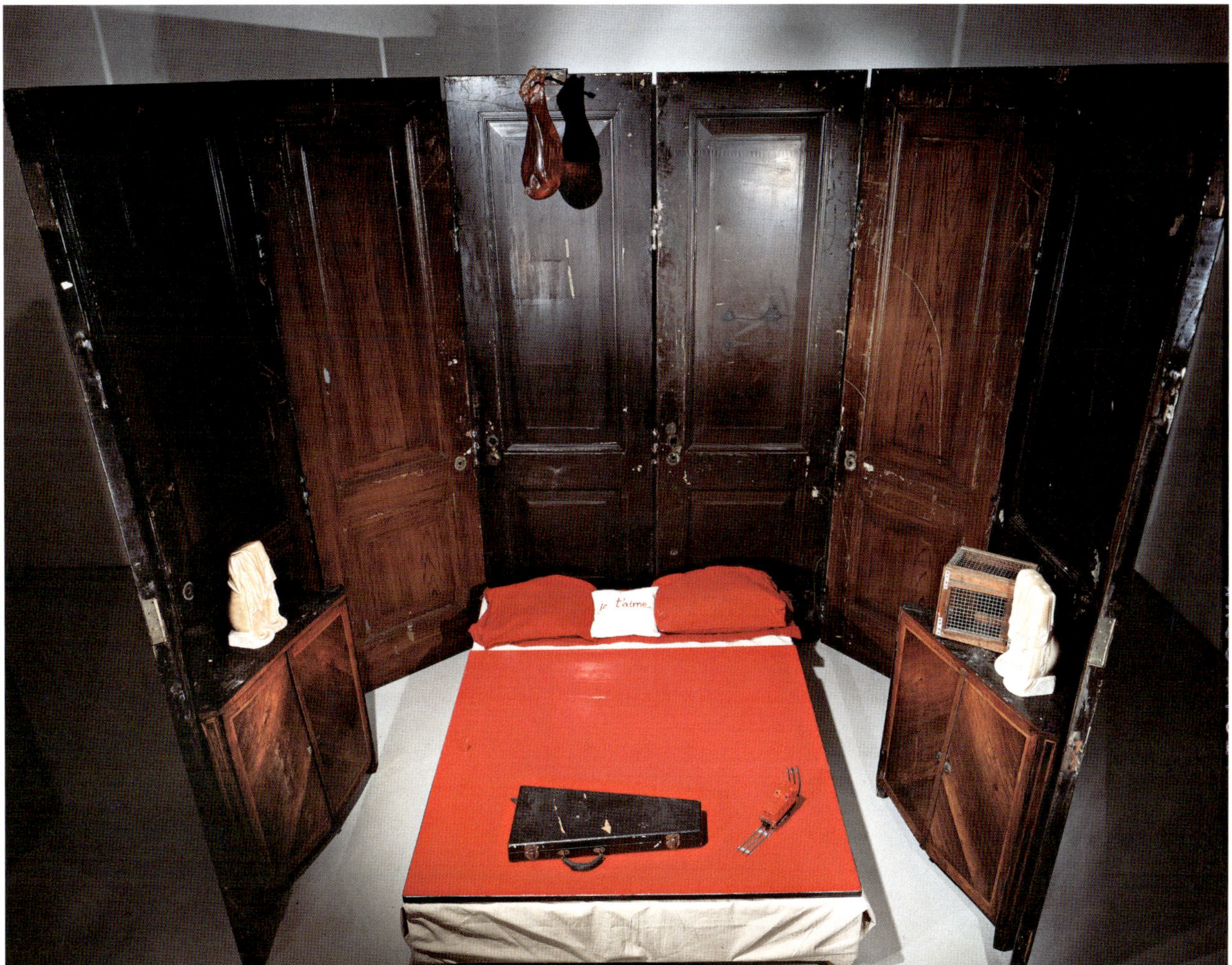

Red Room (Parents)

Red Room (Child), 1994
Wood, glass, thread, metal and rubber
83 × 139 × 108 in.

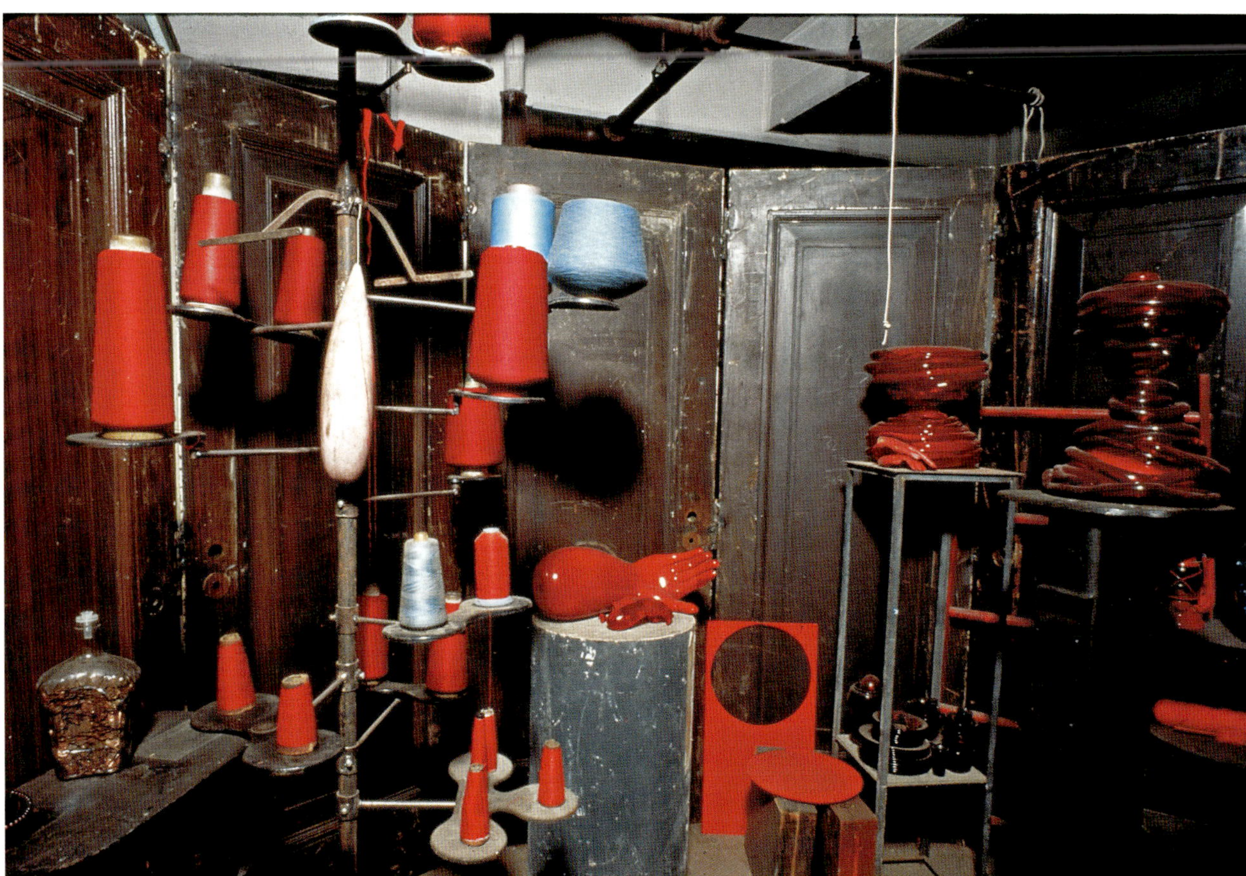

In and Out, 1995
Metal, glass, plaster, fabric and plastic
Plastic: 82 x 65 x 113 in.
Cell: 96 x 96 x 96 in.

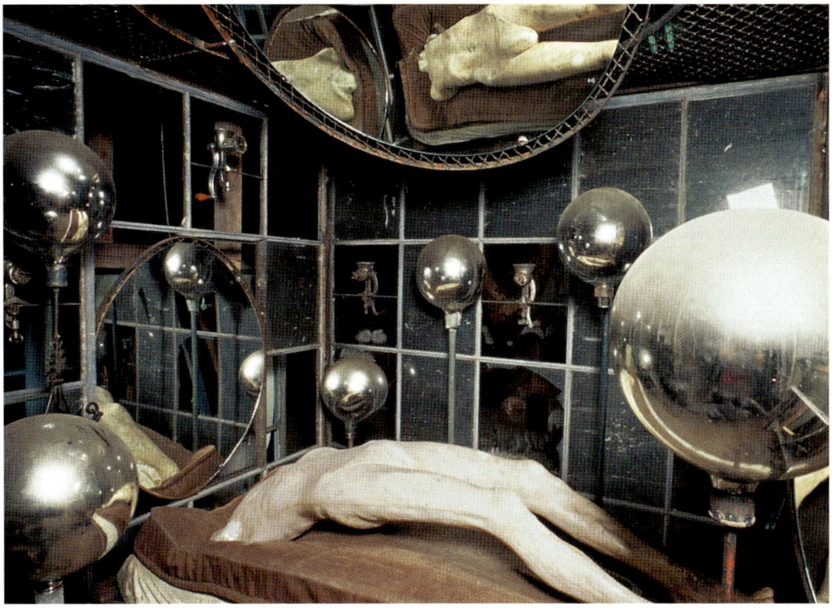

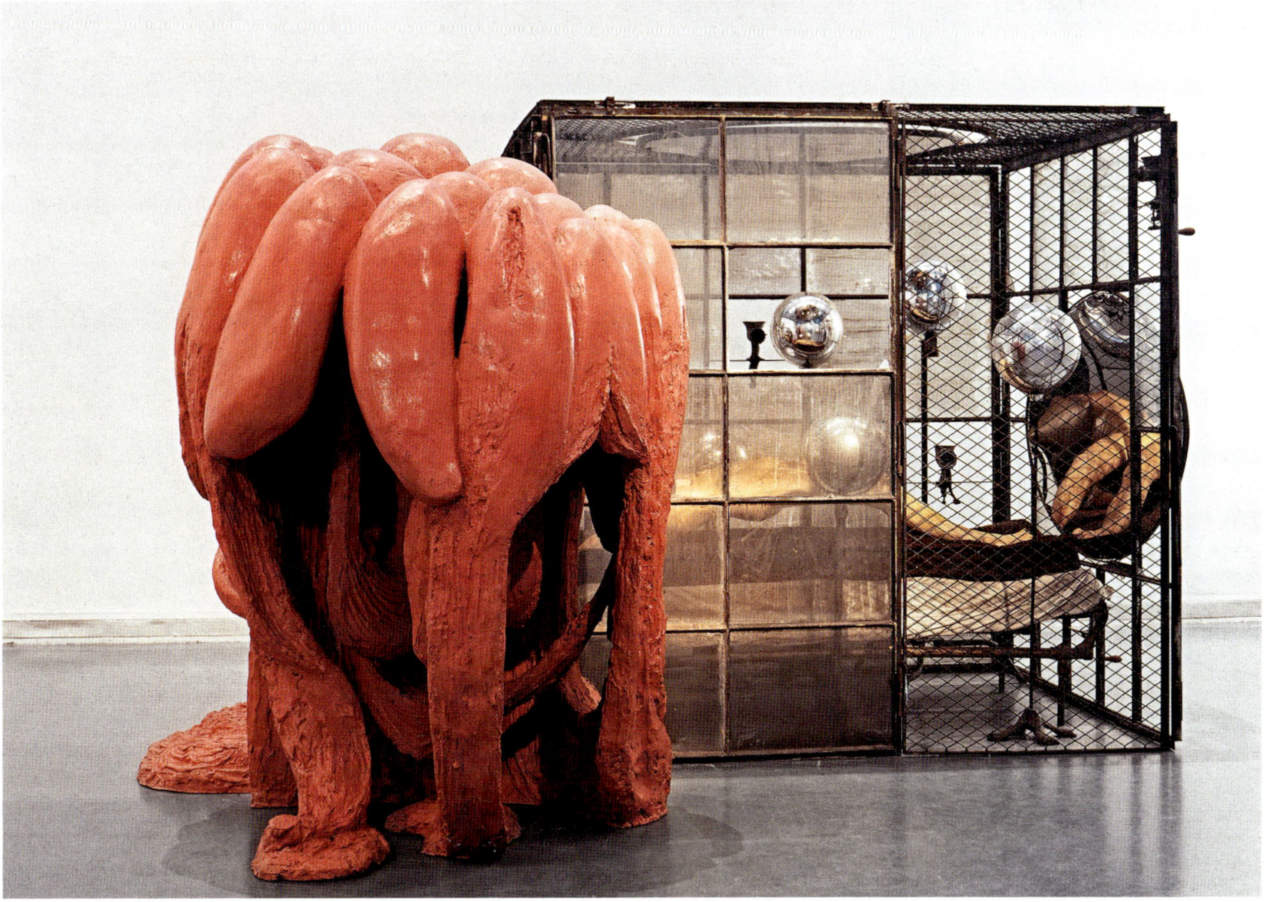

Spider, 1997
Steel, tapestry, wood, glass, fabric, rubber, silver, gold
177 x 262 x 204 in.

Cell (Choisy Two), 1995
Marble, steel, mirrors
95 × 78 × 58 in.

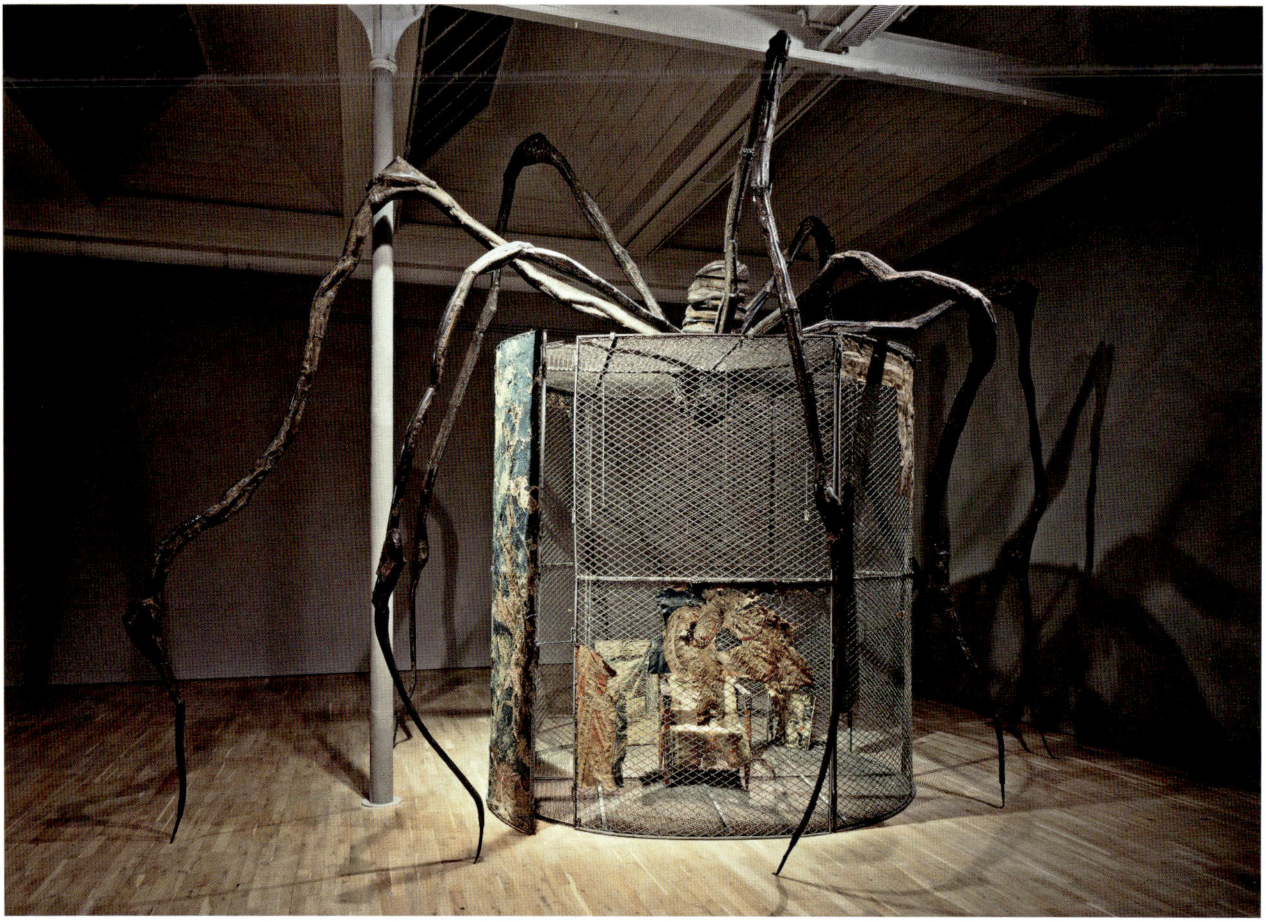

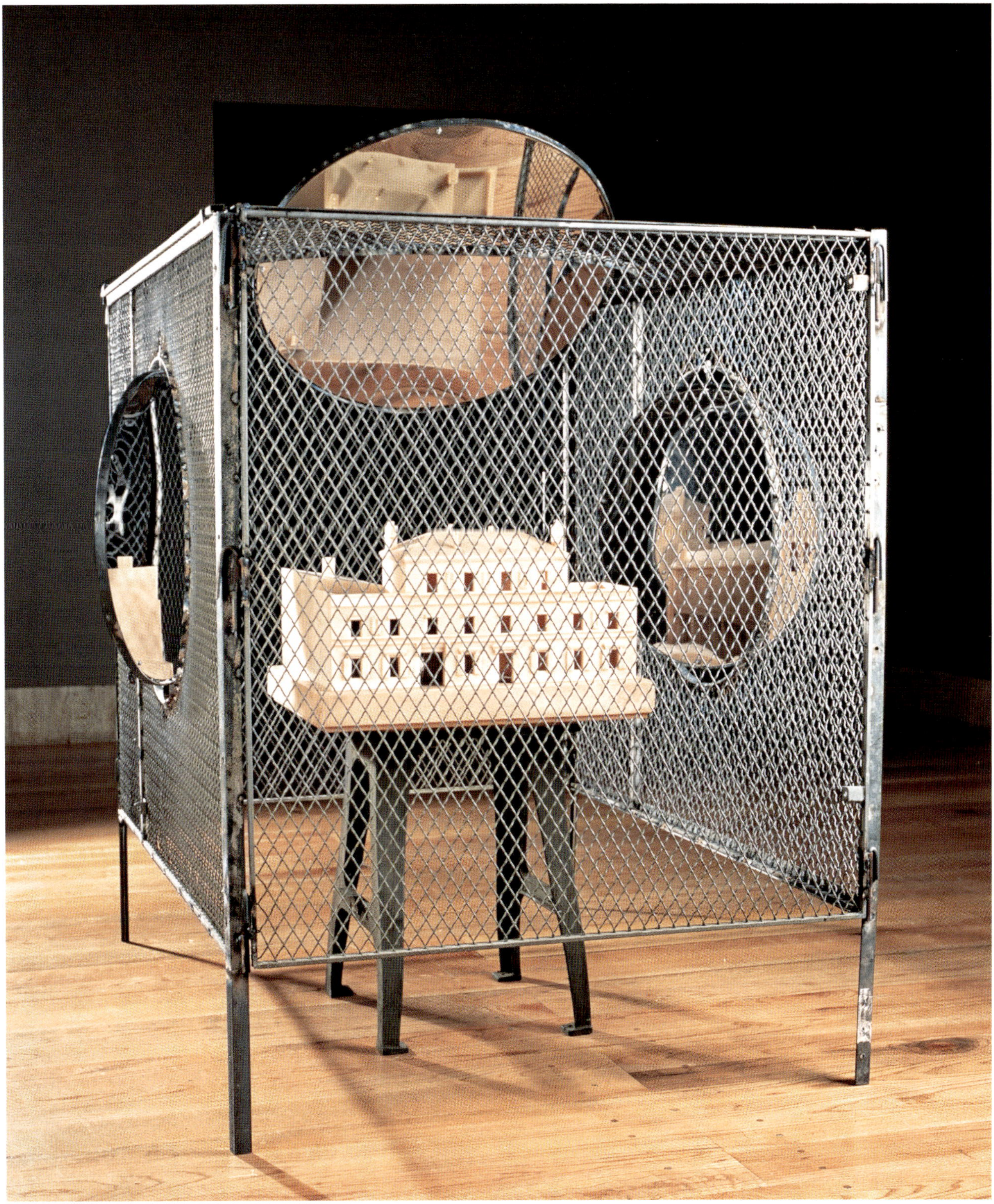

Cell (Hands and Mirror), 1995
Marble, painted metal, metal and mirrors
63 × 48 × 45 in.

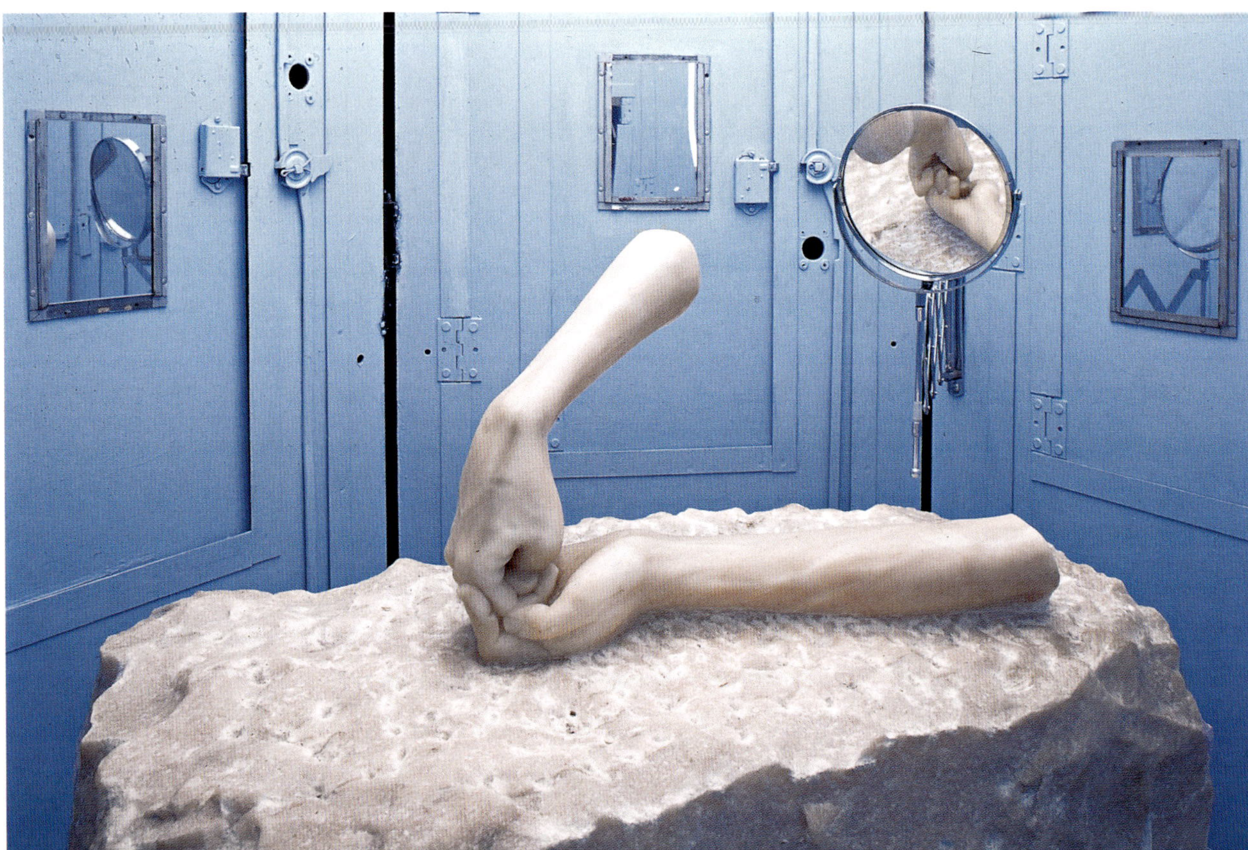

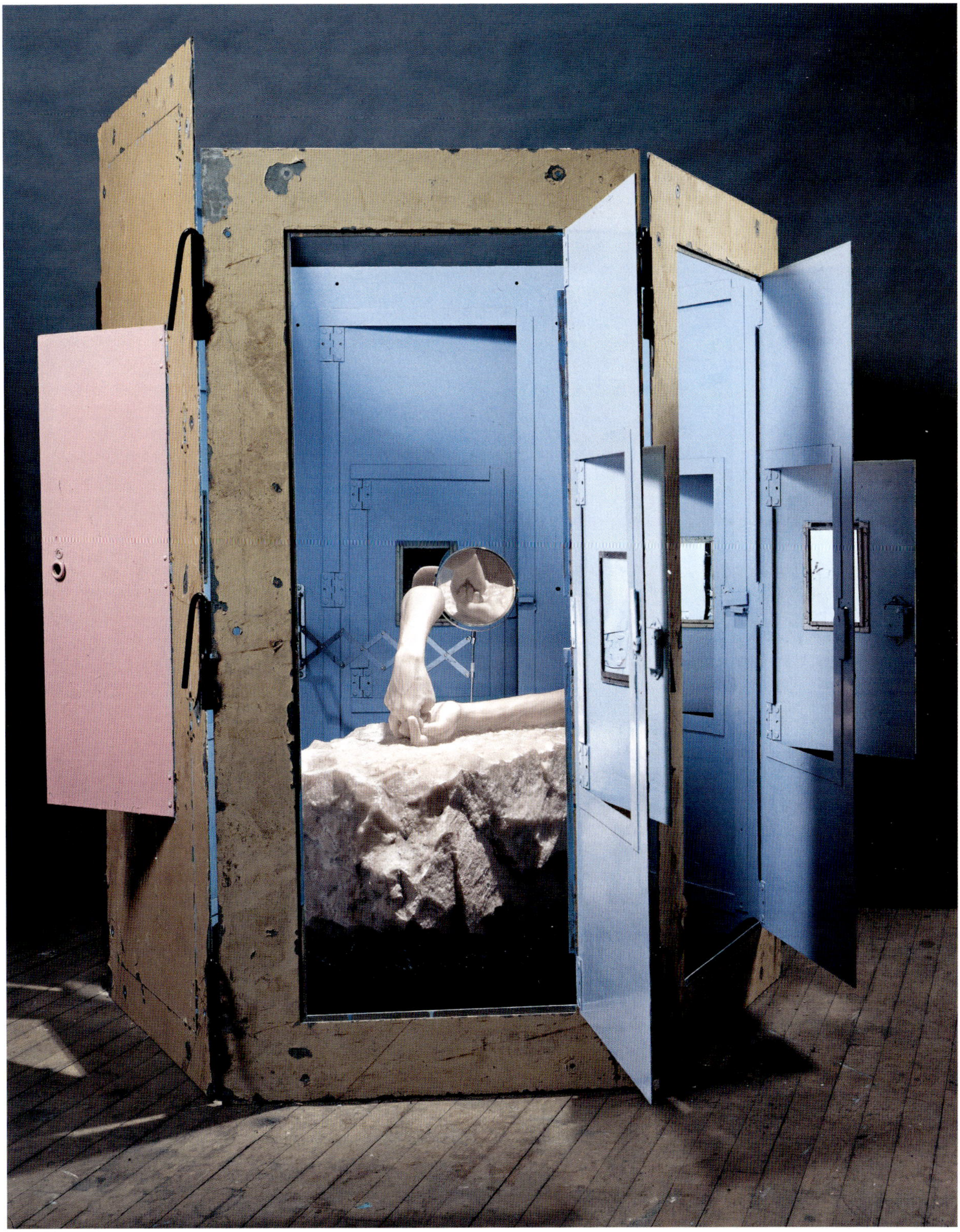

Cell (Hands and Mirror)

Cell (Clothes), 1996
Painted wood, glass, fabric, rubber and mixed media
83 × 174 × 144 in.

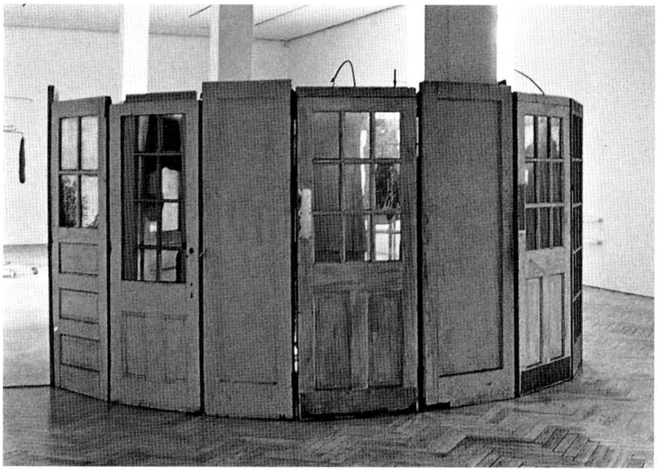

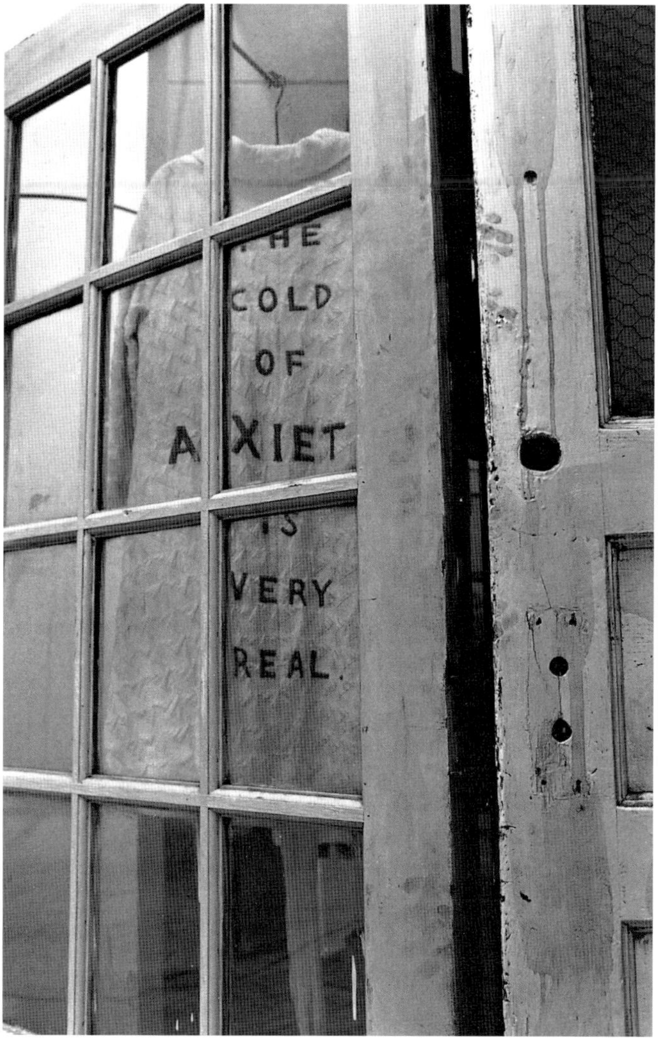

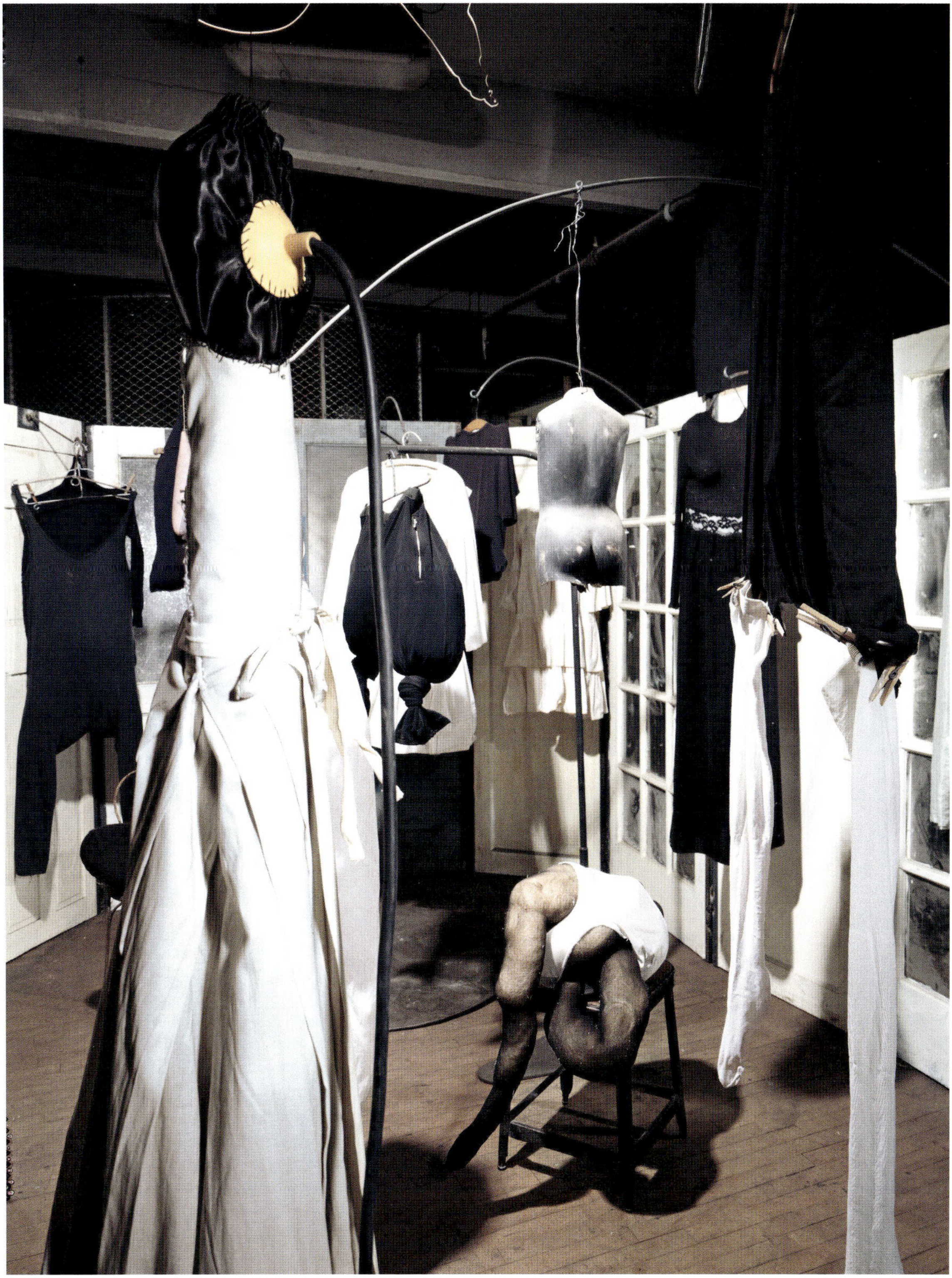

Cell (Clothes)

Cell VII, 1998
Metal, glass, fabric, bronze, steel, wood, bones,
wax and thread
$81\frac{1}{2} \times 87 \times 83$ in.

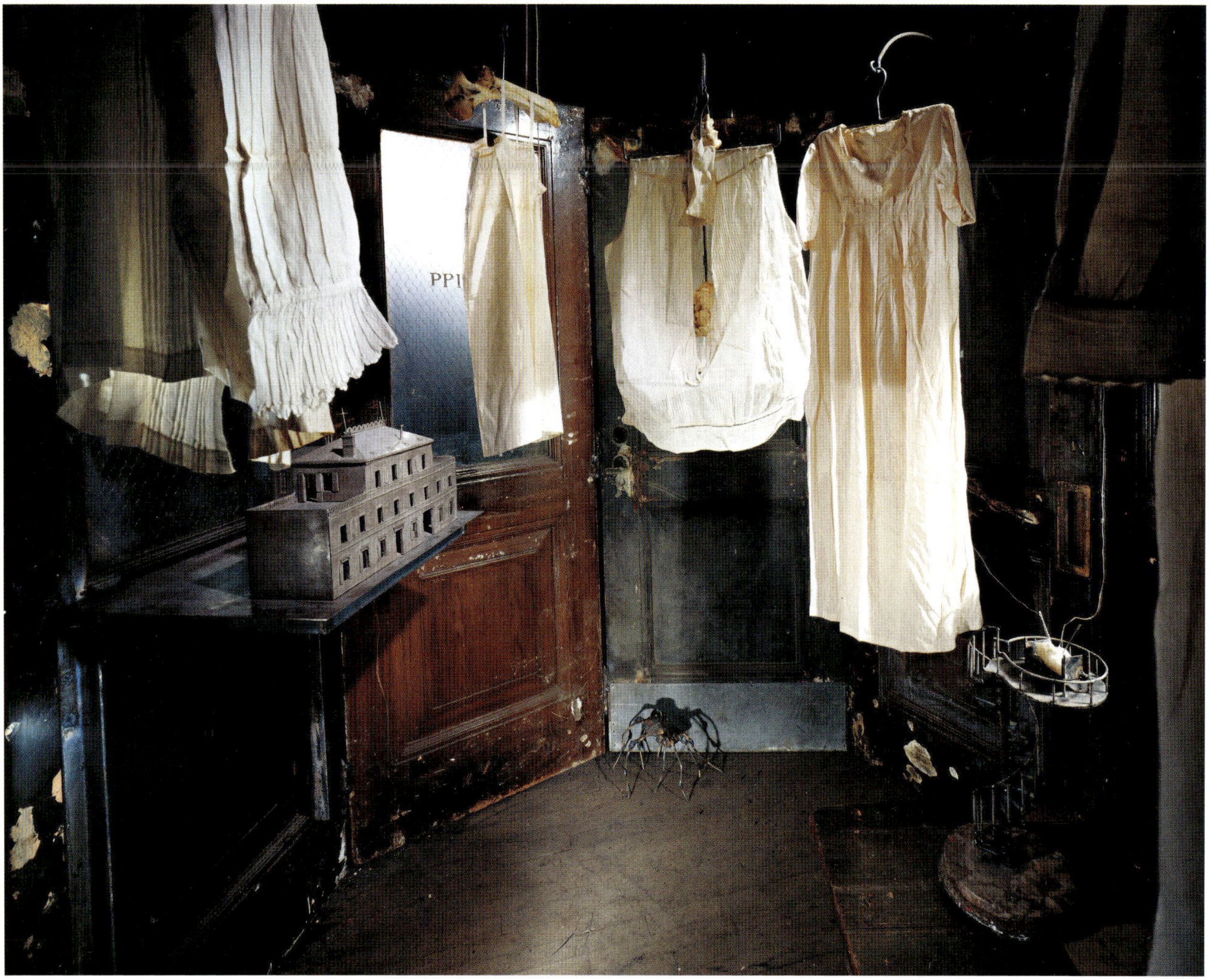

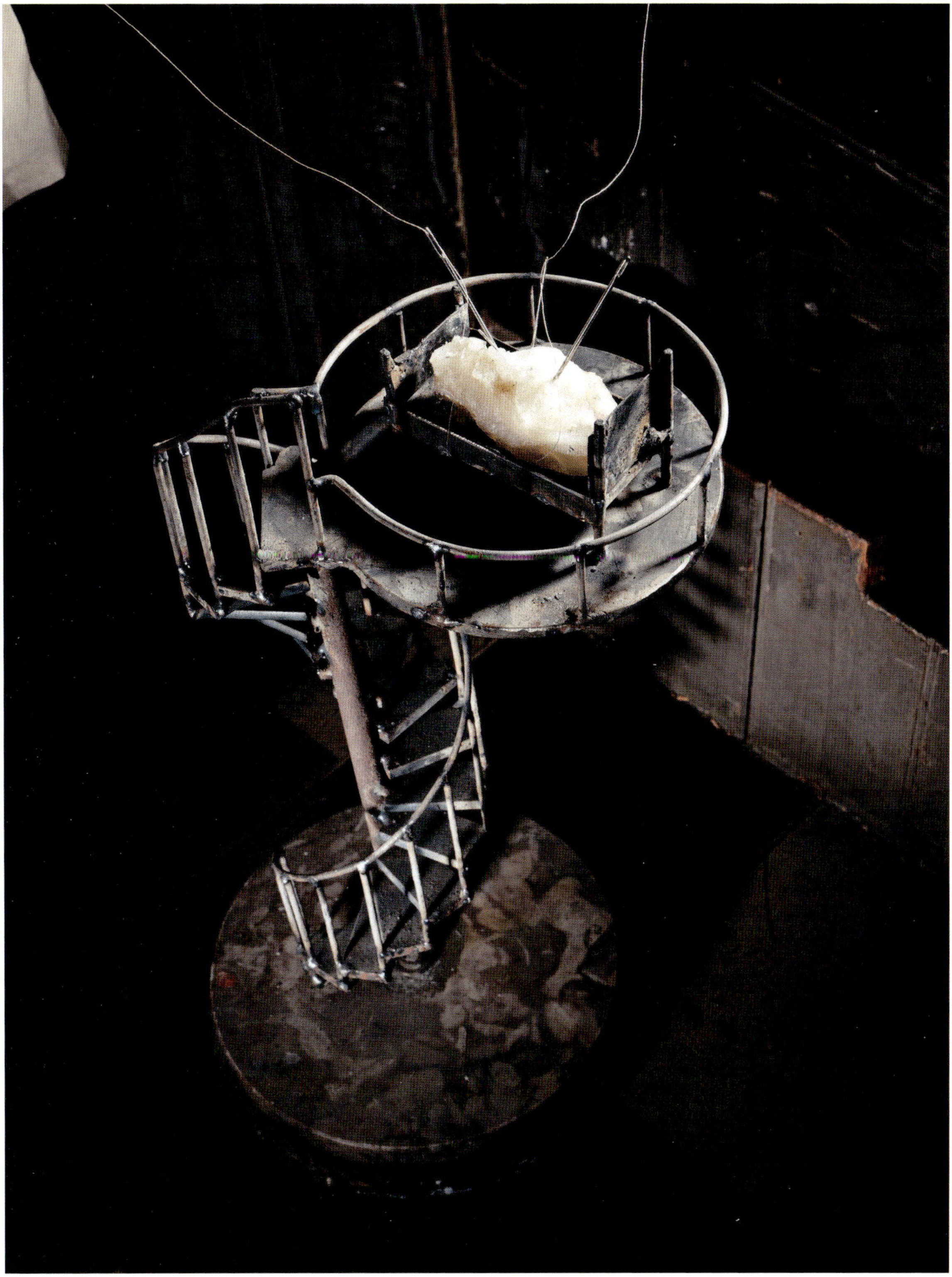

Cell VII

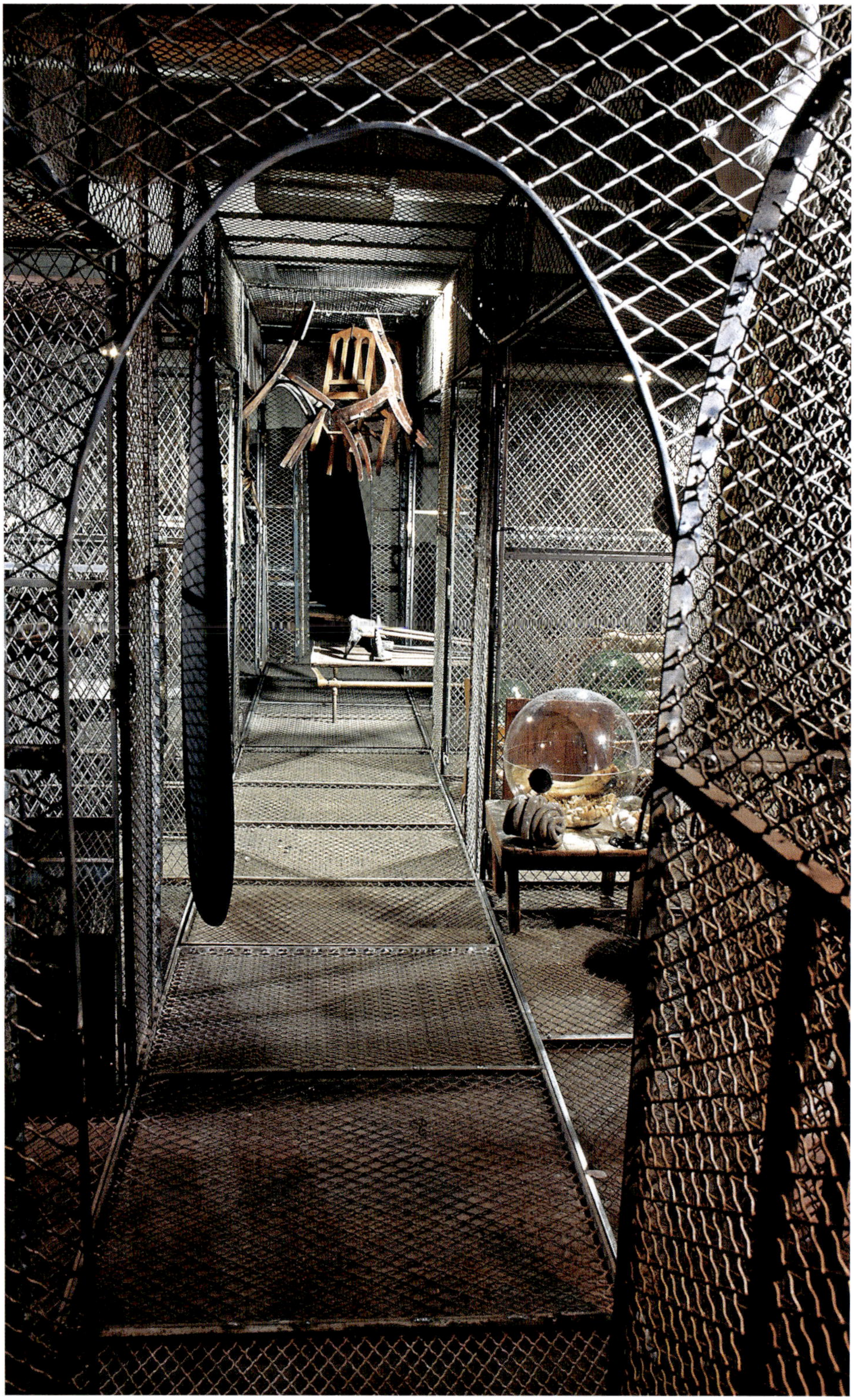

Passage Dangereux, 1997
Metal, wood, tapestry, rubber, marble, steel, glass, bronze, bones, flax and mirrors
104 × 140 × 345 in.

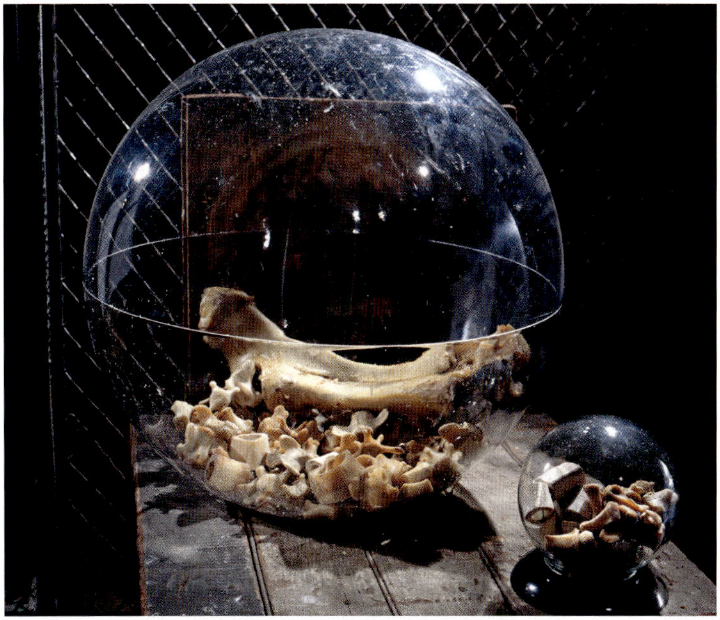

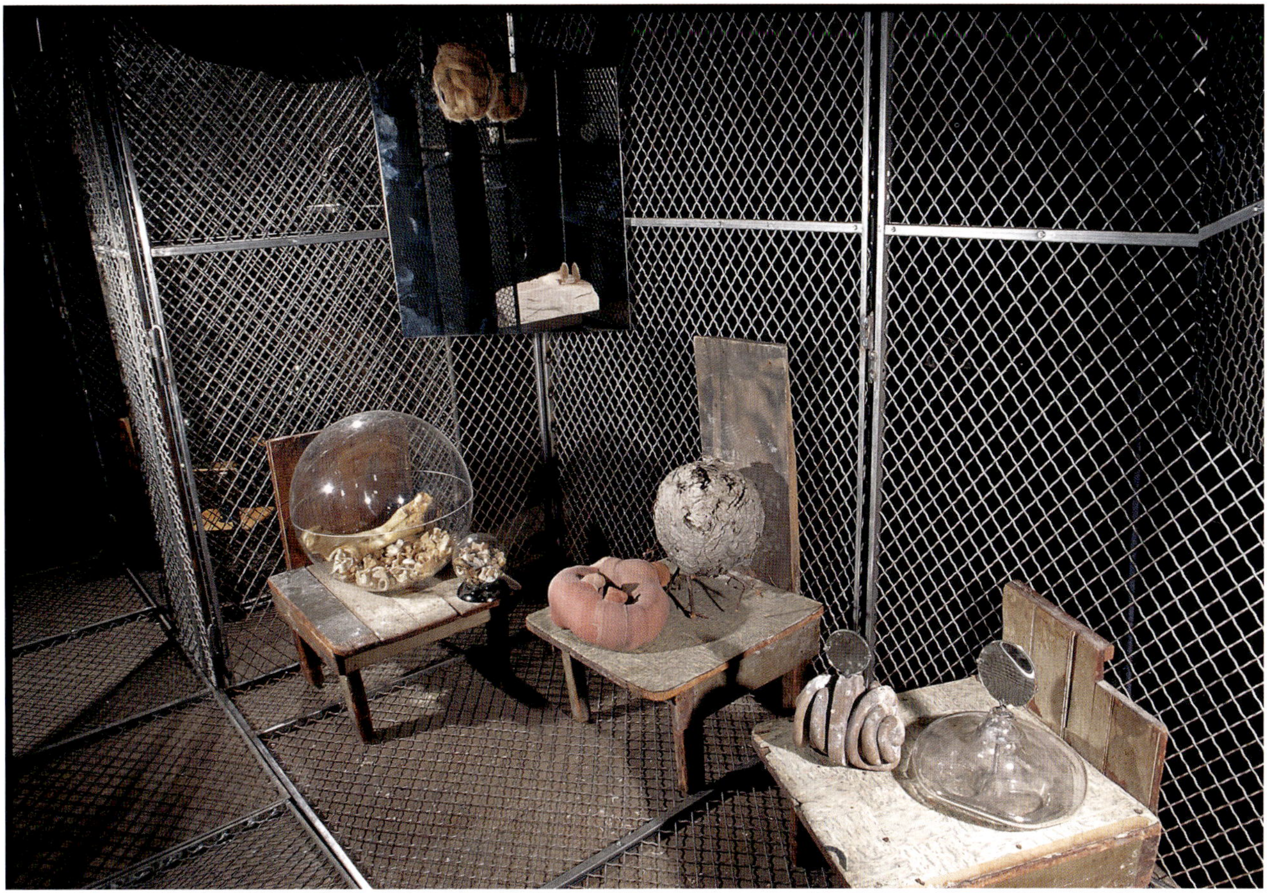

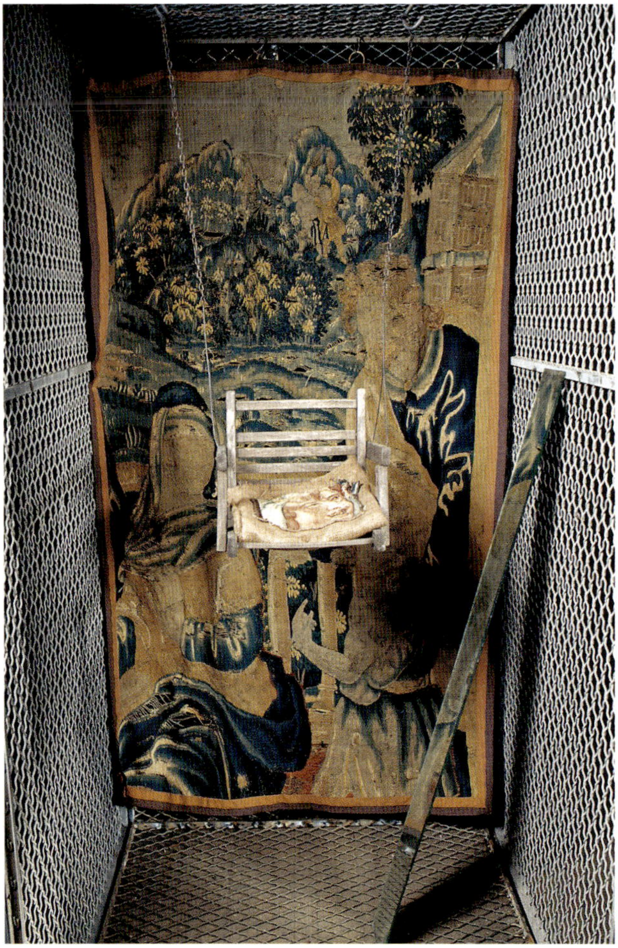

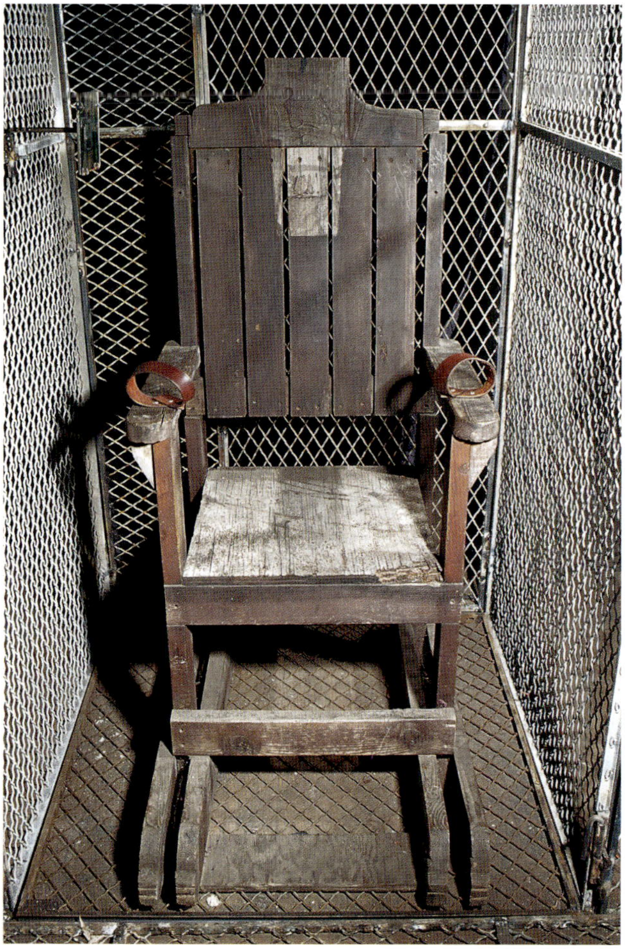

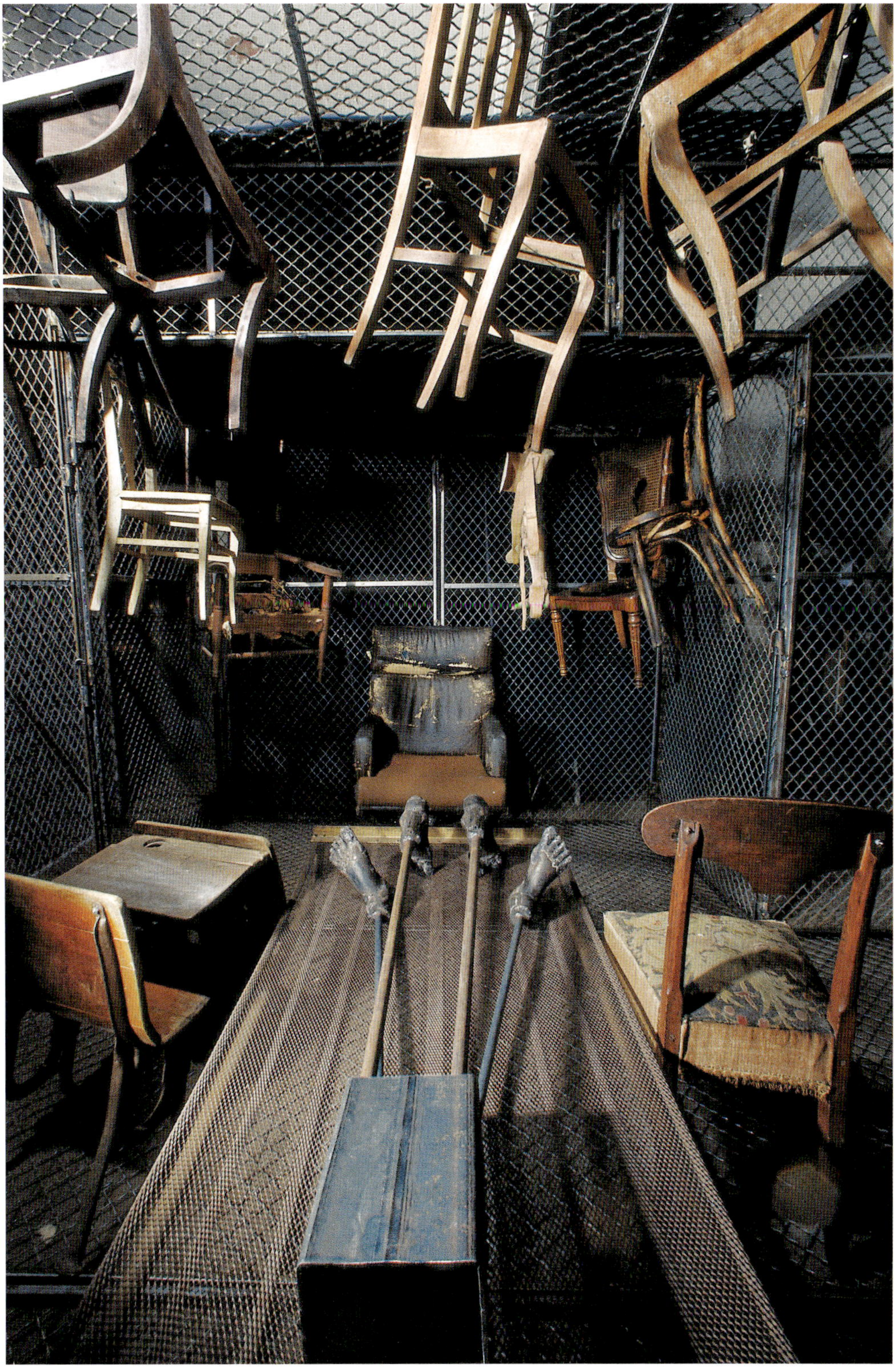

Passage Dangereux

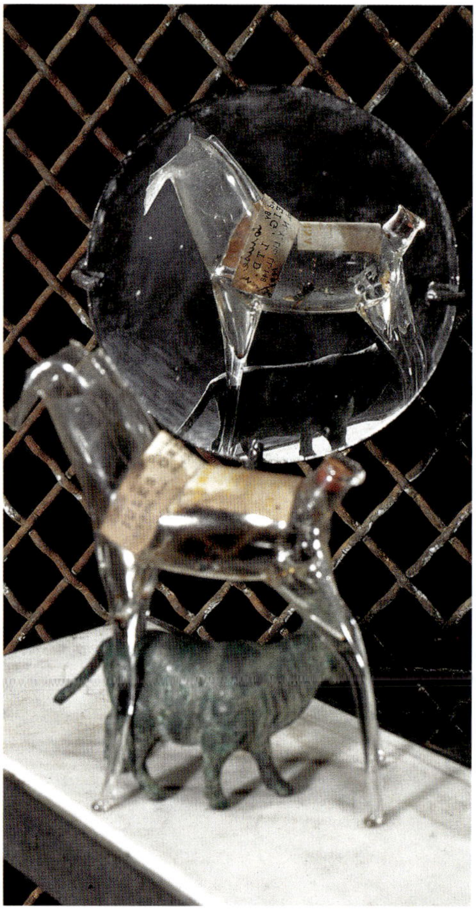

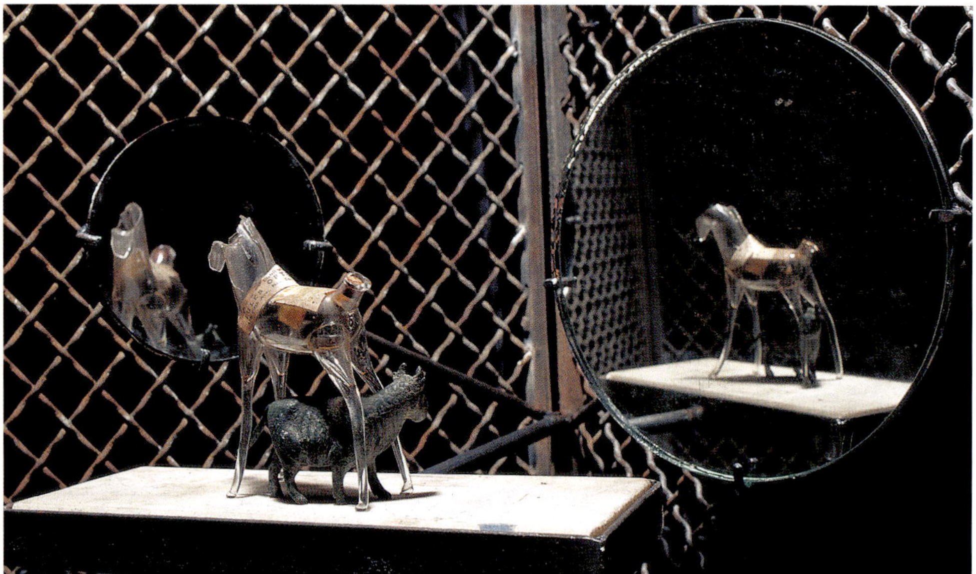

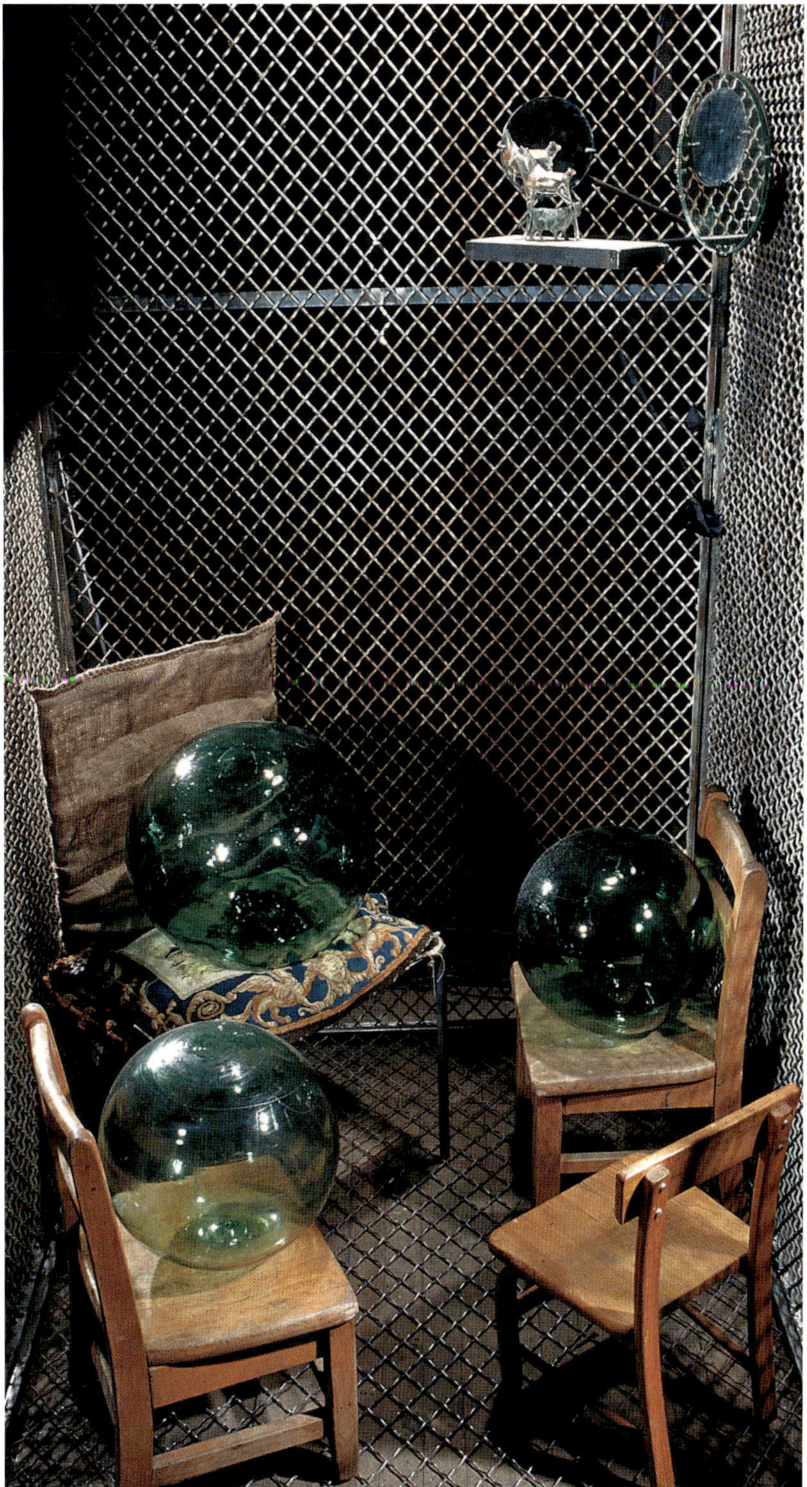

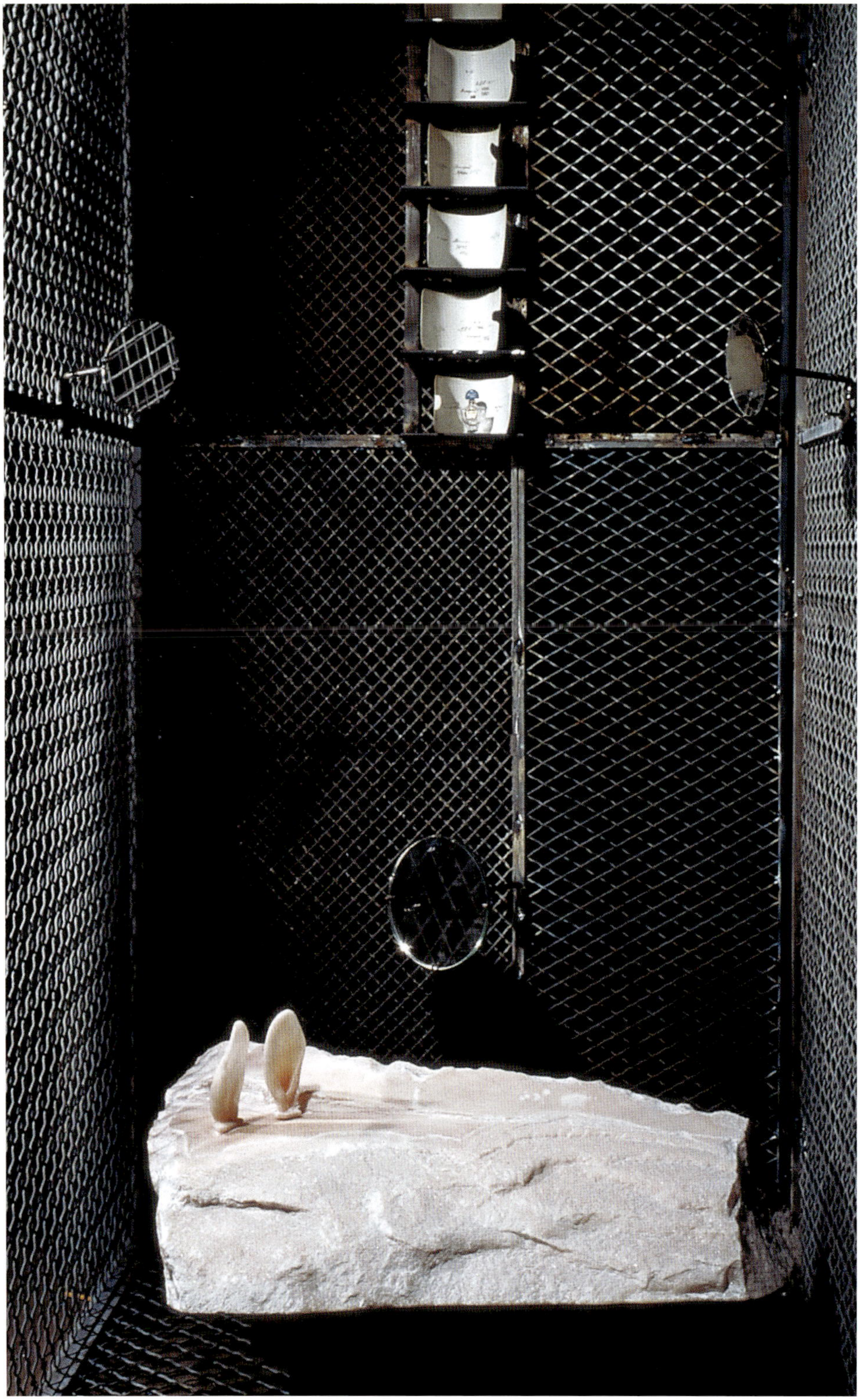

Cell VIII, 1998
Metal, tapestry, fabric, marble and steel
108 × 132 × 100 in.

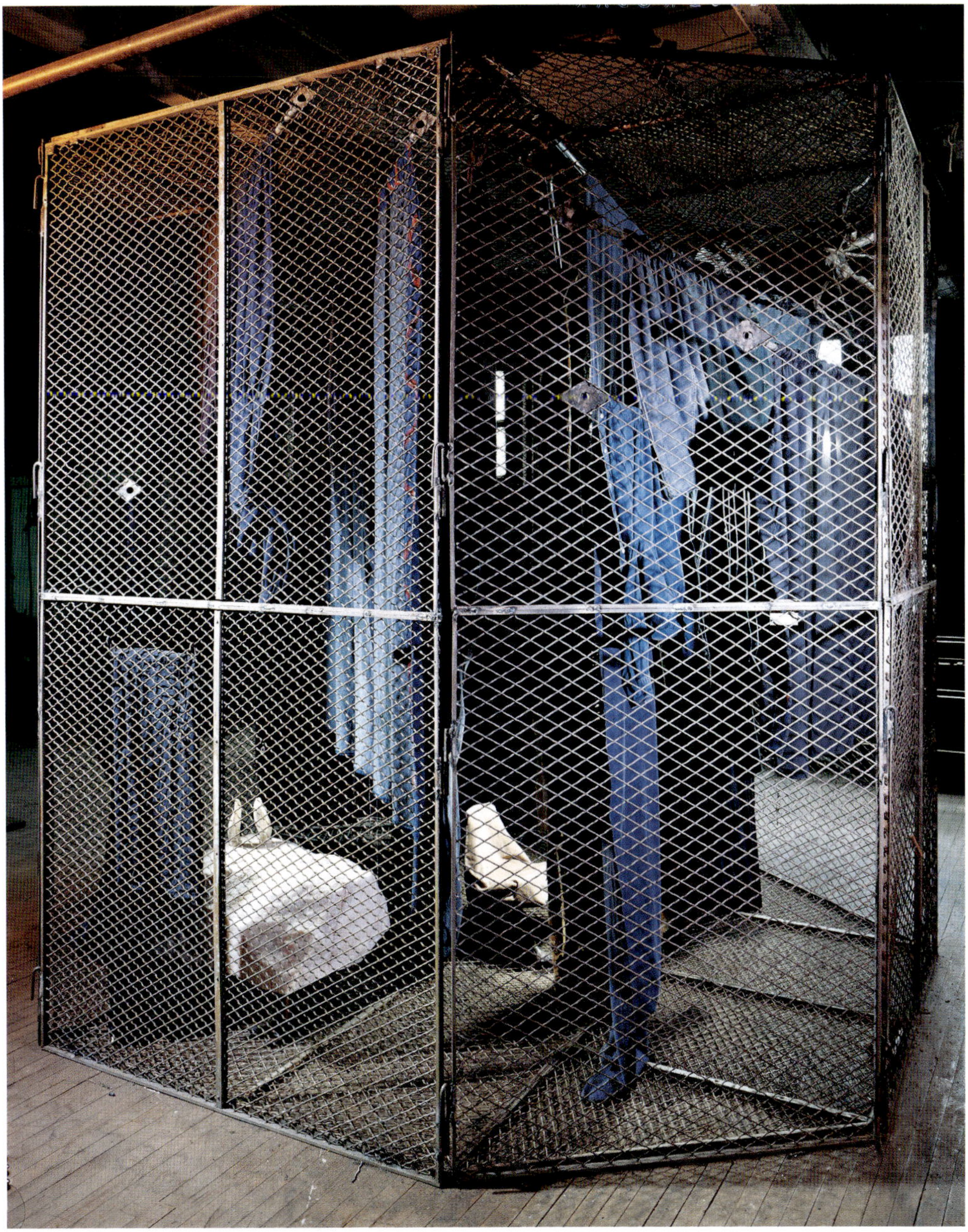

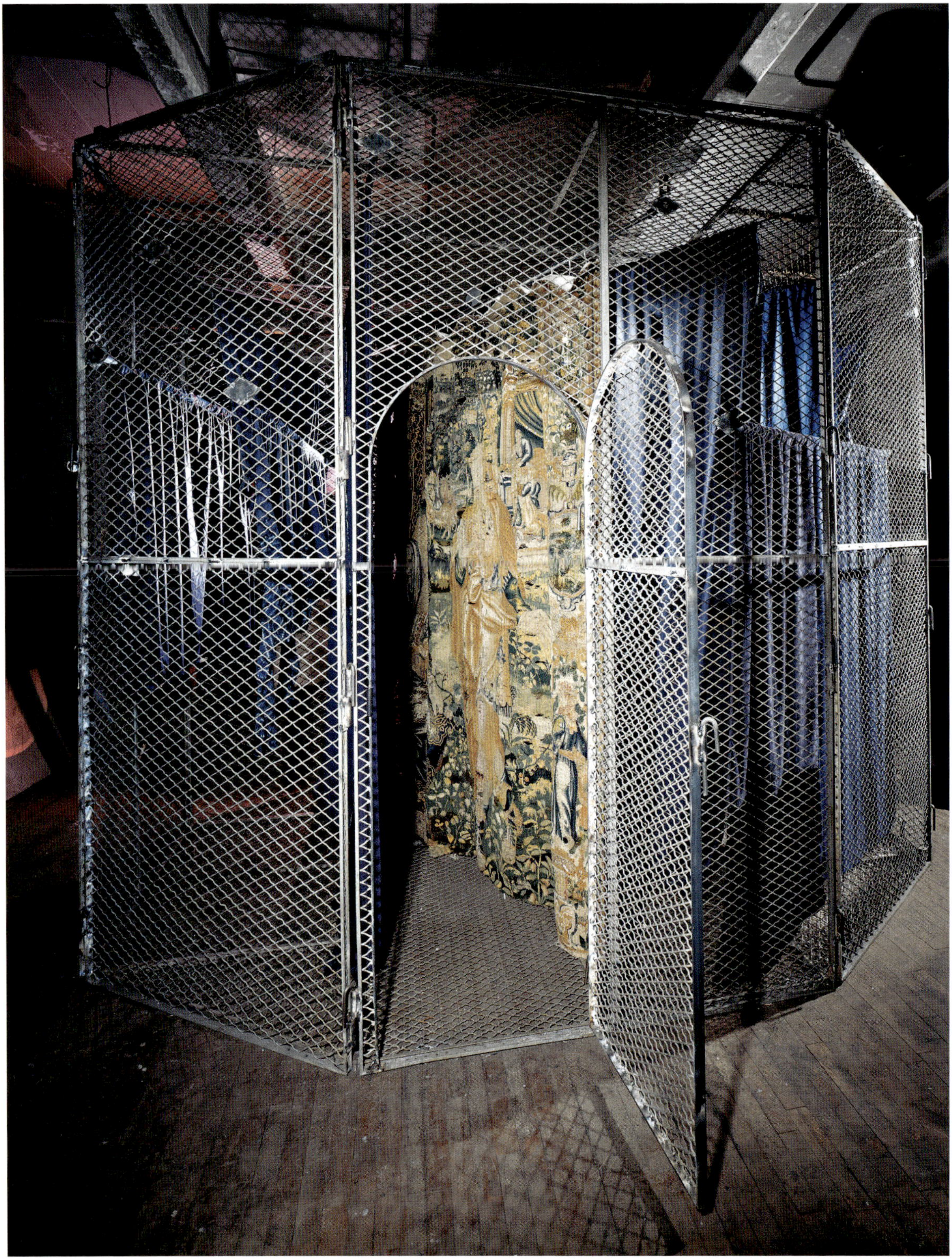

Cell VIII

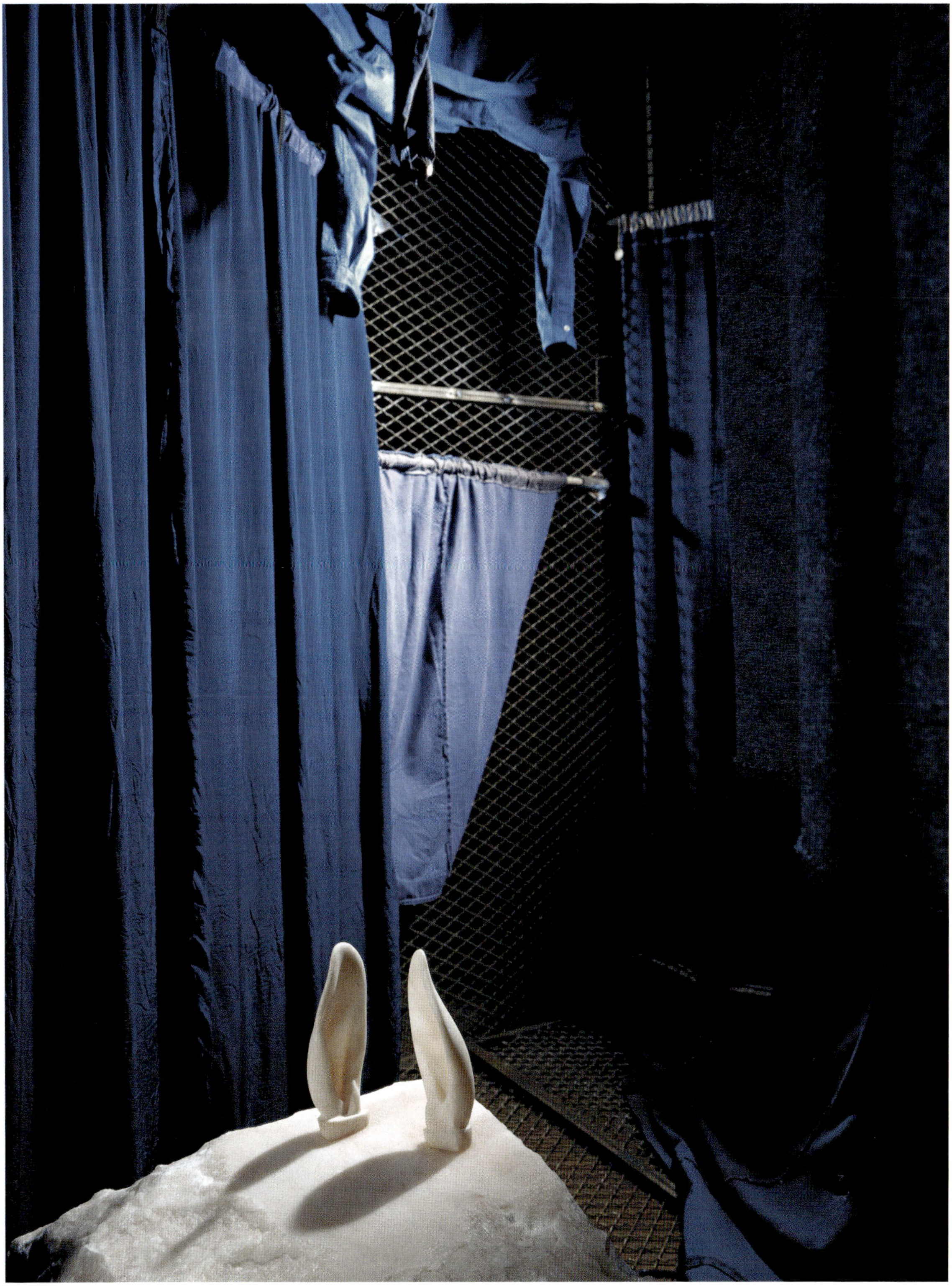

Cell VIII

Cell (Twelve Oval Mirrors), 1998
Steel, aluminum, wood
90 x 96 x 132 in.

Culprit Number Two, 1998
Painted steel, wood, glass, metal and mirror
150 x 114 x 132 in.

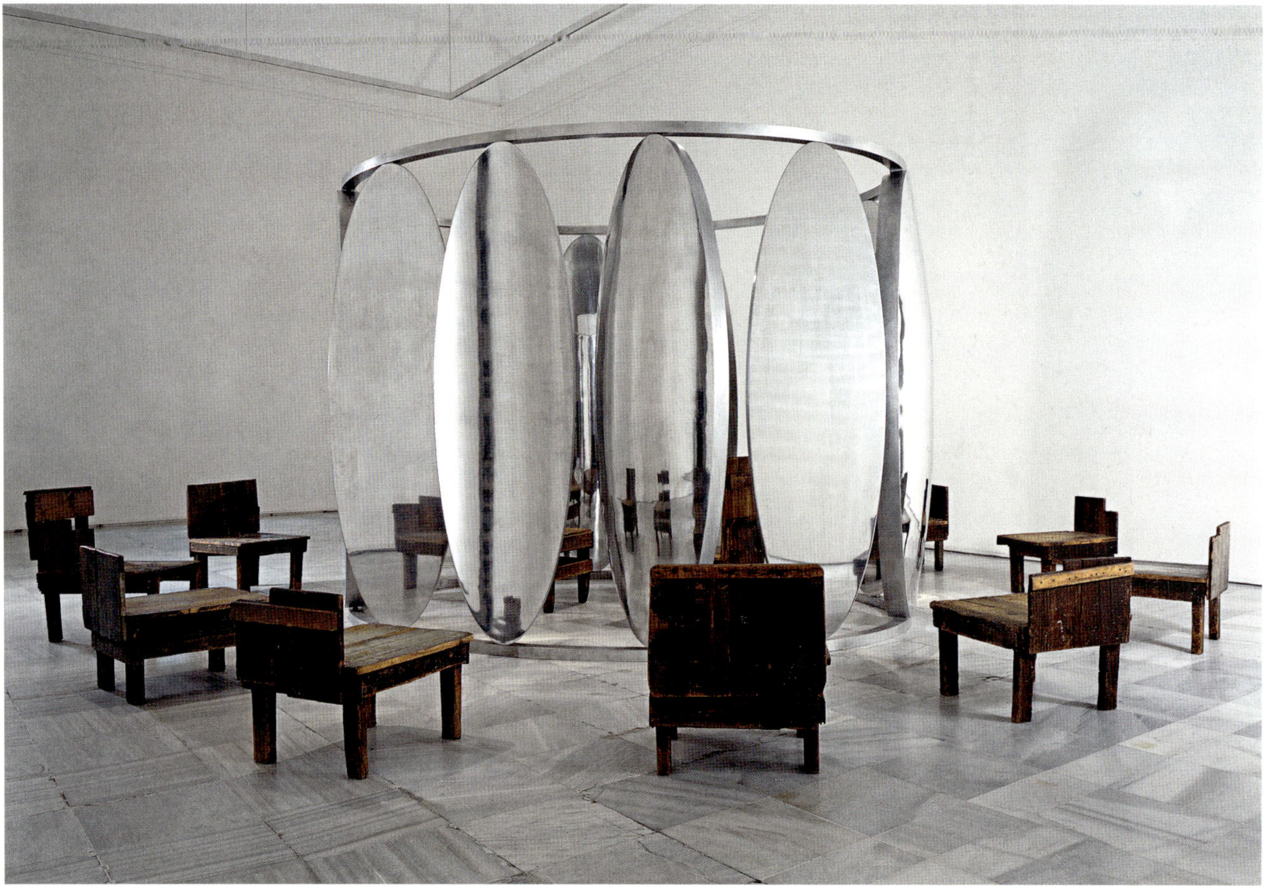

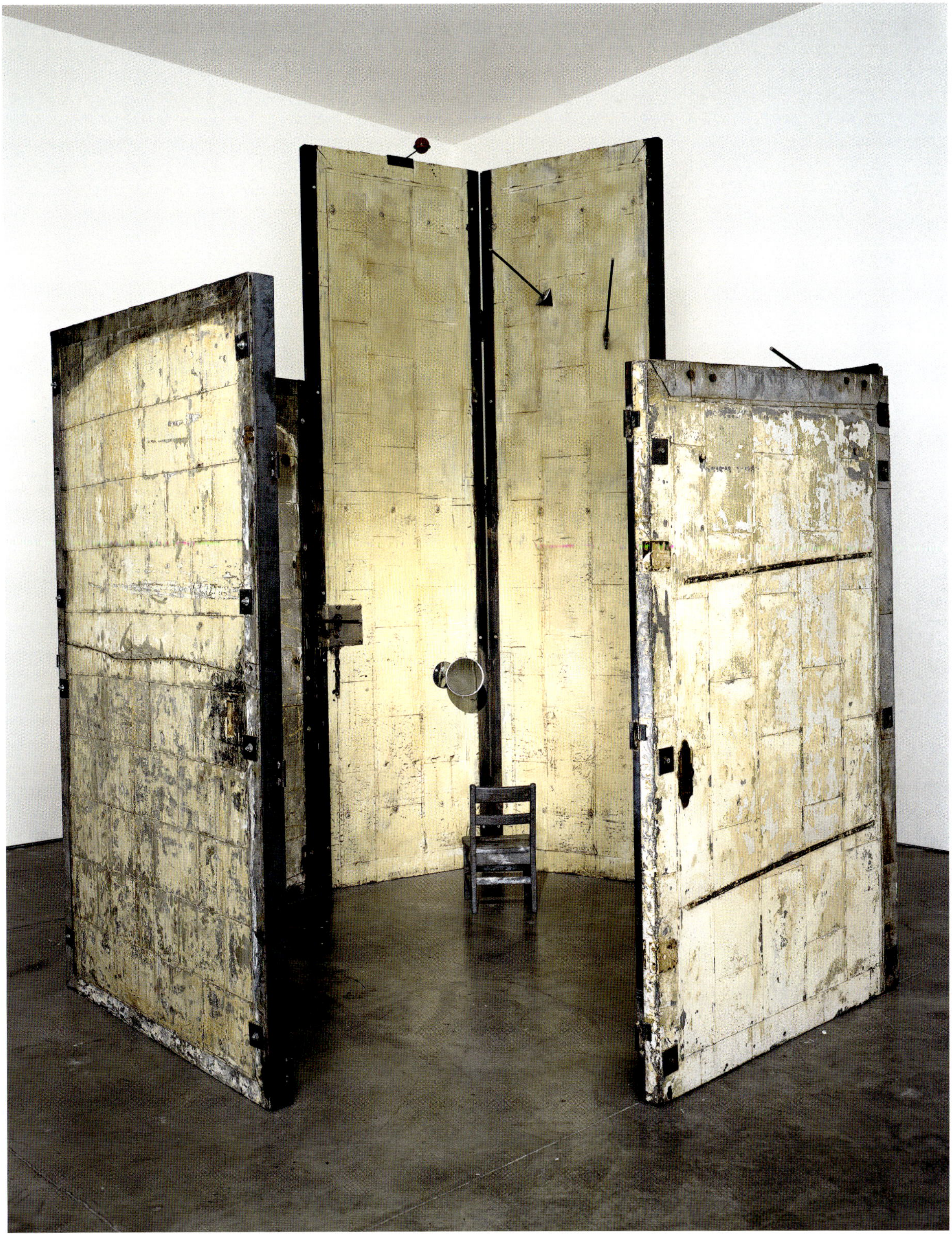

Culprit Number Two

Cell IX, 1999
Steel, pink marble, glass and mirrors
84 x 100 x 52 in.

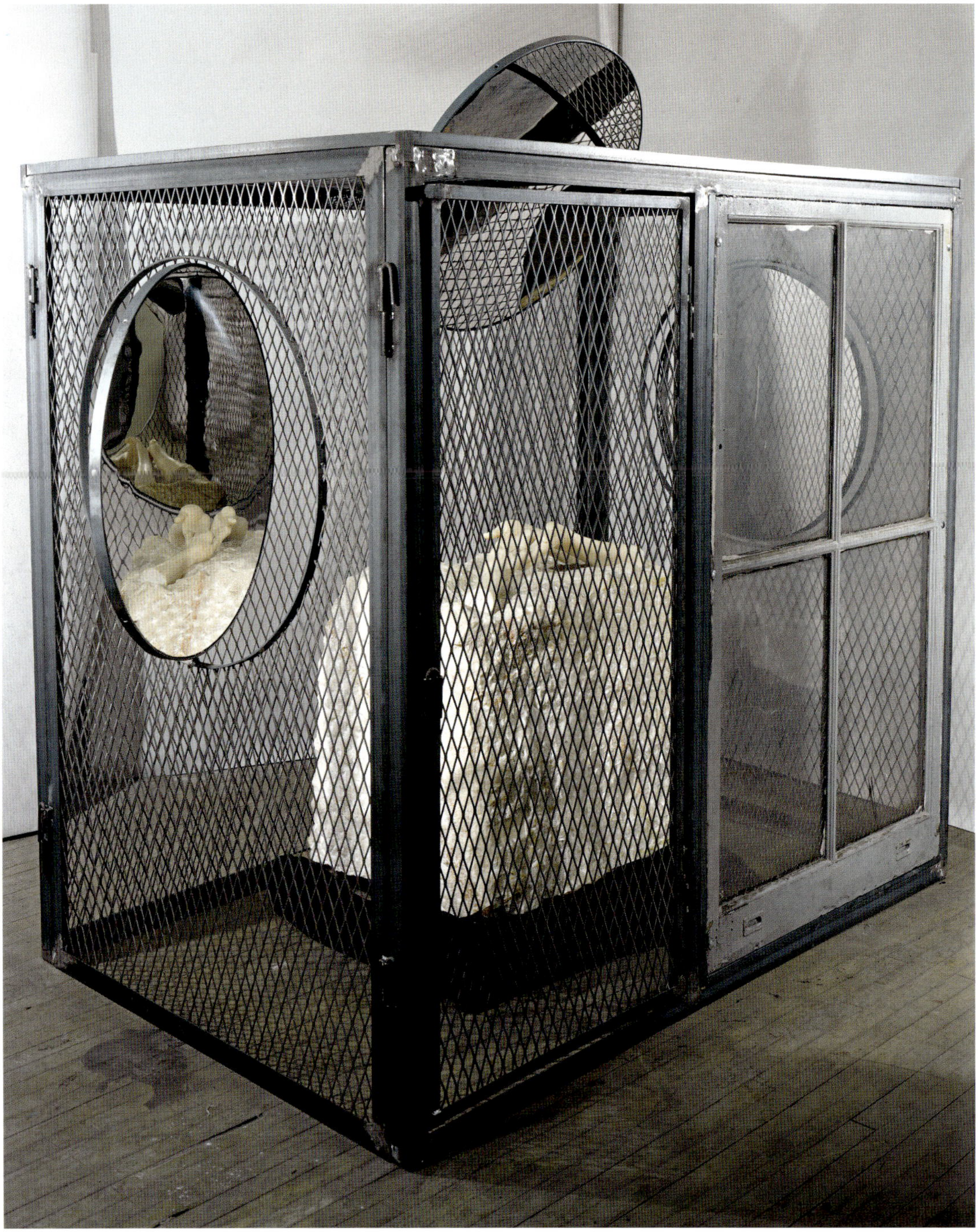

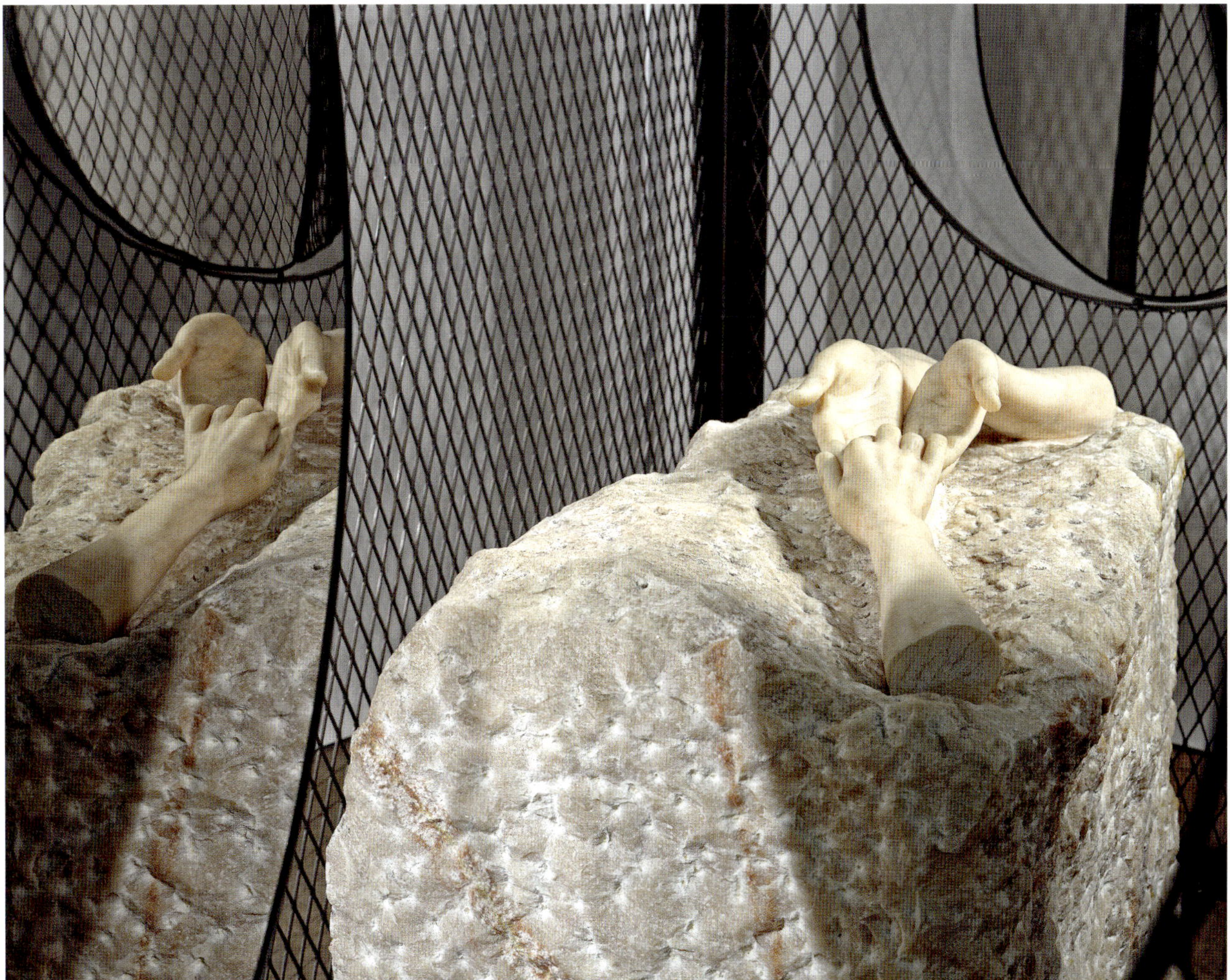

I Do, I Undo, I Redo (1999–2000)
installed in the inaugural exhibition of the
Tate Modern, London, in the Turbine Hall,
May 12–November 26, 2000

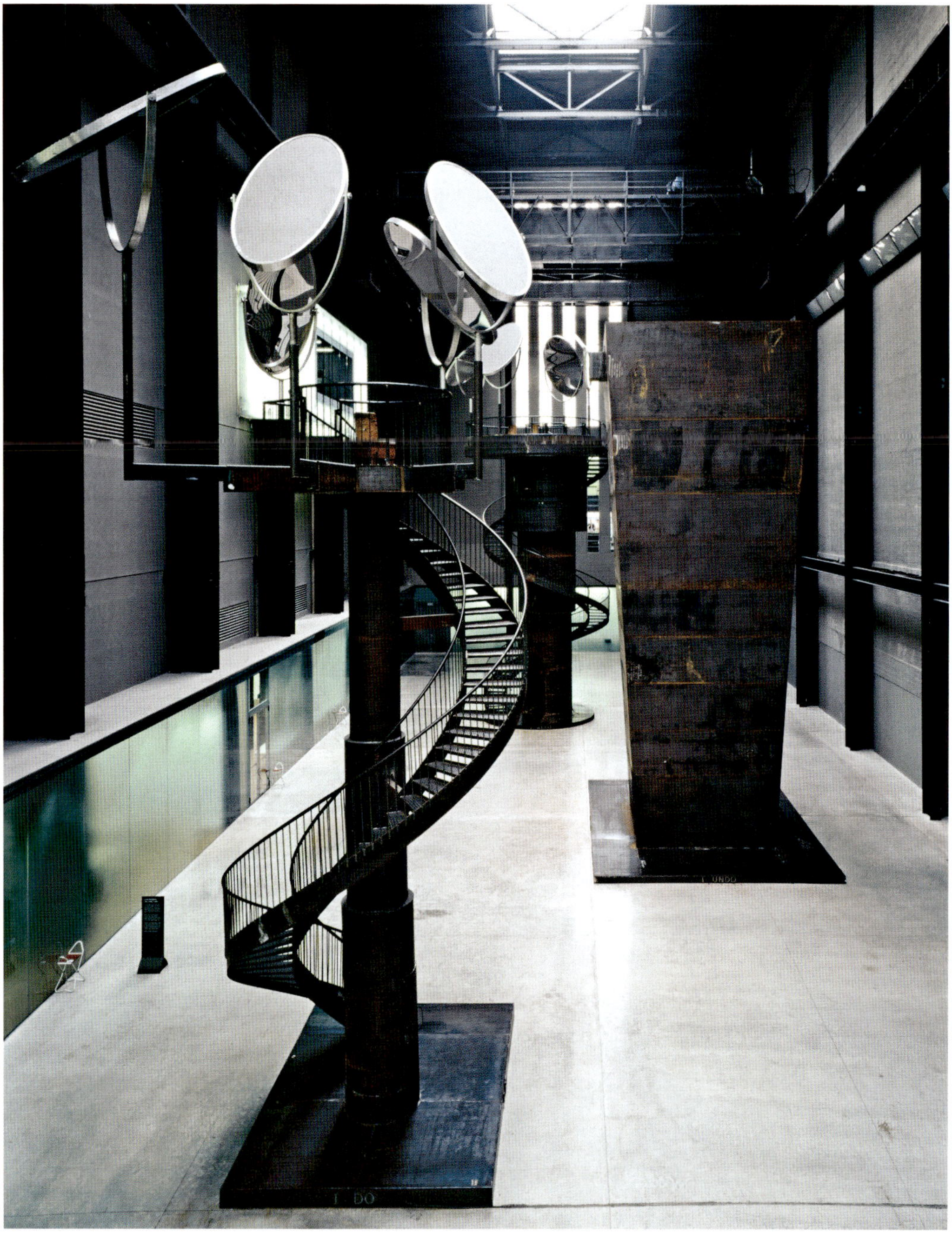

I Do (detail), 1999–2000
Installed at the Tate Modern
Steel, stainless steel, fabric, glass, wood
650 x 236 1/4 x 236 1/4 in.

I Undo (interior detail), 1999–2000
Steel, stainless steel, wood, glass and epoxy
512 x 177 1/4 x 138 in.

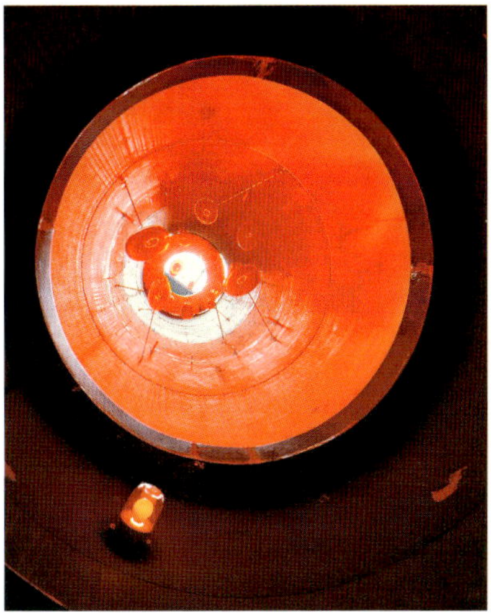

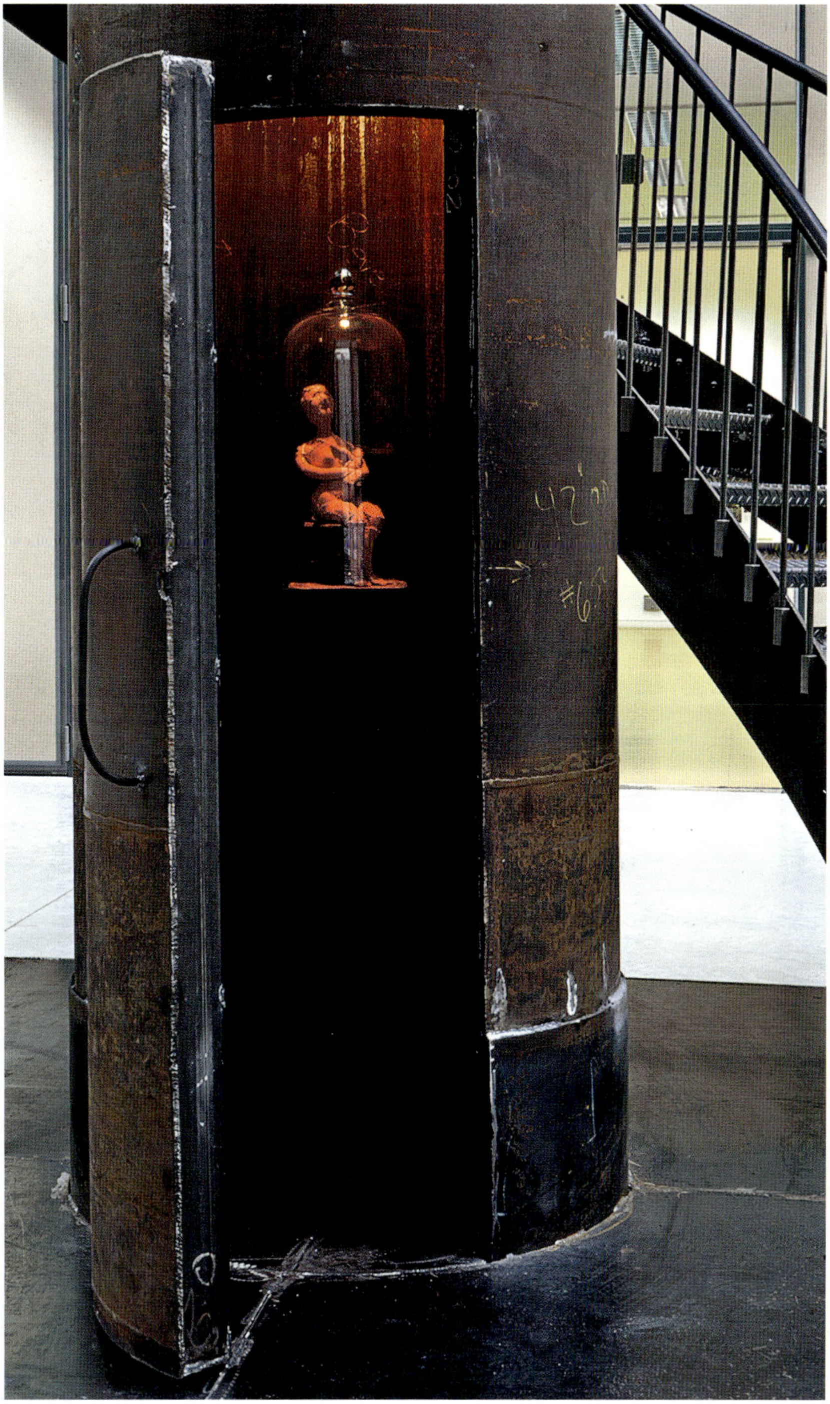

I Undo, 1999–2000
Installed at the Tate Modern
Steel, stainless steel, wood, glass, epoxy
512 x 177 1/4 x 138 in.

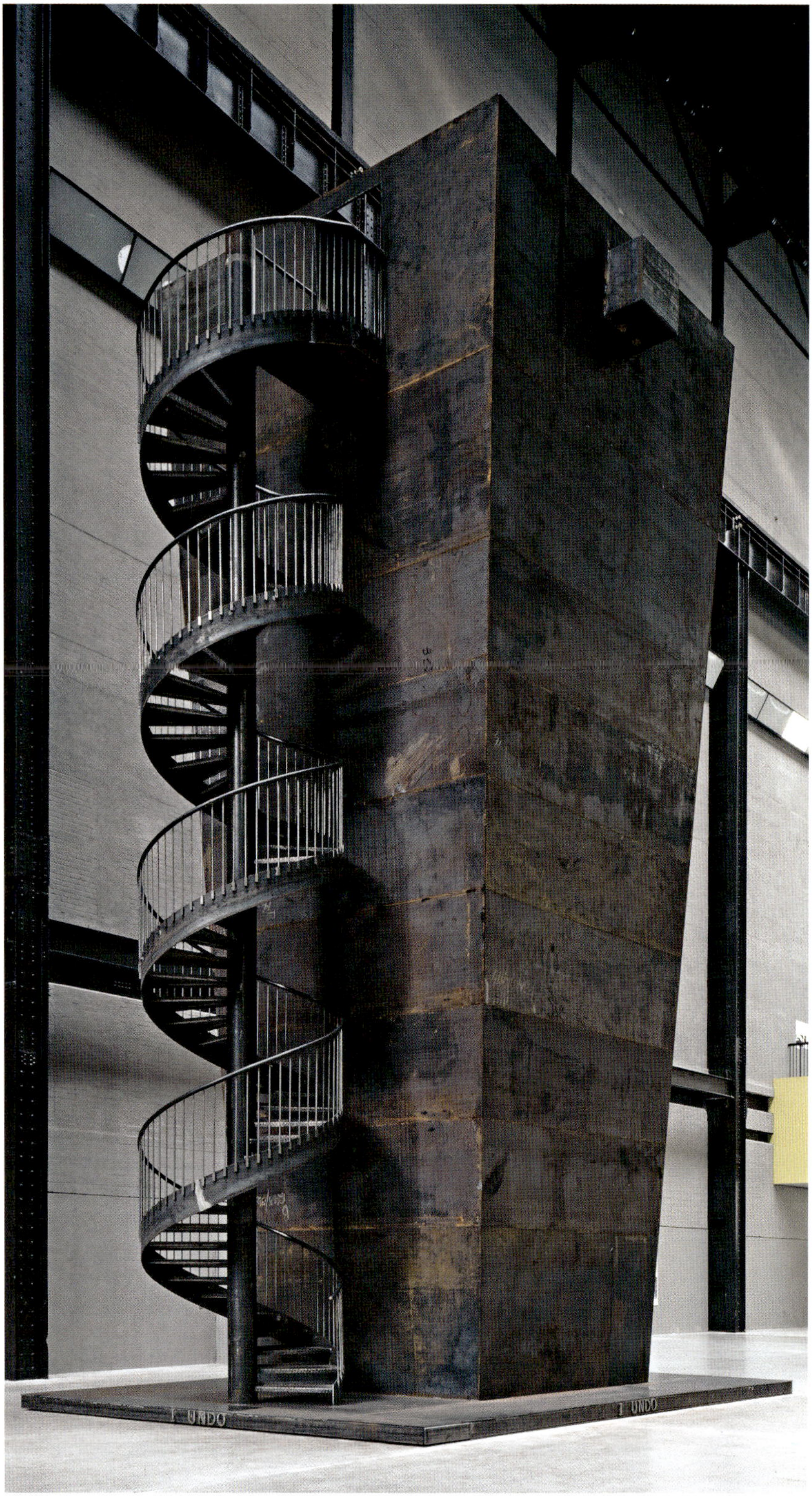

I Redo (detail), 1999–2000
Installed at the Tate Modern
Steel, stainless steel, marble, fabric, glass, wood
698 x 354 1/4 x 236 1/4 in.

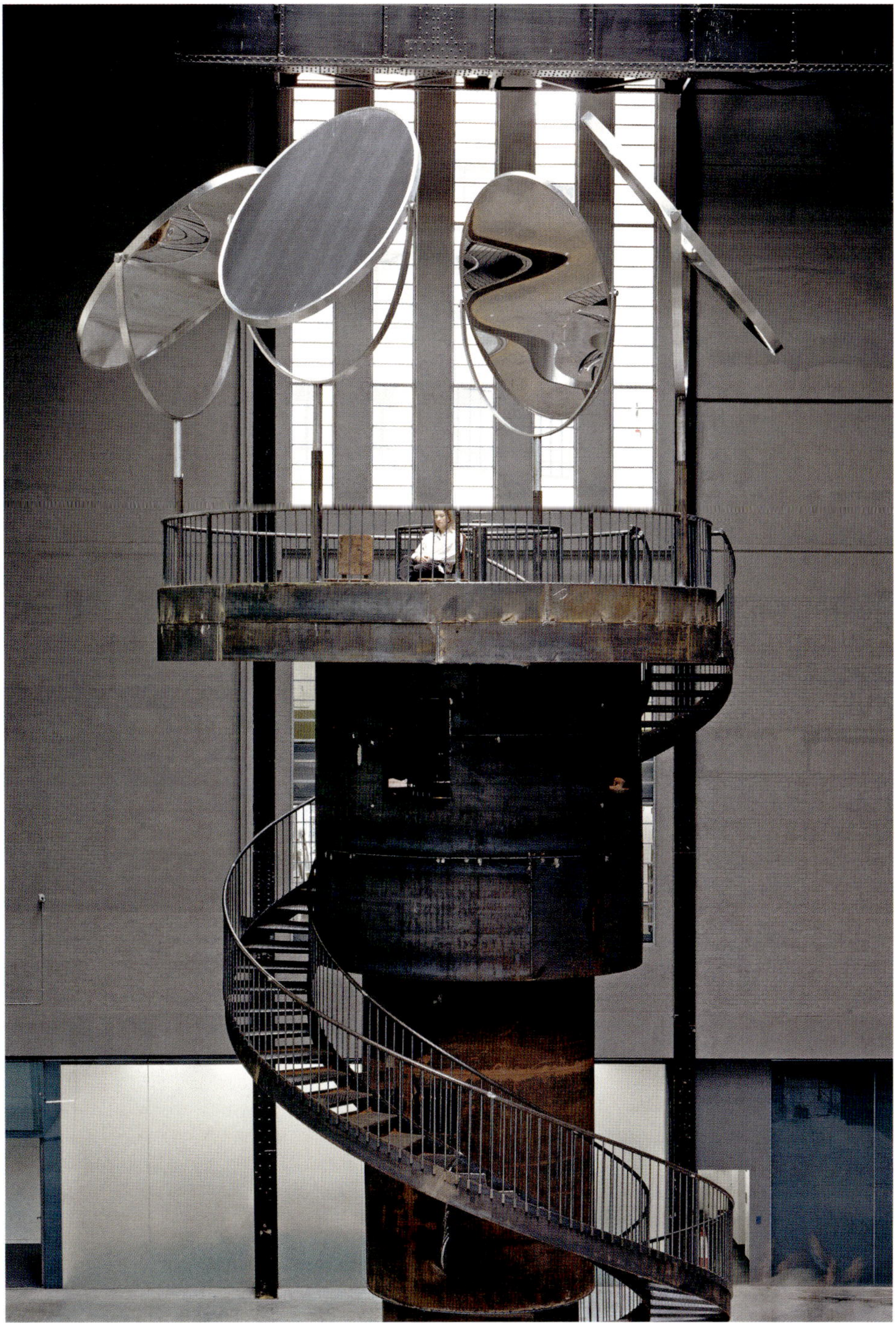

Cell XV (For Turner), 2000
Steel, aluminum, mirrors, glass, metal
and water
108 x 120 x 68 in.

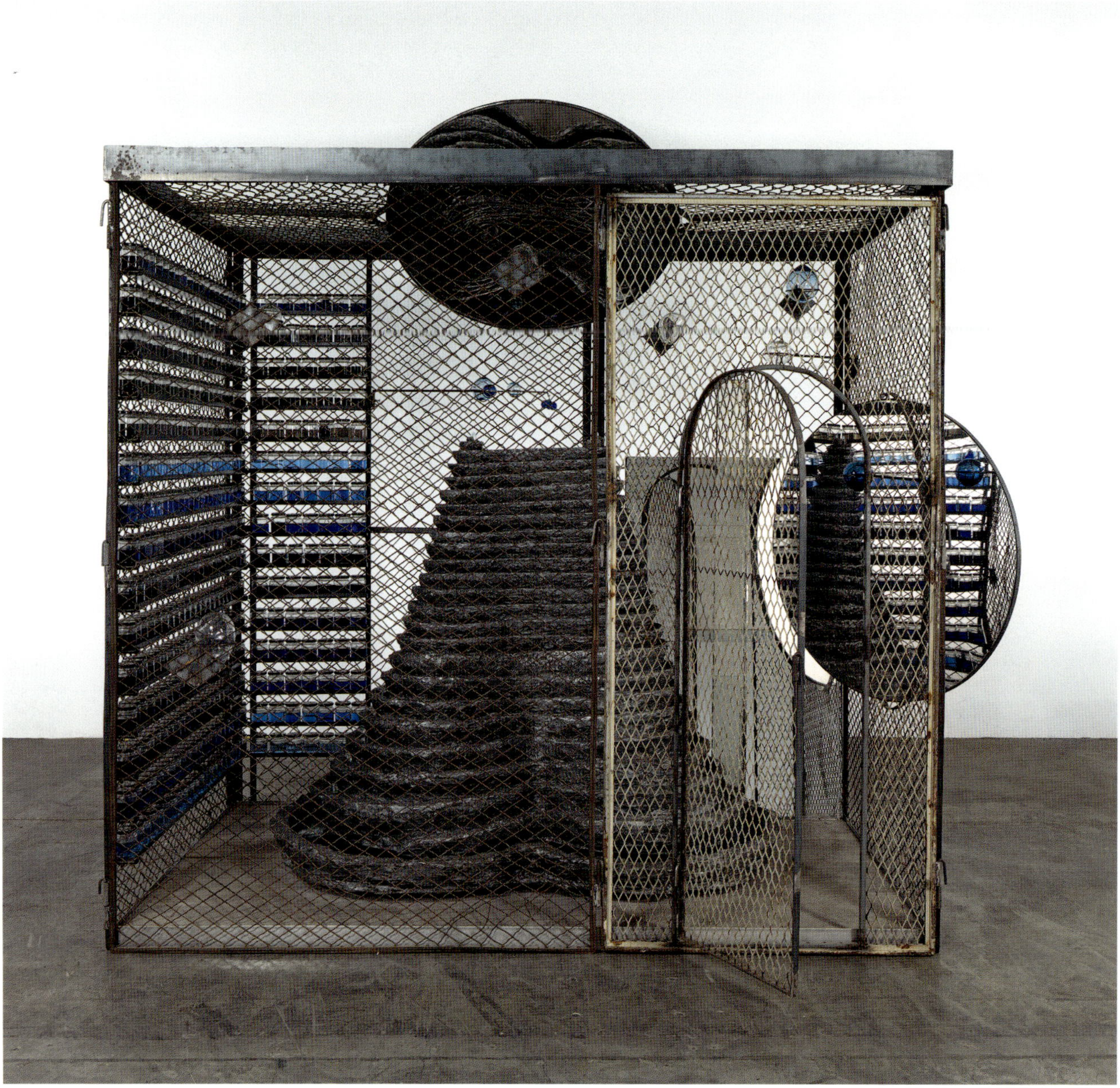

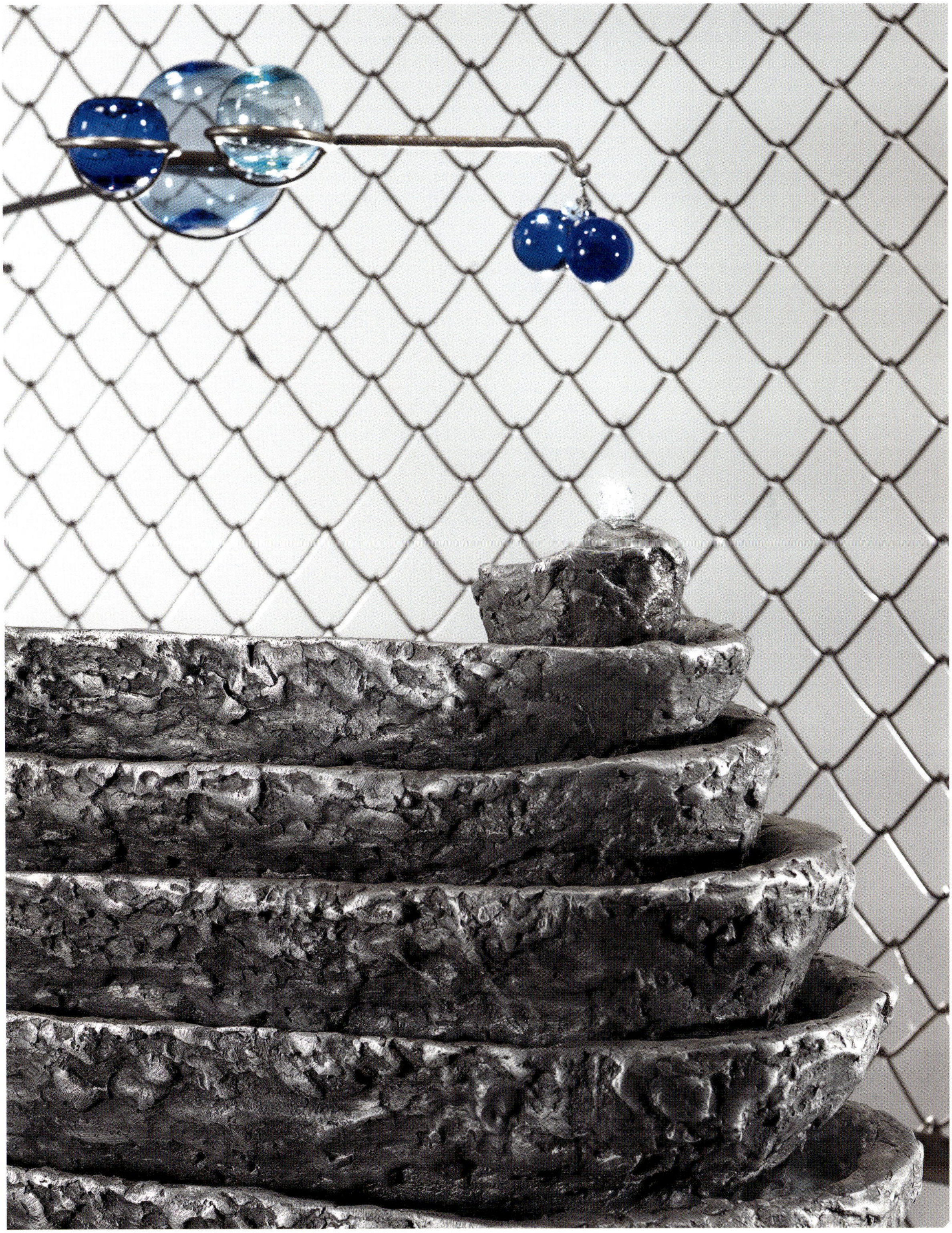

Cell XV (For Turner)

Cell XXV (The View of the World of the Jealous Wife), 2001
Steel, wood, marble, glass, fabric
100 x 120 x 120 in.

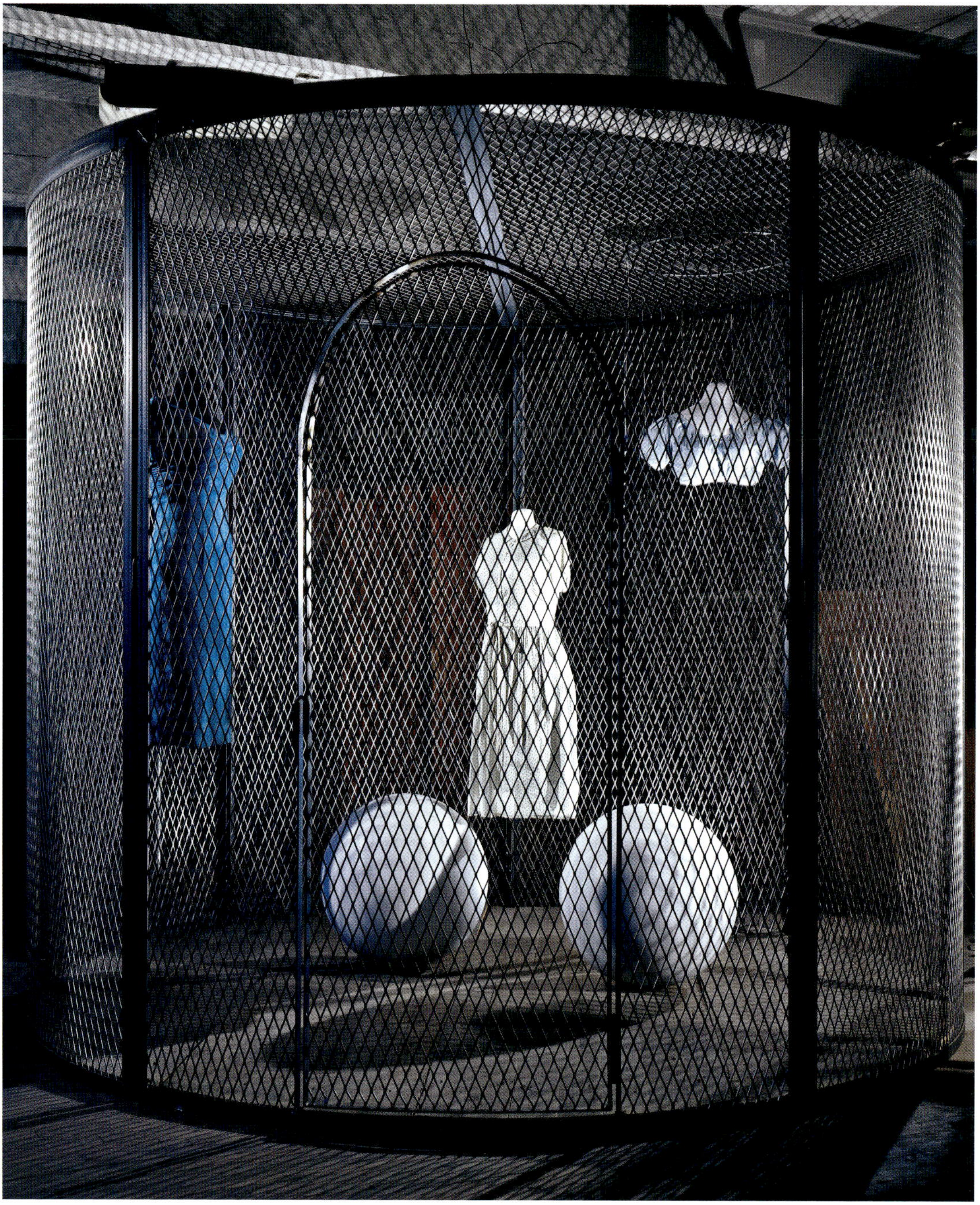

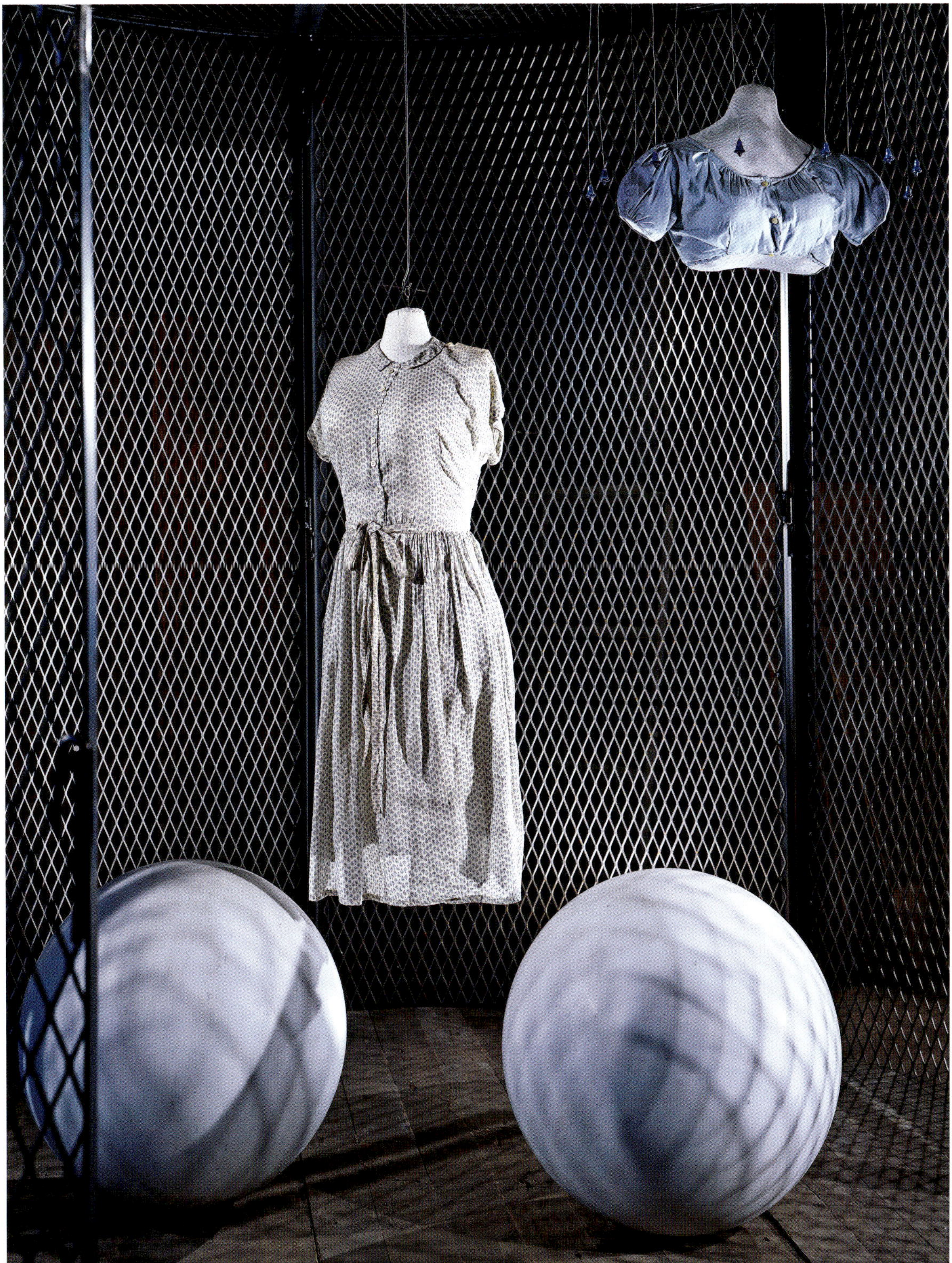

Cell XXV (The View of the
World of the Jealous Wife)

Cell XXVI, 2003
Steel, fabric, aluminum, stainless steel, wood
99 1/2 x 171 x 120 in.

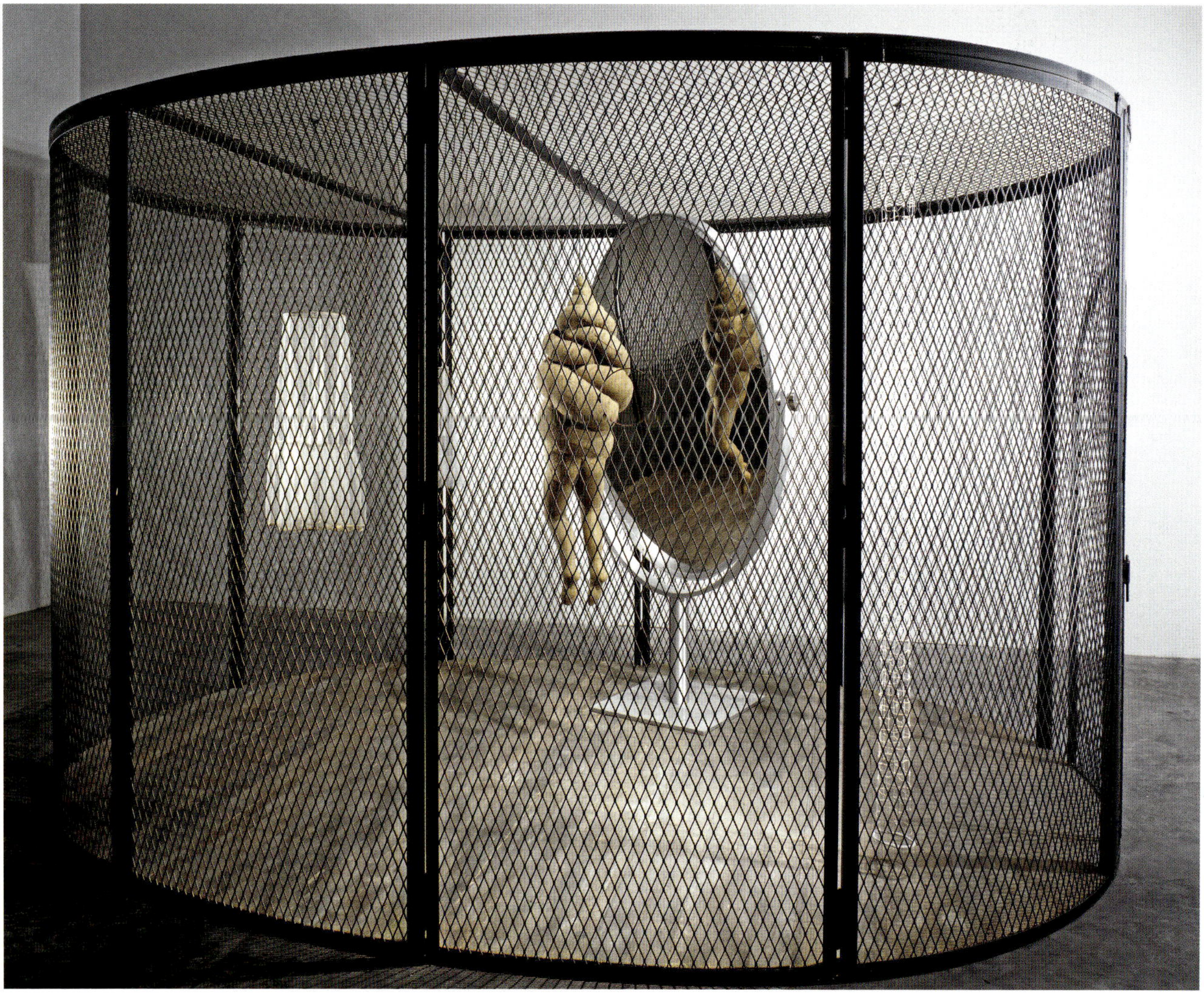

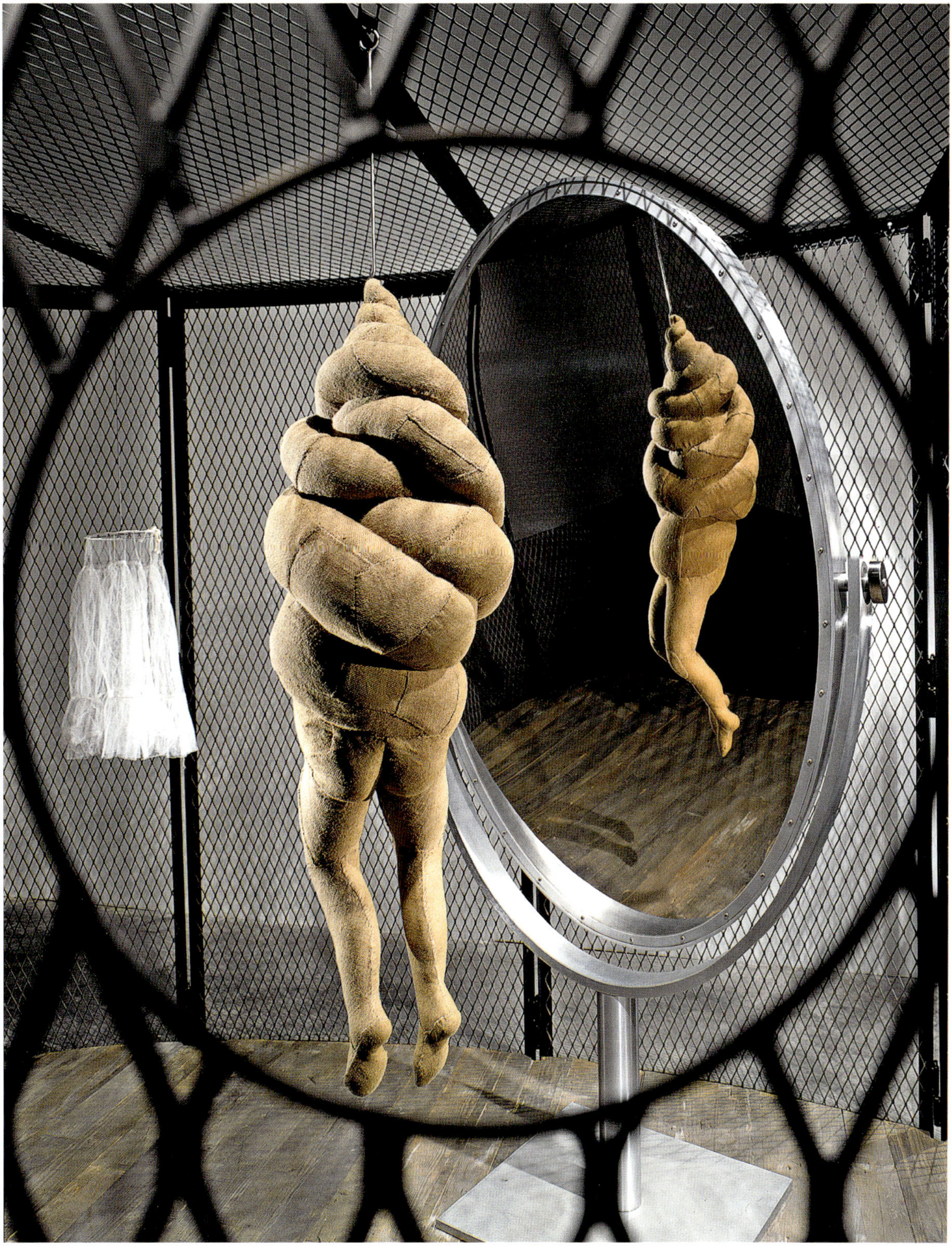

Cell XXVI

Cell (The Last Climb), 2008
Steel, glass, rubber, thread, wood
151 1/2 x 157 1/2 x 118 in.

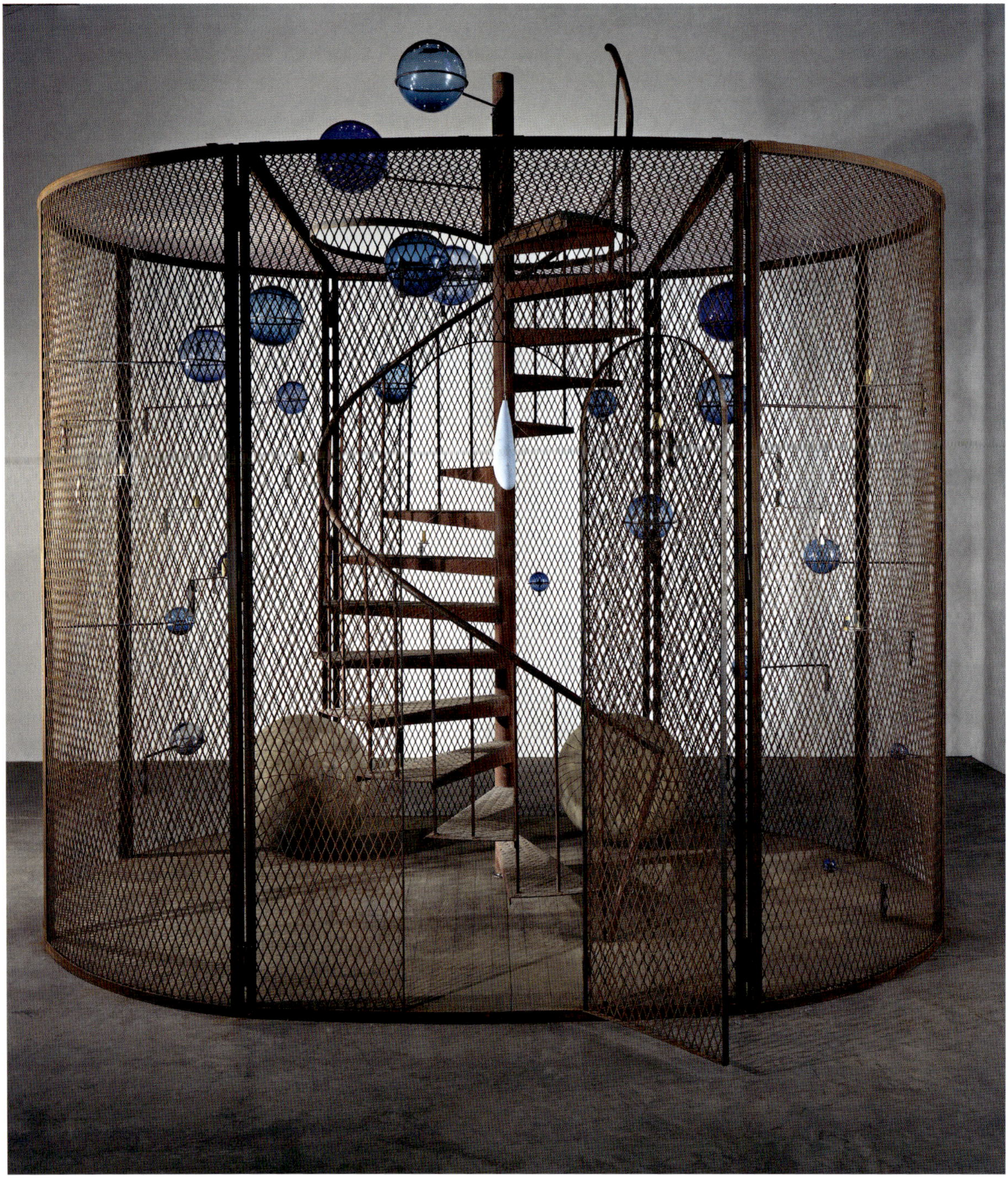

NOTES

1 Louise Bourgeois, source unknown, 1979

2 Stuart Morgan, 'Taking cover. Interview with Louise Bourgeois', in: *Artscribe International*, January/February 1988, p. 32

3 Robert Storr, 'Louise Bourgeois interviewed', in: Carl Haenlein (ed.), *Louise Bourgeois, Skulpturen und Installationen*, Kestner-Gesellschaft Hannover, Hanover, 1994, p. 17

4 Louise Bourgeois in: Marsha Pels, 'Louise Bourgeois: A Search for Gravity', in: *Art International*, October 1979, p. 49

5 Louise Bourgeois in: Jerry Gorovoy, Pandora Tabatabai Asbaghi, *Louise Bourgeois. Blue Days and Pink Days*, exhibition catalog, Fondazione Prada, Milan, 1997, p. 25

6 "There were all kinds of animals. There was a donkey, there was a pig. It was full of guinea hens that always flew – you couldn't get them back – ducks, and families of rabbits. And all these animals. The point of it was to show that all animals can live together in peace and harmony." Louise Bourgeois, *Album*, New York, 1994, unpaged

7 Louise Bourgeois in: Jerry Gorovoy, Pandora Tabatabai Asbaghi, op. cit. (note 5), p. 26

8 Marcel Proust, *Within a Budding Grove. In Search of Lost Time. Vol. 2*, London, 1992

9 Marcel Proust, ibid.

10 Louise Bourgeois, *Album*, New York, 1994, unpaged

11 Louise Bourgeois in: Jerry Gorovoy, Pandora Tabatabai Asbaghi, op. cit. (note 5), p. 21

12 Louise Bourgeois in: Jerry Gorovoy, Pandora Tabatabai Asbaghi, op. cit. (note 5), p. 62

13 Louise Bourgeois in: Henry Geldzahler, *Making It New. Essays, Interviews and Talks*, Turtle Point Press, 1994, p. 285

14 Jerry Gorovoy, Pandora Tabatabai Asbaghi, op. cit. (note 5), p. 56

15 Louise Bourgeois in: Jerry Gorovoy, Pandora Tabatabai Asbaghi, op. cit. (note 5), p. 27

16 Louise Bourgeois in: Douglas Maxwell, 'Louise Bourgeois', in: *Modern Painters*, vol. 6, no. 2, 1993, p. 41

17 "They needed draughtsmen, beautiful draughtsmen, to repair the tapestry. But my father hated those pretentious people who want to be artists. He would say to me: never talk to me about artists – they are parasites. But when M. Gounod, the draughtsman, did not show up, they called on me. I would not say that I was as good as he was, but I wasn't bad. I was a useful person. I never asked to be paid." Louise Bourgeois in: Douglas Maxwell, op. cit. (note 16), pp. 38–43

18 Louise Bourgeois in: Douglas Maxwell, op. cit. (note 16), pp. 38–43

19 Paul Gardner, 'The Discreet Charm of Louise Bourgeois', in: *Artnews*, vol. 79, 1980, p. 84

20 Louise Bourgeois in: Ann Gibson, 'Louise Bourgeois's Retroactive Politics of Gender', in: *Art Journal*, winter 1994, pp. 44–47

21 Louise Bourgeois in: Jerry Gorovoy, Pandora Tabatabai Asbaghi, op. cit. (note 5), p. 72

22 Louise Bourgeois in: Stuart Morgan, op. cit. (note 2), p. 33

23 Louise Bourgeois in: Donald Kuspit, *Bourgeois. An Interview with Louise Bourgeois*, New York, 1988, p. 67

24 Louise Bourgeois in: Donald Kuspit, ibid., p. 51

25 Louise Bourgeois in: Jerry Gorovoy, Pandora Tabatabai Asbaghi, op. cit. (note 5), p. 73

26 Louise Bourgeois in: Donald Kuspit, op. cit. (note 23), p. 26

27 Louise Bourgeois in: Douglas Maxwell, op. cit. (note 16), pp. 38–43

28 Louise Bourgeois in: Donald Kuspit, op. cit. (note 23), p. 52 f.

29 Louise Bourgeois in: Jerry Gorovoy, Pandora Tabatabai Asbaghi, op. cit. (note 5), p. 84

30 Louise Bourgeois in: Jerry Gorovoy, Pandora Tabatabai Asbaghi, op. cit. (note 5), p. 106

31 Louise Bourgeois in: Jerry Gorovoy, Pandora Tabatabai Asbaghi, op. cit. (note 5), p. 18

32 Louise Bourgeois in: Ann Gibson, op. cit. (note 20), pp. 44–47

33 See Louise Bourgeois in: Alain Kirili, 'The Passion For Sculpture – A Conversation with Louise Bourgeois', in: *Arts*, vol. 63, no. 7, 1989, pp. 68–75

34 Louise Bourgeois in: Donald Kuspit, op. cit. (note 23), p. 72 f.

35 'The Irascible 18' was the title of a *Herald Tribune* editorial commenting on the artist's open letter to the Metropolitan Museum of Art

36 Louise Bourgeois in: Robert Storr, 'Louise Bourgeois Interviewed', in: *Galleries Magazine*, June/July 1990, pp. 95–104

37 Robert Storr, 'The discreet charm of Louise Bourgeois', in: *Tate: The Art Magazine*, no. 6, summer 1995, pp. 24–31

38 "La jeune sculpture me paraît plus stimulante que la jeune peinture. [...] Louise Bourgeois, a New York, construit depuis longtemps des *totems* très sommaires mais étrangement doués d'esprit qu'elle appelle 'forme étonnée' ou 'figure endormie'. [...] Son Œuvre rare a exercé une influence évidente sur nombre de jeunes sculpteurs américains." Michel Seuphor, 'Le Choix d'un critique', in: *Œil*, no. 49, January 1965

39 William Rubin, 'Some Reflections Prompted by the Recent Work of Louise Bourgeois', in: *Art International*, vol. 8, April 1969, pp. 17–20

40 See Louise Bourgeois in: Donald Kuspit, op. cit. (note 23), pp. 21–25

41 Louise Bourgeois in: Jerry Gorovoy, Pandora Tabatabai Asbaghi, op. cit. (note 5), p. 142

42 Deborah Wye, *Louise Bourgeois*, New York, 1982, p. 109

43 Louise Bourgeois, source unknown, 1992

44 Donald Kuspit, op. cit. (note 23), p. 57 f.

45 Johann Joachim Winckelmann, 'Gedanken über die Nachahmung der griechischen Werke in der Malerei und Bildhauerkunst', in: Institut für angewandte Kunst, Berlin (ed.), *Johann Joachim Winckelmann. Kleine Schriften und Briefe*, Weimar, 1960, p. 30

46 Louise Bourgeois, 'Freud's Toys', in: *Artforum*, January 1990, pp. 111–113

47 Near the Ancient Greek city of Tanagra, east of Thebes, figures dating from the 4th and 3rd centuries BC were discovered in 1873. These figures are in themselves replicas of even older objects originally made in Athens.

48 Louise Bourgeois, 'Freud's Toys', op. cit. (note 46), p. 113

49 Donald Kuspit, op. cit. (note 23), pp. 59–62

50 Donald Kuspit, op. cit. (note 23), p. 62

51 Jerry Gorovoy, 'Louise Bourgeois and the Nature of Abstraction', in: Carl Haenlein (ed.), op. cit. (note 3), p. 13

52 Louise Bourgeois, in: Susi Bloch, 'An Interview with Louise Bourgeois', in: *Art Journal*, summer 1976, pp. 370–373

53 Louise Bourgeois, in: Robert Storr, op. cit. (note 36), pp. 94–103, 140

54 Louise Bourgeois, 'Brief Account of Career', in: Jeremy Strick (ed.), *Louise Bourgeois. The Personnage*, Saint Louis 1994, p. 9

55 John P. O'Neill (ed.), *Barnett Newman. Selected Writings and Interviews*, Berkeley/Los Angeles 1992, p. 61 f.

56 John P. O'Neill (ed.), ibid., p. 64

57 John P. O'Neill (ed.), op. cit., p. 64

58 John P. O'Neill (ed.), op. cit., p. 65

59 John P. O'Neill (ed.), op. cit., p. 100

60 John P. O'Neill (ed.), op. cit., p. 100

61 John P. O'Neill (ed.), op. cit., p. 100

62 "Alfred Barr told me that at the time the *Demoiselles* was first shown, the reaction, except from vanguard artists, was far from generally favorable and that its acquisition was criticized by some members of The Museum of Modern Art community." William Rubin (ed.), *Primitivisms in 20th Century Art*, New York 1984, p. 76, footnote 46

63 Maurice Raynal, 'Conception and Vision', 1912, in: Edward Fry, *Cubism*, New York/Toronto, 1966, p. 95 f.

64 John P. O'Neill (ed.), op. cit. (note 55), p. 108

65 Louise Bourgeois, in: Robert Storr, as note 36

66 Quoted and translated after Judith Cladel, *Rodin: The Man and his Art*, New York 1918, p. 68 f.

67 Karl Schlechta (ed.), *Friedrich Nietzsche. Werke in drei Bänden. Zweiter Band*, Munich/Vienna 1977, p. 145

68 John P. O'Neill (ed.), op. cit. (note 55), p. 64 f.

69 Karl Schlechta (ed.), op. cit. (note 67), p. 311 f.

70 Louise Bourgeois, source unknown, 1991

71 The title of this work refers to a personal experience of the artist in the Italian village Trani, which has not been further explained. See Marie-Laure Bernadac, *Louise Bourgeois*, Paris/New York, 1996, p. 93

72 Louise Bourgeois in: Jerry Gorovoy, Pandora Tabatabai Asbaghi, op. cit. (note 5), p. 56

73 cf. A. B. Novikoff and E. Holtzmann, *Cells and Organelles*, 1970; M. C. Ledbetter and K. R. Porter, *Introduction to the Fine Structure of Plant Cells*, 1970; S. L. Wolfe, *Biology of the Cell*, 1972

74 source and date unknown

75 Louise Bourgeois, 'Freud's Toys', op. cit.

76 Louise Bourgeois, source unknown, 1992

77 Louise Bourgeois, source unknown, 1997

78 "In bed, crouching in fear, the person in this *Cell* is hiding. What he is hiding is his state of sickness. He is physically sick and afraid of death. But it is not that simple; he has other fears. What is not justified is his fear of people knowing about his sickness. He is afraid of not having any friends or afraid of losing those he has.

Some diseases are considered shameful because sinful. So he is intensely possessive of his privacy and fears the onlookers. He fears people are going to pry into his privacy. Yet he is projecting his fear of being seen, for he himself is a voyeur, a latent voyeur. This is expressed by the windows. If you can look out they can look in. The clear glass represents no secrets.

Sick people die of the need of companionship, a stroking hand, a hungering for compassion. He runs away from people, and people run away from him out of fear of contagion. So he is isolated by his own fear and by that of others.

The transparent glass represents a sickness. When you're sick, people don't like you, you are not desirable. My mother was ill and used to cough up blood; I helped her hide her illness from my father." Louise Bourgeois on *Cell I.*

79 Nulle part trace de vie, dites-vous, pah, la belle affaire, imagination pas morte, si, bon, imagination morte imaginez. Samuel Beckett, *Residua*, Stuttgart 1965, p. 67

80 Christiane Meyer-Thoss, *Louise Bourgeois, Designing for Free Fall*, Zurich 1992, p. 155

81 Ludwig Wittgenstein, 'Zettel', in: *Schriften* 5, Frankfurt a. M., 1970, p. 413

82 Louise Bourgeois in: Jerry Gorovoy, Pandora Tabatabai Asbaghi, op. cit. (note 5), p. 170

83 Samuel Beckett, *From an Abandoned Work*, London, 1958

84 Louise Bourgeois, source unknown, 1988

85 Louise Bourgeois, source and date unkown

86 Louise Bourgeois, source unknown, 1988

87 Hans Blumenberg, 'Ausblick auf eine Theorie der Unbegrifflichkeit', in: *Schiffbruch mit Zuschauer*, Frankfurt a. M., 1979, p. 78

88 Christiane Meyer-Thoss, op. cit. (note 80), p. 105

Cell	Shape	Enclosure	Objects in cell
Articulated Lair, 1986 (Museum of Modern Art, New York) Pages 10, 11, 12, 14, 16, 48, 112, 113	Edged oval, open on two sides and above	46 similar, metal, painted movable doors	Metal stool, black elongated rubber forms
No Exit, 1989 (Collection Fondation Louis Vuitton pour la Creation Paris) Pages 114, 115	Edged three-quarter circle, open on one side and above	6 painted metal doors of varying widths, painted stairs, wooden spheres	Stairs, wooden spheres, white rubber hearts
No Escape, 1989 (Collection Kiasma Museum of Contemporary Art, Helsinki, Finland) Page 116	Edged three-quarter oval, open on one side and above	4 metal doors of varying widths, stairs, wooden verticals	Stairs, wooden verticals, wooden spheres
Cell (Eyes and Mirrors), 1989–93 (Collection Tate Modern, London) Page 118	Closed glass and grating cube	2 glass sides, 2 sides made from woven steel bars, woven steel above with a large, round mirror fitted into it	Standing mirror, make-up mirror, 2 round mirrors and 2 small oval mirrors, granite block with marble spheres set into it
Gathering Wool, 1990 (Collection Louise Bourgeois Trust) Page 117	Open, edged, curved shape	4 metal doors	7 wooden spheres; mushrooms that were originally growing out from the wooden sphere no longer exist
Cell (Choisy), 1990–93 (Ydessa Hendeles Art Foundation, Toronto) Page 119	Closed glass cube	3 glass sides, 1 woven iron side, woven iron above	Guillotine, marble model house
Cell (Glass Spheres and Hands), 1990–93 (National Gallery of Victoria, Melbourne, Australia) Pages 120, 121	Closed glass cube	3 1/2 glass sides, 1/2 side in woven iron, glass ceiling	3 wooden chairs and 2 stools, 5 glass spheres, wooden table, hands (marble)
Cell I, 1991 (Daros Collection, Switzerland) Pages 92, 93, 95, 96, 97, 122, 123	Irregular, edged, oval-like shape, open on one side and above	9 wooden doors, 1 door with windows, all painted	Bed, metal chair, small wooden table, bedside-table lamp, standard lamp, clothes stand, suitcase, test tubes, kitchen utensils, specimen bottle, urinal
Cell II, 1991 (Carnegie Museum of Art, Pittsburgh) Page 124	Hectagon, open on one side and above	3 doors with small panes and 3 wooden doors, all painted	Mirror, plinth, 9 perfume bottles, marble hands
Cell III, 1991 (Ydessa Hendeles Art Foundation, Toronto) Pages 126, 127	Irregular, edged, oval-like shape, open on one side and above	11 doors (2 metal, the rest wooden), all painted	Paper cutting device, foot (marble), figurine (marble), mirror, faucet
Cell IV, 1991 (Collection Louise Bourgeois Trust) Pages 81, 125	Irregular, oval-like form, open on one side and above	9 wooden doors, all painted	Steel gong, wooden clapper, wooden stool and marble block with ear
Cell V, 1991 (Solomon R. Guggenheim Museum, New York) Page 128	Hectagon, open above and closed to the sides	6 varied wooden doors, of which 3 have small panes, all painted	2 wooden spheres
Cell VI, 1991 (Collection Louise Bourgeois Trust) Page 129	Quadrangle, open on one side and above	4 similar doors, all painted	Metal stool
Precious Liquids, 1992 (Centre Georges Pompidou, Paris) Pages 130, 131	Cylinder, open above and openable on two sides, with the inscription: "Art is a guaranty for sanity."	Water tank, cut to size	Bed, glasses, stands, 2 wooden spheres, 2 rubber spheres, coat, embroidered nightshirt, sculpture *Trani Episode*
Bullet Hole, 1992 (Collection Louise Bourgeois Trust) Pages 132, 133	Edged, roughly circular, open on one side. Inscription: "Fears make the world go round. What makes your world go round?"	3 steel doors with wrought iron grills, 1 with steel plate, 2 doors with small panes and steel plates behind with inscription, 1 steel door	3 steel spheres
Cell (Arch of Hysteria), 1992–93 (Centro Andaluz de Arte Contemporaneo, Sevilla) Page 134	Circular, open on one side and above	11 steel doors	Cast-iron cutting machine, bed, mattress, body without arms and head in golden bronze, with patina

Cell (Three White Marble Spheres), 1993 (Saint Louis Art Museum, Missouri) Pages 106, 135	Closed glass cube	3 1/2 glass sides, 1/2 side of openable woven steel, glass ceiling with a large, round mirror set into it	2 larger, 1 smaller white marble spheres
Cell (You Better Grow Up), 1993 (The Rachofsky Collection) Pages 99, 100, 101, 136, 137	Closed cube, glass on one side	2 glass sides opposite each other with mirrors set into them, 2 woven steel sides, woven steel ceiling with a small mirror set into it	3 stool-like stands, 1 ceramic vase with 3 openings, 1 glass vessel, 3 perfume bottles, glass tower, marble block with 3 hands on steel supports
Red Room (Parents), 1994 (Collection Ursula Hauser, Switzerland) Pages 102, 138, 139	Closed, edged, three-quarter oval, open above	13 wooden doors	Bed, toy train, xylophone, 2 commodes, cheese box, 2 marble sculptures, glass, drop-shaped form
Red Room (Child), 1994 (Musée d'Art Contemporain de Montreal) Pages 103, 140, back cover	Irregular, closed, edged, three-quarter circle	13 wooden doors	2 glass, spiral-shaped forms, 2 steel stands, ladder, 3 narrow wooden stands, suitcase, first aid kit, round plinth, sheep's head, 1 large glass hand, 3 small glass hands
Cell (Choisy Two), 1995 (Collection Anthony T. Podesta, Washington DC) Page 143	Cube, open and with grating above	4 woven iron sides, 2 sides with mirrors set into them, woven iron ceiling with mirror	Marble model house
Cell (Hands and Mirror), 1995 (Collection Barbara Lee, promised gift to The Institute of Contemporary Art, Boston) Pages 144, 145	Partly open hectagon, open above	4 painted steel doors with 2 smaller inset openings, 2 painted steel doors with 1 smaller inset opening	Marble block with hands, make-up mirror
In and Out, 1995 (Collection Louise Bourgeois Trust) Page 141	Closed glass cube	3 1/2 glass sides, 1/2 woven iron side, 3 sides with mirrors set into them, woven iron with mirror above	c. 8 meat grinders, 7 silver spheres on stands, an iron bedstead with mattress and plaster body without arms and head
Cell (Clothes), 1996 (Fondazione Prada, Milan) Pages 146, 147	Irregular oval, open above	18 painted wooden doors	About 15 clothes stands, stuffed textile shapes, clothes hangers, 1 iron chair, torso, elongated rubber form, 1 small lamp, 1 flat steel plate
Spider, 1997 (Collection Louise Bourgeois Trust) Page 142	Closed circle with a grate over it, one side covered with tapestry	Closed, barrel-like, with woven iron, woven iron above and below	Steel spheres, bowl, fragments of tapestry, chair
Passage Dangereux, 1997 (Collection Ursula Hauser, Switzerland) Pages 150, 151, 152, 153, 154, 155, 156	Long, barred corridor with wider sections containing diverse objects	35 woven iron sides, 20 woven iron elements on the floor, 20 woven iron elements on the ceiling	Entrance: on the left 1 key welded to the side, on the right above 1 plaster breast. Room 1: 6 cuffs on shelves, on the lowest shelf 1 perfume bottle, 2 make-up mirrors and 1 large mirror, 1 marble block with 2 long ears, 2 metal tubes as base for the marble block. Corridor to room 1: hanging, elongated rubber objects with needles. Room 2: wooden children's swing with tapestry seat, 1 large hanging tapestry, 1 elongated, narrow mirror. Room 3: electric chair, 1 mirror welded to the side. Room 4: 17 hanging chairs, 1 hanging artificial leg, 1 office chair, 1 wooden chair with tapestry cover, 1 children's table and chair, 1 metal bed, 1 copulating couple: feet made of plaster with patina on sticks, thrusting into a steel ring, 1 small steel spider with a leg welded to the side. Room 5: metal chair with tapestry cushion, 3 wooden children's chairs, 3 large glass spheres, 1 small blue glass sphere, 1 steel and marble shelf, on top of it a glass horse, in which there is a fly and scraps of paper with writing on them, underneath the horse 1 bronze bull. Room 6: 3 wooden, chair-like stands; sitting on the first on the left is 1 large plastic sphere and 1 small plastic sphere on a black stand, both containing bones; on the middle stand is a wasps' nest and 1 stuffed stocking; on the right is 1 bronze spiral with a small mirror and 1 glass object, 2 hanging square mirrors in the right corner, in the left 1 hanging flax and steel nest
Cell VII, 1998 (Private collection) Pages 148, 149	Closed circle made of doors	18 wooden doors, some with glass panels	Bronze model house, with patina, 2 blue glass spheres, small steel spider, clothes and bones, spiral staircase with bed on the top platform, wax, needle and thread
Cell VIII, 1998 (Collection Louise Bourgeois Trust) Pages 157, 158, 159	Hexagon made of woven iron	8 woven iron sides, woven iron above and below	Tapestries, blue clothes, roughly cut pink marble block with rabbit-like ears
Cell (Twelve Oval Mirrors), 1998 (Collection Louise Bourgeois Trust) Page 160	Oval, open to space outside by pivoting mirrors	12 aluminum mirrors (concave and convex)	14 wooden benches

Cell	Shape	Enclosure	Objects in cell
Culprit Number Two, 1998 (Collection Louise Bourgeois Trust) Page 161	Six-sided structure with opening	6 steel-covered doors	Chair in lead, mirror, glass ball, steel arrows
Cell IX, 1999 (D. Daskalopoulos Collection) Pages 162, 163	Closed glass, mirror, steel mesh cube	3 mesh wall panels, glass window panel, mesh roof panel, mesh door panel, 3 stainless mirrors	Pink marble piece with 3 hands, 2 steel I-beams, 3 mirrors
I Do, 1999–2000 (Collection Louise Bourgeois Trust) Page 165	Large thin columnar steel tower with exterior spiral staircase and platform at top	Steel tower with lower interior chamber, exterior spiral staircase, platform at top	5 mirrors and single chair on top platform, small pink fabric Good Mother and child under glass dome in the base of tower
I Redo, 1999–2000 (Collection Louise Bourgeois Trust) Page 167	Large columnar steel tower with exterior spiral staircase and platform at top	Steel tower with exterior and interior spiral staircases and platform at top	Exterior spiral staircase, interior spiral staircase, 4 mirrors, 2 chairs, black fabric Janus, 4 marble hand poses, steel and fabric Mother with child suspended by umbilical cord under glass dome
I Undo, 1999–2000 (Collection Louise Bourgeois Trust) Page 166	Large thin columnar steel tower with exterior spiral staircase	Rectangular steel tower, exterior ascending spiral staircase, doorway to interior chamber at top, descending interior spiral staircase	Exterior spiral staircase, interior spiral staircase, Bad Mother with child and spilt milk under glass dome, tiny wood chair, regular wood chair, 19 red glass elements
Cell XV (For Turner), 2000 (Collection Louise Bourgeois Trust) Pages 168, 169	Mirror and steel mesh cube	4 mesh wall panels, mesh ceiling panel, mesh door panel, stainless mirrors for ceiling and wall panel, metal floor	Aluminum fountain, with water, glass jars with ink, steel rods with glass balls, mirrors and glass panes
Cell XXV (The View of the World of the Jealous Wife), 2001 (Collection Ellipse Foundation, Portugal) Pages 170, 171	Closed circular shape with door	6 mesh curved wall panels, 1 mesh door panel, 2 mesh ceiling panels forming circle, circular wooden floor	2 full mannequin forms with dresses, 1 top-only mannequin with blouse, 10 blue glass balls, 2 marble spheres
Cell XXVI, 2003 (Collection Gemeentemuseum Den Haag, The Netherlands) Pages 172, 173	Closed mesh oval shape	10 steel mesh panels, door panel, 4 steel mesh panels form ceiling, wood floor in 4 sections	Stainless steel and aluminum mirror (concave and convex), tan burlap spiral figure, 2 crinoline hanging forms, tubular fishnet fabric
Cell (The Last Climb), 2008 (Collection National Gallery of Canada, Ottawa) Pages 174, 175	Closed oval shape	8 steel mesh curved wall panels, 4 steel mesh ceiling panels, wood flooring	Spiral staircase, 20 glass spheres, 2 wood spheres, 12 spools of thread, 12 sewing needles, 1 elongated rubber shape

INDEX OF OTHER ILLUSTRATED WORKS

Louise Bourgeois

Comparative Illustrations

Unknown Artists

1. SOLO EXHIBITIONS
2. SELECTED BIBLIOGRAPHY
2.1. WRITINGS BY LOUISE BOURGEOIS AND INTERVIEWS
2.2. BOOKS
2.3. CATALOGS
2.4. VIDEOS
2.5. FILMS

1. Solo Exhibitions

1945 *Paintings by Louise Bourgeois,* Bertha Schaefer Gallery, New York

1947 *Paintings,* Norlyst Gallery, New York, 28 October–8 November

1949 *Late Work 1947 to 1949: Standing Figures,* Peridot Gallery, New York

1950 *Sculptures,* Peridot Gallery, New York, 2–28 October

1953 *Louise Bourgeois: Drawings for Sculpture and Sculpture,* Peridot Gallery, New York, 30 March–25 April

1959 *Sculpture by Louise Bourgeois,* Andrew D. White Art Museum, Cornell University, Ithaca, N.Y., 9–25 April

1963 *Recent Drawings by Louise Bourgeois,* Rose Fried Gallery, New York, 14 January–29 February

1964 *Louise Bourgeois Recent Sculpture,* Stable Gallery, New York, 7 January–1 February

1974 *Sculpture 1970–1974,* 112 Greene Street, New York, 14–26 December

1978 *New Work,* Hamilton Gallery, New York, 16 September–21 October

Triangles: New Sculpture and Drawings, Xavier Fourcade Inc., New York, 26 September–21 October

Louise Bourgeois Matrix/Berkeley 17, Berkeley Art Museum, University of California, Berkeley, December 1978–February 79

1979 *Louise Bourgeois, Sculpture 1941–1953. Plus One New Piece,* Xavier Fourcade Inc., New York, 18 September–13 October

1980 *The Iconography of Louise Bourgeois,* Max Hutchinson Gallery, New York, 6 September–11 October

Louise Bourgeois: Sculpture: The Middle Years 1955–1970, Xavier Fourcade Gallery, New York, 20 September–25 October

1981 *Louise Bourgeois: Femme Maison,* Renaissance Society, University of Chicago, Chicago, IL, 3 May–6 June

1982 *Louise Bourgeois: Retrospective,* Museum of Modern Art, New York, 3 November–8 February 1983
Contemporary Arts Museum, Houston, TX, 12 March–8 May 1983
Museum of Contemporary Art, Chicago 3 September–30 October 1983
Akron Art Museum, Akron, OH, 2 November–5 January 1984

Bourgeois Truth, Robert Miller Gallery, New York, 23 November–31 December

1983 Daniel Weinberg Gallery, San Francisco 14 September–22 December

1984 *Louise Bourgeois Sculpture,* Robert Miller Gallery, New York, 11 September–3 October

Daniel Weinberg Gallery, Los Angeles, 17 November–1 December

1985 *Louise Bourgeois: Retrospective 1947–1984,* Galerie Maeght-Lelong, Paris, February–March,
Galerie Maeght-Lelong, Zurich, April–May
Serpentine Gallery, London, 18 May–23 June

1986 *Eyes,* The Doris Freedman Plaza, New York, June–October

Louise Bourgeois, Robert Miller Gallery, New York, 6 May–7 June

Louise Bourgeois: Sculptures & Drawings, Texas Gallery, Houston, 18 November–27 December

1987 *Paintings from the 1940's,* Robert Miller Gallery, New York, 6–31 January

Louise Bourgeois, The Taft Museum, Cincinnati, OH, 5 May–28 June
The Art Museum at Florida International University, Miami, FL, 23 October–18 November
Laguna Gloria Art Museum, Austin, TX, 1 July–28 August 1988
Gallery of Art, Washington University, St. Louis, MO, 18 September–30 October 1988

Everson Museum of Art, Syracuse, NY, 22 November–31 December

1988 *Louise Bourgeois Drawings 1939–1987,* Robert Miller Gallery, New York, 2–30 January

Sculpture by Louise Bourgeois, Laguna Gloria Art Museum, Austin

Louise Bourgeois Works On Paper 1939–1988, Museum Overholland, Amsterdam, 22 November–31 December

Louise Bourgeois Work: 1943–1987, Henry Art Gallery, University of Washington, Washington, 17 November–29 January 1989

1989 *Louise Bourgeois Dessins 1940/86,* Galerie Lelong, Paris, 19 February–25 March

Louise Bourgeois – Sculpture, Robert Miller Gallery, New York, 28 March–22 April

Louise Bourgeois – Progressions and Regressions, Gallery Lelong, New York, 28 March–22 April

Louise Bourgeois: Works from the 50s, Sperone Weestwater Gallery, New York, 16 April–6 May

Louise Bourgeois Sculpture, American Academy and Institute of Arts and Letters, New York 18 May–11 June

Louise Bourgeois: Works from the Sixties, Dia Art Foundation, Bridgehampton, 25 May–25 June

Recent Sculpture by Louise Bourgeois, Art Gallery of York University, North York, Ontario

Louise Bourgeois 100 Zeichnungen 1939–1989, Galerie Lelong, Zurich

Louise Bourgeois Selected Works 1946–1989, Rhona Hoffman Gallery, Chicago, 8 September–7 October

Louise Bourgeois: A Retrospective Exhibition, Frankfurter Kunstverein, Frankfurt, 2 December–28 January 1990
Städtische Galerie im Lenbachhaus, Munich, 14 February–25 March 1990
Musée d'art Contemporain, Lyon, 5 July–20 August 1990,
Fondación Tàpies, Barcelona 6 November–6 January 1991
Kunstmuseum, Bern, 7 March–5 May 1991
Kröller-Müller-Museum, Otterlo, 25 May–8 July 1991

Louise Bourgeois, Ydessa Hendeles Art Foundation, Toronto, June–April 1990

1990 *Louise Bourgeois Drawings,* Karsten Schubert Ltd., London, 24 April–26 May

Louise Bourgeois: 1984–1989, Riverside Studios, London, 2 May–17 June

Louise Bourgeois 1939–89. Skulpturen und Zeichnungen, Galerie Krinzinger, Vienna, 18 May–12 June

Bronzen der 40er und 50er Jahre, Galerie Karsten Greve, Cologne, 13 October–8 November

1991 *Louise Bourgeois L'Œuvre gravée,* Galerie Lelong, Zurich, February–March

Louise Bourgeois Recent Sculpture, Robert Miller Gallery, New York, 15 October–16 November

Louise Bourgeois, Ydessa Hendeles Art Foundation, Toronto, 12 January–20 April

1992 *Louise Bourgeois: C.O.Y.O.T.E.,* Parrish Art Museum, Southampton, NY, 6 June–13 September

Currents 21: Louise Bourgeois, Milwaukee Art Museum, Milwaukee, WI, 18 September–27 December

Louise Bourgeois Drawings, Second Floor, Reykjavík, October–November

Louise Bourgeois, Prints 1947–1991, Barbara Krakow Gallery, Boston, MA, 23 October–24 December

Galerie Karsten Greve, Paris, 24 October–30 January 1993

Installation of recent acquisitions, National Gallery of Art, Washington, D.C., East Wing, November

Louise Bourgeois, Ydessa Hendeles Art Foundation, Toronto, 23 May–6 March 1993

1993 Ginny Williams Family Foundation, Denver, 10 January–31 March

The Brooklyn Museum, New York, 22 April–31 July

The Locus of Memory, Biennale Venice, American Pavillion, 9 June–10 October

The Corcoran Gallery of Art, Washington, D.C., 23 September–15 January 1995
Galerie Rudolfinum, Prague, 15 March–28 May 1995
Musée d'Art Moderne de la Ville de Paris, Paris, 23 June–8 October 1995
Deichtorhallen, Hamburg, 18 January–17 March 1996
Musée d'Art Contemporain de Montréal, Montréal, 25 April–22 September 1996

1994 *Louise Bourgeois: Skulpturen und Installationen,* Galerie Karsten Greve, Cologne,

29 January–14 May
Galeria Karsten Greve, Milan, February

Louise Bourgeois: The Personnages, The Saint Louis Art Museum, St. Louis, MO, 30 June–28 August

Nelson-Atkins Museum of Art, Kansas City, MO, 8 July–4 September

Louise Bourgeois. Skulpturen, Kestner-Gesellschaft Hannover, Hanover, 3 September–30 October

The Prints of Louise Bourgeois, Museum of Modern Art, New York, 13 September–3 January 1995
Bibliothèque Nationale, Paris, 9 February–1 April 1995
Musée du Dessin et de l'Estampe Originale, Gravelines, 28 May–1 September 1995
The Museum of Modern Art, Oxford, 14 October–31 December 1995
Bonnefanten Museum, Maastricht, 20 January–13 April 1996

Louise Bourgeois: The Red Rooms, Peter Blum, New York, 17 September–12 October

The Louise Bourgeois Papers: A Promised Gift to the Archives of American Art, Archives of American Art, New York, 17 November–11 December

1995 L'Ecole Nationale de Beaux Arts de Bourges, January–February

Louise Bourgeois. Pensées-Plumes, Musée National d'Art Moderne, Centre Georges Pompidou, Paris, 1 February–10 April
Helsinki City Art Museum, 28 April–16 July

Louise Bourgeois – Dessins pour Duras, Theatre du vieux Colombier, Paris, 9 March–23 April
MARCO, Monterrey, Mexico, 15 June–5 January 1996
Centro Andaluz de Arte Contemporaneo, Sevilla, February–March 1996
Museo Rufino Tamayo, Mexico City, 4 June–15 August 1996

Louise Bourgeois. Sculptures environnements dessins 1938–1995, Musée d'Art Moderne de la Ville de Paris, 23 June–8 October

Mitsubishi-Jisho Artium, Fukuoka City, 18 August–17 November

Walker Hill Art Center, Seoul, 16 October–14 November

Louise Bourgeois: Hommage à Duras, Galerie Karsten Greve, Cologne, 27 September–4 November

The Museum of Modern Art, Oxford, 14 October–31 December
ORIEL, The Arts Council of Wales Gallery, The Friary, Cardiff, April–May 1996

National Gallery of Victoria, Melbourne, 19 October–27 November 1995
Museum of Contemporary Art, Sydney, 21 December–14 April 1996

Galerie Piece Unique, Paris, 26 October–18 December

1996 *Louise Bourgeois. Der Ort des Gedächtnisses. Skulpturen, Environments und Zeichnungen 1946–1995*, Deichtorhallen, Hamburg, 18 January–17 March

Louise Bourgeois: Drawings, University Art Museum, University of California, Berkeley, CA, 24 January–24 March
The Drawing Center, New York, 17 April–8 June
The List Visual Art Center, Massachusetts Institute of Technology, Boston, Fall

The Art Gallery of Ontario, Toronto, Winter

Installation *Les Bienvenus*, Choisy le Roi, April

Service Municipal d'Arts Plastiques, Choisy le Roi, April

Louise Bourgeois: Arbeiten auf Papier, Galerie Karsten Greve, Cologne, 27 April–29 June

Louise Bourgeois: Spiders, Baumgartner Galleries, Inc., Washington, D.C., 31 May–20 July

Galerie Samuel Lallouz, Montréal, 27 June–31 August

Rupertinum, Salzburg, 27 July–27 October

Gallery Joseloff, Harry Jack Gray Center, University of Hartford, Westford, CT, 1 November–15 December

Galerie Soledad Lorenzo, Madrid, 28 November–18 January 1997

1997 *Louise Bourgeois: Sculpture*, Centro Cultural Banco Cultural do Brasil, Rio de Janeiro, 27 February–6 April

Locks Gallery, Philadelphia, 7 March–12 April

The Drawings of Louise Bourgeois, Centro Cultural da Light, Rio de Janeiro, April–May

Louise Bourgeois: Ode a Ma Mère, The Contemporary Arts Center, Cincinnati, OH, 4 April–22 June

Prada Foundation, Milan, 15 May–20 July

Louise Bourgeois, Yokohama Museum of Art, Tokyo, 2 November–15 January 1998

Chicago Arts Club, Chicago, 12 November–3 January 1998

1998 *Louise Bourgeois*, Musée d'Art Contemporain, Bordeaux, 30 January–26 April
Foundation Belem, Lissabon, 20 June–23 August
Kunsthalle Malmö, Malmö, 11 September–1 November
Serpentine Gallery, London, 18 November–30 January 1999

North Caroline Museum of Art, Raleigh, NC, 7 March–31 May

1999 *Louise Bourgeois*, Jaffe-Friede & Strauss Galleries, Dartmouth College, Hanover, New Hampshire, 16 February–21 March

Louise Bourgeois, Kunsthalle Bielefeld, Bielefeld, 1 March–2 May

Louise Bourgeois: Sleepwalking, *Louise Bourgeois: Topiary*, Pièce Unique, Paris, 5 March–1 June

Wexner Prize Wall, Wexner Center for the Visual Arts, Columbus, 17 April–31 May

Louise Bourgeois Prints: 1989–1998, Maier Museum of Art, Randolph-Macon Woman's College, Lynchburg, Virginia, 17 January–7 March; Cleveland Center for Contemporary Art, Cleveland, 3 September–24 October; Minneapolis Institute of Arts, 4 December–13 February 2000

Louise Bourgeois: Architecture and Memory, Museo Nacional Centro de Arte Reina Sofía, Madrid, 16 November, 1999–14 February 2000

2000 *Louise Bourgeois*, Grafiska Sallskapet, Stockholm, 29 April–17 May; Norrköpings Konstmuseum, Sweden, 7 June–10 September; Göteborgs Konstmuseum, Sweden, 30 September–7 January, 2001

Louise Bourgeois: Inaugural Installation of the Tate Modern at Turbine Hall, Tate Modern, London, 12 May–26 November

Louise Bourgeois: The Space of Memory, National Museum of Contemporary Art, Kyunggi-Do, Korea, 7 September–5 November

Louise Bourgeois: Handkerchiefs, Foundation Bevilacqua La Masa, under the patronage of the Biennale di Venice: Section Architecture, Venice, 2 June–30 June

Installation of The Welcoming Hands, Jardin des Tuileries, Paris, inauguration of permanent installation 29 June

Louise Bourgeois: The Insomnia Drawings, Tate Modern, London, December 2000–May 2001

2001 *Louise Bourgeois: Reconstruction of the Past*, Akademie der bildenden Künste Wien, Vienna, 24 April–27 May; Kunstraum Innsbruck, 6 June–29 September

Louise Bourgeois: Illustrated Books, Miriam and Ira D. Wallach Art Gallery, Columbia University, New York, 25 April–9 June

Louise Bourgeois: Spiders, Rockefeller Center, in association with the Public Art Fund, New York, 21 June–4 September

Louise Bourgeois: Livres Illustrés, Musée d'Art Américain, Giverny, 11 September–30 November

Louise Bourgeois, Guggenheim Museum Bilbao, 2 October–21 April 2002

75th Anniversary Sculpture: Louise Bourgeois, Williams College Museum of Art, Williamstown, Mass., inauguration of large outdoor sculpture commission, 6 October

Louise Bourgeois at the Hermitage The State Hermitage Museum, St. Petersburg, 9 October–13 January 2002; Helsinki City Art Museum, 25 February–5 May 2002; Kulturhuset, Stockholm, 18 May–1 September 2002; Museet for Samtidskunst, Oslo, 14 September–8 December 2002; Louisiana Museum of Modern Art, Humlebæk, Denmark, 15 February–22 June 2003

Louise Bourgeois: Sleepwalking, Williams College Museum of Art, Williamstown, Mass., 24 November 2001–31 August 2002

2002 *Louise Bourgeois: The Early Work*, Krannert Art Museum, University of Illinois, Champaign, 1 May–4 August; Madison Art Center, Madison, Wisconsin, 15 September–17 November; Aspen Art Museum, Colorado, 13 December–2 February, 2003

Louise Bourgeois: Drawings and Sculpture, Kunsthaus Bregenz, Bregenz, Austria, 5 July–15 September

Louise Bourgeois: Childhood, Ars TEOR / éTica Fundación, San José, Costa Rica, 26 August–25 October

Louise Bourgeois: Le Jour La Nuit Le Jour, Palais de Tokyo, Paris; sound installation: 7 October–8 December; film installation: 7 October–12 January 2003; salon: 7 October–6 April 2003

Louise Bourgeois: Recent Sculptures and Drawings, Beaumontpublic, Luxembourg, 18 October–18 January 2003

2003 *Louise Bourgeois: Prints and Illustrated Books*, Centre de la Gravure et de Image Imprimée, La Louvière, Belgium, 31 January, 2003–18 April 2004

Louise Bourgeois, White Cube, London, 4 February–1 March

Louise Bourgeois, Museo Internacional de Arte Contemporáneo (MIAC), Arrecife Lanzarote, Canary Islands, 1 March–31 May; City Hall of Valladolid—Museo de La Pasión, Valladolid, Spain, 5–22 August 2004; City Council of León, Spain, 10 September–24 October 2004; Fundació Joan Miró, Palma de Mallorca, 19 March–12 June 2005; Neue Galerie im Höhmannhaus, Augsburg, Germany, 15 July–11 September 2005

Louise Bourgeois Installation at Inauguration of Dia:Beacon, Dia Center for the Arts, Beacon, New York, 17 May (long-term loan)

Louise Bourgeois: Intimate Abstractions, Akademie der Künste, Berlin-Brandenburg, 3 June–27 July

Louise Bourgeois: Maman, Frederik Meijer Gardens and Sculpture Park, Grand Rapids, 12 June–1 November

Louise Bourgeois: The Insomnia Drawings, Whitney Museum of American Art, New York, 14 June–21 September

A View from the Outside, Louise Bourgeois: The Reticent Child, Sigmund Freud Museum, Vienna, 25 November–29 February 2004

Louise Bourgeois: Stitches in Time, Irish Museum of Modern Art, Dublin, 26 November 2003–22 February 2004; Fruitmarket Gallery, Edinburgh, 5 March–9 May 2004; Centre of Contemporary Art Málaga, Spain, 6 August–7 November 2004; Museum of Contemporary Art, North Miami, 12 February–27 March 2005

2004 Metropolitan State College, Denver, 11 March–24 April

Louise Bourgeois: Emotions Abstracted, Works 1941–2000, Daros Exhibitions, Zurich, 12 March–12 September

Drawings by Louise Bourgeois, St. Louis Art Museum, St. Louis, 23 March–20 June

2005 *Louise Bourgeois: One and Others*, Wifredo Lam Center, Havana, 4 February–26 April

Louise Bourgeois: Topiary, the Art of Improving Nature, Memphis College of Art, Memphis, 18 February–30 March

Louise Bourgeois: Back and Forth, Kunsthalle Wien, Vienna, 24 November–5 February 2006

2006 *Louise Bourgeois: Femme*, Walters Art Museum, Baltimore, and Contemporary Museum, Baltimore, 11 February–21 May

Louise Bourgeois: La Famille, Kunsthalle Bielefeld, Bielefeld, Germany, 12 March–5 June

Louise Bourgeois, The Fabric Workshop and Museum, Philadelphia, 8 July–16 September

Louise Bourgeois: Selected Prints on Fabric, Butler Gallery, The Castle, Kilkenny, Ireland, 1 October–12 November

Louise Bourgeois: The Woven Child (in context), Worcester Art Museum, Mass., 21 October–25 February 2007

2007 *Bourgeois in Boston*, Institute of Contemporary Art, Boston, 27 March–2 March 2008

Louise Bourgeois, Storm King Art Center, Mountainville, New York, 16 May–15 November

Louise Bourgeois: Recent Projects, The Haggerty Museum of Art, Marquette University, Milwaukee, 26 July–1 October

Louise Bourgeois: Retrospective, Tate Modern, London, 10 October–20 January 2008; Centre Georges Pompidou, Paris, 5 March–2 June; Solomon R. Guggenheim Museum, New York, 27 June–28 September 2008; Museum of Contemporary Art, Los Angeles, 26 October 2008–25 January 2009; Hirshhorn Museum & Sculpture Garden, Washington, D.C., 26 February–17 May 2009

Louise Bourgeois: La Sage Femme, Espacia AV, La Región de Murcia, Spain, 22 November–10 January 2008

2008 *Louise Bourgeois: Nature Study*, Inverleith House, Royal Botanical Gardens, Edinburgh, 3 May–6 July

Louise Bourgeois for Capodimonte, Museo Nazionale di Capodimonte, Naples, 17 October–25 January 2009

2010 *Louise Bourgeois*, The Museum of Cycladic Art, Athens, 13 May–12 September

Louise Bourgeois: The Fabric Works, Fondazione Vedova, Venice, 5 June–19 September

Louise Bourgeois: Sculpture and Drawings, Städtische Museen Jena, Germany, 4 September–21 November

Louise Bourgeois: Mother and Child, Nordic Watercolour Museum, Skarhamn, Sweden, 19 September–5 December; Kunstforeningen, Copenhagen, 29 January–15 May 2011

Louise Bourgeois: Moi, Eugénie Grandet, Maison de Balzac, Paris, 2 November–7 February 2011

2011 *Louise Bourgeois: The Return of the Repressed*, Fundación PROA, Buenos Aires, 19 March–19 June; Instituto Tomie Ohtake, Sao Paulo, 7 July–28 August; Museu de Arte Moderna, Rio de Janeiro, 15 September–13 November

Louise Bourgeois: Femme, National Gallery of Iceland, Reykjavik, 27 May–11 September

Louise Bourgeois: À l'Infini, Foundation Beyeler, Riehen / Basel, Switzerland, 3 September–8 January 2012

2. Selected Bibliography

2. 1. Writings by Louise Bourgeois and Interviews

Louise Bourgeois, 'Letter to the Editor', in: *Art in America*, vol. 60, Jan.–Feb. 1972, p. 123

'Artists talk on Art', in: *Women in the Arts Newsletter*, Feb. 1975

Susi Bloch, 'An Interview with Louise Bourgeois', in: *The Art Journal*, vol. 35, no. 41, summer 1976, pp. 370–373

Donald Kuspit, 'Louise Bourgeois', in: *Art in America*, Sept.–Oct. 1977

Marsha Pels, 'Louise Bourgeois: A Search for Gravity', in: *Art International*, vol. 23, Oct. 1979, pp. 46–54

Louise Bourgeois, 'Child Abuse', in: *Artforum*, December 1982

Robert Storr, 'Meanings, Materials and Milieu – Reflections on Recent Work by Louise Bourgeois', in: *Parkett*, no. 9, 1986

Donald Kuspit, *Bourgeois. An Interview with Louise Bourgeois*, New York 1988

Stuart Morgan, 'Taking Cover: Louise Bourgeois interviewed by Stuart Morgan', in: *Artscribe*, Jan.–Feb. 1988, pp. 30–34

Louise Bourgeois, 'Statements', in: *CAA Newsletter*, vol. 14, no. 1, spring 1989

Alain Kirili, 'The Passion For Sculpture – A Conversation with Louise Bourgeois', in: *Arts*, vol. 63, no. 7, March 1989, pp. 68–75

Louise Bourgeoise, 'Freud's Toys', in: *Artforum*, Jan. 1990, pp. 111–113

Robert Storr, 'Louise Bourgeois Interviewed', in: *Galleries Magazine*, June–July 1990, pp. 95–104

Louise Bourgeois, 'Artist's Notes', in: *Dislocations*, exhibition catalog. The Museum of Modern Art, New York, 1991

Christiane Meyer-Thoss, 'I am a Woman with No Secrets, Statements by Louise Bourgeois', in: *Parkett*, no. 27, March 1991, pp. 37–43

Louise Bourgeois, 'Obsession', in: *Artforum*, April 1992

Louise Bourgeois, 'Statements', in: *Balcon*, no. 8–9, 1992, pp. 44, 47

Henry Geldzahler, 'Louise Bourgeois', in: *Interview*, March 1992, pp. 98–103, 127

Christiane Meyer-Thoss, *Louise Bourgeois, Designing for Free Fall*, Zurich 1992

Louise Bourgeois, 'Cellule (tu ferais mieux de grandir)', in: *Biennale d'art contemporain de Lyon*, Réunion des Musées Nationaux, Lyon 1993

Douglas Maxwell, 'Louise Bourgeois', in: *Modern Painters*, vol. 6, no. 2, summer 1993, pp. 38–43

Nancy Spector, Louise Bourgeois, 'Louise Bourgeois at the Venice Biennale', in: *Guggenheim Magazine*, vol. 3, summer 1993, pp. 40–43

Pat Steir, 'Mortal Elements', in: *Artforum*, summer 1993, pp. 86 f., 127

Louise Bourgeois Skulpturen, exhibition catalog. Kestner-Gesellschaft Hannover, Hanover, 1994

Francesco Bonami, 'Louise Bourgeois: In a Strange Way, Things are Getting Better and Better', in: *Flash Art*, vol. XVII, no. 174, Jan.–Feb. 1994, pp. 36–39

Louise Bourgeois, *Album*, New York 1994

Louise Bourgeois, 'Statements', in: *Louise Bourgeois, the Red Rooms*, New York 1994

Louise Bourgeois, 'Young at Art: Miró at 100', in: *Artforum*, Jan. 1994

George Melrod, 'A Conversation with Louise Bourgeois', in: *Atelier*, no. 812, Oct. 1994, pp. 32–44

Louise Bourgeois, Larry Rinder, *Louise Bourgeois, Drawings and Observations*, Boston 1995

Louise Bourgeois, 'Rouge est la Couleur du sang', in: *Louise Bourgeois. Sculpture, environnement, dessin 1935–1995*, exhibition catalog. Musée d'Art Moderne de la Ville de Paris, Paris, 1995

Louise Bourgeois, 'Tender Compulsions', in: *World Art*, no. 2, 1995

Suzanne Pagé, Béatrice Parent, 'Entretien avec Louise Bourgeois', in: *Louise Bourgeois. Sculpture, environnement, dessin 1935–1995*, exhibition catalog. Musée d'Art Moderne de la Ville de Paris, Paris, 1995

Louise Bourgeois, *Destruction of the Father / Reconstruction of the Father* (Writings and Interviews 1923–1997), edited and with texts by Marie-Laure Bernadac and Hans-Ulrich Obrist, London 1998

Louise Bourgeois, *Ode à la Bièvre*, New York, New York 2007

2. 2. Books

Christiane Meyer-Thoss, *Louise Bourgeois: Designing For Free Fall*, Zurich, 1992

Paul Gardner, *Louise Bourgeois*, New York, 1994

Marie-Laure Bernadac, *Louise Bourgeois*, Paris, 1995

Emmanuel Pernoud, *Louise Bourgeois Estampes*, Paris, 1995

Rainer Crone and Petrus Graf Schaesberg, *Louise Bourgeois: The Secret of the Cells*, Munich 1997

Andrea Jahn, *Louise Bourgeois: Subversionen des Körpers*, Berlin 1999

Marie-Laure Bernadac and Elisabeth Bronfen, *Louise Bourgeois: The Insomnia Drawings*, Zurich and New York 2000

Mieke Bal, *Louise Bourgeois' Spider: The Architecture of Art-Writing*, Chicago 2001

Jan Greenberg and Sandra Jordan, *Runaway Girl: The Artist Louise Bourgeois*, New York 2003

Robert Storr, Paulo Herkenhoff, and Allan Schwartzman, *Louise Bourgeois*, London 2003

Mignon Nixon, *Fantastic Reality: Louise Bourgeois and a Story of Modern Art*, London and Cambridge, Mass. 2005

Ann Coxon, *Louise Bourgeois*, London 2010

2. 3. Exhibition Catalogs

Lucy R. Lippard, *Eccentric Abstraction*, exhibition catalog. Fischbach Gallery, New York, 1966

Robert Goldwater, *What is Modern Sculpture?*, Museum of Modern Art, New York, 1969

Madeleine Conway, Nancy Kirk, 'Louise Bourgeois', in: *Artists' Cookbook*, The Museum of Modern Art, New York, 1977

Deborah Wye, 'Louise Bourgeois', in: *From Women's Eyes*, exhibition catalog. Rose Art Museum, Brandeis University, Waltham, MA, 1977

Jerry Gorovoy, *The Iconography of Louise Bourgeois*, exhibition catalog. Max Hutchinson Gallery, New York, 1980

Patrice J. Marandel, 'Louise Bourgeois: From the Inside', in: *Louise Bourgeois: Femme Maison*, exhibition catalog. The Renaissance Society at the University of Chicago, Chicago, 1981

Robert Pincus-Whitten, *Bourgeois Truth*, exhibition catalog. Robert Miller Gallery, New York, 1982

Deborah Wye, *Louise Bourgeois*, exhibition catalog. Museum of Modern Art, New York, 1982

Lisa Phillips, *Twentieth Century Sculpture: Process and Presence*, exhibition catalog. Whitney Museum of American Art at Phillip Morris, New York, 1983

Lisa Phillips, *The Third Dimension: Sculpture of the New York School*, Whitney Museum of American Art, New York, 1984

Jean Frémon, *Louise Bourgeois: Retrospective 1947–1984*, exhibition catalog. Galerie Maeght-Lelong, Paris, 1985

Jean Frémon, Robert Storr, *Louise Bourgeois: Retrospective 1947–1984*, exhibition catalog. Galerie Maeght-Lelong, Zurich, 1985

Louise Bourgeois, exhibition catalog. Serpentine Gallery, London, 1985

Jerry Gorovoy, *Louise Bourgeois*, exhibition catalog. Robert Miller Gallery, New York, 1986

Stuart Morgan, *Louise Bourgeois*, exhibition catalog. The Taft Museum, Cincinnati, OH, 1987

John Cheim, Jerry Gorovoy (ed.), *Louise Bourgeois. Drawings*, Robert Miller Gallery and Daniel Lelong, New York/Paris, 1988

Donald Kuspit, *Louise Bourgeois. Works on Paper*, exhibition catalog. Museum Overholland, Amsterdam, 1988

Peter Weiermair, Lucy Lippard, Rosalind Kraus et. al., *Louise Bourgeois*, exhibition catalog. Frankfurter Kunstverein, Frankfurt a. M., 1989

Henry Geldzahler, *Louise Bourgeois*, exhibition catalog. Dia Art Foundation, Bridgehampton, NY, 1989

Stuart Morgan, *Louise Bourgeois: Recent Work 1984–1989*, exhibition catalog. Riverside Studios, London, 1990

Lynne Cooke, Mark Francis, *Carnegie International 1991*, Vol. I, II, New York/Pittsburgh, 1991

Jan Hoet, Bart De Baere, Denys Zacharopoulos, Pier Luigi Tazzi, Claudia Herstatt et. al., *documenta IX*, Vol. I (Aufsätze und Biographien), Vol. II (A–K), Stuttgart, 1992

Dean Sobel, *Louise Bourgeois*, exhibition pamphlet. Milwaukee Art Museum, Milwaukee, WI, 1992

Charlotta Kotik, *Louise Bourgeois. Recent Work*, exhibition pamphlet for the American Pavillion, New York, 1993

Charlotta Kotik, Terrie Sultan, Christian Leigh, *Louise Bourgeois: The Locus of Memory, 1982–1993*, New York, 1994

Jeremy Strick, *Louise Bourgeois: The Personages*, St. Louis Museum of Art, St. Louis, 1994

Carl Haenlein, Carsten Ahrens, Barbara Catoir et. al. (ed.), *Louise Bourgeois Sculptures and Installations*, Kestner-Gesellschaft Hannover, Hanover, 1994

Deborah Wye, Carol Smith, *The Prints of Louise Bourgeois*, The Museum of Modern Art, New York, 1994

Marie-Laure Bernadac, *Louise Bourgeois Pensée-Plumes*, Cabinet d'art graphique, Centre Georges Pompidou, Paris, 1995

Suzanne Pagé, Beatrice Parent, *Louise Bourgeois: Sculptures, environments, dessins 1938–1995*, Musée d'Art moderne de la Ville de Paris, Paris, 1995

Richard D. Marshall, Paulo Herkenhoff, *Escultura de Louise Bourgeois: La Eleganca de la Ironia*, Museo de Art Contemporaneo de Monterrey, Monterrey, Mexico, 1995

Atsuko Murayama, *Louise Bourgeois*, Mitsubishi-Jisho Artium in cooperation with MOMA Contemporary Co., Ltd., Fukuoka City, Japan, 1995

Jason Smith, Robert Storr, *Louise Bourgeois*, National Gallery of Victoria, Melbourne, 1995

Ian Cole, *Louise Bourgeois Sculpture/The Prints of Louise Bourgeois*, exhibition catalog Museum of Modern Art Oxford, Oxford, 1995

Louise Bourgeois, Larry Rinder, *Louise Bourgeois: Drawings & Observations*, University Art Museum and Boston, Berkeley, CA, 1995

Zdenek Felix, *Louise Bourgeois. Der Ort des Gedächtnisses: Skulpturen, Environments und Zeichnungen 1946–1995*, Deichtorhallen, Hamburg, 1996

Ian Cole (ed.), *Louise Bourgeois*, Museum of Modern Art Papers, Vol. I, Museum of Modern Art Oxford, Oxford, 1996

Paulo Herkenhoff, Angelica de Moraes, *Louise Bourgeois: desenhos/drawings*, Centro Cultural Light, Rio de Janeiro, 1997

Paulo Herkenhoff, *Louise Bourgeois*, Centro Cultural Banco do Brasil, Rio de Janeiro, 1997

Jerry Gorovoy, Pandora Tabatabai Asbaghi, Paulo Herkenhoff, *Louise Bourgeois. Blue Days and Pink Days*, Fondazione Prada, Milan, 1997

Marie-Laure Bernadac, Louise Neri, Paulo Herkenhoff, *Louise Bourgeois*, Musee d'Art, Bordeaux, and Serpentine Gallery, London, 1998

Christiane Terrisse Colomina, Lynne Cooke, Mieke Bal, and Jennifer Bloomer, *Louise Bourgeois: Architecture and Memory*, Museo Nacional Centro de Arte—Reina Sofia, Madrid, 1999

Thomas Kellein, *Louise Bourgeois*, Kunsthalle Bielefeld, Bielefeld, Germany, 1999

Carol Smith, *Louise Bourgeois Prints: 1989–1998*, Maier Museum of Art, Lynchburg, Virginia, 1999

Frances Morris and Marina Warner, *Louise Bourgeois*, The Tate Modern, London, 2000

Sarah J. Suzuki, *Louise Bourgeois: Illustrated Books*, Miriam and Ira D. Wallach Art Gallery, Columbia University, New York, 2001

Julie Sylvester, *Louise Bourgeois at the Hermitage*, The State Hermitage Museum, St. Petersburg, 2001

Josef Helfenstein, *Louise Bourgeois: The Early Work*, Krannert Art Museum, University of Illinois at Urbana-Champaign, Champaign, Illinois, 2002

Eckhard Schneider, Scott Lyon-Wall, *Louise Bourgeois: Drawings and Sculpture*, Kunsthaus Bregenz, Bregenz, Austria, 2002

Martine Schneider-Speller, Jean-Christophe Ammann, Dr. Francis Hermann, Allison Plath-Moseley, *Louise Bourgeois: Recent Sculptures and Drawings*, Beaumontpublic, Luxembourg, 2002

Frances Morris, *Louise Bourgeois: Stitches in Time*, The Irish Museum of Modern Art, Dublin, 2003

Poul Erik Tøjner, Penelope Vending, *Louise Bourgeois: Life as Art*, Louisiana Museum of Modern Art, Humlebæk, Denmark, 2003

Catherine de Braekeleer, *Louise Bourgeois: Prints and Illustrated Books*, Centre de la Gravure et de l'Image Imprimée, La Louvière, Belgium, 2004

Eva Keller, Regula Malin (editors), Robert Storr, Eva Keller, *Louise Bourgeois: Emotions Abstracted, Works 1941–2000*, Daros Services AG, Zurich 2004

Peter Weiermair, *Louise Bourgeois: Back and Forth*, Kunsthalle Wien, Vienna, 2005

Thomas Kellein, *Louise Bourgeois: La Famille*, Kunsthalle Bielefeld, Bielefeld, Germany, 2006

David R. Collins, Peter Stern, Amei Wallach, *Louise Bourgeois*, Storm King Art Center, Mountainville, New York, 2007

Frances Morris, Paulo Herkenhoff, Julia Kristeva, Donald Kuspit, Elisabeth Lebovici, Mignon Nixon, Linda Nochlin, Alex Potts, Rob Storr, *Louise Bourgeois*, Tate Modern, London, 2007

Jean Frémon, *Louise Bourgeois: Moi, Eugénie Grandet*, Maison de Balzac, Paris, 2010

Udo Kittelman, Christina Weiss, Kyllikki Zacharias, Silke Krohn, Elfriede Jelinek, Henry Miller, Hans Bellmer / *Louise Bourgeois: Double Sexus*, Sammlung Scharf-Gerstenberg, Nationalgalerie, Berlin, 2010

2. 4. Videos

Lynn Blumenthal, Kate Horsfield, *Louise Bourgeois*, Interview, 30 min., black/white, Video Date Bank, School of the Art Institute of Chicago, Chicago, September 1975

Louise Bourgeois: Partial Recall, The Easton Foundation, Museum of Modern Art, New York, 1983

Louise Bourgeois, Tape no. 27, Art/New York, 1987

Louise Bourgeois in Lenbachaus, Munich, (Ampex 187, u-matic broadcast videocassette, KCA-40), Videotechnik B. Gürter GmbH, Munich, 1989

Sculpture of the 1980's, Business Arts, Inc., 30 min., 1991

Rosamond Bernier, *Louise Bourgeois at Close Quarters*, Metropolitan Museum of Art, New York, 1995

Rosamond Bernier, *The Many Faces of Louise Bourgeois*, Metropolitan Museum of Art, New York, 2002

2. 5. Films

Camille Guichard (dir.), *Louise Bourgeois*, Terra Luna Films and Centre Georges Pompidou, Paris, 1993

Nigel Finch (dir.), *Louise Bourgeois*, The Easton Foundation, Arena Films, BBC, London, 1994

Marion Cajori (dir.), *Studio Visits with Louise Bourgeois*, Christian Blackwood Productions, New York, 1994

Brigitte Cornand, *Chère Louise*, Les Films Du Siamois, Paris, 1995

Chris Maybach, Paul Gardner (prod.), *ART CITY*, Vertrieb: Twelve Films, 1996

Brigitte Cornand (dir.), *Louise Bourgeois, My Works in progress 1,2, 3*, CAPC de Bordeaux and La Maison Yves Saint-Laurent, 1998

Brigitte Cornand (dir.), *Louise Bourgeois: C'est le murmure de l'eau qui chante / Louise Bourgeois: The Whisper of the Whistling Water*, Les Films du Siamois / Pompidou Center, Paris, 2002

Jill Nicholls (dir.), *Louise Bourgeois: Spiderwoman*, Imagine / BBC One, London, 2007

Brigitte Cornand (dir.), *La Rivière Gentille / The Sweet River*, Les Films du Siamois / Centre Pompidou, Paris, with Harvestworks and Easton Foundation, 2007

Marion Cajori, Amei Wallach (dirs.), *Louise Bourgeois: The Spider, The Mistress and The Tangerine*, Art Kaleidoscope Foundation, New York, 2008

PHOTO CREDITS

Courtesy of Acquavella Galleries, New York: 68 top

Peter Bellamy, New York: 10, 11, 12, 14, 16, 48, 50, 51, 52 o., 53, 56, 59 top, bottom right, 62 bottom, 83, 85, 87, 92, 93, 95, 96, 97, 99, 100, 101, 102, 103, 105, 106, 108, 112, 113, 114, 115, 116, 117, 119, 120, 121, 122, 123, 124, 125, 126, 127, 128, 129, 132, 133, 134, 135, 136, 137, 138, 139, 140, 141 top, 143, 144, 145, 148, 149, 150, 151, 152, 153, 154, 155, 156, 157, 158, 159, back cover

I. Bessi, Carrara: 46 bottom, 63, 71, 77, 105

Ben Blackwell: 161

© Constantin Brancusi: 78 top, 79 top, 80

© Brassaï 1934: 29 top, 30 top

Leo Castelli Gallery, New York: 66 top

Christopher Burke, New York: front cover, frontispiece, 94, 104 bottom, 162, 163, 168, 169, 170, 171, 172, 173, 174

Claudio Edinger: 49

Eeva-Inkeri, New York: 65 top

Allan Finkelman, New York: 54, 55, 57 top, 58, 59 bottom left, 60 left, 61 right, 64 top, 82 top, 84, 85, 86 top, 98, 107

Courtesy of Adolph and Esther Gottlieb Foundation, New York: 68 center

Bruno Jarret, Paris (Musée Rodin, Paris): 73, 74, 75 bottom

Baird Jones, New York: 91

Kate Keller (MoMA) 67 top

Marcus Leith, New York: 118, 164, 165, 166, 167

Lisa Little, New York: 88 right

Rafael Lobato, New York: 160

© Copyright The Robert Mapplethorpe Foundation. Courtesy Art + Commerce: 40 top

Attilo Maranzano: 142, 146, 147

Christian Martin: 141 bottom

H. Messer: 61 bottom

The Metropolitan Museum of Art: 75 top, 76 bottom

© Estate of Peter Moore/ VAGA, New York: 44, 45 top right and bottom

© Peter Moore: 41, 43, 62 top, 88, 98

Inge Morath: 40 bottom, 42, 81

Musée Barbier-Müller, Geneva (Photo: Prestel-Verlag): 67 bottom

Musée de l'Homme, Paris: 79 bottom

Musée Rodin, Meudon: 70 bottom, 72 top

Musée Rodin, Paris: 72 bottom

Hans Namuth, New York: 82 bottom

Beth Phillips, New York: 90

Sebastian Piras: 130, 131

D. R.: 78 bottom

John Seyfried: 66 bottom

Steven Sloman, New York: 88 left

Malcolm Varon, New York: 70 top

Bruce Weber, New York: 110

Zindman / Fremont, New York: 45 top left, 65 bottom, 68 bottom, 69, 86 bottom 89, 104 top

All other material: Courtesy of Louise Bourgeois Trust

Front cover and frontispiece: *Cell (The Last Climb)*, 2008 (see page 174). Photos by Christopher Burke
Back cover: *Cell VI*, 1991 (see page 129). Photo by Peter Bellamy

Prestel, a member of Verlagsgruppe Random House GmbH

Prestel Verlag
Neumarkter Strasse 28
81673 Munich
Tel. +49 (0)89 41 36-0
Fax +49 (0)89 41 36-2335

Prestel Publishing Ltd.
4 Bloomsbury Place
London WC1A 2QA
Tel. +44 (0)20 7323-5004
Fax +44 (0)20 7636-8004

Prestel Publishing
900 Broadway, Suite 603
New York, N.Y. 10003
Tel. +1 212 995-2720
Fax +1 212 995-2733

www.prestel.com

Prestel books are available worldwide. Please contact your nearest bookseller or write to either of the above addresses for information concerning your local distributor.

Library of Congress Control Number: 2011928487

The Library of Congress Cataloguing-in-Publication data is available.
British Library Cataloguing-in-Publication Data: a catalogue record for this book is available from the British Library. The Deutsche Bibliothek holds a record of this publication in the Deutsche Nationalbibliografie; detailed bibliographical data can be found under: http://dnb.ddb.de

Design and layout by WIGEL, Munich
Production by Astrid Wedemeyer
Origination by Reproline Mediateam, Munich
Printed and bound by Druckerei Uhl GmbH & Co. KG, Radolfzell

FSC
MIX
Papier
FSC® C004229

Verlagsgruppe Random House FSC®-DEU-0100
The FSC®-certified paper *Hello Fat Matt* has been supplied by Deutsche Papier

Printed in Germany

ISBN 978-3-7913-4562-8